Life Coaching

FOR

DUMMIES®

2ND EDITION

Life Coaching

FOR

DUMMIES®

2ND EDITION

by Jeni Purdie

A John Wiley and Sons, Ltd, Publication

Life Coaching For Dummies®, 2nd Edition

Published by
John Wiley & Sons, Ltd
The Atrium
Southern Gate
Chichester
West Sussex
PO19 8SQ
England

Email (for orders and customer service enquires): cs-books@wiley.co.uk

Visit our Home Page on www.wiley.com

Wiley also publishes its books in a variety of electronic formats. Some content that appears in print may not be available in electronic books.

British Library Cataloguing in Publication Data: A catalogue record for this book is available from the British Library.

ISBN: 978-0-470-66554-1

ISBN: 978-0-470-66607-4 (ebk), 978-0-470-66608-1 (ebk), 978-0-470-97255-7 (ebk)

About the Author

Jeni Purdie is a coach and facilitator who applies whole life coaching techniques to her work with people and within businesses. Before her own life-changing decision to become a coach, Jeni benefited from a 16-year career with the Hays group, spanning recruitment, sales operations, project management, and people development, where she was lucky enough to embark on a new challenging job role every 18 months or so. It was this experience of discovering that the grass is green wherever you are – if you take proper care of the lawn – that gave Jeni the conviction and motivation to build her purpose around inspiring people to attract and enjoy their own dream life, work and vision of happiness.

In her business Jeni uses best practice coaching techniques together with NLP, and is a licensed facilitator of TetraMap (a holistic model of behaviour; `www.tetramap.co.uk`) and Goal Mapping (a brain friendly technique for identifying and maximising progress towards goals; `www.liftinternational.com`). She is addicted to learning and this helps her add value to her work with clients. But in her moments of brutal self-honesty Jeni will admit that quite a lot of the credit is down to the succession of cats who have owned her, from whom she has picked up a great deal about how to handle the ups and downs of life.*

One of the things Jeni likes best about being a coach is that she feels she always gets as much if not more out of the experience than her clients and she can't thank them enough for the honour of seeing them move themselves from frustration to power. Honestly, it's enough to make you want to write a book about it…

You can find out more about Jeni and her business at: `www.reachfor starfish.com`.

* This philosophy can be summed up as: play, ponder, and when in doubt, take a long nap in the sun or on a comfy bed.

Dedication

To two people who are in my life now in very different ways:

Brian, for your continued encouragement and belief in me.

Ali, for all that you gave and all that you still inspire in me.

Author's Acknowledgements

It's been a delight to work on the second edition of this book. My first thanks remain with the wonderful team at Wiley and especially Rachael Chilvers, who has been my Editor on both editions. You've been a joy once more!

I feel deep gratitude to all the friends and family who have shaped my life, loved and supported me throughout the writing process for both editions.

It's been immensely gratifying to have had such great feedback from readers of the first edition and therefore my heartfelt thanks still go to the people who helped me make it as good as it could possibly be. My original reader group tried out activities, and fed back on sample chapters. Ali, Carol, Margaret, Anne, Pam, Carolyn, Jos, Pennie, Roma, Debbie, Brian, Liza, Sue, Doug, Paul and Tim – I truly valued your contributions and the book would have been the poorer without you all.

During the journey of updating and adding new chapters for the second edition three people in particular have been of significance. Marie Taylor, my business partner at www.livingrightnow.com, who individually and in our work together has shaped my philosophies about living a fully present life. Jules Wyman of www.positive-belief.co.uk who gave valuable input on her core expertise – confidence and self esteem. And Tim Downes of www.trueresults.co.uk who lives and breathes the journey of meaningful success for himself and his clients. Your influences have greatly enhanced the new chapters – thank you, dear friends and fellow coaches.

Final thanks are due to all of the inspirational people who have coached me, especially my current coach Mark Gleave (www.freedomfromthethinking mind.co.uk), to all my clients who have taught me so much, and to readers of the first edition who through their feedback have helped me make this new edition an even more valuable resource for anyone wanting to create and enjoy their best self and life.

Publisher's Acknowledgements

We're proud of this book; please send us your comments through our Dummies online registration form located at www.dummies.com/register/.

Some of the people who helped bring this book to market include the following:

Commissioning, Editorial and Media Development

Project Editor: Rachael Chilvers

Commissioning Editor: Nicole Hermitage

Content Editor: Jo Theedom

Assistant Editor: Ben Kemble

Production Manager: Daniel Mersey

Proofreader: Kelly Cattermole

Cover Photo: © moodboard/Alamy

Cartoons: Rich Tennant
www.the5thwave.com

Production

Project Coordinator: Lynsey Stanford

Layout and Graphics: Carl Byers, Kelly Kijovsky

Proofreader: Lauren Mandelbaum

Indexer: Ty Koontz

Contents at a Glance

Introduction 1

Part I: The Basics of Life Coaching 7
Chapter 1: Introducing Life Coaching 9
Chapter 2: Deciding What You Want to Take from Coaching 25
Chapter 3: Preparing for Coaching 39

Part II: Your Life Coaching Journey 51
Chapter 4: Becoming Your Best Self 53
Chapter 5: Choosing Your Beliefs 67
Chapter 6: Discovering the Values that Motivate You 81
Chapter 7: Stocking Up on Powerful Questions 95
Chapter 8: Taking Stock of Now 105
Chapter 9: Exploring Your Options 119
Chapter 10: Planning Effective Action 131

Part III: Focusing on the Elements of Your Life 145
Chapter 11: Career and Work..147
Chapter 12: Money, Wealth and Abundance 167
Chapter 13: People and Relationships 179
Chapter 14: Physical, Mental and Emotional Well-being 193
Chapter 15: Developing and Growing 207

Part IV: Working with the Themes of Coaching........... 219
Chapter 16: Attracting the Life You Want 221
Chapter 17: Coaching Yourself to Happiness 231
Chapter 18: Defining True Success 245
Chapter 19: Tackling Common Blocks 257

Part V: Creating a Harmonious Whole Life................. 269
Chapter 20: Achieving Balance 271
Chapter 21: Making a Life-Changing Decision 285
Chapter 22: Applying Your Coaching Skills More Widely..............299

Part VI: The Part of Tens **311**
Chapter 23: Ten Life Coaching Beliefs about Yourself.............................313
Chapter 24: Ten Questions to Keep Your Life on Track......................319
Chapter 25: Ten Daily Balancing Acts 325
Chapter 26: Ten Inspirational Resources 331

Appendix: Considering a Future as a
Professional Life Coach **337**
Index **345**

Table of Contents

Introduction 1

About This Book 1
Conventions Used in This Book...2
Foolish Assumptions...2
How This Book Is Organised 3
    Part I: The Basics of Life Coaching 3
    Part II: Your Life Coaching Journey...3
    Part III: Focusing on the Elements of Your Life............................3
    Part IV: Working with the Themes of Coaching 4
    Part V: Creating a Harmonious Whole Life 4
    Part VI: The Part of Tens...4
Icons Used in This Book 4
Where to Go from Here...5

Part I: The Basics of Life Coaching 7

Chapter 1: Introducing Life Coaching 9

A Brief Definition of Life Coaching 9
What Life Coaching Is Not 10
Living Your Best Life 11
    Getting ready for change 12
    Presenting the passport for your coaching journey 14
Choosing Life Coaching for Long-Term Results 15
Tuning In to Your Inner Coach 16
    Introducing your split personality!..16
    Giving yourself the gift of your own good opinion 17
    Turning up the volume on the voice of your inner coach.............18
    Having a coaching conversation...19
Identifying Your Current Priorities for Coaching 20

Chapter 2: Deciding What You Want to Take from Coaching 25

Assessing the Benefits and Challenges of Coaching...........................26
    Attaining goals..26
    Achieving balance...27
    Finding purpose 28
    Changing your mindset 28
    Growing through self-awareness 29
    Enjoying the journey 29
    Considering the challenges of coaching 30

Deciding on a Coaching Method...30
   Finding the right coach 31
   Considering co-coaching.......................................35
   Deciding to self-coach 36
Making a Promise to Yourself 37
   Checking out your current life conditions...............37
   Framing your coaching promise 38

Chapter 3: Preparing for Coaching **39**
Getting Ready for Your Coaching Session...................39
Beginning Your Coaching Journey 40
   Seeing the big picture..41
   Packing your survival kit 42
   The stages of your journey...................................43
Knowing Where You Are on the Road 44
Marking Your Progress..45
   Using milestone goals to celebrate success............45
   Giving yourself a pat on the back 47
   Choosing people to cheer you on..........................47
   Anticipating setbacks and relapses 48
   Keeping a record...49
   Painting a picture..49

Part II: Your Life Coaching Journey **51**

Chapter 4: Becoming Your Best Self **53**
Considering Your Unique Gifts 53
   What do you do really well? 54
   How do you do that thing you do?
      Boosting your competencies 55
Noticing Your Preferences 58
   Looking out or looking in? 59
   Finding your behavioural styles 60
   Adding new behaviours 64

Chapter 5: Choosing Your Beliefs **67**
Understanding How Your Beliefs Shape You.................67
   Where do your beliefs come from?.........................68
   What are your beliefs?...69
   What do your beliefs give you?.............................70
Changing Your Beliefs..72
   Reshaping a limiting belief...................................72
   Getting under the skin of your most stubborn limiting beliefs......73

Learning to Manage Your Fears..75
    Identifying fears that drive you and fears that block you 76
    Recognising your fear foes 76
    Minimising your fear foes 78

Chapter 6: Discovering the Values that Motivate You 81

Navigating with Your Own Coordinates 82
    Reading your personal road map 82
    Knowing what your needs are..84
Getting Clear on Your Values...86
    What are your values?...87
    Reflecting on your values..91
Sorting Through Conflicts of Motivation 92
    Looking out for your heart's desire..93
    Dealing with changing priorities 94

Chapter 7: Stocking Up on Powerful Questions...................95

Delving into the Power of Asking Questions.....................................95
    Heeding hesitation...96
    Confronting confusion...97
    Fighting frustration...97
Don't Get Stuck Asking the Wrong Questions!.................................98
Asking the Right Questions 99
    Moving down the funnel 99
    Finding your most powerful questions 101
Listening to the Answers 102
    When you don't know the answer 102
    Tuning into energy levels to find the answers.............................103

Chapter 8: Taking Stock of Now 105

Practising Awareness...105
    Taking short cuts without cutting corners....................................106
    Balancing assets and liabilities 106
    Redefining success 108
    Focusing on outcomes 110
Tapping into Your Intuitive Self...112
    Trusting your gut feeling..112
    Living with a light heart 113
    Cultivating a relaxed focus 113
Knowing What You Really Want 114
    You don't have to have what you've always had 116
    You're creating your future now..116
    Visualising your whole-life goals...117
    Placing your whole-life goals on your horizon 118

Chapter 9: Exploring Your Options **119**

Moving from Problems to Possibilities 120
  Avoiding the 'yes, but' game 120
  The desert island scenario 121
Assessing Your Stock of Resources 122
  Building supportive networks 123
  Increasing your resources 123
Expanding Your Range of Options 124
  Developing a creative approach 125
  Playing with unlimited options 126
  Choosing the best fit 128

Chapter 10: Planning Effective Action **131**

Smarten Up Your Goal Setting 131
  Putting theory into practice 136
  Smartening up to lose weight 138
Matching Your Options to Your Goals 139
  Setting milestones for your journey 139
  Taking baby steps 140
Keeping Your Promise to Yourself 141
  Thinking like a hero 141
  When life gets in the way of living 142
  Exploding the myth of will-power 143
  Dealing with jealousy from others 144

Part III: Focusing on the Elements of Your Life 145

Chapter 11: Career and Work **147**

Assessing Your Attitudes to Work 148
  Playing your part in different work roles 148
  Balancing your different roles 148
Setting Your Work in Context 151
  Making a conscious choice 151
  Evaluating your job 152
  Making adjustments at work 153
Improving Your Current Job 155
  Keeping your focus 155
  Dealing with negative situations 157
Finding Your Dream Work 158
  Knowing your job-search goal 159
  Working the market 160
  Using your networks 161
Getting Recognition for Your Work 161
  Getting feedback 162
  Promoting your personal brand 163
Looking to the Future 164

Chapter 12: Money, Wealth and Abundance....................167

Defining the Role of Money in Your Life 168
Being Financially Secure..169
    Drawing up your financial ground rules 169
    Developing your financial survival plan..............................171
Living Your Chosen Lifestyle 172
    Counting the true cost of your lifestyle 173
    Permitting yourself to be rich 174
Cultivating a Feeling of Wealth and Abundance......................175
Giving It All Away..177

Chapter 13: People and Relationships 179

Enjoying Loving Relationships..179
    Creating a relationship with yourself.................................180
    Finding your soul mate..181
    Building and maintaining a strong partnership 182
    Deciding to leave a relationship 184
Nurturing Family Bonds...184
    Setting family ground rules..186
Giving and Receiving Friendship 186
    Maintaining lifelong friendships 187
    Staying open to new friendships..189
Building Productive Networks...190
    Widening your circle of influence 190
    Getting into the networking groove....................................191
    Taking a role in your world 192

Chapter 14: Physical, Mental and Emotional Well-being.........193

Choosing Your Health Goals 193
    Defining your health goals...194
    Digging deeper into your motivation 194
Looking After Your Body..196
    Avoiding illness and disease 197
    Filling your body with the best fuel....................................197
    Avoiding sweat and tears: Finding the best exercise for you 199
    Building energy, strength and fitness.................................200
Taking Care of Your Mental and Emotional Well-being 202
    Managing your emotions 202
    Getting out of getting into a state 204
    Developing mental resilience 205

Chapter 15: Developing and Growing 207

Thriving on Learning 207
    Being your best 208
    Harnessing your brain power..209
Playing in the Game of Life..211
    Benefiting from a playful approach 212
    Making the most of your leisure time.................................213

Getting in Touch with Your Spiritual Side..................................215
What is spirituality for you? 215
Accessing your spirituality.......................................216
Exploring spirituality through coaching..........................217

Part IV: Working with the Themes of Coaching 219

Chapter 16: Attracting the Life You Want 221

Mastering the Art of Acceptance...221
Letting go of resistance...222
Being present 223
Wanting What You Have 226
Practising gratitude...227
Tuning into your positive emotions 228

Chapter 17: Coaching Yourself to Happiness 231

Discovering Your Happiness Formula 232
Getting into the flow 232
Delving into positive psychology................................233
Identifying the elements of happiness for you....................235
Discovering Optimism 239
Taking charge of your mindset 240
Practising the positive 240
Planning Your Happy Life..241
Making time to be happy 242
Keeping faith and focus on happiness 243

Chapter 18: Defining True Success........................... 245

Knowing Your Value in the World...245
Adopting the personal qualities of success 246
Modelling excellence...249
Getting the Results You Want..251
Developing your inner success compass 252
Thinking Yourself to Success...252
Observing your thoughts 253
Creating positive outcomes.......................................254

Chapter 19: Tackling Common Blocks 257

Kicking Procrastination into Touch..257
Getting to the root of why you procrastinate 258
Maintaining momentum 260
Sorting out wishing from wanting 260

Clearing Up Confusion 262
    Knowing why you feel conflicted 262
    Finding common ground for forward motion 263
Transforming Self-doubt into Self-esteem 264
    Accepting yourself as you are 264
    Knowing that you're worth it 266

Part V: Creating a Harmonious Whole Life 269

Chapter 20: Achieving Balance 271

Finding Your Balance 271
    Integrating the Goldilocks theory of balance into your life.......... 272
    Checking out your daily energy balance............................ 274
    Centring yourself 276
Regaining Your Balance 277
    Managing yourself and your time 277
    Learning to love delegation 279
    Choosing to let go.. 280
    Saying what you mean... 281
Managing Longer-Term Stress 282
    Spotting your danger signs.. 282
    Coaching your way through stressful situations.............. 284

Chapter 21: Making a Life-Changing Decision 285

Knowing How Your Stage of Life Affects Your Attitude to Change....... 286
Recognising Your Need to Make a Radical Change................. 289
    Moving from pain to pleasure and purpose 289
    Noticing the clues in your emotions 290
    Deciding to be your authentic self..................................... 292
Making Your Best Decision 292
    Fixing it 292
    Fleeing from it 293
    Building on strength.. 294
Letting Go and Integrating the New 295
    Working through the change 295
    Evolving to the next stage... 297

Chapter 22: Applying Your Coaching Skills More Widely 299

Thinking beyond Self-Coaching 299
Developing Key Skills for Coaching Others............................. 302
    Hear, hear! The art of listening... 302
    Building rapport... 303
Using Your Skills Ethically.. 306

Developing a Coaching Role in Your Life 306
    Coaching friends and family... 307
    Building coaching into your job... 308

Part VI: The Part of Tens 311

Chapter 23: Ten Life Coaching Beliefs about Yourself 313
You Are Unique..313
Your Whole Life Is the Canvas for Coaching....................................314
You Hold Your Own Agenda 315
You Are Resourceful 315
You Are Capable of Great Results 316
You Can Generate the Right Solutions for Yourself.......................316
You Are Free from Being Judged 317
You Can Make Powerful Choices 317
You Take Responsibility for Your Results 318
You Trust Your Senses 318

Chapter 24: Ten Questions to Keep Your Life on Track 319
What Would I Do If I Knew I Couldn't Fail?..320
Who Am I Becoming? 320
What Am I Doing Right Now to Honour My Core Values? 321
What Am I Settling For?...321
What Is My Legacy?..322
Where Do I Focus My Attention? 322
How Am I Using My Gifts?..323
What Am I Holding on to That I No Longer Need? 323
How Much Time Do I Spend with People Who Inspire Me? 324
What One Thing Would I Change for the Better? 324

Chapter 25: Ten Daily Balancing Acts 325
See a Clear Vision 325
Take a Gratitude Tonic 325
Do a Kind and Thoughtful Act 326
Soak Up Wise Words 327
See-saw between Action and Reflection 327
Take a Deep Breath 327
Share a Smile 328
Give Yourself a Treat 328
Stretch Out 329
Get Natural 329

Chapter 26: Ten Inspirational Resources 331
Your Life Is a Journey 331
Get Out of Your Mind..332

See Things as You Want Them to Be 332
Choose Happiness 332
Feast Your Senses...333
Value Your Life Experience 333
Poetry Creates Motion 334
No Place Like Home...334
Your Life Is Significant 335
Let Your Inner Coach Come Out to Play...335

Appendix: Considering a Future as a Professional Life Coach *337*

Getting Started 337
Considering Your Niche..339
Doing the Business 340
Marketing Yourself 342
    Knowing your offering..342
    Choosing the right marketing methods for you 342
Making Up Your Mind 344

Index *345*

Introduction

A few years ago I left my well-paid and prestigious job with a global corporation to venture into the scary world of self-employment as a life coach. Many of my colleagues who I'd come to know and love over the years wished me well and asked exactly what I'd be *doing*. 'Well,' said I, 'I suppose what I'm really interested in is inspiring people to find the right balance, enjoyment, and meaning in their lives.'

'Oh,' they replied, and a faraway look came into their eyes, 'I could really do with some of that.' Then their gaze focused back on their overflowing desk and the ringing phone. 'But I don't see how I can possibly give up my job.' And they smiled, reached for the phone, and did what they knew they did best. I found their response very interesting because it summed up the precise feelings I'd wrestled with for three long years before finally taking my personal plunge. I began working closely with people from widely different backgrounds, with widely different reasons for coming to personal coaching. And I discovered that when you take the time to question and challenge your own assumptions, to focus on working out what your own life is really about, rather than what you or others think it *should* be, things start to make a lot of sense. You begin to get more balance, enjoy yourself more, and work out the meaning of life for you (for fans of *The Hitchhiker's Guide to the Galaxy*, the meaning of life does not appear to be 42, by the way, however comforting that thought may be to those of you in search of certainty).

Coaching is like using a really efficient search engine to help you work out what you really want. Coaching gives you the keywords to finding meaning in your life, like nothing else I've ever discovered. That's why I wrote this book – so that you can have that power too.

About This Book

This book is about coaching yourself to greater balance, enjoyment, and meaning. You can also use this book as background inspiration if you're already working with a life coach. And professional life coaches can suggest this book to your clients to act as a virtual coach between sessions. You can also find information here about helping others through using your coaching skills.

Conventions Used in This Book

Breathe a huge sigh of relief – this book is a jargon-free zone. Some books about life coaching can spin your head, but this book sets out the information in a practical way so that you can quickly and easily start to make a difference in your life. When I do introduce a new term, I *italicise* and define it.

The only other conventions in this book are that web addresses are in `monofont`, and the action part of numbered steps and the key concept in a list are in **bold**. I alternate between using female and male pronouns in even and odd chapters to be fair to both!

Foolish Assumptions

I assume, perhaps wrongly, that some of the following applies to you:

- You've heard the term *life coaching* and think that behind the rather airy-fairy, fluffy name something useful and practical may be in it for you.

- You gravitate towards the personal development/peak performance/ self-help sections of train station newsagents and sneakily take pop-personality and lifestyle quizzes on a regular basis.

- You're fed up with gurus in the media telling you they've found the holy grail to personal fulfilment. You reckon you probably know more about it than they do (you do, actually).

- You're committed to being your best self but get a bit frustrated at times that it seems so hard.

- You're hungry for inspiration and practical guidance on how to fit all the pieces of your life jigsaw together, but you don't have time to attend motivational seminars.

This book is for anyone who *has* a life and wants to really *live* that life.

How This Book Is Organised

This book is divided into six parts, each covering a broad subject area.

Part 1: The Basics of Life Coaching

This part explains what life coaching is and what it isn't. You discover why and how life coaching works. This part helps you decide what you want to get out of coaching and how to set yourself up for success.

Part 11: Your Life Coaching Journey

Part II takes you on a whistle-stop tour of your *natural behaviour preferences*, the beliefs you have that can either propel you forward or hold you back, and the things that really get you going in a positive direction. You find out how to build your own stock of powerful coaching questions to help you on your journey. The chapters in this part encourage you to set your goals and create a robust strategy for seeing your plan through.

Part 111: Focusing on the Elements of Your Life

Part III homes in on the different areas of your life that may need the most attention:

- ✔ Career and work
- ✔ Money and wealth
- ✔ People and relationships
- ✔ Health and wellbeing
- ✔ Personal growth

The chapters in this part cover your options in the daily challenges you have in these different areas.

Part IV: Working with the Themes of Coaching

In Part IV you discover how to really appreciate the present moment and attract good things into your life. You find out about the happiness formula (yes, it really exists), and the factors that are proven to contribute towards individual happiness . . . you may be surprised by the results.

In this part you also explore your definition of success; what success really means to you. Finally, I offer some tips for tackling common blocks to living your best life, such as procrastination or a lack of confidence.

Part V: Creating a Harmonious Whole Life

Fixing on one bit of anything can sometimes throw the whole system out of balance. In this part you examine what balance means to you and how you can work out the best way to find equilibrium in your life.

You can also ponder on how to make a really big life-changing decision safely, if you feel that change is on the horizon.

This part also explores the wider role that coaching may play in your world in the future.

Part VI: The Part of Tens

Here you find the ten core beliefs about you that can sustain your progress, the ten most powerful questions you can ask yourself to help you develop, ten things to do each day to stay in balance, and ten inspirational resources to keep at your fingertips.

Icons Used in This Book

All *For Dummies* books feature icons to draw your attention to special paragraphs. In this book you find these icons:

The placard highlights activities – some fun, some more serious – to help you on your coaching journey. Jump to these if you love filling out those personality questionnaires in magazines!

I've witnessed some amazing transformations as a result of coaching. The inspiration icon shares what real people have done and how they have done it. Their experiences can give you clues to your own way forward.

This icon draws your attention to an important point to bear in mind, often one that's been discussed in another chapter when I want to make sure you've got the connection in case you're wandering randomly through the pages. (If you are, no turning down of page corners, now. Oh, all right, you can if you want to. It's your book.)

Coaching yourself is all about finding your own answers. The springboard icon signposts you to a great website, resource, or longer activity that can take you to another level in your knowledge or thinking.

This icon highlights practical tips to help you on your life coaching journey.

Where to Go from Here

'We're all individuals,' as the crowd shouted in unison in the Monty Python comedy *The Life of Brian.* And you don't have to live your life or read this book in a conventional way. You can take detours, zigzag back and forth, and get pleasantly lost in admiring the terrain along your way. You can choose to start at Chapter 1 and follow the chapters in order. Or you can dip in and out of the book as you like.

You may want to go straight to the Part of Tens and get a flavour of the life coaching beliefs, or just dip in and see what you find. After you've devoured this book you can check out my website for additional resources, information, and goodies (www.reachforstarfish.com).

It's your book, your choice, your life. Make the most of it.

Part I
The Basics of Life Coaching

The 5th Wave   By Rich Tennant

"I'm tired of everyone pulling my strings."

In this part . . .

From finding out what life coaching actually is,
through deciding how it's going to work for you, to
laying the foundations for your own success, the chapters
in this part focus your mind on how to get the best out of
the journey ahead.

Chapter 1

Introducing Life Coaching

. . . .

In This Chapter

▶ Knowing why coaching works

▶ Meeting your inner coach

▶ Coming to terms with change

▶ Working out your current life priorities

. . . .

*P*eople talk lots of hokum about life coaching. Life coaching television programmes, magazines and newspaper columns range in quality from the powerful and inspirational through to the downright misleading and dangerous. True life coaching isn't about some guru telling you how you should live. Yes, you may be tempted to bask in the comfort of an expert who can fix your life, your fashion sense, your body flaws and your emotional angst. But these fixes are too often like an elegant sticking plaster. Changes don't last, unless a real change has come from deep within you. True life coaching enables you to call on your very own inner guru, any time, any place, with or without the support of another human being.

This chapter explains how coaching can work its magic for you and how it can help you manage the changes in your life, not just right now, but through all the shifting priorities of your journey.

A Brief Definition of Life Coaching

Here's my definition of life coaching:

> *A purposeful conversation that inspires you to create your best life.*

You have conversations all the time (unless you're a hermit in a cave). Your conversations are chit-chat to pass the time and get along with people, or purposeful talks where you clarify thought processes, resolve problems, reach agreements and commit to actions.

Life coaching uses dialogue as well to move you along in the right direction. When you engage in a purposeful conversation with your coach – who is a skilled professional or simply that part of *you* that already *is* your coach – you cut through all the chit-chat and get to the root of everything. You may discuss the following topics, for example:

- ✔ Why you act in the way that you do.
- ✔ Which beliefs about yourself stop you from taking certain actions.
- ✔ What your options really are.
- ✔ How you can best go about getting the right results for you.
- ✔ How you can maintain your motivation.

Coaching conversations leave you refreshed, inspired and ready for action. Life coaching is more than inspiring you to live the life you *want*; it's even better than that. Sometimes your best experience of life comes from facing up to living through the parts that you really *don't* want and understanding the lessons within them. Coaching conversations help you identify how to live your very *best* life, the one that taps into all your potential and strengthens you.

Life coaching can help you form the questions that lead to answers that are right for you, which is a lot better than taking someone else's answers. Many books claim that they can guide you to The Magic Formula for Happiness, Success and Fulfilment in Life, but this book is a little different. Here, I guide you to the source of your *own* magic formula. The answers aren't out there – you already have them all and life coaching shows you how and where to find them.

What Life Coaching Is Not

In its purest form, life coaching is a technique that uses powerful questions to facilitate you in finding your own answers. It does, however, draw on and can work alongside many other similar approaches. This section explores the distinctions between coaching and its close relations.

Here are some things that life coaching is *not*:

- ✔ **Coaching is not counselling or therapy.** Counselling and therapy typically start from the perspective that something needs fixing. While many therapies are firmly rooted in present action and forward motion, their focus is more towards understanding what went wrong and achieving acceptance with that in order to move forward. With coaching, the bias is towards working from the perspective that you are fundamentally whole, healthy and strong enough to deal with the challenges of coaching.

✔ **Coaching is not mentoring.** Working with a mentor is a great way of developing yourself. You find someone who is farther ahead on the road than you are in some important respect – skills, knowledge, awareness – and model yourself on the best that you see in them. A mentor freely passes on wisdom, and you then choose whether or not to accept it. A mentor may also coach you to draw on your own inner resources – but the function of mentoring tends to focus on building your capability in an informal way.

One of the possible outcomes from self-coaching is that you decide to find yourself a mentor to model. Perhaps someone you work with who can pass on their wisdom in a very specific work context. Or it could be a person who you respect for their overall attitude to life – maybe some-one who excels at building strong, positive relationships, or who always exudes an air of calm and balance. You can actively work with a mentor or simply observe a strong role model rising to life's challenges so that you can adapt your own style to theirs.

✔ **Coaching is not giving advice.** A coach doesn't give you advice. A coach may discuss and suggest options for you, but essentially coaching facilitates your own thought processes. In this book I offer you practical principles, which act like coaching to prompt you to let the voice of your own inner coach speak out. When you coach yourself, listen to your inner coach but don't lecture yourself.

A *non-directive* coach is someone who steers away from intervening, mentor-ing and giving advice. When you coach yourself, always give yourself the space to work things out calmly and objectively, based on what you really want and need.

See Chapter 2 for more guidance on choosing the right professional coach for you, which is a great way to experience how non-directive coaching works before trying it out for yourself.

Living Your Best Life

John Lennon wrote, 'Life is what happens when you are making other plans.' I bet you often feel that you're so busy doing all the things you have to do that you never get a chance to enjoy the fruits of your labours – or simply *be*.

Your happiness in life hinges on maintaining a delicate balance:

- ✔ *Doing* **the tasks and filling the roles you have to fulfil each day.** These tasks are things that maintain you and keep your life running smoothly, such as your job, shopping, mowing the lawn and loading the dishwasher. The doing category also includes the big things you do and achieve, such as running a marathon or honing a skill.

- ✔ *Having* **the things you enjoy in your life.** These things may be material possessions, such as a house, a fancy car or a pair of designer shoes. Or they can be intangibles like security, peace of mind and love.

- ✔ *Being* **content and enjoying your experiences from all that you do and have.** *Being* means having a sense of who you are – a feeling of being comfortable in your own skin. You often sense that you are simply being in those quiet (and maybe rare) moments with yourself when you feel that you are the right person, in the right place, at just the right time.

When these three aspects of your life are in tune with each other, your life feels just right.

Life coaching doesn't turn your life into a super-charged roller-coaster of an experience – unless that's what you really want. It does help you to work out your unique gifts and your true priorities, and it does support you in eliminating anything blocking you from doing, having and being what you want. And life coaching provides that sprinkling of magic action dust that can transform your current life into something even better than your wildest dreams, because those dreams are rooted in your ideal reality.

Chances are that you want both happiness and success in your life. Sometimes those two things can seem contradictory, yet through coaching yourself to your unique definition of each, you can make them a harmonious whole. Check out Chapters 17 and 18 for insights and techniques to create your happy success.

Getting ready for change

Perhaps you picked this book off the shelf because you're totally fed up with where you are in your life. Or you may have a nagging feeling that more potential for happiness and fulfilment is out there for you. Obviously you're ready for change – after all, you don't want your life to stay exactly the same, so that means change, right?

Maybe. Think carefully. The results you get from coaching depend to a large part on where you are in terms of readiness and willingness to change, and although you may feel that you want to change, you may not be quite ready to do so.

Most New Year's resolutions fail because the goals you set aren't always linked into your state of readiness. Unless you've done the work to seriously consider your options and prepared the ground for action, your laudable resolution to lose 20 pounds, or give up smoking or find the man/woman of your dreams is likely to lose momentum well before the end of January. If that's the case, nothing is wrong with you, you just haven't geared yourself up to sustain your promise to yourself.

Here are the stages you can work through to make any change effective:

1. **Drag yourself out of the Bogs of Denial.** If you bought this book, you're probably not in denial about an aspect of your life that you want to change. Through coaching, you may find that you're stubbornly resisting change in another aspect of your life. Denial is a tough phase, not least because its existence is hard to recognise in yourself. You need to look for the clues in your communication with other people. Do you get defensive when people say that you smoke or drink too much, or are working too hard? If you do, you may be in some state of denial. You can stay in denial just as long as it takes for you to see the need for change, but this book, and especially Chapter 5, can help you get out of the bogs quicker.

2. **Take a good look around the Plateau of Contemplation.** After you climb out of the Bogs of Denial, you can't just rush into making changes; although many people do, if they get a sharp enough shock about the behaviour or thing that needs to change. Usually, you want to play around with the *idea* of change. You may start admitting, even if only to yourself, that perhaps you're a bit of a workaholic and promise yourself to address your work-life balance sometime sooner or later. You look around at your options and possible choices and you weigh up your desire to change against the things that are keeping you stuck. Reading this book can really help you take strides along the Plateau of Contemplation. After you communicate your intent to some trusted people, you're ready for the next stage. Read Chapter 9 for more about contemplating your options.

3. **Assemble the Kit Bag of Preparation.** Consider your plan of action. How can you go about making changes in your life? What tools do you need? Who can support you? You don't need to stay too long at this stage – all planning and no action get a similar result to all action and no planning, and that's not the result you want! But the preparation needs to be right for you, whether that be emptying the house of all forms of chocolate temptation if you decide you want to lose weight, or drawing up a full-blown, all-singing, all-dancing project plan complete with bells and whistles. The coaching approach of exploring your options is invaluable here to ensure that you can check off the items you need for your change. Chapter 10 has more planning suggestions for you.

4. **Climb the Mountain of Action.** You're all prepared and you're ready to go! You're firing on all cylinders and you feel like an unstoppable force. You appreciate all the benefits of having worked through the first three stages now, because your strength, will and resolve increase with every step towards your goal. Take note of what happens along the way and expect a few sidesteps, too, in order to move forward. Check out Parts III and IV to see how the actions you take can affect different areas of your life.

5. **Claim the Flag of Consolidation.** Your life change only becomes embedded when you work out how to maintain it over time. Perhaps you'll fall back into an earlier stage of change (such as back into contemplation) from time to time – that's a normal part of consolidation. Think of this relapse as a way of fully integrating your changes into your life for the long term. Coaching is wonderful at maintaining and renewing your promise to yourself to change, not simply when doing so is easy.

Presenting the passport for your coaching journey

You already have everything you need to get started on the process of changing your life. The gifts that you may discover on your coaching journey are ones that you already have, although you may not yet recognise them. These gifts fall into three main areas:

✔ **You are unique and no one but you is so well equipped to create the life you want.** Consider what you need to live a whole and full life.

You have to put yourself first, without being selfish, in order to be of service to anyone else.

✔ **You are infinitely resourceful.** You're capable of more than you usually achieve. Allow yourself to take control of your life and you get even better results.

✔ **You have choices and freedom.** Even at times when you feel a little trapped by circumstances, you can take responsibility for your own attitude towards those barriers. You can trust your senses and tap into what helps you make the right choices in the future.

Chapter 23 can inspire you with more life-coaching beliefs.

A brief history of life coaching

Coaching has been around for a long, long time. Certainly Plato's *Dialogues* from fourth-century BC Greece have many elements of what we think of as coaching – challenging assumptions, exploring ideas, making sense of the real world.

Modern coaching owes much to the American sports coach. Think of the baseball coach cheering on his team, dispensing advice and motivation.

Coaching in business has become increasingly popular over the last decade. A business coach works in much the same way as a sports coach – encouraging performance and outcomes, and building skills and talent.

Whole-life coaching emerged more recently and is now gaining popularity in the business world as well as with private individuals. If you're also a manager you may find that the ideas in this book are ones you can bring into the workplace surprisingly easily. Many organisations recognise that if their staff are happy, then business productivity goes up. Senior people in companies sometimes work with a coach who not only supports them to achieve business excellence, but also takes a whole life perspective on areas like work-life balance and personal fulfilment.

My website guides you through the different kinds of coaching interventions that you may come across if you decide you want to work with a professional coach: www.reach forstarfish.com.

Choosing Life Coaching for Long-Term Results

Plenty of places offer you solutions to life's challenges. You can attend a training course and come away with practical options. You can read a great book and be inspired. You can talk to wise friends and get guidance. You can find a role model and kick-start your motivation. These options are highly effective in their own ways, but they do have drawbacks. In order for any or all of these strategies really to work, you have to do two things.

1. First, you have to make those options, inspiration, guidance and motivation your own.

2. Then you have to commit to carrying out the plan of action, even when your motivation wavers.

Be honest now. How many times have you made a commitment to change and found that, sooner or later, the resolve that you had at the start has deserted you, or that the methods you've chosen seem too hard? That wavering point is where coaching steps in to strengthen your resolve.

Life coaching generates in abundance all the inspiration, motivation, guidance and practical options that you need. At the end of a coaching conversation or activity (with a professional coach or simply with yourself) you come away with an action plan that you are genuinely excited about and can't wait to start (see Chapters 2 and 3). Life coaching constantly supports you in finding the right solutions for you as you eliminate limiting beliefs about what is possible in your world.

Tuning In to Your Inner Coach

You can move your life forward with the help of your very own inner coach. You may know this inner coach already, but I'm guessing that you don't yet give it the respect it deserves. And the reason you don't is because you've spent far too long listening to the whining voice of your inner critic. Well, it's time to make a change and let your inner coach come out to play! You can start by understanding more about these two aspects of yourself.

Introducing your split personality!

Your inner critic loves to talk, warning you of all the terrible consequences of everything you do. Your inner critic speaks from your past and selectively recalls only those things that went wrong – when you failed an exam, when you didn't get the date with the love of your life and when you were made redundant. So your inner critic tries to makes your present and your future safe and problem-free by wrapping you in cotton wool and persuading you to take as little action in the present as possible so that you don't trip up. And yet all the negative conversations you have with your inner critic make you feel miserable and stifled in that cotton wool instead of all warm and cosy. And that's not the worst. Your inner critic is quite prepared to use nasty tactics to hold you back from living out your dangerous dreams for yourself. It distorts and stretches reality so that it focuses only on what you think you *can't* do or be. Your inner critic is not afraid to speak its mind and tell you you're not good enough, you're too fat or too stupid.

The good news is that you also have an inner coach, cheering you on to have a go and celebrating your progress. The inner coach speaks from your future. That version of you who knows how it all turns out and is bursting to tell you that everything is going to be just fine! Yes, you had some hard challenges along the way and even periods when you felt deeply unhappy or frustrated. But your inner coach looks back along your life and sees a great deal more to celebrate – lots of fun and growth and love and happiness. Even what you thought were catastrophes turned out to be blessings in disguise. For example, getting made redundant resulted in a total career change where you discovered your true calling. And how lucky that the love of your life didn't agree to that date, because you then went on to meet the *real* love of your life, someone who you didn't, at that time, find remotely interesting!

The job of your inner coach is to encourage you to create a great future by taking positive action in your present. Your inner coach wants to tell you that you can trust yourself, because as long as you take positive action, everything will be okay. You can work out how to deal with any false steps along the way and, instead of feeling miserable and stifled wrapped up in all that cotton wool, you can feel energised and free, breathing in the fresh air and looking forward to your next adventure.

You may not hear the voice of your inner coach very often because that of your inner critic is so strident and ever-present. And when you do hear your inner coach, your inner critic is quick to slap down the wisdom, labelling the viewpoint as unrealistic or even self-indulgent.

Inner critics are fantastic at their jobs and convince us that worry, cynicism and doubt are the only real things to be guided by, and that optimism and self-belief are delusions. But both voices come from you and both perspectives have value, in the right proportions. Sometimes your inner critic points out something useful that you really need to take account of. (Inner critics do often start with a grain of truth to lure you into a dialogue where they can really go for the full guilt trip.)

You may not even know that your inner coach has a voice you can trust – you may simply let your inner critic run on autopilot so that the inner coach never gets a chance to fly the plane. You can get far better results in your life if you switch their roles so that your inner coach is the captain of the plane and your inner critic has a turn only in support and under strict supervision!

Giving yourself the gift of your own good opinion

Your inner coach – just like a professional coach if you decide to work with one – supports you in the following ways:

- ✔ Encourages you to set challenging and inspiring goals for your life that are in tune with your values
- ✔ Believes you can do it!
- ✔ Expects the best from you and knows you can meet that expectation
- ✔ Explores options with you
- ✔ Helps to generate action steps that work for you
- ✔ Keeps you moving forwards

✔ Celebrates your accomplishments along the way

✔ Delights in the positive results you get for yourself

Your inner critic, on the other hand, seeks to do the opposite of all that and delights in the times when you indulge in self-sabotage, keeping you stuck in loops that go nowhere.

Who would you rather listen to?

Turning up the volume on the voice of your inner coach

The first step in engaging with your inner coach is letting its voice come through loud and clear amid all the white noise created by your inner critic. Try this activity:

1. **Set aside 15 minutes in a place where you won't be disturbed.** Let your thoughts wander freely for a few moments, maybe bringing your attention to something you have experienced recently, perhaps a project at work or an exchange with a friend or loved one.

2. **Start to listen to the voices that come through.** Can you hear the voice of your inner critic? What does it sound like? What does it say? How often does it use negative language? Do you hear a lot of 'should', 'ought' or 'must'? Is it taunting, mocking, strident, bitchy, sarcastic? Or is it sorrowful, fed-up, depressed, dejected? Or something else entirely?

3. **Now imagine a voice that is the opposite.** How does it sound? What does it say? Is it a voice you know and love or one that is delightfully fresh to you? If you turn up the volume on this voice, how do you feel? Does your inner critic complain? If so, let it fade away and fizzle out all by itself and keep turning up the volume on the voice of your inner coach. What new insights does it offer you? What feelings does it produce for you?

4. **Practise this activity frequently.** Fifteen minutes a day over a period of time can soon have you tuning in at will to what your inner coach has to say.

When Jo came to coaching, she found that writing in her journal most effectively helped her to recapture the voice of her inner coach. It also did the trick for taming her inner critic. Whenever she felt an inner critic attack coming on, she stopped and found a few moments to write out what she was feeling. The crazy, spiteful words of her inner critic often seemed ridiculous written out on the page in black and white. Within five or ten minutes of doing this, she found herself starting to write down the wisdom coming from her inner coach. She said that for her, writing out the dialogue in her head acted almost like a meditation and she could always get back into the swing of things feeling refreshed and energised.

Having a coaching conversation

If you choose to work with a professional coach, the coaching conversations will have certain characteristics. You can incorporate these characteristics into your own self-coaching. Here's what makes a coaching conversation so uniquely purposeful:

- ✔ The focus is on knowing what you want to get out of the conversation itself. Your inner coach encourages you to set a goal for the session itself, for example, 'By the end of this time I've set aside with myself, I want to have clarified and fully understood my limiting belief about my ability to close a sale.'

- ✔ Your inner coach asks you many powerful questions that get you thinking deeply about what's going on and what's important. Some of these questions may be ones you've never considered before or dared to ask yourself.

- ✔ A fair amount of clarification occurs during the conversation. Communication can be a slippery beast and a good coach never assumes too much. Your inner coach listens out for the voice of the inner critic and notes those times when you lapse into shoulds, coulds and woulds, because that's a sign that you don't really *want* to do something but think you really *ought* to!

- ✔ The coaching conversation involves a strong call to action, but this doesn't always mean that you identify a full-blown plan. The action may be that you need to explore more options, do some more research or even reflect more on the issue in hand. But the call to action from your inner coach ensures that you move yourself and your thinking forward.

- ✔ The focus is fully on your current agenda, within the context of your whole life. If you decide that your burning priority in life is perfecting your golf swing, then that will be the focus until you choose to move to another aspect of your life. But because coaching tends to highlight the connections – or lack of them – in your whole life, you're likely to change your agenda fairly frequently for yourself when other priorities take over.

Identifying Your Current Priorities for Coaching

Knowing where to start with applying coaching techniques to the elements of your life may seem hard. Sometimes you get a clear sense that one particular area, your work or career for example, is the one that requires the most attention. At other times you have the general feeling that all areas of your life need a good overhaul or boost of momentum.

This section enables you to really home in on the area of your life in which coaching can provide the biggest and most immediate benefits. You can keep coming back to this section to update your goals every so often, because one thing's for sure – your priorities change over time, and that's just as it should be.

Dividing up your life into handy compartments may seem simplistic. Your life is full of connections and consequences, so you don't really move attention from your career to finance issues to relationships throughout your day, even if your diary indicates that you're at work from 8 a.m. until 6 p.m., with a lunch appointment with your accountant and an evening spent with your family. All areas of your life intrude on and complement each other. However, when applying coaching techniques dividing these distinct areas of your life into separate compartments is helpful so that you can be very specific about the changes you want to make and the actions you need to take. You can then think about the impact the changes may have on other areas of your life.

Working out what's really important to you (your core values in life) gives you a great entry point into coaching, because doing so can highlight common themes or specific areas of your life that are out of kilter. Read Chapter 6 for more about identifying your core values.

The following activity helps you to identify your compelling current priority for life coaching if you haven't identified one yet.

1. **In Table 1-1, mark in the second column (A) how important each factor is to you.** Three ticks indicate that the factor is very important to you, two ticks mean that it is moderately important to you and one tick means that it's not very important to you.

Table 1-1	Identifying Areas for Coaching	
	A. How Important Is This to Me?	*B. How Satisfied Am I with This Right Now?*
Career and work		
I enjoy my work and get satisfaction from it.		
I receive appropriate recognition for my work.		
I have enough opportunities to develop myself in my work.		
Money and wealth		
I am financially secure.		
I have enough money to live the kind of lifestyle that I want.		
I am creating wealth for my future.		
People and relationships		
I enjoy loving family relationships.		
I have close and supportive friendships.		
I have access to beneficial networks and communities.		
Health and well-being		
I take care of my health to prevent illness.		
I am fit, strong, flexible and energetic.		
I am emotionally and mentally resilient.		
Learning and growing		
I have enough fun and leisure in my life.		
I am constantly learning and developing myself.		
I have a sense of purpose and meaning in my life.		

2. **Consider what areas, if any, have appeared as priorities for you.** You may be surprised that one or two areas don't warrant three or even two ticks. Or maybe everything has three ticks for you, but you have a sense that some ticks carry more importance for you than others. Don't worry; that's natural. But have a sense of what, when push comes to shove, are the factors that most sustain you.

3. **Consider each statement in the light of your current level of satisfaction.** Mark three ticks in the third column (B) if you're very satisfied, two ticks if you're moderately satisfied and one tick if you're not very satisfied.

4. **Look at your results and see how many three-tick matches you have.** Well done if you have a total of six ticks in some areas (the combined ticks in the two columns). This shows that you're getting high satisfaction from an area of your life that is very important to you.

   Are you getting a high level of satisfaction from an area that is quite low in importance to you? That's okay – but perhaps you can consider whether you can shift the balance a little so that your higher-priority areas get some more attention. Or maybe this highlights that something great is going on in your life that you've begun to take for granted.

   Look out for the areas that only get one or two ticks on a satisfaction level. These are your more urgent priority areas of focus as you apply coaching techniques to your life.

You can find lots more practical help in Part III, which looks closely at the different life areas. If the activity has got you thinking about how unbalanced your life is, hop straight to Chapter 20. Chapter 21 can help you if the activity highlighted a big area of change that feels a little scary.

When you begin highlighting areas of focus for coaching in this way, you may uncover a particular block that affects one or more areas of your life. Three of the most common blocks are:

✔ **Procrastination.** Putting off starting or completing tasks and actions.

✔ **Feeling conflicted.** A part of you wants one thing, while a part of you wants something else.

✔ **Lacking confidence.** Holding back in all sorts of ways because you don't feel up to the challenge.

All three of these blocks can stop you in your tracks. If any of these have cropped up for you here (or you simply recognise them already as they play out in your life), head to Chapter 19 where I look at ways to zap these blocks so you can get on with creating your best life!

Pinpointing priorities

Lauren completed Table 1-1 with some surprising results. She felt that her working life was the priority area for her to address, so she was expecting the importance/satisfaction gaps to be pretty big. Surprisingly, only one area had a real shortfall – her sense of recognition for her efforts. Lauren found that recognition was highly important to her at work and she was very dissatisfied with that aspect, even though she scored three ticks each for enjoying work and her potential for skills development. Before she analysed work in this way, she would have said that she was generally very unhappy with all aspects of her work. Lauren's feeling of not being recognised was affecting her positive feelings about the other aspects. Not feeling recognised at work was linked to some of her own negative beliefs about herself – 'Unless people tell me so every single day, I don't feel that I'm doing a good enough job.'

Coaching helped Lauren accept that external feedback may always be erratic and may not always relate to how good a job she was doing. The internal recognition she could give to herself was within her control and, with coaching, began to feel more satisfying. As a result, she was able to ask for feedback more openly because she felt surer in herself.

Lauren had allocated two ticks to family, and this took her aback. She'd always thought of herself as *very* family-oriented. Over the years, family had become less important to her than friends and even than her wider networks. Lauren was getting high satisfaction from the connections she had with her parents and siblings, and she began to wonder if she wanted to address this lowering in importance. Her family was very good at making time for her, and yet she'd reduced the time she gave back to her parents and siblings. Lauren found that this issue had become one of the most compelling for her to address.

Lauren's priority order for these actions turned out to be as follows:

- Examining and working on changing her negative beliefs about herself at work.
- Improving the quality of her communication with her family.
- Getting recognition at work through feedback.

Chapter 2

Deciding What You Want to Take from Coaching

. . . .

In This Chapter

▶ Knowing the benefits of coaching

▶ Choosing a coach

▶ Making your promise

. . . .

*O*ne of the most surprising things about life coaching is that you don't have to know at the outset exactly what it is that you want to fix or improve in your life for the magic to work. Having a specific goal in mind (such as getting fit) or at least an area of your life that you want to improve (such as your relationships) does help the coaching process. But you can also use coaching to help you identify that vague, nagging feeling of dissatisfaction that you have and what needs to change in your life to restore your vim and vigour. In fact, sometimes having too fixed a goal in mind distracts you from enjoying the many benefits of the process. I've found that many clients who had a very clear objective about change in a specific area of their lives later identified that what they thought was the problem or goal wasn't at all, or was secondary to something else. So if you're worried that you don't have a clear enough idea of what's wrong or could be better – relax! Whole life coaching is the perfect medium for exploring what's really going on.

Because coaching has a wonderful way of giving you many more goodies than you set out to acquire, keeping a completely open mind helps you appreciate those goodies when they pop up. Life coaching shows you how connected your life really is. Maybe you have a specific goal to use coaching to improve your assertiveness at work, but you'll almost certainly discover that, as a result, you find new ways of improving your personal relationships too. Or, in taking a close look at the problem you have getting fit and healthy, you may discover fresh sources of motivation that result in better work performance and perhaps even a promotion.

You can use the ideas in this chapter to help you get a feel for some of the main benefits of coaching so that you can begin your journey with a sense of what you want to achieve, and equally, so that you can prepare for some of the consequences of the process. It helps you work out the best way for you to go about coaching and prepares you for the commitment you're about to make to yourself and your life.

Assessing the Benefits and Challenges of Coaching

All coaching gets results but not all coaching results look the same. You get more out of the process if you have the right expectations about what you want to achieve. Your coaching results may be very tangible and visible – a new job, or a trimmer waistline. Or your results may be reflected in changes in the way you think and behave that make you happier in your daily life. The biggest benefit of coaching is that it brings more self-awareness and makes you at peace with your life choices. Think about the following benefits of coaching and decide which ones are priorities for you.

The act of reaching for your goals creates a great deal of the enjoyment in your life.

Attaining goals

Coaching is a very effective mechanism to support you as you identify and attain your goals. Perhaps you're aiming for a specific outcome or outcomes from coaching, such as wanting to:

- Change your job or embark on a new career
- Establish your own business
- Improve a personal relationship
- Get fit and healthy
- Become a non-smoker
- Increase your personal wealth
- Become more self-confident

The list could go on and on. You can tackle anything tangible that you want to change or improve in your life through coaching. If you have a long list of goals, decide how they stack up on your priority scale, because you can't achieve everything all at once. Coaching can help you decide on these priorities too – and what you think is the compelling issue may turn out to be rather less critical after you've turned the spotlight on it through coaching.

Part III helps you to decide on the goals that you want to achieve in very specific areas of your life:

- ✔ Career
- ✔ Money
- ✔ Relationships
- ✔ Health
- ✔ Personal growth

The following activity helps you focus on the main benefits you want to take from coaching.

Think about some broad outcomes that you hope to achieve through coaching:

- ✔ What goals do I want to focus on?
- ✔ How do I feel about my whole-life balance?
- ✔ Do I have a sense of purpose, and if not, is this a key area for me?
- ✔ How do my thought and behaviour patterns get in my way?
- ✔ How often do I question myself and my actions without being self-critical?
- ✔ How focused am I on enjoying the present moment in my life?

When you have some answers, even though they may not yet be very specific, ask yourself which of these areas are the most compelling for you. What benefits do you get if you choose to focus on these areas? What challenges do you think lie ahead?

Achieving balance

You may feel pretty happy with what you've got in your life – perhaps you have too much of everything apart from time! Coaching can help you work out what balance means to you and devise a strategy to rebalance yourself when you feel out of kilter. Coaching can help you find ways to manage your life and your resources more effectively, or assist you in working out your true priorities so that you can decide what you can let go of.

Chapter 20 looks specifically at issues of whole-life balance and provides a simple diagnostic tool for you to assess where the balance is in your life at any point in time.

Finding purpose

Perhaps you've already achieved all your goals and have worked out how to balance your time and resources. Yet you may still have a nagging feeling of discontent or a sense that something is missing. You may feel unfulfilled – certainly not miserable, but not fully alive.

If this description fits you, you're probably searching for meaning and purpose in your life. Coaching is a great way of exploring your unique gifts and what your contribution to the wider world can be. Life coaching can be the start of a spiritual journey for you, or it may help you identify and secure the work or activity that makes your soul sing. Often, this search for meaning and purpose means that your life undergoes a big change in its direction or structure, although sometimes the changes are more subtle and interwoven into the threads of your current way of living.

Through coaching, Sally found that her job as an IT consultant didn't feed her soul, and so she resigned from her job to concentrate full-time on her passion, landscape photography. Sally's conviction that she was on the right path sustained her through a few years of financial hardship until she became established.

Pete's search for purpose took him right back to his family unit and his desire to be the very best father he could possibly be to his two young children. This shift in emphasis was relatively easy to integrate into his life.

Chapter 21 explores ways of working through periods of major change as a result of this shift in focus.

Changing your mindset

You may have come to coaching because you've identified that the way you think or behave isn't making you happy. You may have achieved what look like fantastic results in your life, and yet you're miserable because you have a tendency to be too hard on yourself and underrate all your achievements. Or you may have fallen into patterns of behaviour that work up to a point but mean that you feel bad about yourself in some other way.

One super-salesperson I met was consistently top of the sales league tables, but she confessed to me that she was deeply unhappy because the only way she could find to achieve this success was to play against her colleagues, taking advantage of their good natures, so that she would always be the one to get the sale. She recognised that this strategy was not only making her unhappy, but also meant that her jobs had a short shelf life because she felt she continually had to move elsewhere for fresh victims.

Coaching works on the premise that you can always get as good or better results through approaches that are congruent with what is truly important to you. Some very deep-rooted thought and behaviour patterns are sometimes best tackled through counselling or therapy, but often coaching can be the most effective method of holding a mirror up to unhelpful thought and behaviour patterns, and devising a workable strategy for replacing them with healthier approaches for yourself.

Part II of this book has information about how you can work to change the way you think about yourself and your life so that you can move forward more positively.

Growing through self-awareness

All coaching offers you the possibility of growing through becoming more self-aware. Think of yourself as an onion with many, many layers to uncover (not a very flattering image, I know!). As you peel back the layers, you reveal more of your true self until you get to the fullest understanding of who you are and what you're capable of. Some people describe this as a feeling of coming home to themselves. This understanding is like spending a long time away travelling, soaking up new experiences and finally arriving home richer for your travels. Home is still the same, yet you see it with new eyes because of all the things you have seen, done and learnt.

Throughout this book you discover how coaching allows you to reflect and take new meanings from the things that are most important to you.

Enjoying the journey

Coaching is a combination of getting the results you want and taking steps to get those results. Sometimes the goals in themselves may turn out to have limited power to make you happy. Have you ever worked really hard to achieve something and then found that the reward at the end was somehow not as satisfying as you'd hoped? Often the *challenge* of attaining your goals makes you really come alive as you stretch yourself and your abilities. The joy you experience as you cross each finishing line is more likely to be lasting if you've been fully engaged in everything leading up to that moment. Coaching can become addictive, because the process of setting and reaching for your goals in a way that's meaningful to you gives you the most benefits as you begin to see and experience all that you're capable of. The great results then become a wonderful bonus!

Finding a meaningful way to achieve your goal is especially important if your goal is to give up a bad habit. Successful non-smokers who make a determined plan to focus on being a new, healthy version of themselves and use the savings from their old habit to fund a gym membership enjoy the challenge *and* stick with the goal. Someone who doesn't replace smoking with a positive distraction mopes around thinking about how much pleasure they're giving up. Being realistic in your coaching journey means knowing that you need a massive effort to get to your goal, as well as appreciating the pleasure of the process that gets you there.

This book focuses on getting your expectations of coaching right and prepares you for the ups and downs of the road to your new self.

Considering the challenges of coaching

Not all the results of coaching feel positive at the time. Like any process of self-development, you need to prepare yourself for hard work and effort, and perhaps some frustration and disappointment along the way. Perhaps you have to let go of something that has acted as a comfort blanket for you, and maybe you also face up to some tough facts about yourself and your choices to date. Don't think that these challenges are depressing – there's way more on the positive side to make your life coaching journey all worthwhile. Knowing in advance that a few thorns lie in the bed of roses helps to keep you grounded.

Deciding on a Coaching Method

This section helps you to decide whether you want to engage a professional life coach, find someone with whom to co-coach or begin to self-coach. There is no single best way – the decision you make depends on many factors, including your own preferred style of self-development.

A good idea is to work with a professional life coach for a period early on in your coaching journey, and to return to working with a coach at times during your life when you need extra support. Coaching is a skilled profession, and the investment of time and money is well worth it. You can especially benefit from engaging a trained life coach for a while if the areas you think you want to focus on are changing your mindset, achieving whole-life balance or finding meaning and purpose. You may find these areas complex to work through on your own. Experiencing coaching in this way helps set a standard for you to develop your own self/co-coaching style.

If you already have some experience of coaching, maybe at work, or have acquired knowledge, perhaps through this book or other resources, then co-coaching or self-coaching may be quite appropriate. Co- or self-coaching is especially appropriate if the area you want to focus on is a specific goal such as getting fit or managing your time.

Keeping vigilant

Even when the issue you're addressing seems simple and straightforward, the process of coaching can reveal more complex matters. If you are co-coaching or self-coaching, you must be very vigilant during the process to ensure that you are giving yourself or your co-coach the best possible support. Watch out for warning signs that you're getting out of your depth – feeling uncomfortable, not making progress or extreme negative emotions. Remember that overlaps exist between coaching and the therapeutic professions, and it's not always clear at the outset if an issue is going to fall into an area best dealt with by an altogether different specialist. This is where working with a trained coach offers greater protection than going it alone.

Remember that sometimes people turn to coaching when they're very low as a more 'acceptable' way of getting help rather than visiting a doctor or other therapist. Coaching someone who has clinical depression is not appropriate. Instead, sensitively help the person you're with to seek the right kind of support to move her forward. Visit www.nhs.uk/depression to understand more about the common symptoms of depression.

Finding the right coach

Life coaching has only been around in its current format in the United Kingdom in recent years, and the professional framework is taking a little while to settle into its final form. Currently the coaching profession as a whole is unregulated, which means that anyone can set themselves up as a coach and charge whatever hourly rate they like, subject to market forces. No single recognised programme of study leads to a definitive qualification in life coaching, and nothing stops anyone from designing and offering a programme of coach training.

However, a number of excellent companies and colleges are working to provide quality training programmes for life coaching and credible professional bodies are working hard to formalise best practice. Go to the Appendix for more guidance on coaching qualifications and programmes.

You can find more information about choosing a training course on my website at www.reachforstarfish.com.

Be aware that a minority of individuals are practising as life coaches who do not have the requisite skills, experience and training. This section helps you find the right questions to ask to make sure you don't put your trust in someone who may not be able to work in your best interest.

From notice boards to word of mouth

How do you go about finding a coach? If you want to get fit and healthy, then you can start with your local gym, doctor's surgery or even your local health-food shop to see if they hold the names of coaches you could approach.

If your coaching goal is more general or still undefined, then an Internet search on life coaching is a good start. Remember that much professional coaching is done over the telephone so unless you want to have face-to-face sessions, location needn't be a stumbling block to working with a coach.

Word of mouth is a good approach to finding the right coach for you because you already have the assurance that the coach has done a great job for someone you know.

Fixing terms and conditions at the first session

Many initial consultations with a life coach are free of charge and usually last about 30–60 minutes. The initial session allows you to find out exactly what's involved and whether you and your coach have a good rapport for your work together. (If the coach feels that her own skill set and style are not the best matches for you, she may refer you to a colleague, associate or other specialist.)

A professional life coach explains terms and conditions clearly to you at the outset and confirms them in writing. Pricing is normally based on hourly rates and usually differs depending on whether the coaching is carried out on the telephone or face to face. Telephone-based coaching has the advantage of convenience for both parties and is often more cost effective because the coach has no travelling time or costs. The price the coach quotes you normally doesn't include the cost of the telephone call (because usually you call your coach), but your coach should explain that at the outset (some coaches do offer an all-inclusive rate).

Charges for coaching are often a little higher than the therapeutic professions (counselling/therapy) and may be more akin to business consultant rates for a top coach. Rates vary dramatically and typically range from £50–£150 ($100–$300) an hour. Coaches who are still in training may charge less than this range and highly experienced and skilled coaches charge a lot more. Shop around and talk to a number of different coaches to ensure that you make the most appropriate choice for you and your budget.

Many coaches offer a range of programmes based around a set number of sessions with the view of setting specific realistic objectives, so that you always know exactly what you're signing up for and how much the total cost is. For example, you may begin with a 12-week programme of between 9 and 12 sessions. Or your coach may offer a taster programme of 2–4 sessions. Most coaches work quite flexibly and can discuss the best option for you at the end of an initial consultation – one size doesn't fit all in this respect.

Your coach may ask you to sign a brief contract or agreement. In general, coaches recommend that you do not work with one coach for very extended periods. How long is too long? Well, that depends on you and how much value you're getting from the relationship, but in general, review things every three or four months. If you work with the same coach for a year or more without any break, then the relationship may become too comfortable and lack challenge. One of the goals of coaching is to build your self-reliance and ability to self-coach, so most coaches do set regular review points. Coaching is such a great experience for most people that it can be tempting to continue working with a coach for longer than you really require. Both parties need to be vigilant that the process is producing tangible benefits.

Any agreement you make with a professional coach carries cancellation charges (if you're not making time for your sessions and cancelling at the last minute then your commitment to yourself is not 100 per cent). But beware of non-refundable deals. You should have the right to terminate the relationship at any time. Only work with a coach who is clear on the ground rules.

Qualifications

Many life coaches possess a Certificate or Diploma in Life Coaching from a reputable training provider or educational establishment. A *Certificate in Coaching* is an entry-level qualification whilst a *Diploma* is a more thorough period of study. If you want to take a rather more theoretical and academic route, you can now complete a postgraduate degree in coaching with a number of institutions in the UK.

By no means all coaches are qualified in this way. Many coaches are qualified by their experience in practical coaching alone, or have other qualifications in areas such as neuro-linguistic programming or psychotherapy, more general qualifications in human resources or training, or certification to administer and interpret psychometric tests. Ask what qualifications your coach possesses and make sure that she explains clearly why and how the qualification is relevant to the work she does in general and specifically to what you want to achieve from the coaching. A trained and experienced life coach has a wide range of skills and expertise that she continually updates according to the best possible practice.

If you are not familiar with your coach's qualification, ask for a website or head office address for the awarding body or training provider and do a little research to check the qualification out. It's perfectly appropriate to ask to see copies of any relevant certificates.

Qualifications aren't always the most important factor to consider, but they're a good indicator of professional integrity and demonstrate a commitment to the coach's own professional development. A formally qualified coach who is active in her own profession is likely to have up-to-date best practice at her fingertips. If your prospective life coach doesn't possess any kind of relevant formal qualification, you may want to ask her why she decided not to go down that path and what she's done instead to ensure that she's well trained and developed as a coach. She may cite membership of an association that supervises her. *Supervision* simply means that she gets support from another coach who is trained to help her maintain the best technical quality standards and develop her competence.

Don't rule out a coach simply because she lacks a qualification. Many excellent life coaches have extensive relevant life and business coaching experience rather than a formal qualification, and it is this that qualifies them, along with their natural attributes, to work with you.

Experience

Ask your prospective life coach what kind of work she has done and what sort of results she can facilitate. Most life coaches who have been practising for any length of time have a clutch of testimonials from their past and current clients, and you can ask to see some of these. You can also ask if you can speak directly to a couple of clients to find out more about the coach's process, style and approach. (This may not always be possible due to client confidentiality.)

Specialist areas

Whole life coaching is not the same as business coaching. Coaches who are used to working in the corporate field may focus exclusively on performance in a work context, and while this very often encompasses aspects of personal development, it is not the main intent of life coaching. Probe your prospective coach about whether she specialises in business or whole life coaching. If you're interested in engaging a coach whose main work is in the business arena, take extra care to get testimonials from and speak to personal clients who she has coached.

Coaching approach

You are best served by a coach who has a *non-directive* coaching approach. This means that the coach supports and facilitates you to identify your own answers and does not impose her own solutions on you. She uses her skill to help you think through your issues and ideas, and may suggest and discuss options with you, but she never recommends the one best way forward because there's no 'one size fits all' when it comes to coaching. If you choose to work with a directive coach, the results you get may be less tailored to your needs.

You can identify a non-directive coaching approach because it involves the coach asking many open questions, actively listening and offering broad ideas and suggestions to help you generate a range of options. Non-directive coaching also involves some very specific techniques to focus you in your decisions, and it should always be challenging. A directive coaching style may appear to generate results more quickly, but the solutions may be less effective for you, so it's rarely the best approach in the long run.

Keeping your options open

Give yourself plenty of choice and speak with two or three prospective coaches before making your decision. On a practical level, this helps you confirm that the prices you're quoted are all in the same ball park. More importantly, shopping around allows you a better chance of finding the coach who fits best with your needs at any one time. Over the lifetime of your coaching experience, you may find that you need different styles depending on where you are in your life and the different challenges you experience.

Best fit

A competent coach is skilled at maintaining rapport with a wide range of different clients. During your initial consultation you have an opportunity to assess for yourself the style of your prospective coach and see whether it matches your needs and preferences.

Ask yourself the following questions:

- ✔ Do I feel comfortable with this person?
- ✔ Do I trust that this person has my best interests at heart?
- ✔ Am I confident in her abilities and skill?
- ✔ Do I feel challenged?
- ✔ Do I feel supported?
- ✔ Do I feel encouraged and inspired to action?

Considering co-coaching

Co-coaching is a great way to capture some of the objectivity that you get when working with a professional coach, which you can't always get if you self-coach. The idea is that you team up with like-minded people and swap roles with them. The group may be as small as two, with one of you taking the role of coach for one session and then the role of coachee the next. Co-coaching can work equally well as a trio arrangement, with one person acting as an observer. Or you can apply coaching principles in a small group, perhaps by focusing on an area of common interest such as getting fit.

Co-coaching can help build motivation and momentum. It's part of the thinking behind most slimming clubs, where you get to share experiences and ideas and other members of the group support you.

Unless you are already a trained and experienced coach, co-coaching has some limitations. The skills of empathy and objectivity take a while to develop to the full, and you can all too easily rush straight into dispensing sympathy and advice. (Co-coaching with your close friends and family can turn out to be a bad idea if they're unable to stop themselves from rushing into sorting your life out for you!)

You can use and adapt all the ideas in this book as part of your co-coaching practice.

Here are a few simple guidelines for setting up a co-coaching group:

- **Be clear that the objective of co-coaching is to support each other to generate the right solutions for the individual, without judgement.** Get your friends to read this book to understand the difference between coaching and giving advice.

- **Don't involve too many people.** Co-coaching works well with two people taking turns to coach each other. You can also try a trio arrangement, where you each take turns being coach, coachee and observer. The observer comments on what seems to work well and helps you improve your coaching skills. Many coach training programmes use this method to build practical coaching skills.

- **Use the phone too.** Face-to-face coaching works well if you can all get together fairly frequently, but you can also consider three-way calling via your telephone provider.

- **Keep the sessions regularly spaced.** Aim for a minimum of a week and no more than a month between sessions. You want enough time to take your actions following the session but not so much that you lose momentum.

- **Consider working with a professional coach before or during co-coaching.** You can pick up tips and help to ensure that you're getting the best out of your informal arrangements.

Deciding to self-coach

Self-coaching is a way of using coaching that you can adopt at any time and in any place, and this book is particularly designed for you if you want to self-coach. Indeed, one of the main goals of any coaching is to help you develop a sense of your inner coach so that you are self-reliant. You may want to try self-coaching based on the ideas in this book before deciding whether to engage a coach or organise co-coaching. While self-coaching involves no cost and relatively little resources – apart from the time commitment – it's not necessarily the easiest method because you need to work hard to be objective. As with co-coaching, you'll probably find that you also want to consider working with a coach from time to time.

This book offers guidance on listening to the voice of your inner coach so that you can become more objective during self-coaching.

Making a Promise to Yourself

You may be wondering if you can maintain the commitment to your goals that you feel right now. You've probably experienced the disappointment of setbacks before and know how hard it feels to maintain motivation long after the mood in which you first made your commitment has gone. Why are things different for you now?

For the things that are really important to you, think in terms of making a serious promise to yourself about the changes you want to make. This is different to a simple commitment, which you can measure in milestones and outcomes. The promise you make to yourself in coaching may involve allowing yourself to learn and grow from the process, to persist despite setbacks, to be honest with yourself about what is truly important and to stop beating yourself up when you get it wrong. Within this promise you make commitments that you aim to fulfil. But the big picture of your promise is to commit to making the changes and choices that are best for you and that move you forward.

Checking out your current life conditions

Are your current life conditions right for you to begin your coaching journey? Coaching can be challenging, and you should only begin if you're already feeling pretty strong and capable. Everyone suffers from low self-esteem and a lack of confidence at times, but if your current emotional state is very negative, or even depressed, you may want to consider a different kind of help, such as counselling, to get you to the point where you're ready for coaching.

Perhaps a lot is going on in your life at the moment and you're under an unusual amount of pressure. You may be tempted to look on coaching as the answer to your prayers, but if your life balance is so out of kilter that you can't make time for coaching and find that you cancel appointments – with yourself or your coach – then it's time to ask yourself some hard questions.

Ask yourself if you're ready for coaching now. Maybe you want to take a session with a coach to discuss and decide this. A half-hearted commitment can be worse than no commitment at all, and you needn't feel bad if your current life conditions don't allow you to be whole-hearted about coaching yet. You may simply have to go with the flow of what's happening in the here and now for a while. Think about what other support mechanisms are around for you, read this book to get you into the right frame of mind and make a promise that when the time is right for you, you *will* take the first step.

Framing your coaching promise

You can make a real commitment to coaching by framing your own coaching promise. Think about the traits that, in your heart of hearts, you know have most held you back in seeing through commitments in the past. Now take yourself back to the feeling you had when you last made a solemn promise. What was it that gave you the conviction that you would see that promise through? How can you access that feeling of conviction again?

Here are some examples of coaching promises that you can make:

- ✔ I promise to take responsibility for discovering the solutions that are right for me and that allow me to be the best I can be in my life.

- ✔ I promise to be open and honest with myself and trust that as long as I am taking positive action, I am making progress.

- ✔ I promise to commit to developing my awareness of myself so that I can replace habits and behaviours that are destructive with ones that are creative and productive.

- ✔ I promise never to accept second-best for myself.

- ✔ I promise to seek to learn from all my experiences and actions.

What is your coaching promise to yourself?

Chapter 3

Preparing for Coaching

- -

In This Chapter

▶ Identifying your milestone rewards

▶ Planning for setbacks

▶ Introducing your coaching journey

- -

*P*reparing for coaching helps you to enjoy the process of achieving your goals. Getting ready for coaching is partly about getting into the right mindset and feeling confident about your promise to yourself to achieve a certain goal. But it's also about getting the little things right and understanding some of the stages you go through on your journey to achieving your goal.

In this chapter I show you how to ensure that each step you take is a positive one through ongoing review and celebration of your achievements. I also give you an overview of what's ahead to help you decide the areas you want to focus on the most, whether you are self-coaching or working with a professional coach. (If you haven't decided between working with a professional coach or self-coaching, refer to Chapter 2.)

Getting Ready for Your Coaching Session

If you decide to work with a professional coach, your coach will discuss with you at the outset how to get the most out of your sessions. If you're self-coaching, you can benefit from setting some ground rules for yourself to help you get into a good coaching pattern. Here are some general guidelines to consider:

> ✔ **Schedule your coaching time in your diary or calendar and treat it as a priority.** You may be guilty of putting your own needs last – don't! You're better prepared to face the emergencies of your life if you give yourself the calm space of coaching. (Okay, at times you really will have to cancel the session because of unforeseen events, but thinking of your coaching as a major priority in your life helps you to challenge yourself when you're tempted to sacrifice the coaching time for something else.)

✔ **Ensure you have a quiet physical space for your coaching session.** If you have a telephone session with a professional coach, you need to know that you won't be disturbed and that nothing will distract you. You may want to have some soft, calming music playing very low in the background and light a candle to create a special atmosphere.

✔ **Take a few moments to review your goals from the last session and the actions you've completed or attempted.** You usually discuss these early in the session with a coach, but reflecting quietly to yourself beforehand makes this part of the coaching more focused and gets you into the right frame of mind. If you're self-coaching, you can close your eyes and review your goals for a few moments.

✔ **Keep a journal between your coaching sessions to keep track of your progress.** You can use your journal to make notes of what you discuss during coaching or to complete exercises and record answers to powerful questions (see Chapter 7 for more about powerful questions).

✔ **Complete your assignments between sessions.** Many professional coaches like to suggest ideas for homework between sessions. This may be as simple as reflecting on an idea or new belief, or it may involve a specific exercise or piece of research to help you move closer to your goals. If you're self-coaching, you may want to complete some of the activities in this book or have a stockpile of inspiring resources to dip into to keep your motivation high.

✔ **Spend a few moments after the session drawing your thoughts together and refining your actions.** If you're working with a professional coach you can drop him an email confirming the actions you agreed, and if you're self-coaching, send the email to yourself! Simply confirming your commitments like this is a fantastic way to make them feel real and significant.

Beginning Your Coaching Journey

You may be quite familiar with concepts of personal development, having read other books, attended programmes or worked through your own goals. Or maybe this is the first time you've had much exposure to the idea of personal development. But the great thing about coaching is that you enter into the process at the level you're currently at. Coaching works as a mechanism for harnessing everything you've learnt about yourself so far and all the great self-development ideas that other people have found to work.

Seeing the big picture

Your coaching journey isn't a straight line. Take a look at Figure 3-1. Central to life coaching is building your self-awareness. This begins with seeing how and why you behave in certain ways and how you can adapt and change that behaviour to improve your life. Moving to the second ring, you then begin to think about what makes you uniquely you – your beliefs, needs and values.

Armed with a clear idea of yourself, you can enter into the journey at one of the three stages of the third cycle. Perhaps you begin by noticing the results that you have achieved in your life so far; by working out what's working, maybe you then move on to exploring your options. Then you're ready to take action, which leads you back into noticing your results, and so the cycle continues. All this activity is surrounded by the outer ring – the skill of asking yourself searching and empowering questions that assist you in the journey and feed back into your self-awareness.

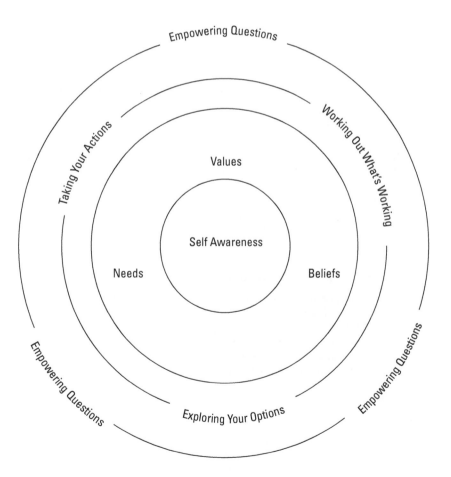

Figure 3-1:
The life-coaching circle.

I explore these cycles in more detail in the following sections.

Packing your survival kit

To begin your journey, you need a kitbag of qualities to develop and hone along the way. These qualities sustain you on your journey and help you navigate the twists and turns of the road. Your particular kitbag will be stuffed full of self-awareness, positive self belief, motivation and an impressive array of powerful questions to help you reach your destination.

Stocking up on empowering questions

Coaching takes you back to the habit you developed as a child of questioning everything around you. As an adult, you may be out of the habit of questioning and exploring, because you begin to think that your questions should be intelligent and sensible – no one wants to look stupid. And you find that you get by in the world even though you sense that you don't know quite enough about some stuff. Life coaching helps you to recapture your child-like curiosity so that you can get to what's really going on for you. Stock up on questions to direct your life in a helpful direction, such as 'What will happen if I don't make this change in my life?' And check out Chapter 7 for how to frame the empowering questions that are powerful navigation aids.

Choosing your beliefs

You have helpful beliefs about yourself but also destructive beliefs. For example, I think of myself as good with words but tend to hold a belief about myself that I'm hopeless with numbers. The positive belief gave me the confidence to write this book – great outcome! – but the negative belief causes me to procrastinate on doing my accounts – disastrous outcome! Life coaching helps you to increase the power of your positive beliefs and minimise or reject the negative limiting ones, breaking free of any self-doubt that stops you from getting what you want in life. I talk more about beliefs in Chapter 5.

Building your motivation

Values, as well as beliefs, are in the second inner ring of the coaching circle (refer to Figure 3-1). The values you hold about what is important to you, and, to a great extent, the needs you have, drive you forward. You create this motivation inside you as you seek to shape your world. Understanding how your values and needs work for you is a powerful tool to propel you forward. Turn to Chapter 6 for more.

Becoming self-aware

At the centre of the coaching circles is *self-awareness,* an understanding about yourself and how you respond to your world. The more self-aware you become, the more you're able to understand others, which helps you in many ways. You work more effectively with colleagues, and your personal life benefits too because you have a better idea of how people tick.

Achieving the highest level of self-awareness is the most beneficial outcome of all personal development, and coaching is a great medium to achieve this. Through self-awareness, you can begin to change aspects of your behaviour that don't serve you well, you can identify what it is that truly makes you happy, you can become realistic about what you're not prepared to sacrifice and you can ultimately achieve inner peace and harmony with who you are and what your place in the world is. Chapter 4 has more about understanding yourself, your preferences and your attitudes.

A client of mine said to me at the outset of a coaching programme that her goal was to work out a way of balancing the demands of her career and family life, or to accept that she needed to make a small sacrifice somewhere and to be happy with that decision. Sometimes you have to recognise that you can't always have your cake and eat it, and be at peace with your decision; this too is part of self-acceptance and self-awareness.

The stages of your journey

Kitbag packed? Good. Time to take the first steps. This section provides an overview of the stopping off points of your journey. Remember that the journey is circular. In general though, you start by thinking about what you want to change, move on to considering your options and choices, and then you take your actions.

Working out what's working

During coaching, you spend time thinking about what's working well in your life, as well as what's wrong. Shifting the focus in this way still allows you to see what you don't want, but puts you in a more powerful frame of mind to take action. Do more of what you do well and enjoy, and you discover that many other things fall into place. You still encourage yourself to change and adopt new behaviours, but your focus is on identifying positive new habits, not condemning yourself for old, bad ones. Chapter 8 helps you to develop the awareness you need to work out what's working in your life.

Exploring your options

On your life-coaching journey, you encourage yourself to experiment and try new approaches to reaching your goals. Acting in the same way as you always do generally results in the same outcomes, so flexibility, creativity and imagination become your new friends as you step outside your comfort zone a little and try new options. Chapter 9 explores your options in more detail.

Taking your actions

Having identified what you want more of or a specific goal and explored ways of achieving that, you can begin to take actions that move you one small and significant step at a time towards your goals. I describe planning effective action in Chapter 10.

Knowing Where You Are on the Road

Where are you now? Because you're creating this coaching journey, you get to choose where you start. Your starting point depends on what you need right now. Are you feeling stuck in a rut and bereft of choices? Perhaps you want to turn first to working out what you really want and building up your motivation. Or you may have a plan but lack the confidence to carry it out, in which case you may want to check what beliefs are holding you back. Equally, you may find that your commitment to seeing through the goals you set for yourself tends to waver, so perhaps your action strategies need the most attention.

The following activity can help you discover where you are the road.

In order to begin your journey towards self-awareness, ask yourself the following questions:

- ✔ How well do I understand why I behave the way I do? (Chapter 4)

- ✔ Do I know which of my beliefs help me and which ones hinder me? (Chapter 5)

- ✔ What's my true motivation in my life? What needs do I have and how do I meet them? (Chapter 6)

- ✔ How effective are my self-questioning skills? (Chapter 7)

- ✔ Do I know what works well for me and why? (Chapter 8)

- ✔ How flexible am I in exploring options and potential solutions? (Chapter 9)

- ✔ Am I effective when I decide to take action? What strategies do I employ? (Chapter 10)

Keep in mind that you move through the levels of the coaching circles even within all these stages. Just because you spend some time thinking about what motivates you and identify some answers doesn't mean that you've discovered everything about your motivation. Your self-awareness continues to grow. You may not experience radical change, but you may see more deeply into your own understanding.

Imagine that you're walking up a mountain. The air becomes less cloudy, and as you get higher, you see more of the landscape around you. Moving through the levels means that you begin to make more connections and feel more congruent with yourself as you see how everything links in for you. Accept that you may move quickly through the levels for some things – perhaps your understanding of your motivation – and get stuck at fairly low levels on others for a lot longer – perhaps in the area of your beliefs. You make progress at different rates in different areas, and that's fine.

Marking Your Progress

Coaching often produces results that are hard to measure. If your goal is to get a promotion, you know you're there when you're holding the new contract. But what if you take a year to get there? And if you don't achieve the promotion, have you failed? You may acquire even more goodies in the form of personal development as a result of the journey to get a promotion than if you actually get the job. You can always find ways to mark your progress so that you can look back at any stage and see how far you've come, which particularly helps you when the going gets tough.

As you change and develop, you set ever higher standards for yourself, so sometimes it's easy to forget where you started from. Have you ever been involved in a house renovation project? The work can get more frustrating as you get closer to completion, and you have to look at the photos of digging the foundations and clearing all the dirt and rubble to get a sense of the transformation.

Using milestone goals to celebrate success

When you set yourself a significant goal you probably can't achieve it overnight. Start thinking early on about how to celebrate success along the way. Getting fit, working towards a promotion, tackling an unhealthy habit – all these goals produce benefits for you during the journey as well as when you reach your destination, so why not celebrate these milestone benefits? Your milestones are individual to the task you set yourself. They may be tangible, such as going down one dress size (even though your ultimate goal is three sizes smaller!), or completing a great CV to submit for a new job. Your milestone goals can be process goals – maintaining your commitment to staying alcohol- or cigarette-free for a month.

Attaching rewards to milestone goals helps you to keep a focus on the here and now, not just the future, which bolsters your commitment.

What is a reward for you? Naturally, achieving your goal is a great reward, but perhaps you set a long-term goal. Waiting months or even years to breathe a sigh of relief and congratulate yourself for a job well done isn't really the best way to sustain your motivation. Instead, you can set milestone goals that you link to smaller rewards to sustain your enthusiasm.

Choose milestone rewards that don't go against your ultimate goal. If you want to lose weight, allowing yourself to binge on your favourite food every time the scales show a loss is likely to be detrimental. Aim for rewards that are healthy and nurturing for you. They needn't be expensive either, although you can push the boat out a bit when the milestone you achieve is especially significant. Here are some examples:

- A couple of hours with a good novel.
- A long, relaxing bubble bath.
- A round of golf.
- Watching your favourite sports on television.
- An evening at the theatre or cinema.
- Buying yourself something special that you've had your eye on for ages.
- A weekend away with a friend or loved one.
- Something you haven't done before that gets the adrenalin going and energises you, such as a helicopter ride, trip in a hot-air balloon or a day spent go-carting.

Think about the treats that you tend to put off because other responsibilities come first. A reward feels more like a treat when it's something you don't do every day or don't always make time for.

Why not introduce an element of surprise to your rewards? Ask a friend or partner to hold your list and choose items off it at random for you at the appropriate milestone. Or write out each reward on a separate card and post it in a box that acts as your Rewards Bank. Every time you decide to celebrate a milestone achievement, take out a card at random and treat yourself.

I cover milestone goals in greater depth in Chapter 10.

Giving yourself a pat on the back

One of the simplest ways of marking your progress is simply to notice when you move forward and take a few seconds to give yourself a pat on the back. A former boss of mine is one of the happiest people I know, and his secret is that he makes a point of looking out for small things that he's proud of during the day and mentally saying to himself, 'Well done!'

Most people are unused to paying themselves compliments, and you may have to do battle with your inner critic (see Chapter 7 for more on your inner critic). But try it – anything from finding a parking spot in a crowded high street to pulling off a brilliant presentation to a client deserves a quiet acknowledgement to yourself that you have added to the smooth running of your day. As patting yourself on the back becomes a habit, you find it easier to take those few moments of reflection to celebrate the small and significant steps you make towards the big goals in your life.

Choosing people to cheer you on

Not everyone you know will be as wholehearted about your commitment to change as you are. Accepting that you're changing can be hard for people watching from the sidelines, especially if they aren't on the same page as you with your need for change, or if they actually feel that it disrupts their own world to some extent. Read Chapter 10 for more about dealing with jealousy from others.

Identify in advance people to cheer you on in your coaching. Maybe they are people who are also going through changes and can empathise with and support you in your ups and downs. Or they may be people who are thoroughly delighted to see you taking positive steps and are always ready with words of encouragement. Knowing who your supporters are in advance and telling them what you're planning can be a great way of pinning your colours to the mast. After you've made an open declaration of your intent you're even more likely to carry through your aim and you can enjoy telling these people what progress you're making.

By the same token, avoid telling the whole world about your goals in an attempt to make yourself guilty enough to follow through. Guilt is a poor master when it comes to coaching yourself through change, even though it sometimes seems to get results. Some people do feel the need to tell as many people as possible, even those who they suspect may secretly want them to fail. A kind of 'I'll show them!' theory operates in these circumstances. My own experience, and that of most of the clients I work with, is that positive reinforcement has a much more powerful long-term impact than provoking yourself into action with guilt.

Anticipating setbacks and relapses

Take a long view and accept that you experience setbacks when attempting change. Gridlock and deadlock aren't disastrous when you think through in advance the keys that open them up. Seven helpful guidelines to bear in mind when you anticipate the challenges ahead are:

- ✔ **Remember that change requires effort and can cost more than you think** – shaping the life you want is worth the investment, so think about the resources, especially of your time, that you are putting into your change programme. Trying to take short-cuts may result in longer periods where you stay stuck.

- ✔ **Choose the methods that are right for you, not the latest 'get rich and happy quick' theory.** And if something you try doesn't work, be prepared to reflect on the reasons and try something different.

- ✔ **Realise that willpower is over-rated!** Almost no one can sustain strong willpower in the face of temptation. So avoid actions, no matter how small, that may jeopardise your goals, such as keeping tempting foods in the house when you're working to lose weight (even if you tell yourself that the biscuits are for unexpected visitors!).

- ✔ **Accept that you almost certainly don't make it first time every time.** If you're training for a race, you expect to reach your best time after preparation, practice and experimentation – not on the first day of your training programme. Of course, you easily achieve some goals at your first attempt, and you feel exhilarated at your hole-in-one, but they may be the exception.

- ✔ **Expect the unexpected.** The journey to change isn't a straight line. You may encounter surprises, go back on yourself, zigzag around, lose your way in the dark corners and suddenly find you're back in the same spot – but armed with a lot more knowledge and maybe a level up from where you started out.

- ✔ **Don't forget that your emotional state matters.** Sometimes you need to retreat and recuperate because you feel somewhat battered by events. Perhaps the struggle has got you down a bit, or maybe an upsetting life event has thrown you off course emotionally. Whatever the reason, you must anticipate that you need to let yourself off the hook at times and take care of your emotional state to gather strength for the next phase of the journey.

- ✔ **Stay curious!** Lapses do not mean that you've failed; they simply indicate that some reflection and adjustment are needed. Stay open to the lessons you can learn from your relapses and you begin to develop a helpful curiosity that allows you to step beyond gridlock and deadlock and move to the next stage.

Keeping a record

As you work through activities in this book, you may find that the simple act of writing down your thoughts and reflections really helps to clarify your understanding of your goals. Consider starting a coaching diary or journal to record your progress. Your journal can take many forms. Some clients push the boat out with leather-bound, handmade journals and write with an expensive pen. Others prefer a simple ring binder. Still others carry around a small notebook to jot down ideas and reflections as they go about their day, while the technology lovers tend to deploy their PDAs or laptops.

Writing in your journal enables you to:

- ✔ Capture your reflections on what you learn from your coaching sessions, helping you to build up a bigger picture over time and make connections between your thoughts, feelings, actions and behaviours. You see trends developing that aren't always obvious until you write them down!

- ✔ Track your goals and results so that you can look back on what you've achieved. This alone can be a significant motivator in your journey.

- ✔ Write out inner critic attacks. Sometimes just seeing the nonsense that your inner critic comes up with in black and white on the page is enough to break the spell and restore your confidence in yourself.

Painting a picture

A record of your progress need not be expressed only in words. Many people get more meaning from pictures and images. Consider collages, scrapbooks or drawings that represent the stages of your journey. If you have a room of your own, you can even create your own timeline on one wall, representing the stages you go through. Or why not invest in a flip-chart pad and get creative on a large scale?

You can also use objects to remind yourself of goals and reflections.

Exploring the significance of objects

Early on during a coaching workshop I attended, the group facilitator asked us all to take a 15-minute break in the grounds of the beautiful hotel we were staying in. He asked us to reflect on three examples of events or things:

- ✔ Something from the past that had affected us greatly

- ✔ Something in the present that we were proud of

- ✔ Something in the future that we were drawn to

The facilitator suggested that as we reflected, we look out for objects that represented these things for us and that, on our return to the session, we explain to the rest of the group why the objects had significance for us in the context of those events.

The results were very powerful. Some people brought back oak leaves or stones, while others produced car keys or a wallet. Each object had a story that helped the person to clarify their understanding of an event that had happened to them or that they were looking forward to. For example, the oak leaf represented a desire to act in a more natural way, and the car keys signified a sense of freedom. Not only was it easier for many people to talk about important things in their life when they represented them in this way, but the objects also continued to remind them of their ideas long after the event was over.

Part II
Your Life Coaching Journey

The 5th Wave   By Rich Tennant

"If I'm supposed to be so over the hill, how come it feels like I'm still going up one?"

In this part . . .

In these chapters you consider your strengths. You examine which of your beliefs are ready for throwing out, and you work out how to navigate with your own co-ordinates by focusing on the values that really drive you. You question, and then question some more. You concentrate your gaze on what's working, what your options are, and what your best plan is. And you figure out how best to keep your promise to yourself.

Chapter 4

Becoming Your Best Self

. . . .

In This Chapter

▶ Putting your best foot forward

▶ Expanding your range of behavioural skills

▶ Introducing your inner coach

. . . .

*I*n this chapter you take the first steps of your coaching journey by developing your self-awareness. You start to think about your strengths as valuable resources you can draw on at will and you see why those traits that you perceive as your weaknesses are far less significant than you may think. You find out more about some behaviours that you may like to adopt, such as becoming more organised or having the confidence to deliver a speech, and start to experiment with trying out new approaches. Above all, you begin to recognise that you really do have your own unique style and you can develop this to become your most authentic and best self.

Considering Your Unique Gifts

When you were a child learning to walk, you didn't think for a minute that, just because you were exceptionally good at crawling, you were destined to crawl for the rest of your life because, well, crawling was your major strength. Even if when learning to walk you fell over more than most of the toddlers in your playgroup, you didn't let that put you off for long. Sooner or later you developed the ability to walk just as competently as you could previously crawl, and chances are you were a lot less anxious about the whole experience than your fond parents were.

Trouble is, most people get rather bogged down in attaching labels (such as 'I'm a hopeless speller') to themselves as they get older. You start noticing things that seem to come easier to you and begin to ignore the stuff that is a bit harder. Other people, perhaps your teachers and parents, reinforce this behaviour by telling you how good you are at music but maybe art isn't your *thing*. And because you learn early on that doing things well gets approval and rewards, you tend automatically to shoot for maximum points in the areas that feel most comfortable to you.

Nothing wrong with that, of course, and it's probably got you a lot of goodies so far in your life. Passing an exam in your best subject with flying colours? Winning at your favourite sport? A rapid promotion through using your natural abilities at work? Hardly results to be sneezed at!

But you've probably also had a few frustrations along the way, feeling that some things just seem to be out of your grasp. Maybe, no matter how hard you try, you still feel like a nincompoop around computers, or you're on your seventh driving test and it's not funny any more. People are very good at adapting, though, so you come up with solutions that mean you don't have to do the things you don't like or find tricky. You leave the computing to your partner and get to know the bus timetable by heart. You can avoid and evade, and often other people don't even notice. But you don't fool yourself, right?

Now imagine you felt able to tackle anything and everything. Picture yourself with loads of things you are really good at and also some other things that are as yet undiscovered talents. Envisage that your 'weaknesses' are just an aspect of you, and not the most significant aspects by a long way. You can begin to change your mindset by thinking about the following:

- ✔ There are many more things that you *can* do than things you can't.

- ✔ The things you can't do are often simply skills that you haven't yet mastered or prefer to avoid. You have the choice to put in the time and the effort to become competent at almost anything, within the bounds of what's realistic and achievable for you.

- ✔ By focusing on your positive unique qualities, you make more progress than trying really hard to excel at something you're less strong at. And the confidence this gives you makes tackling those trickier challenges easier because you're in a more relaxed and productive state of mind.

What do you do really well?

How easy is it to concentrate on your strengths? You may find this a difficult area, for any or all of the following reasons:

- ✔ **You take your strengths for granted.** *Doing this well is just a minimum standard. To be really excellent, I have to be better than everyone else.*

- ✔ **You always qualify your strengths with a weakness or time when you messed up.** *I'm really good at getting people involved in meetings, but I often run over time as a result.*

- ✔ **You don't know how good you are.** *I can't be doing very well because no one ever gives me any feedback.*

- ✔ **You get embarrassed about blowing your own trumpet.** *I don't want to be one of those bores who is always on an ego trip.*

Notice how a lot of the thoughts you have when you consider strengths are about what other people think? Or about comparing yourself to others? Or that no sooner do you hit on a strength than you think of something that spoils it? That's because thinking of strengths and weaknesses in this way is like sitting in judgement on yourself with a pair of scales. You feel that the scales need to be balanced, so you make quite sure you've got some good solid negatives to weigh down the positives. And you may have become so used to focusing on what isn't working for you that your self-esteem has taken a big dip – take a look at Chapter 13 for tips on building your self-esteem.

Instead of thinking about your good points and bad points, consider the question: 'What are my unique qualities?' That's a very different kind of question, even though to answer it you think about many of the same traits. The whole focus of the question is on what makes you uniquely *you*. It's a lot easier to be confident about the positives and stay more objective about the rest.

Seen from this perspective, *everything* about who you are is key to being your best self. Instead of worrying about your weaknesses, you can begin to think in terms of your opportunities to develop what you like about yourself and what works for you, and to change the stuff about you that gets in your own way. A character trait that you may think of as a weakness may turn out to be one of your biggest strengths, when you find out how to apply it in the right way. A former colleague of mine used to worry that she was very nervous when meeting a new client and found it hard to speak up in an initial meeting. Then she received some feedback that her clients respected her for her empathy and listening skills and felt they had more rapport with her in these meetings than many of her more confident co-workers.

Two of the basic life-coaching truths support the idea that you're already good enough – 'You are resourceful' and 'You are already capable of much more than you know'. (See Chapter 23.)

Thinking about how you do what you do well is an essential part of the life-coaching process.

How do you do that thing you do? Boosting your competencies

Apart from being a good way to boost your reserves of confidence, taking a close look at the times in your life when you achieved great results is an effective way to find out more about yourself in all areas of your life. A great result certainly doesn't have to mean winning the Nobel Peace Prize. What you can focus on is any event that turned out the way you wanted it to, as a result of *something you did*. I talk about defining success in Chapter 8.

Take a look at this list of accomplishments. You may be able to add some or all of them to your own list:

- ✔ You passed your driving test.
- ✔ You got a job offer from an interview.
- ✔ You asked someone out on a date.
- ✔ You learned to ride a bike.
- ✔ You mastered a foreign language.
- ✔ You made a successful sales call.
- ✔ You became computer literate.
- ✔ You wrote a complex report for your boss.
- ✔ You navigated your way round a new city on a walking holiday.
- ✔ You cooked a fancy three-course meal from scratch for the first time.

If you were to tell the story of exactly how you did anything on that list, your story would be different to anyone else's, although the nuts and bolts of the task may be pretty much the same. Even the simplest of these examples can take an impressive array of skills and knowledge. But *how* you go about getting and using those skills and knowledge is what makes the difference.

As well as skill and knowledge, *competency* – the behaviour or *how* of carrying out an action – is the magic third ingredient you need to achieve a great result in whatever you put your mind to. Writing that complex report? Maybe you already have enough technical knowledge, but you've never written a formal business report before. So you might apply your competency of persuasion to get the help of a team member who's done this before.

Your competencies can often compensate for shortcomings in your skills and knowledge. Knowing how to apply your competencies can help you find new ways to hone any skills and knowledge you think you lack. The really great news about competencies is that far from being qualities that only get dusted off at your annual work appraisal, they apply to all the different areas of your life with just a few tweaks here and there. Table 4-1 gives some examples of using competencies.

Table 4-1	Examples of Using Competencies	
Competency	*At Work*	*At Home/Socially*
Communication skills	Writing a report	Giving your opinion about a news item to friends
Getting results	Winning some new business	Completing a do-it-yourself project in time for a housewarming party
Team work	Working on a departmental budget with others	Cooking a big family meal together
Planning and organising	Drawing up a staff rota	Organising a family party
Flexible/adaptable	Taking on additional work duties	Adapting to a major change in your life circumstances
Developing others	Training and coaching staff	Teaching a child to ride a bike
Problem solving	Fixing a jammed photocopier	Arranging some private space in the house for a teenager
Building relationships	Meeting new clients	Joining a club or society

Other competencies include:

- ✔ Creativity
- ✔ Determination
- ✔ Initiative
- ✔ Self-reliance
- ✔ Persuading and influencing
- ✔ Negotiating
- ✔ Empathy

You can find a comprehensive list of common competencies on my website www.reachforstarfish.com.

Make a list of your competencies. A good way to begin your competency list is to ask a friend or family member to describe you. Your friend or family member is very unlikely to tell you what they think you *can* do and much more likely to talk about *how* you do it. (Beware of asking this question when she is just a *teeny* bit annoyed with you for leaving all the washing-up in the sink overnight . . .)

Life coaching involves looking for ways to develop your inner resources to create the results you want. When you try out new things, it sometimes feels scary, because you know you don't have the appropriate knowledge or skill yet. But, armed with a well-developed set of competencies, you can truly tackle anything.

Follow these steps to find out more about the resources of skill, knowledge and competency you already have in the area of getting results in your life.

1. **Create your own Great Resources list by thinking of ten examples of things you have accomplished.** Remember to include examples from your work, home and social life.

2. **Now choose one of your examples and think about what skills you used to accomplish it.** For becoming computer literate, maybe you already had good keyboard skills. What new skills did you learn? Perhaps you learnt to surf the Web. What knowledge did you have at the start, and what did you know at the end? What competencies did you apply to the task? List as many different examples as you can think of.

3. **Do the same with the other nine items on the list.**

4. **Stand back and admire the impressive array of skills, knowledge and competency that you already have!** And that's from only ten accomplishments! Imagine what the list would look like if you did this activity on all your accomplishments?

5. **Consider what you want to do with this knowledge about yourself.** You can look at the skills you have in certain areas that transfer to other parts of your life. And you can consider the goals you have and which of your unique qualities will best help you achieve them.

Noticing Your Preferences

Have you noticed how easily you fall into a familiar pattern of behaviour, or *comfort zone*, as you go about your daily tasks? You may, for example, always take the same seat round the table at your team meeting. Maybe you have a certain routine for getting out of the house in the morning and feel mildly panicked whenever that gets disrupted? Life can often be so chaotic that, consciously or unconsciously, people like to have certain things that they always do in the same way. Following patterns of behaviour is a very effective strategy for dealing with times when you feel under stress or have to make difficult decisions that take you into unfamiliar territory.

These preferences are a bit like a comfy woolly cardigan that you pull on for a day home alone when you don't want to think about picking out coordinated clothing. And like the comfy cardigan, your preferences are right at home in that situation, but aren't always appropriate in other circumstances.

Looking out or looking in?

The two basic behavioural preferences are *extroversion* and *introversion*. Extroverts like to experience their world externally, through thinking aloud and interaction with others, while introverts prefer to make sense of their world through inner reflection, independent of others.

Just in the same way that everyone possesses some element of every competency, everyone has aspects of their personality that they express in an extroverted way and other aspects that are more introverted. Perhaps you are by preference more extroverted than introverted. You love meetings where lots of people talk through ideas and brainstorm, generating high energy but not much in the way of paperwork. But part of your role is to prepare a detailed budget report that means you have to lock yourself away in a room by yourself for a day a month and concentrate. You may really dislike this part of your job and feel that it isn't your strongest area. To improve the results you get at work, you can adapt your approach to ensure that you develop the introverted skills, even if they are not as strong as your more extroverted qualities.

You can take yourself out of your comfort zone from time to time, which helps to build your flexibility muscle. Doing so stops you from only achieving results in certain areas.

Changing the hand you write with is a simple example of showing you how you can step out of your comfort zone and try something you're less comfortable with. Have a go at the following activity.

1. **Take a pen and write your signature as you normally do.** How does that feel? Comfortable? Automatic?

2. **Now change hands and write your signature holding the pen in your other hand.** What's the difference? The action is probably a lot less comfortable. You're certainly going to be more conscious of what you're doing. How does your signature look? Would you get away with it as a forgery?!

3. **Now try again, six more times, changing hands each time.** What differences do you notice? You are probably beginning to feel more comfortable and the results are starting to look a bit better. If you carry on practising this every day, you eventually start to get results that are equally good and feel almost as natural as writing with your leading hand.

The more you do a certain job or activity, or use a particular character trait or competency, the more comfortable you become because you *already* have some ability in the area. You always enjoy the comfy cardigan, but the feelings of comfort from that and from the smart suit start to feel more similar. And you make a much better impression on a new client in the smart suit!

Finding your behavioural styles

Your preferred behaviours have another dimension besides favouring introversion or extroversion (refer to previous section). You may gravitate more towards the *task* in hand or the *people* who are involved. For example, you have a strong focus on task if, as a manager of a business, you tend to think first of the business results, and you consider the people in the business as part of the systems and the processes that get those results. A people-focused manager, on the other hand, thinks of people first and then considers how to make the systems and processes work with those people. Both approaches have advantages and disadvantages at the extremes, and a good manager works to compensate for their own strong preference by adapting their behaviour and/or ensuring that other team members can balance it.

When you add the preference you have for extroversion or introversion together with your preference for tasks or people, you get a certain style or way of being that you can also recognise in other people. Knowing your style is invaluable in working out which of your behaviours you want to develop, as well as predicting how people around you might respond to your behaviour and actions. Awareness of these behavioural styles is helpful in three key ways:

- ✔ You can come up with action steps for your goals that fit with the way you like to do things, which means that you can accomplish these goals more effortlessly and enjoyably.
- ✔ You can identify people who have a different behavioural style to you. You can model how these particular people accomplish their goals in areas in which you may not feel strong.
- ✔ You can better understand why people around you react in certain ways to your behaviour, and you can deal with resistance and conflict as you make your life changes.

You can find many ways to help you understand your particular behavioural style. The following activity in Table 4-2 is a very simple exercise that gives you a quick sense of your main preferred behavioural style.

1. **Look at columns A and B. Tick the extreme of each pair that you're most like.** For example, you may sometimes take risks and sometimes avoid them, but if in general you tend to be more risk averse than risk attracted, tick the response in column A. Enter the total number of ticks for each column underneath in the space provided.

2. **Now do the same for columns C and D.** If you see yourself as 'relaxed and warm' rather than 'formal and proper' most of the time, tick the response in column C. Again, enter the total for each column.

3. **Take your total score for column B and make a cross on the horizontal line at the appropriate number in Figure 4-1.** This score shows your tendency towards an extroverted or introverted behavioural style.

4. **Take your score for column D and make a cross on the vertical line.** This shows your preference for task or people.

5. **The intersection of the two crosses show you which of the four behavioural styles you tend to feel most comfortable in.**

Table 4-2	Finding Your Behavioural Style
Column A	*Column B*
Avoids risks	Embraces risks
Slow to decide	Quick to decide
Indirect	Direct
Easy going	Impatient
Prefers to listen	Prefers to talk
Reserved	Outgoing
Keeps opinions to self	Expresses opinions often

(continued)

TOTAL A SCORE:

TOTAL B SCORE:

Table 4-2 (continued)

Column C	Column D
Relaxed and warm	Formal and proper
Opinion oriented	Fact oriented
Open	Reserved
Time flexible	Time disciplined
Relationship focus	Task focus
Shares personal feelings	Keeps feelings to self
Intuitive	Analytical

TOTAL C SCORE:

TOTAL D SCORE:

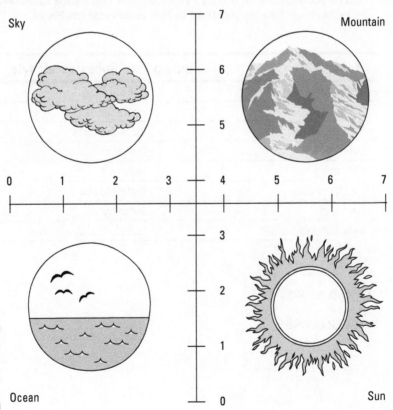

Figure 4-1:
Finding your
behavioural
style.

If your style is Mountain:

- ✔ You like to focus on tasks and results in an outgoing (extroverted) way.
- ✔ You favour taking action, decisiveness, effectiveness and getting results.

If your style is Sun:

- ✔ You like to be around people and prefer to behave in an outgoing (extroverted) way.
- ✔ You favour spontaneity, enthusiasm, having fun and collaboration with others.

If your style is Ocean:

- ✔ You like to be around people and tend to be more reflective (introverted) in your style.
- ✔ You favour patience, sensitivity and support.

If your style is Sky:

- ✔ You like to focus on tasks and results and prefer to be more reflective (introverted) in your style.
- ✔ You favour thinking things through, structure, planning and being thorough.

What did you notice when you did this activity?

- ✔ Perhaps it was difficult making a choice between the pairs. Sometimes you feel you are spontaneous, sometimes cautious. You are a complex human being, and all your responses vary to a degree. Variety is what makes you unique.
- ✔ If you had very high total scores that placed you squarely in a certain style, did you feel quite dismissive about the opposite style? Did you feel that your style is definitely the best? Being your best self certainly means celebrating your unique positive qualities – and it also means being aware of those that you can develop. Opening your mind to the benefits of your opposite qualities can be extremely liberating!
- ✔ In contrast, did you look at your opposite style with some regret, wishing you were more like that? Other people may well be doing the same with you – start to value the great qualities you have, knowing that you can expand your range if you choose.

This exercise gives you a sense of the general behavioural arena that you prefer to operate in. If you meet other people who also like that general arena, they may seem different to you in some respects yet you probably have quite a strong rapport with them because they are, in essence, rather more like you than some other people you meet. And you may struggle to get rapport with people of the opposite style to you for the same reason. On the other hand, many successful marriages and partnerships are formed on the basis of opposites attract, because we instinctively seek out those aspects of our style that are different to us, perhaps as a way of achieving a complete whole.

Knowing your preferred style is a great starting point for self-awareness. You can look at some of the behaviours of your opposite style and begin to experiment with ones that you think may serve you well, much like the idea behind practising writing with your non-dominant hand. Try reflecting a little more before you give an opinion perhaps, or speaking out even if your idea feels not quite fully formed. You can do this because you already have in you some element of the whole range of behaviours and you can make an informed choice that you are going to step into another style and see how that changes the results you get. Flexibility is the key!

More detailed *psychometric tests* (tests that measure personality traits) can give you a fascinating guide to how you really see yourself. These tests are based on a principle known as *self-report*, which means that you answer the questionnaire based on your own perception of what you're like. Most tests have to be administered and interpreted by a licensed practitioner and incur a fee. Free unlicensed products may not be subject to the same quality and validity controls. And as with the activity above, the results won't be completely accurate, so use the tests as a guide and starting point for self-awareness. You can find out more about psychometrics and how they work by visiting the following websites of the British Psychological Society: www.bps. org.uk and www.psychtesting.org.uk.

Don't box yourself in with personality profiles! You may be tempted to take them too literally and ignore the fact that you are a unique and complex individual who can flex and adapt to the full range of human behaviour. Personality profiles are most useful to identify where your strong preferences currently lie as a guide to help you develop and grow. Don't let them allow you to cling to a rigid 'take me as you find me, warts and all' mindset.

Adding new behaviours

Being your best self doesn't mean that you have to change how you do things, but rather adapting some of your behaviours to help you get even better results.

In fact, a willingness to develop yourself is a fundamental part of coaching – but are some people *unable* to change? You probably know people who've made major changes in their lives yet appear to have ultimately reverted to their old behaviour. Examples are the smoker who quits for a decade and then suddenly starts again, or the calm and controlled individual who reverts to anger after years of managing their unhelpful emotions. This seems to be pretty discouraging evidence that a leopard never changes its spots!

The process of change is often tough and challenging. However, even repeated relapses into old behaviour patterns do not in any way mean that you are unable to change. Indeed, every fresh attempt simply provides new information about what's working and what's not, so you get ever closer to lasting change. Think of Thomas Edison and the invention of the light bulb: it's believed he made close to 10,000 attempts to create a light bulb, and he still refused to see any of them as proof that he couldn't succeed, choosing to regard each failure as a step closer to success by eliminating what *wasn't* going to work.

Fundamentally, the essence of *you* never changes. Alcoholics Anonymous works on the premise that someone may always *be* an alcoholic, but that they always have the power to change their behaviour so that they do not *live* as an alcoholic. Although this might seem depressing on the face of it, it's a pretty encouraging fact – you can choose your best life and be your best self and that's when your real strength shines through.

Start to think of the change process a little differently. See yourself *adding* new habits rather than fighting to eradicate old unhelpful ones. Anyone who has ever successfully lost weight will tell you that simply cutting out favourite foods only goes so far, whereas building regular exercise into your schedule not only promotes weight loss, but also cuts down on the times when you're available to snack on unhealthy foods (unless you are very adept at slurping ice cream while you're on the treadmill!).

Think of your state of mind when you choose to do something that is positive, enjoyable and easy for you. Then think of the opposite of that – the feeling of deprivation you get when you're trying really hard to kick a bad habit. The truth is that *doing* something is almost always more enjoyable than *stopping* something.

As you open your mind to *choosing* new behaviours rather than stifling old ones, you begin to *want* to choose the new, empowering behaviours over any old, destructive habits that have been restricting you from living your best life.

Chapter 5

Choosing Your Beliefs

. . . .

In This Chapter

▶ Recognising and reshaping your limiting beliefs

▶ Harnessing power from strong positive beliefs

▶ Managing your fears

. . . .

*P*erhaps you have a pretty clear idea of what you want to change or improve in your life, such as becoming more assertive or starting your own business, and you've had a good look at your options. You may even have formulated a plan, but somehow you never really got going with it. You feel frustrated, because the plan's a good one, and you really want to put it into action. But you find yourself procrastinating, thinking of reasons not to start or getting discouraged along the way. You say to yourself that you don't have time or that you need to do other things first.

What's going on? Are you simply weak or lazy? I'd guess you've beaten yourself up on this count a number of times in your life. The good news is that the reason you're blocked may have nothing to do with weakness or laziness, or any other nasty trait you choose to label yourself with. You may well be blocked because, deep down, maybe you don't believe you're capable of executing your plan. Or even worse, you don't really believe that you deserve to be happier than you are at the moment.

In this chapter I talk about having the power of a strong belief system to catapult you into action. I show you how you can choose the beliefs that will support you and how to turn down the volume on the beliefs that hold you back.

Understanding How Your Beliefs Shape You

You can lack resources and your plan can be no more than a few random scribbles on the back of an envelope, yet if your motivation is right and you really believe you can do it, you can make your plan happen. History is full of men and women who have defied the odds and overcome seemingly immovable obstacles to reach their goals, and these people all have one thing in common – an unshakable belief that they are exactly the right person at exactly the right moment in time to achieve whatever they set out to do, be it scaling an impossible mountain or winning a marathon.

In life coaching, a *belief* is simply a feeling of conviction about something, specifically about yourself – and strong positive beliefs about something are the foundation for action. Holding negative beliefs or beliefs that no longer serve you well has the opposite effect and keeps you stuck. Your inner critic specialises in these destructive beliefs and can produce them at the drop of a hat.

Beliefs are tricky things; they always appear to be logical and watertight – that's their nature – but whole communities have built their worldview based on beliefs that were later proved wrong. For example, the world isn't flat, but people used to believe that it was and wasted a lot of energy in elaborate strategies to avoid falling off the edge.

Where do your beliefs come from?

Some beliefs you hold go right back to your childhood. When you were very young you genuinely believed that your parents knew the answer to everything. And what about your belief in Santa Claus or the Tooth Fairy? Some beliefs you picked up in childhood are harmful. What about the school report that left you with a belief that you're lazy and easily distracted? Okay, you sometimes behaved that way in class, but these kinds of labels have a habit of sticking with you as part of your identity long after you've also become hardworking and focused. Beliefs learnt or given to you in childhood can be very powerful indeed, and if the beliefs are negative, they can really hold you back from seeing and then fulfilling your true potential.

But sometimes beliefs can be overturned in an instant. Do you remember the film *The Matrix*? Neo, the main character, is stunned to discover that the world is not what he thought it was, that it had been elaborately constructed in a certain way for a sinister purpose. His *inner* world, his whole frame of reference, is certainly never the same again after he starts to hold his new beliefs. And in the real world, scientists are constantly making surprising discoveries about 'facts' that have always been held to be true about our external world and the internal workings of the human consciousness.

Have *you* ever experienced a time when something you utterly believed in turned out to be different to what you thought? Perhaps you've read true stories where someone discovers that their partner of many years has been leading a double life for decades. Having a core belief overturned like this cuts to the quick of your belief system and makes you begin to question many things you've always held to be true.

They said it couldn't be done

Some of the greatest achievements in history have been things that were considered impossible. Whenever you feel that you can't overcome your limiting beliefs, remember:

✔ Thomas Edison persisted in his many-thousand attempts to invent the light bulb in the face of sceptics who said that gas-light was the only feasible option.

✔ Roger Bannister ran the four-minute mile despite the medical experts who said that the human body was not capable of the feat.

✔ Neil Armstrong walked on the moon.

And from modern business, in the face of overwhelming market evidence and belief:

✔ James Dyson created a vacuum cleaner that never loses suction.

✔ Sony created the Walkman, the first pocket-sized music system.

✔ First Direct pioneered 24/7 banking without branches.

Sometimes beliefs you pick up may be incomplete or misleading. Perhaps you formed ideas about someone from what a friend told you and then found out that there was a lot more to the situation than met the eye. What do you believe about the stories you read in the newspapers? The media can be very compelling and authoritative, yet only reflects a tiny proportion of the whole truth of the matter, if that.

Realising that your beliefs can be wrong doesn't mean that you need to walk around in some kind of conspiracy theory state, challenging everything that comes your way. But you can see how strongly held beliefs propel you into acting with conviction, for good or ill. Choosing different beliefs that move you forward isn't being naive or thinking positive – it's simply plain good sense.

The belief that's holding you back is no truer than a belief that spurs you into positive action, so choose to focus on the beliefs that get you great results!

What are your beliefs?

Many of your beliefs are so much a part of you that you rarely have a good, objective look at them. A quick glance isn't always enough, because on face value all your beliefs may look perfectly reasonable to you. Building a strong positive belief system starts with dusting off your beliefs and pinning them up on your mental washing line to let some air get to them.

You need a pen and paper or your journal for this activity. Set aside some quiet time and ask yourself the following questions. Write down everything that occurs to you as you answer your questions. Don't worry too much at this stage about the whys and wherefores. Simply capture what seems to you to be the truth, pleasant or unpleasant. You look more closely at these beliefs in an activity later in this chapter.

- ✔ **What do you believe about yourself?** For example, *'I'm smart.' 'I'm lazy.' 'I can't sing a note.' 'I'm lovable.'*

- ✔ **What do you believe is possible in your world?** *'I can do anything I set my mind to.' 'I'll never kick my smoking habit.' 'The job market is too competitive for me to succeed in getting the job of my dreams.' 'Hard work always pays off.'*

- ✔ **What do you believe about other people's relationships to you?** *'People are generally supportive.' 'Work colleagues don't co-operate with my plans.' 'I'm lucky to have great friends.' 'People I date are put off by my reserve.'*

What do your beliefs give you?

All the beliefs you hold are likely to feel very real to you. Even negative and destructive beliefs exist for a reason. At some point you've gathered evidence that supports everything you believe. If you're convinced that you're hopeless at sports, that's because you've got a stack of compelling examples, such as missing an easy goal or coming in last in a race. You have more negative examples than you have instances where you performed well, so you get used to looking only for the evidence that supports your negative belief about your sporting ability. Holding on to this belief protects you from failing or looking stupid, because by doing so you can choose to avoid sports. In reality, you're almost certainly able to become very good at sports if you want to do so badly enough and are willing to put in the practice and effort required.

Your most limiting beliefs about yourself get in the way of the action you need to take. But many people are surprisingly attached to their limiting beliefs and are reluctant to let them go. That's because all your beliefs serve you in some way. If you believe that you're not bright enough to get a promotion, then you can give yourself permission not to try. If you believe that all the men or women you date are selfish and untrustworthy, you can build up a comfortable protective armour so that you don't get hurt. Your limiting beliefs have a function, but a very limited one. Your empowering beliefs, on the other hand, serve you far better by helping you to expand the range of what is possible in your world.

Still got that list of your beliefs from the last activity? Good. Now try this.

1. **Draw two columns, as shown in Table 5-1.** Head the first as 'My beliefs'; the second as 'My payoffs'.

2. **Take your original list and enter all your beliefs from the three questions, both limiting and empowering, into the first column.**

3. **Consider what your payoffs are for each of these.** What does this belief give you? Be specific. Is it a feeling of pride, or safety, or love? The comfort of not having to try too hard? The certainty of the devil you know? Payoffs for your positive beliefs are often all good – but watch out for some that are less so. Maybe believing that you're smart allows you to feel smug at other people's expense? For your negative beliefs, is the payoff worth it? Does holding that belief give you enough of a payoff to justify keeping it in your life? Or is the payoff something that makes you feel okay in the short term but doesn't move you forward in the long term? Table 5-1 shows a completed example.

Table 5-1	Beliefs and Payoffs
My Beliefs	*My Payoffs*
I am smart	I feel confident that I can hold my own
I am lazy	I can let myself off the hook
I can't sing a note	I don't have to risk embarrassing myself
I am lovable	I feel secure
I can do anything I want to	I feel powerful
I'll never kick my smoking habit	I don't have to try
The job market is too competitive for me to succeed in getting the job of my dreams	I can stay in my comfort zone in this job that's going nowhere
Hard work always pays off	I like finding the staying power to complete tasks
People are generally supportive	I enjoy a feeling of trust
Work colleagues don't co-operate with my plans	I can allow myself to enjoy a good grumble
I'm lucky to have great friends	I can enjoy and appreciate them to the full
People I date are put off by my reserve	I can hide behind my reserve and not risk them rejecting the real me

You can do some personal research by asking some of your friends and loved ones what makes up their belief systems. You're likely to get a fascinating cross-section of views demonstrating that everyone has their own unique map of the world. We all see a different version of fact and reality. This activity can demonstrate how arbitrary some beliefs are, and it can also aid you to a better understanding of what drives your nearest and dearest. No arguing now! Your friends and loved ones are just as entitled to their maps as you are to yours.

Changing Your Beliefs

Sometimes, simply by recognising a limiting belief, you take all its power away. You can then see it for the false friend it really is. Whatever you believe about yourself ('I'm deceitful', 'I'm unattractive', 'I'm stupid') you can always find plenty of evidence to support that belief if you look hard enough. Your brain seems to actively seek out that evidence and ignore the contrary evidence that says you're also truthful, attractive and smart.

You are a complex human being who at times may behave in a deceitful way and at other times in a truthful manner. But what defines the essence of *you* isn't your behaviour. Nevertheless, your behaviour does tend to define the results you get, and those results determine how good you feel about your life. Changing your beliefs allows you to act in different ways more of the time. The more you choose positive behaviours, the better the results you get and the better you feel. It's a virtuous circle.

Reshaping a limiting belief

Can you simply decide in an instant that you no longer hold a limiting belief, even if you feel as if you're playing mind games with yourself? Yes, absolutely!

You can defeat your limiting belief through regularly repeated *affirmations and mantras*, powerful, positive, present-centred belief statements that help to change your thinking patterns. For example, 'I radiate energy and vitality' is a great affirmation to use if you're working to cut out unhealthy foods that make you feel sluggish. Your brain believes what you tell it. So a great starting point is to experiment with simply switching the language that you use from negative to positive. You may feel a little as if you're kidding yourself, but over time, the new belief becomes embedded and you begin to gather more evidence to support it than you previously had for the old limiting belief. So instead of always seeing the evidence that you're lazy (spending all afternoon on the sofa) you begin to notice and focus on the contrary evidence (when you take a walk, clean out a cupboard or knuckle down to a work task).

The following activity helps you to zap those limiting beliefs about yourself.

1. **Take your list of negative limiting beliefs and decide which ones you want to eliminate (hopefully all of them!).**

2. **Write out your negative beliefs again on the left side of a sheet of A4 paper.** Keep the sentences simple, such as 'I am stupid' or 'I am deceitful'. You already know that these statements are at best partial truths. Seeing them written in black and white like this can't help but make your brain protest a little!

3. **Now think of the opposite statement to each negative belief and write it on the right side of the page.** Use the first person ('I') and again keep the statements simple and unqualified, such as 'I am intelligent' or 'I am honest'. Take care to write the positive statement larger and bolder than the negative statement; use coloured pens if you like.

4. **Go back to the negative statements and strike through all the negative words one by one, with a thick black pen, leaving incomplete sentences.** This helps your brain to demolish the negative association.

5. **Read your positive statements again. Then read them out loud 10 times, hearing your voice get stronger with each repetition.** Have some fun with this. Imagine you're at a rock concert and you're swept along with the elevated mood of the crowd. Ten thousand other people are shouting out your positive beliefs along with you and you feel great!

6. **Refer to your list daily for at least the next 15 days.** Take time to find a few moments each day when you can shout out your new beliefs at the top of your voice. (Don't try this in company unless they've been to the same metaphorical rock concert as you!)

You need time and practice to embed a new habit. Research suggests that you need to do something between15 and 20 times before it becomes a part of you. This varies according to what it is you are trying to do and how deeply ingrained your old habit is. The best approach is to keep practising the new habit until you catch yourself doing it three times in a row without having to *make* yourself do it. And then carry on!

Getting under the skin of your most stubborn limiting beliefs

What happens if restating your limiting belief simply doesn't work? This probably means that you need to go deeper to get to the root of your real fear, which is always at the bottom of limiting beliefs. Sometimes you know when you get to your real fear, because you feel a sense of relief and amazement as you recognise the feeling for what it really is. This can even result in immediate clarity about how you can let go of the limiting belief, but more often you'll want to explore it further to prove to yourself that you don't need it any more.

Your inner coach guides you to asking yourself probing questions – what's the real truth here? And what's beneath that? You don't need to worry so much about *why* you have this fear, simply knowing the truth can be enough. After all, you are not your past; your past is the things you've done and experienced up to now in your life. Your concern is to be at peace with the experiences of your past and be focused on your present – the here and now that creates your future.

Sometimes you do have to make peace with the past before focusing on the present. If you have beliefs associated with a strong childhood trauma that cause you distress, then counselling or therapy may be the appropriate route to help you first understand how that belief was formed and come to accept its effect on your life.

Kate thought she knew her limiting beliefs very well indeed and had done a lot of work over the years to replace them with positive, empowering beliefs. But she had come to accept that a few negative beliefs were so completely ingrained that she may never fully lose them, even though she considered that she had made a lot of progress and was moving forward in her life. During a coaching session, Kate decided to focus on the area that she felt was most holding her back. She had been self-employed for two years and was frustrated that she wasn't yet taking the action that she knew she needed to take to move her business to the next level in the mainland European market. Her coach asked her what belief she held about this.

'That I'm not capable of sustaining the success I know I can generate,' she responded.

Her coach asked her to think of a couple of other life areas or situations that were also proving stubborn, but that weren't necessarily related to her example. After some thought, Kate said, 'I want to procrastinate on things all the time. It's linked to the business thing of course, but actually I do it in all areas of my life sometimes, and it drives me mad!'

'Anything else?'

'Yes – this one is a bit embarrassing. I'm not an alcoholic, I hope, but I do seem to need to drink a lot at times. I think I need it to change my mood when I'm feeling low. Of course it isn't healthy and it never really works, so why can't I just control it? I'm weak-willed.'

Her coach then asked Kate to think of each limiting belief behind these three different areas in turn and ask herself what fear was beneath it. She started with the business one, since that was the most frustrating for her. After a moment she said, 'My fear is that I don't have the ability to run a successful business – that I'm not good enough.'

'And what's the specific fear beneath that?'

Kate pondered. At first nothing came to her – after all, not being good enough was pretty terrifying in itself. But the more she relaxed and considered what the truth really was for her, the closer she felt to an answer. Suddenly she blurted out, 'I'm afraid that I'm weak!'

This somehow felt like a breakthrough. Kate then found that this fear of weakness was beneath all three of her most stubborn limiting beliefs. She'd amassed evidence in the past of not cutting it in her job, being undisciplined with tasks and weak-willed in the context of alcohol (all her own labels). As soon as she understood that her real fear was feeling weak, she was able to see how crazy it was. Kate could see lots of evidence that she could also be strong in all these areas, and that this was always her choice to make.

Kate was even able to guess at one reason why she was so focused on these labels of weak and strong – as a child she'd been the little princess of the family, cared for and cosseted and absolutely loved. She thought that she had built up a belief that she had to be protected and had unconsciously allowed herself to create the circumstances for her to make herself into someone who was vulnerable from time to time. So from time to time she'd held back from tackling a challenging task and relied on others to see it through. Kate's new awareness about this was significant enough to squash the negative belief and she didn't feel the need to over-analyse it. She realised that, as an adult, she simply didn't need to be protected in this way and the limiting belief of 'I'm weak' no longer served her. She replaced her deepest fear with the positive and empowering statement, 'I am strong and make powerful choices'.

Learning to Manage Your Fears

All limiting beliefs stem from some kind of fear. Strange as it seems, fear is often a good thing. The physical symptoms you get when you're scared silly are exactly the same ones that accompany extreme excitement. Compare the butterflies in your stomach before you're about to speak in front of a crowd of people with the butterflies you get when you meet the person of your dreams on a date. The *meaning* you attach to the feelings can cause the poor outcome. Athletes and stage performers have long learned to channel their natural fear into excited anticipation before they're required to perform at their peak. And having no fear of any kind in your life isn't as great as it sounds. People seem to love the thrill of the chase and are hardwired to respond to challenges. So even when the feelings are unpleasant, your mind and body may choose a state of fear over that flat feeling that nothing exciting is ever going to happen to you.

Fear gets in the way when you allow it to stop you from taking action and achieving things. Managing your fear stands you in good stead as you coach yourself to your own success.

Identifying fears that drive you and fears that block you

Fear can be your friend when fear of an outcome allows you to get leverage on yourself to take action. For some people, imagining the shame of failure helps them to perform better than they think possible. If you're prone to move away from what you *don't* want more than you move towards what you *do* want, then you're using fear to spur yourself into action. Giving up smoking, for example, may be tough for you if you focus only on the benefits to your health of stopping. You can gain motivation by thinking instead about the negative consequences of continuing to choose to smoke. And the crunch time for you may be when your small child appeals to you to stop because he or she doesn't want you to die.

Using your fear of consequences may seem a good strategy to employ on yourself, but it comes at a cost. Using guilt, fear and shame as mechanisms to make you take action may work in the short term, but the negative messages you are setting up for yourself can do you more harm in the long run. Going on an extreme crash diet because your partner thinks you look fat isn't likely to have long-term benefits for you. Your overall health may suffer and you may feel resentment as well as low self-esteem, which won't give you the best chance of success in keeping the weight off. Your inner critic loves to guilt-trip you in any way possible and even puts up with times when the guilt produces a positive result for you, because beating yourself up as you get this result can undo a lot of its benefits.

Take care with using fear to generate your results. Keeping a focus on what you really want in your life, rather than what you really don't want, is always the most effective and healthiest leverage in the long run.

Recognising your fear foes

Putting a name to something can take away its power. Naming and shaming your fears is amazingly liberating – it's like facing up to the dust under your bed that you've been ignoring for a year, or clearing out old junk that you've been hiding away in a cupboard which has been quietly draining your energy.

You can experience four main types of fear – fear of failure, fear of embarrassment, fear of rejection and fear of achievement. You may be fascinated to find out which ones are the biggest fear foes in your life – they may not be what you expect!

Fear of failure

Most people can relate to this one. Perhaps your biggest fear is failing and so proving that you're not good enough. Certainly failure often has undesirable consequences, and most people enjoy being successful much more. But your real fear may be that not being good enough means that you won't be loved. Conquering this fear means embracing some or all of the following new beliefs:

✔ Failure is simply part of my discovery process and success comes from being willing to gain knowledge.

✔ I am always good enough, even when the things that I do don't work.

✔ I always succeed when I do my best with good intention.

✔ Avoiding failure means closing myself off to new possibilities I may never otherwise experience or know.

If you fear failure because you're worried you'll let people down, remember that self-love is the best starting point for being all that you can be to yourself and others. See Chapter 13 for more on this.

Fear of embarrassment

Sometimes you avoid things because you don't want to look stupid or exposed. Perhaps you hold back from speaking up at a meeting with a different point of view because you fear ridicule. You may avoid speaking in public because you worry that you'll literally fall flat on your face as you take the stand. We learn in childhood that not everything we do is universally applauded, and we are made to feel foolish instead of creative and innovative. So it's easier to stay out of the limelight in case we feel embarrassed again. Fight your fear of embarrassment with the following self-talk:

✔ Everyone admires someone who has the courage to say what they think, even if they don't agree with it.

✔ What's the worst that can happen? If I make a fool of myself it breaks the ice and people warm to me.

✔ There are no stupid questions – I bet everyone wants to know the answer and is afraid to ask.

Fear of rejection

Fear of rejection is connected with the deep desire we all have to be loved and liked by everyone we meet. Successful salespeople find ways to overcome this basic fear in order to make the hundreds of calls that generate the one sale they need. Accept that rejection is an inevitable part of life – you can't be loved and liked by everyone you come into contact with and even if it were possible, you would make yourself miserable trying to be all things to all people. Make it easier on yourself to handle rejection by adopting the following attitudes:

- ✔ When my ideas get rejected, I get the benefit of more information about what isn't going to work, and that takes me closer to a successful outcome.

- ✔ Nothing people do to me is personal – they have their own reasons and anxieties that make them behave badly towards me at times.

Fear of achievement

Fear of achievement seems an odd fear to have, yet it holds everyone back at some point in their lives. Doesn't everyone want to achieve things? Yet often you don't do something that you know you're capable of because you want to fit in with the crowd and, even more importantly, you don't want to be left alone and isolated because of your success. Being good at something can seem like a lonely place to be and the expectations that people have of you sustaining your success can seem overwhelming. Sometimes you find it easier and more comfortable to avoid being the best you know you can be.

Fear of achievement can be the trickiest fear to recognise in yourself because it seems quite unselfish – don't blow your own trumpet, be modest, avoid pride. But it's a false friend. Marianne Williamson, in her book *A Return to Love*, says: 'Your playing small does not serve the world. There is nothing enlightening about shrinking so that other people won't feel unsure around you.' Get comfortable with your own success with the following thoughts:

- ✔ Holding myself back doesn't help others and only harms me.

- ✔ I'll develop the skills of dealing with my success as I go along.

- ✔ I can be a shining example to others and will experience much more joy from this than pain.

- ✔ I'm worth going the extra mile for.

Minimising your fear foes

Ironically, reducing the impact of fear in your life means inviting it in to play and taking a good look at it. You can eliminate fear over time by experiencing the reality, rather than what your imagination conjures up. As you gain confidence, you start to realise that, more often than not, you don't fail, get embarrassed, get rejected or end up lonely and alone. And you begin to appreciate all the great things that come out of having a go, taking a risk and trusting in yourself.

Try to perceive fear as just another powerful emotion that can serve you in some way – if you let it. In fact, sometimes fighting against things increases their resistance. You can think of your fears as comic book monsters. Why not have some fun by creating your own personalities – be inspired by the wonderful un-scary scary monsters in the Pixar film *Monsters, Inc.* Seeing your fears in this way takes a lot of the power out of them. Do your fear foes have names? Does giving them a personality that's faintly ridiculous allow you to laugh them out of existence, just as the monster moguls in the film discovered when they saw that laughter generated far more power than fear ever did?

Chapter 6

Discovering the Values that Motivate You

In This Chapter

▶ Creating your personal motivation map

▶ Getting clear on your needs and values

▶ Sorting through conflicts of motivation

*Y*ou sometimes do things for the strangest of reasons. Factors that seem to be strong motivators for you, such as the pursuit of money, can turn out to be empty and shallow as you realise that you really want more time. You may find that things that you may have side-lined, like having enough fun in your life, can really get you going. You have to motivate yourself to get through your day successfully, but you don't always use the same motivators in the context of your whole life.

You're clear on your goals, you have strong positive beliefs and you have a plan to be proud of (if you don't have these things yet, head to Chapters 5, 8 and 10). The vital ingredient for success that you'll discover in this chapter is ensuring that you're really motivated to see through your promise to yourself, no matter what obstacles and challenges get in your way.

The word *motivation* stems from the Latin for movement, *motivus*. All change requires movement, so along with your beliefs (which can propel you forward or hold you back) your motivation is one of the most important elements of your coaching journey. In this chapter you discover how to tune into your significant motivators so that you can harness all that energy to make the changes you want in your life. You begin to see why your values can cause conflicts in your motivation and how you can hold up a clear, shining beacon of motivation to guide you to what you most want to happen in your life.

Navigating with Your Own Coordinates

Dozens of theories exist about the different ways in which people can be motivated. If you work in a sales or customer service environment, you may well associate motivation with incentives – targets to hit to win prizes – and many people do derive some forward motion from the combination of a competitive environment and a glittering prize at the end. But many people are indifferent to these techniques or even find them demotivating. That's because motivation is a complex beast that's different for everyone.

Many theories of motivation describe strategies that may motivate some groups of people and other strategies that motivate different groups. Yet you can't predict what works for any one individual, unless you really know the mix of needs and values that drive that individual, and the priority they allot to those needs and values. Your individual motivation is as unique to you as your fingerprints.

Certain behaviours are recognisable styles that show broad similarities between certain groups of people (refer to Chapter 4). But you can choose to adapt and flex all the behaviours to create the unique person that you are. You can apply the same principle to your motivation.

Want to understand more about the different theories of motivation? Check out the following website where you can find lots of examples of motivation theories and a huge range of related resources and ideas, all set out in easy-to-understand language: www.changingminds.org.

Reading your personal road map

Coaching yourself through change requires you to navigate in a forward direction, and you need a good map to do so. Some of the false steps that people take in their journey to change happen because they are relying on someone else's map without realising it. You may have a great role model for some aspect of your life, perhaps a peer or boss at work. That role model may seem similar enough to you for you to have confidence that their motivation stems from the same root as yours. So you may decide to apply some of their strategies to motivate yourself to make your changes. Yet you find that the results you get are poor, certainly not as good as those of your role model. Then, when that happens, you use the poor results as an opportunity to berate yourself for not trying hard enough or not having enough will power.

The truth is that you are just a few coordinates off course. As any traveller knows, it doesn't take much to take you in the wrong direction before you end up way off course. All successful journeys start with knowing where you want to go and gathering the tools to keep you on course. Creating your personal motivation map and learning to read it accurately is a sure-fire way of navigating using your own coordinates.

David was successful at his job as a technical manager, but felt that the time was right for him to develop more entrepreneurial skills that would allow him to move away from his narrow specialist field and set up his own business as a freelance technical consultant. He was very clear about his goals. The main driver behind his goals was to build greater financial security and plan for his family's future. David knew a number of people who had successfully achieved financial security for themselves and their families through establishing their own businesses, and he had decided that this was the way forward for him too. During coaching, David admitted that the prospect of selling himself as a consultant scared him quite a bit and over a few sessions he successfully dealt with many of these fears. Then the day came when he said he was ready to hand in his notice. However, when the time came for serious action, he hesitated.

At his next coaching session, David said he wanted to try to understand what was stopping him from taking this important step in realising his dream goal. One of the things his coach asked him to consider was this question: 'What excites you most about the prospect of running your own business?'

'Well,' David responded, 'mainly the financial security, the sense of pride I'm going to get.'

'So what are you least looking forward to?'

'I guess it's going to be really hard work, and I'll be pretty much on my own for a while. That will be tough.'

The language he used was certainly revealing. His coach wondered if David saw himself not really enjoying this challenge much on a day-to-day basis. 'Remind me why you want to start up on your own, David?'

David began to repeat the same broad objectives as before, and then stopped himself mid-sentence. 'Actually, I don't want to *do* this at all – I want to have already *done* it! And that's not enough for me! I see other people who love running their own businesses and I really would like to be like that, but it feels wrong now. I can't see myself enjoying it like they do. So what now?'

As soon as David came to the realisation that he had been trying to squeeze himself into a motivation map that didn't fit him, his instinctive creativity opened up. Within a few minutes he began to come up with a new strategy involving his current employer, one that he had summarily refused to consider so long as he had his mind fixed on someone else's motivation map. David set his sights on being promoted to Technical Director in his present company instead of starting up on his own, and he quickly achieved this goal in the following months. He used the same motivation as before (financial security), but created his own road map.

Knowing what your needs are

The first stage of creating your motivation map is recognising your *emotional needs;* the things you feel you must have to make you happy in some way. Some of your basic emotional needs may be:

- ✔ To be loved
- ✔ To be safe, secure and certain
- ✔ To comfort and please your senses
- ✔ To feel special and important
- ✔ To experience new things

You also have higher needs that make you feel good and may also benefit others or develop you in some way:

- ✔ To make forward progress in your life
- ✔ To make a difference in the world

Meeting some of these needs all the time can be a tough trick to pull off and may come at a price. Your need to feel loved may make you try so hard to please people that you fail to stand up for your own best interests. Your need for safety may stop you from trying new things. Your need to feel special and important may drive you to seek out a promotion at work that ends up making you miserable. Your need to experience new things may result in you cheating on your partner out of boredom after many years of marriage.

Your higher needs – making progress and making a difference – are more likely to result in overall good results for you, yet even here, when they are combined with more basic needs in the wrong way, they can have undesirable consequences. Imagine that you have a strong need to make a contribution to your community, so you volunteer your time and talents in the cause of a local charity. All good, right? But imagine also that you have an even stronger need to feel special and significant! Perhaps you throw your weight around at committee meetings and this creates upset and disharmony in the group. Can you see how perhaps that need may cause you to behave in a self-important way as you carry out your voluntary duties? The good that you do isn't cancelled out, of course, it's just that there may be other, less pleasant results for you and other people because of the way you feel you need to behave to get the notice you think you deserve.

A sweet story

A woman approached Gandhi and said, 'Master, tell my boy to stop eating sugar.'

Gandhi looked at the chubby six-year-old and replied, 'Bring him to me again in four weeks' time.'

The woman was surprised, but did as she was told. Four weeks later she brought the boy again. Gandhi looked at him forcefully and said, 'Stop eating sugar!'

'Why didn't you tell him that a month ago?' the woman asked.

Gandhi replied, 'Because four weeks ago I myself was eating sugar.'

Your needs, like your beliefs, have the potential to steer you off course as much as they have the potential to keep you moving forward. The trick is to recognise what drives you and ensure that your needs are met in ways that fit with your values. If you have a strong need to feel loved and enjoy the thrill of romance, then the best way to get this need met that sits well with your value of building a strong relationship is to talk to your partner about how they can do this for you, rather than, say, flirting with a work colleague. And you can still feel significant while you contribute to your community, without that resulting in behaviour that rubs other people up the wrong way.

You're entitled to have needs; it's part of who you are. You can also find ways of meeting your needs that are life enhancing, not destructive. And sometimes you'll let go of needs that hold you back from being your best self.

In this activity, think about the needs you have and how they're met. Answer the following questions and think carefully about the impact your behaviour has when you act in certain ways to meet your needs. Do you indulge in temper tantrums to get your way (destructive, mostly), or do you clearly and positively state what you need from a certain situation (constructive)?

- ✔ What are your needs?
- ✔ Which are the most important needs to you?
- ✔ How do you currently meet your needs? How many of your needs do you meet in ways that are destructive to others or to yourself?
- ✔ How can you find ways of meeting most of your needs in a healthy way most of the time?

What actions do you want to take as a result of this activity?

Getting Clear on Your Values

Your values are the principles that are most fundamental to you. Your values do link into your needs, yet they can be independent of them. Your values truly steer your motivation in a forward direction. You can have a strong need to feel loved that drives you to tell little white lies to your friends when the honest truth is far kinder but may cause them to be upset with you. And at the same time you can hold the value of honesty, which tells you that lying is wrong. In this instance, a good way to satisfy both the need and the value is to hold the importance of honesty with the gift of compassion, so that you look for kind ways to tell your friends the direct truth. This approach also feeds your need to be loved because your friends respect and honour you for your caring.

Some of the values that you hold may be:

- To be compassionate
- To lead and inspire
- To experience and create joy
- To love and be loved
- To be the best you can be
- To make a contribution to the world
- To provide for your loved ones
- To leave a legacy for people to remember you by
- To create wealth

You are likely to have many, many more values, and each value means something different to you. My website www.reachforstarfish.com has a comprehensive list of values to get you thinking about your own mix.

Some values appear on the list of needs too. However, values and needs have a subtle difference. A true value generates positive forward motion, helping you to fully enjoy your life and develop yourself and may also allow you to benefit those around you or the world in general. Think about the pleasure you get when you sit and watch TV passively for several hours. Sometimes you need it to comfort, relax and amuse you – but it doesn't usually open up your horizons much. On the other hand, watching a challenging film or reading a book that fascinates you often helps you to feel that you're more fully engaged with your world. You feed your value of growth or self-development.

Meeting only your needs can sometimes take you further into yourself so that you may behave in a more selfish way. When you're living a life that is in tune with your values – no one else's – you often find that you're in harmony with the world around you. You don't suddenly become a saint overnight, but when everything in your life is in synch with your values, you enjoy yourself so much that you want everyone else to be as happy as you are. And being motivated to make that happen feeds your happiness even more. A virtuous circle! (Chapter 5 has another virtuous circle.)

Living up to your own values isn't always a bed of roses. Tough and painful decisions and actions are part of the deal. But you'll find a world of difference between the discomfort that accompanies being true to yourself and the pain that goes with avoidance. Some types of depression may be caused by avoiding living according to your values – in *depressing* your instinct to be truly yourself, you cause a physical depression, which is your mind and body telling you to step up and take notice of your true values.

What are your values?

The names you attach to your values aren't really important. One person may describe a particular value as 'integrity' and another as 'honesty', when in fact the two individuals mean the same thing. On the other hand, you can have two people who say that the value of 'respect' is key to them and discover that their definition of respect couldn't be further apart!

In this activity, pay close attention to the words that occur to you first, and the pictures, sounds and feelings attached to those words. That helps you get to a definition of what that value actually means to you in a practical sense.

Stage one: Identify the values that motivate you

1. **Draw up a table with three columns, as shown in Table 6-1. In the first column, write the answers to the following question:** *What people, places and things are most important to me in my life right now?*

   Your answers may include things like 'my job', 'my kids', 'my sports car', 'the Italian Riviera' – any person, place or thing that you value. Note everything that is important to you.

2. **In the second column, write your answers to the following question:** *What positive benefits does this person, place or thing give me?*

   Identify the value or benefit that you get as a result of having this person, place or thing in your life. You may have many benefits associated with one factor – your job may give you security, respect, a sense of growth and a feeling of excitement. Focus on the good things here – your job may also give you frustration and stress at times. (I talk about the warts and all aspects of your life in Chapter 8.) If you find that you're identifying benefits that are also a person, place or thing (such as 'money' or 'my company car'), list them separately in the first column and consider what actual benefits you derive from these tangible things. Money may give you 'security' and your car may give you 'excitement'.

   Do this for all the things on your list.

3. **Consider your second list.** You should have a great many values on that list by now. Go through the list and circle those that come up more than once. Then link together any that mean the same thing to you. For example, you may have used the word *honesty* in one context and *integrity* in another. These words may mean pretty much the same thing to you or they can be very different. It's your definition, so feel free to combine things that essentially mean the same to you and choose a value word to describe them that's meaningful to you.

4. **Write out the most frequently occurring values in the third column.** Look at the remaining values and decide which ones are the most significant for you. Enter up to ten emotions or values in this third column. Don't try to prioritise them yet, simply pick out the top ten, the ones that make your heart and soul sing. These represent the true values that have deep meaning for you.

Table 6-1	Identifying Values that Motivate You	
People, places and things that are most important to me right now	*Positive value that I derive from this person, place or thing*	*Most important values*
My family	Security, peace, fun, love	Security
My job	Security, creativity, making a difference, fun	Fun
Money	Enjoyment, security	Enjoyment
My friends	Fun, enjoyment	Peace
Travel	Enjoyment, fun	Making a difference
My home	Security, peace	Love

Stage two: Review your list for completeness

Step back and look at your list and see how complete it is. Have you identified values that are really more like needs? Perhaps your meaning of 'love' is that you are the receiver of love and not the giver? This may indicate a strong *need* to be loved rather than a *value* to give and receive love. Refer to the earlier section 'Knowing what your needs are' if you like. If you do identify qualities that are needs rather than values, remove them from your list for separate consideration. And remember, it's okay to want to get your needs met – you simply have to look for healthy and constructive ways to do that.

Your top ten values are all true values, in the sense that they meet your own needs and allow you to meet the needs of others or positively affect your world in some way too. For example, your value of security drives you to create a safe haven in your home and with your family, giving you all peace of mind. Think of values as mainly outward looking and forward moving.

Are any values that are vital to you missing from your list? Perhaps you have a value of 'making a contribution' that is very strong for you but doesn't appear on the list because you don't currently have a person, place or thing that allows you to express that value? The absence of this value in your life is almost certainly causing you frustration, sadness or stress. If this is the case, you can ask yourself two questions about this missing value:

> *If I don't have a way of expressing this value now, is it really important to me, or do I think that it 'should' be important, because of someone else's expectation of me?*

If your answer to this question is that the value is truly important to you, ask yourself:

> *How can I find a way of expressing this value in my life?*

Make a note in your journal to come back to these very important questions at the end of this activity when you review what you have discovered.

Now that you've removed your needs from your list and added any missing values, you have a definitive list of up to ten values that are truly important to you right now. It's time to get a handle on which are the most important for you so that you can align your goals to this essence of who you are.

Stage three: Prioritise your true values

1. **Draw up a table like Table 6-2.** Enter your top 10 values in the first column, in any order. (Examples are given here; your own list will be unique to you.)

Table 6-2	Prioritising Your True Values
Value	*Total*
Respect	
Love	
Integrity	
Fun	
Learning	
Joy	
Accomplishment	
Balance	
Wisdom	
Friendship	

2. **Take the first value and compare it to all the others on the list, one by one.** Ask yourself questions in the following way:

   Which is more important to me right now, respect or love? If respect is, place a tick in the first column next to respect. If love is more important than respect, place a tick in the first column next to love. You may find this a difficult question to answer – these values are all important to you after all – but getting clarity on your current priorities is crucial to helping you chart your course.

   Note the language you use here. You want your unconscious and conscious mind to answer this question truthfully for you, as you are *right now*. Your values may well shift in priority over the years. Your motivation map always looks slightly different over time. In order to move forward you need to be clear about the priority of your values right here, in the present.

   Then ask yourself, is respect more important to me than integrity right now? Is respect more important to me than fun right now? And so on. Each time, you place a tick in one of the right-hand columns.

3. **When you've worked all the way down the list comparing respect to all the other values, you now take the second value on the list and do the same with all the values below it.** So your first question is: Which is more important to me right now, love or integrity?

   Make sure that you always compare a value with those below it or you end up double counting!

4. **When you finish this exercise you can see which of your values have the most ticks in your boxes.** (Note that no one value can have a score of more than nine.) Now you can draw up a ranking from one to ten. You may find that some rankings are equal. You can go through the process again with these closely ranked values by asking yourself the choice question. Many people find that they end up with a final absolute ranking from one to ten. Some people find that they don't, and they feel happy that some values are clustered together in importance for them. It's absolutely your choice; they are your values!

5. **Now that you have your values prioritised in this way, you can write in your journal your thoughts on the following questions:**

   • Are there any surprises or even shocks for me in doing this exercise?

   • Are some values lower down the list than I thought they would be? Are others much higher than I would have expected?

   • How happy am I with the way I am living my values every day?

   • How well do my current life goals align with my values as they are right now?

Stage four: Define your values

You now have your top ten list, and you can start to define precisely what your values mean to you in the way you live your life. This produces the detailed coordinates for your motivation map.

You can write out a definition or get creative and draw or collect images, just as long as the definition is meaningful to you and you can clearly see how it translates into action. For example, some definitions might look like this:

> *My value of honesty means that I never avoid telling myself the truth even when it is painful to admit.*

> *My value of fun means that I look for ways to laugh with team members every day and I spend an hour each day playing with my kids.*

You don't have to come up with some kind of all-embracing mission statement for your life. You are creating a map for the here and now, so let your instincts tell you the most important definition for your values for how you *want* to be right now.

You may choose to create a glorious collage of pictures cut out from magazines to define your value of excitement as it relates to your love of foreign travel. Whatever method you choose to define your values, make sure that it is something you can actually see at will, so that you can call on the image or written definition to inspire you on your journey. Your definition can even be a mental image, be associated with a specific piece of music or be a clear feeling that you associate with that value. It's your choice!

Reflecting on your values

Although the activity in the preceding section focuses on defining the values that motivate you, you may have found it hard not to think of the things that you *don't* want in your life. You may have realised that a certain aspect of your job causes you pain. Perhaps you feel you have to follow a sales technique that you hate – and when you dig underneath for the reason it turns out that complying with this technique takes something away from your sense of honesty or your compassion. And you may also have discovered that those values of honesty or compassion featured very strongly on your list of values. So this tells you that in order to be true to yourself, you have to find new ways of honouring the positive value that you hold as well as ceasing to *dishonour* that value in a specific part of your life. That doesn't always mean you have to jack in your job! Quite often you can find a solution that allows you to have what you have, yet in a different way, when you realise the things that need to change. You could challenge the sales technique that's causing you trouble and suggest different ways of approaching the task that allow you to express your values more fully.

You now have ten clear and specific definitions of things that you can do in your life to satisfy the most essential part of you. How does that map across to your current goals? Most people get so caught up in the busy whirl of their lives that they don't realise how little time and attention they give to the things that are truly important to them. And yet the things that are really important to you don't actually require you to get yourself motivated – they feel natural and effortless. You may want to spend a little time writing your thoughts in your journal. Ask yourself the following questions:

✔ How many of my goals are driven by my most important values?

✔ How can I prioritise my goals so that they fit my motivation map?

✔ How can I incorporate the things that really drive me into the process of getting to my goals?

As you do you may begin to discover ways in which you can bring your life goals into alignment with your true values. After you've done that, give yourself the gift of taking some immediate small, significant steps on the new routes that you have discovered for yourself, which I go into in Chapter 10. I hope you feel really motivated now!

Sorting Through Conflicts of Motivation

Getting clarity on your motivation map is a great feeling and very often things simply click into place at this point so that you know exactly the route you need to take. Often, though, you discover conflicts of priorities within you that keep you feeling stuck. Perhaps you have a strong need to feel special and important and the job you do feeds this need. This job may also give you payback in some of your deepest values of growing as a person and making a contribution. At the same time, the commitment you give to your work may have some negative consequences. Perhaps it prevents you from honouring your value of being there for your family and may even negatively affect your need to be loved, because you have to deal with family members being unhappy that you don't give them the time they deserve. Skip to Chapter 19 for more insight and tips on those times when you really feel conflicted.

The priority you place on your values changes, sometimes from moment to moment, as your life changes around you. At times this can feel confusing, frustrating and disorientating. You can feel that you are being pulled in different directions.

Looking out for your heart's desire

If you had to pare down your life to its very essence, your heart's desire that you wouldn't ever let go of, what would it be? Perhaps you'd pick love, or a sense of inner peace, or a feeling of accomplishment. Your heart's desire can also be a dream of how your life could be – a way of living or a way of expressing yourself fully, perhaps in a creative sense. You may take your whole life to work out your heart's desire, or you may already know it. But the key to your heart's desire almost certainly lies in your most important values.

Your most significant values may remain broadly the same throughout your life, even though you experience subtle changes. This is why developing a supporting awareness is so important – noticing how you feel about the things that are most important to you, seeing what holds true for you over time and what changes. The awareness you develop helps to guide you when you are uncertain and need motivation.

Supporting awareness is about really seeing what's going on, with no judgement, so that you can make the best possible decision about how to move forward. The questions in the following list can help you develop awareness:

- ✔ Which values keep coming out for you again and again in many areas of your life? For example, do you get a sense of honouring your value of integrity in your home life, your family and your friendships?

- ✔ Which values make you feel fully alive when you honour them? People can hold values that are difficult to honour and may involve some pain, inconvenience and discomfort, yet they have a sense that they always get more out of the experience than they put in. So it's worth it.

- ✔ Which values give you a sense that your life is complete? A perfect life where nothing ever goes wrong and where you are never challenged may in fact fail to make you happy. In contrast, a life where you feel fully yourself, where you are making progress and where you are contributing in some way to your world may be perfect for you.

- ✔ Which of your life goals meet all your needs and values without in any way conflicting with other important things in your life?

- ✔ What are the things that you want to do, that you are excited about doing and that you don't need to procrastinate about because you can't wait to get going?

Staying focused on finding your heart's desire means giving yourself the gift of taking action on the goals that feed these values. It doesn't mean that you have to abandon every other responsibility you have or sacrifice others in your wake. You owe it to yourself to take the first step, even if it is a baby step, because being on the right route for you helps to make sense of everything else in your life.

Dealing with changing priorities

No man or woman is an island. You need to take account of the motivation maps of the people around you, and this may require you to think differently about how you honour your values. Ask your nearest and dearest to work through these ideas for designing their own personal motivation map to help you all get clarity on the bigger goals that you need to tune into. As you do this, you may enter a state of confusion for a while as it may seem that you all want different things. Stay with the process and you will probably discover many ways for you to pull together in your individual journeys so that you end up at the same destination. And if this proves not to be the case – well, better to find that out sooner rather than later so that you can make the right decisions and accommodations about how you want to live your lives.

Does discovering the values that motivate you and your loved ones mean that life becomes easier? In one sense yes, because knowing is always preferable to not knowing. But as your priorities and those of your loved ones become clearer, you may face hard choices that you have previously been able to ignore. Sometimes you have to accept that some of your needs may not be met, or at times you may want to sacrifice your own needs for a greater good to you or to the people you love, as much as you really want to have your cake and eat it.

Chapter 7

Stocking Up on Powerful Questions

. . . .

In This Chapter

▶ Introducing the effective question funnel

▶ Knowing what you need to ask

▶ Making sense of the answers

. . . .

A surprising amount of the success you create for yourself as an adult comes from the times when you think carefully about the questions you ask of yourself and others around you, and then listen hard for the right answer. Figure 3-1 in Chapter 3 shows empowering questions as the outer ring in the life-coaching circle; the first step towards self-awareness.

Think of using questions as you use a good search engine – the right keywords get you to the result you want. You still have to be discriminating with the information you get, but you can master the skill of knowing how to phrase your request with the help of this chapter, and you're then better placed to sort out the wheat from the chaff.

Delving into the Power of Asking Questions

Questions are the starting point for discovery in your life. Since you were a small child, you've known the power of asking the right question. The first time you discovered effective questioning was probably when you stumbled across the 'why' word, and this stood you in good stead for a while – until your fond parents resorted in exasperation to the answer 'just because!'

You live in an age of unprecedented availability of information. Not all the information that's available to you is good, honest, valid or useful, yet it's sometimes hard to distinguish what's beneficial from what's positively harmful. You need good questioning skills to tell the difference.

So how do you *know* when you should be asking yourself questions? Well, I'm glad you asked! Ask yourself questions all the time, but most especially when you feel like maybe you ought to. The following sections go over some situations that should trigger you to begin asking yourself questions.

Heeding hesitation

Hesitation, confusion and frustration are good indicators that you should be asking yourself questions about a situation. Your hesitation may be down to uncertainty about what's really going on, or the options you could consider, or the steps you have to take.

Start to use hesitation to your advantage by identifying what hesitation is and what it means for you. What are the signs? Is it a break in your thought processes; feelings of discomfort, or even fear; a sense of going round in circles? And what does it mean? What is it you don't want to do when you feel hesitant? What one thing could transform your hesitancy into clarity? It may be a different thing every time – get into the habit of simply asking yourself questions about your hesitation and you can often break the deadlock.

You can pick up hesitation quite easily in a telephone conversation with another person. You hear it in the silence sometimes, or the tone of voice, or the words the person uses. Hearing it in yourself is a little trickier. You tend to want to make your inner dialogue flow and get to the answers you need quickly. Rushing your thoughts like this can mean that you sometimes end up with a vague feeling of dissatisfaction and a sense that you missed something.

Suppose someone at work asks you to help him out with a report and it means you missing your train and staying late to work with him on the task. You hesitate initially but then say yes, partly because he's helped you in the past. When you examine your thinking later (after you've made some excellent contributions to the report!) you realise that your hesitation wasn't to do with being reluctant to repay the favour, or even the missed train. Your gut hesitation was because your colleague always takes a lot more credit for a team effort than he really deserves, whereas you're always completely upfront if you've had help on a project. Your hesitation was telling you to set the ground rules at the point of the request so that you could offer your help with an open heart.

Question any hesitation you feel about a situation, because you're much more likely to state your needs assertively to get a good result than if you tackle it after the event.

Confronting confusion

Confusion leads you to ask yourself questions such as, 'Which option is best?' because you may have conflicting or incomplete evidence about a situation or course of action. Sadly, this particular question can be really difficult to answer! Usually, you need to step back and ask yourself what exactly is causing your confusion. Is your lack of knowledge making you feel confused? Maybe you can't decide on a career move because you don't know how you stand in the internal job market in your own company compared to the outside world. Do conflicting emotions about your options add to your confusion? For example, what's the best approach for your old friend who's going through a hard time and is making it worse by wallowing in it – tea and sympathy or helping him face some hard facts? Or perhaps your values and needs are in conflict, so you don't know which way to turn. Perhaps you're attracted to someone who's exciting to be with and boosts your ego, but whose values of care and consideration for others are very different to yours.

You can help to clear up confusion if you delve a little deeper for more information and imagine the outcomes of your potential actions. When you have apparently conflicting options, ask yourself the following questions of each option:

What will happen if I do this? What will happen if I don't?

What will I gain? What will I lose?

Make a pros and cons list for each option to help you reduce the mist of your confusion and see clearly to your best first step.

Chapter 19 takes you deeper into clarity from confusion.

Fighting frustration

You feel frustrated when you think you've exhausted all your options and have reached dead-end street.

Harry, an excellent salesman, hit a dry spell in his performance. He redoubled his efforts in all the things that usually worked for him – he spent longer on the phone talking to prospects, he called in all his goodwill with former clients, practically demolished a small rainforest sending out mail-shots advertising his services and clogged up thousands of in-boxes with sales messages. But the dry spell persisted.

'I've tried everything, and nothing's working!' Harry finally bemoaned to his boss at his one-to-one review.

His boss replied calmly, '*Everything? Really?*'

In fact, this super salesman had indeed tried everything that he *knew* – and he'd also asked the advice of other colleagues, so he'd incorporated a few new ideas as well. But he hadn't exhausted the limits of possibility of the approaches he could take. Harry got thinking about a really new strategy involving social media, one that pushed him away from his tried and tested techniques and into territory that initially felt uncomfortable to him. The result was astounding – within a few weeks he was back up the league tables and his new-found enthusiasm went down a storm with a new batch of clients who'd previously remained resistant to his old approaches. Harry had been stuck in a bit of a rut without realising it, and hadn't taken the time to question himself until he suffered the pain of frustration.

When it comes to fighting frustration, ask yourself:

> *What can I do differently to get a new and better result?*

As the old saying goes, if you carry on doing what you always did, you'll always get what you always got. Sooner or later, you risk ending up boxing yourself into a corner with no obvious escape route.

Don't Get Stuck Asking the Wrong Questions!

Some questions lead you down the garden path and you go nowhere useful. A prime example of such a question is one that reinforces your limiting beliefs about yourself, for example, *'Why do I always mess things up?'* There's no good response to that apart from the one your inner coach provides – *'Really? Always? What about the times when you have made a success of things?'* But your inner coach sometimes has to shout pretty loudly over the persistent whiny voice of your inner critic who is more than happy to step in with lots of reasons why – you're stupid, you're unlovable, you're lazy . . . frankly, you're just a messer-upper!

Instead of asking yourself unhelpful questions, stock up on lots of resourceful questions – they're the keys to unlock the garden gate and allow you to get out onto open terrain so you can begin your self-coaching journey.

Asking the Right Questions

Questions are an open invitation for more information or a call to action. Closed questions – those that generate a yes or no response – aren't bad questions at all – in the right place, closed questions have a vital role to play. In general though, work with a kind of funnel approach, where you start off with broad, open questions (generally beginning with who, what, how, where or why). Then move on to probing questions to find out more; perhaps ask a few clarifying questions to check your understanding; and finish off with closed questions to confirm action. The idea is to funnel your thinking so that you cover all possibilities and get to the best solution as quickly as possible. Figure 7-1 illustrates the question funnel.

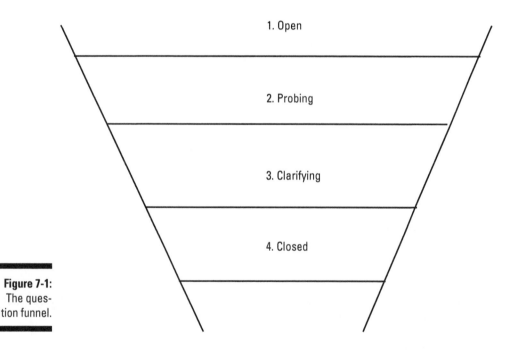

1. Open

2. Probing

3. Clarifying

4. Closed

Figure 7-1:
The question funnel.

Moving down the funnel

You don't have to be rigid about using the question funnel by starting at the top with open questions and finishing at the bottom with a closed question. More likely you'll experiment with moving up and down the funnel to get the results you need. The trick is to make sure that you've covered all the levels before proceeding to action.

Open questions

Think about a goal of getting fit. The first open question you ask yourself may be:

> *What does getting fit mean to me?*

Your answer may include gaining energy, strength, looking good in your clothes, avoiding illness and disease.

Probing questions and statements

Probing questions invite you to explore more about the situation or objective. You may examine your priorities for getting fit:

> *Which of these health objectives are most important to me and for what reasons?*

You may discover that 'looking good' is connected to a need to feel attractive and that avoiding illness and disease is associated with living a full life with your children. Knowing the value you place on these two things helps you sort out your motivation. (Refer to Chapter 6 for much more on pinpointing the values that motivate you.)

Clarifying questions and statements

A good clarifying question is often more of a statement and its purpose is to keep you on track and stop you from wasting time:

> *So, what I really want from my fitness programme is . . .*

Although it may sound odd, asking yourself a clarifying question just as you're about to go on to action planning can make you stop, think and reconsider. Your plan of action may not be what you really want after all. Asking a clarifying question is a way of re-stating your objectives and checking if anything is missing.

You may be surprised at how often your objective or action gets tweaked at this stage. Clarifying moves you nicely onto closing.

Closed questions

Closed questions are great for closing the funnel with a commitment or action. A closed question often generates a yes or no answer, so you may simply ask yourself if you're 100 per cent committed to the action. In coaching, a closing question also means a specifically focused question designed to generate that action, for example:

> *What's my best first step?*
>
> *When will I make the call to the gym?*

Closed questions are directed towards a clear decision rather than options.

Finding your most powerful questions

The right questions asked at the right time are always empowering, but some questions have even more impact. *Reflective* and *presupposing* questions are two special types of questions that effectively challenge your thinking when you coach yourself.

Reflective questions

A reflective question is a probing or clarifying question used very frequently in coaching because of its almost magical properties in getting to the heart of a particular issue.

Reflective questions allow you to reflect inwards and consider possibilities in a certain way. By crafting a tightly focused reflective question and thinking about its context, you can often gain a real light-bulb moment when something just clicks into place. Ask yourself these reflective questions:

- ✔ **What will make me most comfortable with this action/decision/ situation?** This question reminds you to make the most of your unique strengths and preferences (Chapter 4).

- ✔ **What stops me from taking action?** This question helps you identify beliefs that may be holding you back (Chapter 5).

- ✔ **What would achieving this goal give me?** This directs you to considering the link between your goal and your needs and values (Chapter 6).

- ✔ **What tells me that this is what I'd achieve?** This question helps you tune into your intuition or the evidence of your senses (Chapter 8).

- ✔ **What's great about the option I'm considering?** This question helps you reflect positively on the solutions you're generating (Chapter 9).

- ✔ **How will I know when I've reached my goal?** This question keeps you focused on positive actions, milestones and results (Chapter 10).

Presupposing questions

Presupposing questions are a form of probing or hypothetical question and fall mainly into the context of generating solutions. These coaching questions presuppose that you can form a bridge over a limiting belief, and they show you what you can achieve on the other side. They give you the safety of simply putting aside for a moment the need to believe in whatever may be holding you back and imagining what your world would look like. Here are some presupposing questions:

> *If I knew that I couldn't fail, what would I do next?*

> *If I could have my perfect state of health, what would that look and feel like?*

> *If it were possible to combine the security of my current job and the freedom of self-employment, how would I be working right now?*

Coaching with my clients, I find this type of question to be one of the most powerful in helping them set aside their limiting beliefs. Even if a client has a deeply embedded belief, their attitude towards that belief always changes after answering a presupposing question so that they can approach the limiting belief with new, more effective strategies.

Listening to the Answers

If questioning is one of the most important skills you can apply in your life-coaching journey, listening is probably the most underrated! The quality of your life improves dramatically if you spend more time listening both to other people and to yourself. Everyone loves to be listened to. You've probably met someone who is a good listener and thought afterwards what an interesting person they were – even though they may have said very little. The truth is that they were allowing *you* to be interesting, so you naturally warmed to them.

Turning that charm on yourself works in the same way. It feels wonderful to ask yourself empowering questions and really listen to the answers, as long as the voice you hear is your inner coach and not your inner critic.

When you don't know the answer

One frustration you may have when you start to use your communication skills in an advanced way is that you sometimes feel you really *don't* have the answer. No matter how hard you try to get yourself into a resourceful frame of mind, no matter how well-framed your questions to yourself are, no matter how willing you are to believe that the answer is inside you – sometimes you simply draw a big fat blank. Don't worry. That's okay, and sometimes it just means that you need to search around for a different question, or try again another time or go off and do something different to change your state of mind. The answer sometimes comes when you least expect it.

 What do you do if the answer doesn't come to you? Try this very simple technique and amaze yourself at the number of times it gets you unstuck. When you have asked yourself a question and you really, truly don't seem to know the answer, ask yourself this:

>*What would the answer be if I did know it?*

This question may sound daft to you, but be reassured that it works in almost all cases. Why it works is a bit mysterious, but it has something to do with reaching down a level to your unconscious thoughts and knowledge. And on a superficial level, it also lets you step back from the anxiety of not knowing to the possibility of 'what if?' You can also think of it as the answer that your inner coach provides for you.

Tell me your secret

You need the willing participation of a couple of friends for this activity; an amusing exercise that makes a serious point about how well people use the questioning funnel. It's similar to the game Twenty Questions.

1. Ask your two friends to sit back to back and nominate one person to be the questioner (A) and the other to be the holder of a secret that you are going to give them (B).

2. Give person B a slip of paper that you've prepared with their secret. This secret can be quite bizarre, for example, 'I'm the person who counts all the dents on a golf ball.'

3. Person A then has to identify the secret through questioning alone. The only questions that are out of bounds are 'What is

your secret?' or 'What is written on your piece of paper?'

4. Listen carefully to the range of questions that person A uses – how many open, probing, clarifying and closed questions they use. The most effective questioners, who move up and down all levels of the question funnel (Figure 7-1), often get to the answer surprisingly quickly, no matter how bizarre the secret is!

Sometimes simply identifying that you have a tendency to skip probing questions or never seem to get to a closing question can be enough to sharpen your questioning skills and help you craft more meaningful dialogues with yourself.

You can try this out on other people too and watch their expression change from confusion to delight as they come up with the answer they really didn't think they had in them.

Tuning into energy levels to find the answers

Your energy levels contribute significantly to how good you are at making sense of your answers. You can ask yourself great questions and even generate great answers, but if your mood is low, or you're tired and worn out, or feeling particularly stressed, you may not hear those answers for the gift they really are. Your inner critic loves those days when you are drained of energy and takes every opportunity to beat you up for not even having the spirit to make the changes you say you want.

Recognising that you're feeling low or stressed is the first stage of solving this problem. At certain times in your life you get caught up in one long vortex of stress and activity and never seem to find the time and energy to really listen to yourself. Because you are strong and resilient, you can cope with this in the short term but sooner or later you need to call a halt and find some mental and physical refuge – the second stage of solving the problem. Your refuge can be as simple as a quiet hour alone with yourself or as extensive as a long holiday or sabbatical. Chapter 20 has more ideas on managing stress.

Thankfully, most energy lows are short-term and you can plan times to coach yourself when you feel strong, positive and alert.

Chapter 8

Taking Stock of Now

In This Chapter

▶ Seeing what's really working for you

▶ Accessing your intuition

▶ Visualising your whole-life goals

'The unexamined life is not worth living.'

— Socrates

Your life changes whether you want it to or not. Choosing to stand still means that in fact you go backwards, because your world changes around you. And when your world changes, even in small ways, you eventually get dragged along, sometimes kicking and screaming because not everyone embraces change. Just recognising that change is inevitable can be a relief. Putting yourself in control of the changes you experience makes the journey a lot more enjoyable. You may have tough work to do along the way, and a fair sprinkling of discomfort to accompany the exhilaration and accomplishment, but *you* are in the driving seat, focused on the road ahead. And while you're moving up the gears, you need to see what's going on clearly and objectively so that you can make the best possible choices for your route.

This chapter explains how you can develop a supportive awareness about the things that are happening in your life so that you can make better decisions about what's not broke, what needs fixing and what exactly is going to take your life to the next level.

Practising Awareness

I'm sure that some things that are going on for you are pure, unalloyed success. Others are mixed blessings. Yet others seem to be clearly big, bad mistakes. When you analyse your life without supportive awareness, you can tend to feel like prosecuting counsel and defence lawyer at the same time – imposing the death penalty on yourself while being convinced that you're really the innocent party! Your inner judge rushes into sentencing before really seeing what you are getting out of the situation, good and bad, in an objective and calm way.

Taking short cuts without cutting corners

Relying on other people to help you decide what's the best next step or the thing that you should change can seem easier than doing it yourself. After all, that's what friends are for, right? If you're agonising about whether or not to take a job offer, end a relationship or just buy that lime-green spandex T-shirt that may make you look trendy or jaundiced, asking for advice may seem the quickest way to clear your indecision. You have limits on how often you can loop the same arguments around in your head and get different answers. You haven't really got the time for navel-gazing and you just want practical advice.

Asking for advice very definitely has its place. The problem with this short cut, though, is that advice, however well intentioned and wise, sometimes makes your dilemma worse. Advice can increase your confusion, make you doubt your own certainties and can even be plain wrong! Until you get used to taking advice from yourself from that part of you that knows the answers, other people's opinions always have the potential to throw you off track. Seeing what's really going on, even when a situation is confusing, is the first step to allow you to take short cuts without cutting corners. Really listening to yourself enables you to make quicker and more effective decisions from your options without going round and round the same old loops in your head. In the context of this new way of seeing and hearing, you can then take advice and guidance on board without it throwing you off course.

Balancing assets and liabilities

Think of yourself and your life as a business, with assets and liabilities. Assets add value and appreciate over the years. Liabilities are those things that come at a cost and tend to deplete you over time. No business runs without liabilities – it's the cost of showing up in the game – but a healthy company is rich in assets and manages its liabilities properly. Some of your assets you already know, because they represent the things that are important to you, your true values, such as the fun and support you get from your friendships, for example. But seeing only the positive side of the balance sheet isn't going to get you where you want to be. The first step in supportive awareness is to start thinking about how your own balance sheet looks, right here, right now. The following activity helps you to identify your assets and liabilities.

1. **Draw up a table like the one in Table 8-1.** In the first column list all the things you consider to be your assets. Assets can be tangible things (in the case of a business, perhaps an office building; in the case of yourself, perhaps your job) or they can be intangible things ('goodwill' is considered an asset on a company balance sheet, whereas 'my self-confidence' may be a prominent asset on yours).

2. **Do the same for liabilities in the second column.** You may have the same thing in both columns; in fact, it's normal for many aspects of your life to have both positive and negative sides. Your job may be the best job in the world on some days and feel like a weight around your neck on others.

3. **Consider the third column and ask yourself the question, 'What does this thing (asset, liability or bit of both) give to me and what does it take away from me?'** Pay attention to your first instinctive response, even if you are tempted to spend a while balancing up the arguments.

4. **In the fourth column, consider what the main feelings or emotions that accompany this asset or liability are for you.** If there are both positive and negative emotions, which seems to be the stronger? Don't completely reject the weaker of the two emotions though; list both if they are equally strong.

Table 8-1	**Your Assets and Liabilities**		
My Assets	*My Liabilities*	*What Does it Give Me/Take Away from Me?*	*Primary Emotions*
My job		Money, status, structure and routine.	Pride, sense of security, sense of certainty.
	Also my job!	Time from leisure interests and family.	Frustration, sometimes boredom.
My enthusiasm		Helps me win allies at work and make friends in my personal life.	Builds my self-esteem.
	My lack of assertiveness.	Drains my time and energy because I commit to things I should say no to.	Makes me feel less powerful.

How did you do? Some common results from this activity are:

✔ You find that many things in your life have both positive and negative pay-offs for you. You can see from Table 8-1 that a job has both a negative and a positive impact.

✔ You notice that some things seem to stem from the same cause – perhaps you see a link between the lack of time you make for family and fitness, and the time you devote to your work.

✔ You may be pleasantly surprised or frankly shocked at the balance between your assets and liabilities.

✔ You may find it tricky to decide which emotions and feelings are to the fore, especially for the greyer areas of your life where both good and bad exist.

In addition, you may have found yourself rushing into some kind of action plan as you articulated what is going on for you. For example, the judge in your head may already have decided that in order to free up time to spend with family and improve your fitness, you absolutely have to reduce the hours that you put in at work. Already you may be getting into that loop in your head where you try to work out how you can possibly do that and still maintain your performance at work. If this is the case, stop right now! The process of supportive awareness has only just begun. You can look more closely at what options you have in Chapter 9, but for now, you can be pleased that you have clearly identified some things you like about your life at the moment and some things you most certainly don't like!

In the business of your life, you don't need to strike out your liabilities and focus only on your assets; your aim is to pull together a business plan that allows all aspects of the 'company' to work together in harmony towards the same goal.

Redefining success

Did you attach mental labels such as 'success' or 'failure' to anything in Table 8-1? It's natural to do this, but as you may have seen from the exercise itself, it's not always helpful. How can you possibly evaluate how successful you are in your life? Think for a minute about all the possible ways you *could* count up your success score:

✔ You *could* give each asset and liability a point score and add up the total. But what do you do to balance up the really powerful assets against a large number of smaller liabilities?

✔ You *could* measure your achievements against some standard of what most people consider to be success. But what standard do *you* use and how do you make sure that your sample includes people similar enough to you for it to make sense?

✔ You *could* go by how you feel about things that have happened. But you've already noticed that you tend to be harder/easier on yourself than some people seem to be.

✔ You *could* compare your own perception of being successful to how it was five, ten or twenty years ago. But you're different now, and so is the world you live in.

Now, are those really the ways you want to view your successes?

Success is really impossible to quantify in these ways. So is failure. Your definitions of both success and failure change with time, experiences and circumstance. What may have been a major failure in your early twenties – failing to get a promotion, for example – may in fact have been the catalyst you needed to change jobs and really find your professional niche. It's just not possible to tally up the success of your life while you are right in the middle of it, because you don't yet know how or what you are going to learn from events, and what action you are going to take as a result. Life is unfinished business – you don't yet know how *you* are going to influence what happens. You may have heard the expression, 'There is no such thing as failure, only a result or outcome from which we can learn.' Perhaps you thought that sounded like a nice platitude to make people feel better about failing. It isn't. Because really what that expression means is, 'There is no such thing as failure, *or success*, only a result or outcome from which we can learn.'

So does what you do really matter? Oh, yes! A scene in the old television series *Angel* shows the team facing the fact that they will almost certainly fail to vanquish the forces of darkness, no matter what action they take. Angel affirms:

> *When nothing that you do matters, the only thing that matters is what you do.*

Maybe this seems a little bleak to you, but looked at from another perspective not only is it realistic, but also it's actually quite liberating. You have very little real control over how the world responds to your actions. What you consider to be a rousing success may fall like a damp squib and a task that you think you have made a mess of can sometimes be loudly applauded by others, to your utter mystification. You can in fact only have control over the integrity of your intention, the action that you then take and your response to situations or events. The result you get from your actions is for you alone to interpret and learn from, and this is entirely separate from the judgements and opinions of others. Certainly you may have to take other people's judgements and opinions into consideration as you examine your results, but they should always be secondary to asking yourself the questions: 'What does this result tell me? What can I learn from it? What do I want to do more of, or less of, to change and improve the result I get next time?'

What a relief to suspend all that judgement for a while and simply be interested in what's actually going on. The experience is similar to being suddenly airlifted from a heated argument between two good friends, where you are trying to keep the peace and support both of them at the same time. Looking down on the argument raging below, you can hear what's being said, you can observe your friends' body language, you can even smile at some of the crazy things they say to each other in the heat of the moment. And you have some breathing space to work out how you can best help your friends to move on.

You may be worried at this point that the sudden disappearance of success labels from your life takes all the buzz out of your efforts – fear not! Trying to assess what's going on as success or failure in this way – as if your life were no more than a simple scorecard – actually distracts you from the *business* of achieving real success – the success that is defined in your own unique way. As the actress Ingrid Bergman once said, 'Success is getting what you want; happiness is wanting what you get.'

Chapter 18 helps you coach yourself to a meaningful definition of success in your life.

Focusing on outcomes

Being self-aware allows you to see the results of your life objectively and in perspective. You may have a tendency to label certain events that happened to you 'good' or 'bad' based on how you felt about them at the time. In reality, events are mixed, and you even change how you feel about them over time. For instance, you may look back and smile about an embarrassing first date where you seemed to say all the wrong things, although at the time you wanted the ground to swallow you up.

The following activity gets you to think differently about some significant events in your life to practise getting curious about outcomes of your actions.

Think of some events in your life that were significant for you. Start by considering an event that has happy associations for you and where you got a result that pleased you. Perhaps passing an exam, getting a promotion, accepting a job offer or taking a trip abroad. Ask yourself the following questions:

✔ Were there any results from this action that were less than satisfactory?

✔ What other options did I rule out for myself by the action that I took?

Now repeat the exercise with an event that didn't turn out well for you. Maybe a poor performance at a meeting, failing your driving test or even a relationship ending. Ask yourself:

✔ What came out of this experience that turned out to be good?

✔ What did I learn from the experience that has stood me in good stead since?

Curiosity never killed anyone – not even the cat. Thinking about the choices you make in your life in a curious way doesn't mean that you always have regrets that your actions can never produce 100 per cent good results. It does mean that you begin to relax, knowing that whatever choice you make, you always open up for yourself the possibility to choose again and perhaps choose differently. When you focus on outcomes, you find that you automatically start to become interested in the puzzle, curious about how it's going to be solved and fascinated by the new end result. This is a great state to be in, because it's almost always a better way of getting the answers you need than agonising that you messed things up – and it's certainly a lot more fun.

Become more curious in your own life. Stand back a little as if you were a benevolent observer and take a look more often at what's really going on for you.

Focusing on the results or outcomes of your life is a great technique of life coaching. What happens when you do it? Lots of positive things:

✔ You take the emotion out of things for a while. It's like being your own best friend – you're interested and engaged but not self-obsessed about the highs and lows of your life.

✔ You get to play detective on your life, looking for clues and trends that help you build up a picture to guide you.

✔ You start to see your life as a whole – a constantly changing balance sheet, where your assets and liabilities shift around and develop. You realise that, as in the corporate world, even going out of business for a while doesn't stop you from refinancing and getting back in the game.

✔ You discover surprises and make connections that are simply not possible when you're intent on adding up your running scores as if you were sitting the final exam for passing your life.

✔ You begin to realise that many possible interpretations of events exist and you can see the right solutions when you open yourself up to changing your perspective.

Talk to people you know who have to use and develop curiosity in their jobs and professions. Thinking like a scientist, inventor, detective or trouble-shooter can add intriguing dimensions to how you approach the big issues in your own life. How do these different job roles employ curiosity? How can you find ways to harness these methods of discovery in your life?

Tapping into Your Intuitive Self

Curiosity is a wonderful thing to have in your life-coaching toolkit as you develop supporting awareness. It's a free, enjoyable way of analysing your results. You can take curiosity to a new level by taking steps to find out just how intuitive you are and how powerful intuition can be in helping you see what aspects need addressing in your life.

Everyone has intuitive powers. Mostly you pick up evidence through your five senses – you consciously notice the clues in how you feel and what you see, hear, touch and taste. But have you ever had that 'aha!' moment where your conscious mind is distracted from the task in hand? Maybe you are taking a shower, waiting for the kettle to boil, laughing and joking with friends. But suddenly, out of nowhere, you get a new insight that helps you solve a problem you've been chewing over for ages!

Intuition is incredibly valuable for supportive awareness and can provide you with solutions that are light years better than some of the solutions you analyse and agonise over. Trusting your instincts, living with a light touch and tapping into the power of relaxed focus are some of the most effective ways to become more intuitive and can really benefit the quality of the decisions you make in your life.

Trusting your gut feeling

In his book about developing intuition, *Blink: The Power of Thinking Without Thinking*, Malcolm Gladwell talks about the concept of *thin-slicing*. Thin-slicing is the way in which humans often instinctively come to make decisions and judgements within seconds. Thin-slicing means that you quite unconsciously make intuitive assessments about something or someone from tiny bits of information, often in what feels like a nano-second. For example, you meet someone for the first time and know that something isn't quite right, that you don't quite trust that person. You pick up cues that you don't even notice on a conscious level and later you may find the tangible evidence that backs up your intuitive flash. Of course, that doesn't mean that you should always trust your first impressions – whole romantic dramas warn you of *that* danger! But it does mean that listening to what your instincts tell you may often work better for you than trying to analyse and gather facts.

How can you develop intuition? It's one of those elusive traits that defies a structured approach, but you can become more aware of how finely tuned your intuition is with these suggestions:

✔ Start to predict who's on the end of the phone when it rings and note how often you're right. You may find your hit rate starts to improve for no reason other than that you're focusing on it.

✔ Intuition is strongly linked with creativity (Chapter 9) and playfulness (Chapter 15). Take a hop and a skip to these chapters to find out more about how to become more creative and playful in your daily life.

✔ Becoming more present-centred assists you in tuning out conscious thought and tapping into what's going on in your unconscious – the source of your intuition. See Chapter 16 for more on living in the present.

✔ Finally, simply notice what results you get over time when you go with your gut compared to the times when you carefully weigh up evidence. Do you see any trends developing?

Living with a light heart

Life can be a serious old business at times, but taking every little setback to heart drains your energy. Laughter is truly one of the best medicines, and after you've done what you can to resolve a bad situation, you can help yourself best by seeking out ways to lighten your mood. Your brain works more efficiently when the negative emotions of worry and anxiety aren't weighing you down. You can see what's going on in a difficult situation far more easily if you can tune into the lighter side of your day. Situation comedy is so popular because it gives people just this kind of release. Watching the antics of ordinary people going about their daily lives and being able to laugh at and with them is incredibly therapeutic.

How can you find ways to introduce a lighter touch to your day? Sharing a laugh or joke with work colleagues or catching up with friends at the end of a busy day is great for lightening the mood. And when your day threatens to become tense and over-serious, you can recall a time when you enjoyed a good old-fashioned belly laugh to help you recapture a sense of perspective.

Cultivating a relaxed focus

Have you ever been in the middle of a task and lost all track of time? Not only that, but also you know that your thoughts, actions and emotions are in tune with each other as you go about the task. You feel as if you are in slow motion, yet you are working effectively, even speedily, and without effort. You're in what athletes call *the zone,* and it's a wonderful state to be in. You are totally absorbed in what you're doing and your awareness of everything else going on around you seems heightened at the same time. Your conscious mind is utterly absorbed in the task in hand, and your unconscious mind is free to play along, providing all sorts of unexpected insights and knowledge. Your inner critic is dozing and your inner coach is proudly cheering you on from the sidelines! At these moments you feel invincible and you get a sense of how powerful and talented you really are. This kind of relaxed focus helps you perform better, make better decisions and enjoy your life more.

How can you harness a relaxed focus in your life? Start by thinking of the times when you've experienced a relaxed focus. Be specific. What sort of things were you doing? Was it work or play? What were the feelings and sensations that went with the experiences? If you think about these experiences, can you recall those feelings and sensations? If so, you already have a great tool for changing your state of mind.

You may be able to recreate this feeling of relaxed focus, or being in the zone, during the following activities:

- Driving or cycling
- Running or jogging
- A special hobby you are passionate about
- Reading
- Meditation and contemplation
- Yoga, Pilates, t'ai chi and many other mind/body practices
- A long walk outdoors

If recapturing those feelings and sensations doesn't come easily to you, look for ways to recreate the experiences that created them in the first place. As you get more practice at recalling your resourceful states, you find you can enter into relaxed focus at will, instantly allowing you to notice what's going on with alertness and a sense of calm.

Knowing What You Really Want

What does your awareness of now tell you about where you're heading in your life? If you carry on doing the things that you're doing, will you be able to look back and see a life that you have designed, with all its joys and challenges?

When you're clear on what you're getting from the actions you take and the decisions you make, you find it much easier to answer the big questions of what you really want in life. You can be more objective about the bad habits that get in the way of your full enjoyment, such as procrastination, negative self-talk or always running late. And you can prepare to replace them with habits that enhance your life. Yet even when you are crystal-clear on the most important things in your life, it can be tricky to sort out the ones that form the biggest goals. You may have achieved a big goal and felt somehow a little flat and empty afterwards – a kind of 'what now?' feeling. Perhaps working towards your goal was more enjoyable than actually attaining it.

These feelings are normal, and in fact the most compelling reason to set goals is to propel you into action to create, which is where the real rewards in life often come. In fact, the more you coach yourself to set and achieve your goals, the more you're likely to find that the feeling of forward movement and progress gives you the most satisfaction. This is one reason why starting to think about your next big goal before you've completed the one you're currently working towards is a great idea.

Sometimes the things you thought you really wanted turn out to be not so wonderful after all, which can be confusing. A coaching client of mine focused obsessively on her forthcoming house purchase – a significant symbol of her corporate success. However, on the day she moved in, her enthusiasm fell to rock bottom. She discovered that the thrill of the renovation project was what she really wanted, although she'd mistaken it for the end goal itself. This realisation caused her to rethink her career direction and five years later she's carved out a stimulating sideline in property development.

Enjoying the journey

Think of your future life goals as if they are features on a far-distant horizon. You can see, way ahead of you in the distance, the shapes and colours of a mountain, or a lake, or a village. But nothing is in sharp relief because you're too far away. You can choose to head towards the mountain, or the lake, or the village – whichever seems the most appealing to you from where you are now. As you get closer, you begin to see the terrain on the mountain, the eddies and whirls of the lake, the houses and buildings of the village. You get a stronger sense of whether your choice to head for the mountain was the right one, or whether, now that you can see a little more in focus and have gathered speed along the way, the lake or the village seems to be a better destination. You can still change course, even quite late in the day, and make your final decision about your destination. You may even notice something that you couldn't see from your starting point. Just around the corner from the mountain is a valley that looks appealing. And when you finally reach the destination that you've chosen, you have no regrets because you've had the most amazing journey along the way.

You don't have to have what you've always had

You are not your past, just as you are not your future. If you dwell on the past, you tend to rely on your past experiences too much to make your decisions. That's like saying that ten years ago you drove a Ford Cortina with limited speed and power capability and now you own a Ferrari but still drive it like a Ford Cortina. You've acquired skills, learned lessons, gathered wisdom – you're capable of more than you achieved in the past.

What you really want in your life now may have changed dramatically from old goals. If you neglect to question yourself about this, you can easily end up following an old pattern. When Christine decided to move into a new profession in her late thirties, she automatically thought of going back to college to get a formal qualification before she started putting out feelers for new roles. She'd grown up surrounded by the strong values of her parents that higher education was the proper foundation for a career, and that was the route she took for her first career. But as she coached herself through her decision, Christine realised that she had a strong preference for practical application and really wanted to be as hands-on as possible as quickly as she could. She found that she could build on her existing experience and secure a starting position with a company who would train her on the job.

You're creating your future now

In the very first *Back to the Future* film, the character Marty goes back in time to before he was born to ensure that his parents meet and fall in love, despite the odds against them, or he simply won't exist in his own future. As he takes actions that move him by turn towards and then further away from his goal, you can actually see the images of Marty and his sister fading in and out of the family photograph that Marty carries with him. Marty was able to adjust his actions because he had a very clear idea of what he wanted to achieve and could clearly see how certain things were taking him off course.

Although you don't have a crystal ball to see how your life will turn out (or a Hollywood scriptwriter!), you can keep a focus on the kind of future you want to create. This focus can act like a beacon that helps you walk your chosen path. Is one of your long-term goals to create enough wealth so that you can retire early and run a small hotel on a fabulous tropical island? If so, the avoidance habit you may have in the here-and-now of never opening your bank statements isn't going to help you create that future.

The action you take in the here-and-now creates the many possible futures that can exist for you.

Visualising your whole-life goals

Achieving what you really want depends on creating some kind of vision for yourself that you can begin to shape into tangible goals with a clear route to reaching them. At this stage your vision for your life may be clear, but equally it may be quite general or vague. Now that you're truly getting in touch with knowing your values (refer to Chapter 6), you can describe many of the things that have to be present in your future life. You can also get clearer on some other details too.

The following activity helps you to get your whole-life goals clearly in sight.

Imagine that you turn on your computer one morning and pick up a series of emails from your inner coach. Remember that your inner coach exists now, in your present, and at all stages of your life in your future. Your inner coach wants to tell you all the things you've accomplished in your life and so has decided to write you emails from five, ten and twenty years in the future.

Look at the following list of different areas of your life. Maybe some areas are more of a priority to you than others, so you may choose to focus on just a few for now. You may want to work through the activity for each key area in turn, or alternatively discover that looking at your life as a whole is the right way for you. Both approaches work very well. Where do you see yourself in five, ten and twenty years time in terms of your:

- ✔ **Health.** Your physical, mental and emotional well-being and health.
- ✔ **Career.** Your job, work or career, paid or unpaid.
- ✔ **People.** The relationships and people in your life.
- ✔ **Money.** Financial security and lifestyle choices.
- ✔ **Growth.** The way you learn and develop as a person.

In terms of people, you may see yourself as a parent in five years. In the area of growth, your inner coach may tell you that you've travelled the world. In 20 years you may be enjoying a comfortable retirement.

Happy writing and happy reading!

(Note for technophobes: you can quite simply type or handwrite your messages, which works just as well as doing them on the computer!)

Placing your whole-life goals on your horizon

After you have a vision of your whole-life goals, you can frame them into a desire statement in preparation for generating options and an action plan. A *desire statement* is a simple expression of a vision for yourself for your future.

What did you see when you emailed yourself as your inner coach? Perhaps you saw yourself running your own business? Maybe you got a vision of a wonderful family life? Or did you see yourself using a talent or passion in a certain way?

Time to place your goals on your horizon with the following activity so you know where you're heading!

1. **Take each of your whole-life goals and condense them into a short desire statement.** Your desire statement for wealth may look something like this example:

   I want to be a successful and talented businessperson, creating the wealth that I need to provide my family with the lifestyle that we all want.

2. **Think of the time period in which you want to achieve your whole-life goals – it could be a year or 20 years – and choose an image to represent your path.** You may like the idea of a mountain range to represent your ultimate destination, or perhaps the point where the sea and sky meet in a coastal landscape. Maybe you'll choose the night sky and focus on the furthest star.

3. **Place each of your whole-life goals on the terrain ahead of you, approximately where you think they'll be in the time when you achieve them.** As you place them, think of the images and feelings associated with each goal and repeat your desire statement to yourself. For example, you may get an image of your perfect home that represents for you a goal of family life, or a trophy to symbolise a sporting achievement like running a marathon.

4. **Recall this visualisation regularly to keep your own big-picture vision for your life sharply in focus.**

This activity may already get you thinking about how you are going to fulfil your whole life goals. Chapter 9 tells you how to generate options so that you can turn your desire statement into a present-centred goal that you can begin to take action on right away.

Chapter 9

Exploring Your Options

· ·

In This Chapter

▶ Getting into the possibility mindset

▶ Developing your range of options

▶ Generating and choosing your preferred option

· ·

*Y*ou've got your compelling whole-life goals clearly in sight and your kitbag is stocked with strong, positive beliefs, inspirational motivation and a curious, questioning outlook (read Chapters 5 and 7 if you're not there yet). One of the best ways of exploring options is by stepping into the unknown and trying out a few for size.

On the other hand, you may feel a little hesitant because you want to consider the different routes open to you more thoroughly. Perhaps your whole-life goals are big and bold, and you find it hard to see exactly how you're going to travel the distance from your present position to the lofty heights of the mountain range on the horizon. Or perhaps your whole-life goals are perfectly achievable in scope – maybe you simply want to regain a little more balance or have more of what you've already got. What's going to be the best and most efficient route for you to reach that pleasant valley?

This stage can feel deeply frustrating because you can *see* your ideal life beckoning invitingly at you, yet you may still feel trapped and powerless to move forward. Everyone feels like that at times, which is one reason why some people stay locked into jobs they hate or relationships that drain them of their spirit, even though they know they could have a better way of living.

These feelings of being trapped are normal. But you can deal with them. The surest way of breaking the deadlock is to start exploring options that you *could* take . . . even if part of you wants to reject the options as impossible dreams, unrealistic or otherwise non-starters. In this chapter you discover how you can challenge your own assumptions and begin to come up with exciting alternative routes for your journey.

Moving from Problems to Possibilities

One of the things that can keep you feeling trapped in a life that's a little out of kilter is the natural human tendency to see problems instead of possibilities. This section identifies ways for you to see possibilities in both situations and deep within yourself too.

Avoiding the 'yes, but' game

Joe often complains to his friend Mark that, at the age of 42, he's beginning to feel out of condition and unhealthy, and he wants to regain the fitness levels he had in his twenties. The following conversation illustrates the 'yes, but' mentality that sees problems instead of possibilities.

Mark: Well, how about taking up sport again to get fitter?

Joe: Yes I could, but I just don't have the time – I'm working crazy hours and I'd never be able to commit to anything regular.

Mark: What about swimming with the kids? Don't you take them every Saturday morning to the pool?

Joe: Well, yes, but it's not really proper exercise. I have to keep my eye on them the whole time.

Mark: OK, can you join the Wednesday lunchtime running club at work? I know the managing director goes regularly, so I suppose it wouldn't do your career prospects any harm either.

Joe: You know, that's a really great idea! But I can't run since I tore that ligament in my knee – it's too weak. If I tried I'd make myself look stupid in front of the boss!

Mark: Well, if exercise is tough for you, what about losing a few pounds? That would help you feel better to start with and you could see how you feel about exercise after that. Have you thought about this new diet that all the blokes in the office seem to be doing?

Joe: Losing a few pounds would help, but I hate the idea of a faddy diet.

Mark: You can ask your doctor to recommend a diet programme.

Joe: Have you tried getting an appointment with our doctor recently? It's like getting an audience with the queen! Besides, I don't think dieting is the way to go. I really wish I could find the time to exercise, but I've been through all my options, it's just too difficult . . .

Joe's objections aren't bad in themselves – all are genuine reasons why he still sees the whole issue of getting fitter as a problem with no solution for him. And he really does wish he could change. Yet he is playing the 'yes, but' game, which stops him from seeing all the possibilities associated with many of the options Mark suggests (even the added bonus of raising his profile with the managing director). The 'yes, but' game shuts down the range of options like a series of closed questions and helps Joe stay confined in his trap – a feeling that, although unpleasant, at least confirms that he is right. Joe is so focused on coming up with a 'but' that he fails to explore other ways to overcome his problem. Maybe a trip to a physiotherapist can help him sort out his ligament problem so he can join the running club.

If Joe allows himself to see possibilities, his wish to be different starts to become a goal that he can set his sights on accomplishing.

When, and in what way, do you find yourself playing the 'yes, but' game? What possibilities do you close down for yourself by playing that game? Try 'yes, *and*' for a change and notice the difference.

The 'yes, and' game forces you to think of positive solutions. When Mark suggests swimming with his children, Joe comes up with an objection because he plays 'yes, but'. Substituting 'but' with 'and' is more likely to get Joe thinking of how it could work, for example, 'Yes, and I could ask my wife to come along so we can take it in turns to watch out for the children.'

The 'yes, and' attitude won't feel all that natural to you if you're used to finding reasons not to do something. A big part of decision-making is assessing realistic risks and making sure you don't fall into any traps. But keep in mind that until you take the first steps, you're not committed to anything (and you can always retrace your steps) so playing out the possibilities that 'yes, and' offers you breaks your mental deadlock in the safest possible way.

The desert island scenario

If you keep coming up against situations where you don't feel able to tap into just the right thing to move you forward, look deeper within yourself as well as taking a good look around, because the answers aren't always obvious.

Imagine you're stranded on a desert island like the team in the hit television series *Lost*. Your normal life is light years away and you're understandably scared at the prospect of surviving day to day and somehow planning your escape or rescue. Yet can you imagine how to ultimately pull out of yourself strength and resourcefulness you never knew you had? What role would you play if you were lost in this way? Would you be a leader, a worker, a planner, a supporter? What would sustain you and drive you? You don't think you're capable of extreme resourcefulness? Think again!

Cast away

In the film *Cast Away*, Tom Hanks plays FedEx employee Chuck, whose plane crashes, stranding him on a remote island where he has to learn to survive alone for four years. Before he is cast away, Chuck is an ordinary man leading a normal life – certainly no prime candidate for extreme survival. He's overweight, prone to wearing thick knitted jumpers and seemingly obsessed with time management in his highly targeted job. Despite many setbacks and fears, he rises to the challenge of survival and over time he discovers many new ways to be resourceful. Opening some FedEx packages cast adrift in the wreck, Chuck finds a pair of girls' ice-skating boots. He quickly works out how to use the blade for cutting, as a mirror and even to perform emergency dental surgery on himself!

Watching the film, you can see how Chuck uses the skills he already has in a completely new environment, and also discovers some strengths within himself he had no idea he possessed. As a result, his life changes forever, in more ways than one.

Have you ever been in a real-world desert island situation, where you had to deal with something you felt completely unprepared for? Perhaps you had to give a speech at the last minute without any preparation or notes. Maybe you've been stuck on a mountain in a white-out while skiing and had to find your way home with no visibility. Or perhaps you've even been called on to put your old first-aid skills to saving someone's life. Can you remember the exact moment when you decided that you were going to get through the situation? Chances are you felt that you acted on instinct and maybe you can't begin to explain how you summoned up resources you didn't know you had.

That kind of talent is in everyone, and you can be confident that resourcefulness exists for you to access when and if you need it. Know the wealth of talent you already have at your disposal – skills, knowledge and competencies that you can apply to many different areas of your life (refer to Chapter 4).

Assessing Your Stock of Resources

You have powerful resources already within you – your current skills and talents as well as your potential ones. And you also have access to external resources that you can tap into at will. Take some time to develop these and they'll pay you dividends when you're investigating your options for change.

Building supportive networks

Although you may be able to survive alone on a desert island if you absolutely have to (see the preceding section), having a bit of company to support, motivate and inspire you would no doubt lift your mood considerably. Your options open up when you engage other people in your journey, not only because those people may have different talents to complement your own, but also because the more you can tap into a supportive network, the more opportunities you have for unexpected help.

While writing this book, I made sure that lots of people knew about my project, and I asked everyone to keep their eyes and ears open for anything that they thought might help me to make the book the best it can possibly be. People offered to read chapters and comment, friends sent me magazine articles and emailed inspirational quotes, and lots of folks suggested I speak to so-and-so who was doing some interesting work in such-and-such an area. Everything that my networks sent my way proved to be interesting and useful in some way. The result was an amazing writing journey that has resulted in a book I am proud of and an experience that has enriched my professional and personal life in many ways. And to think that I nearly locked myself away in a room for six months to write about what I know!

Have you heard of the game of six degrees of separation? The idea is that you are only ever five other people away from anyone else in the world because you know someone who knows someone else and so on, until you reach the person you had in mind. So with the right networking, theoretically you could be enjoying a casting interview with Steven Spielberg or taking tea with the Queen of England! On a serious note, think about the many people you know who may hold a small piece of your jigsaw. Perhaps an acquaintance knows someone who can help you get funding to turn your hobby into a home business. Or maybe a neighbour can show you how to get started with woodworking. Or you can consult a former work colleague who has travelled extensively in the very country you've got your sights set on for a holiday home purchase.

If you have a specific goal in mind, you can consider setting up a personal website or blog and asking people you meet to visit the site and contribute their advice. Or you can make a note of the contact details of the people you meet who have resources that you think may be useful to you in the future.

Increasing your resources

What do you instinctively reach for when you want more information about a topic? Are you a dedicated web surfer or more of a book addict? What external resources inspire you and develop your ideas? When you're generating options for yourself to achieve your goals, increase the sources of information and inspiration you use so that you maximise your chances of finding useful data. Think about *how* you use your resources too. Leisure pursuits are often comfort-based activities. For example, you may love reading and tend to choose your favourite authors over a new genre. Or you may always visit the same websites because you know exactly what's in store there. Doing so is perfectly fine for relaxation purposes, but stay open to the possibilities these resources offer to expand your mindset. Consider mixing it up a little just to see what transpires. You may find some surprising new avenues that can broaden your range of options for your life goals.

A colleague of mine spent months agonising over her website, hoping to get it just right, and inevitably putting off the go-live day when the website would become available to view. She suddenly discovered the world of *blogging* (keeping an online diary) and after a brief period of cynicism she started experimenting. She was delighted to find that, not only was blogging an easy way to get up and running with communicating to her clients, but it also helped her increase her determination to finish her website because the visitors to her blog were clamouring for more information.

For the next week, take particular notice of the influences that you receive from the world around you. What television programmes, videos or DVDs do you choose to watch? What books are you reading? How do you spend your time surfing the net? Which radio stations do you tune into? Do you read a newspaper or magazine and if so, which ones, and which sections attract you? Think about trying something different from time to time to open up your mind to different options. Perhaps read a non-fiction choice instead of a novel, or spend some time surfing the Internet for a change. Expanding your range of resources may help you in other unexpected areas of your life.

Expanding Your Range of Options

When you visit a favourite restaurant, do you often order the same meal as last time? Partly the sheer busy-ness and uncertainties of life in general make you do this – little acts of routine can help make you feel safer and more secure. Plus you know you enjoy that meal, right?

Maybe you prefer a simple menu that's easier to choose from. But you get bored after a while. If you then go to a restaurant that offers a huge range of choices, you may panic and make the wrong choice. But the more you experiment and try other options, the more knowledge and power you have about what you like. Okay, you sometimes make a wrong choice, but one day you may even make the surprising discovery that you actually *like* stir-fried liver after years of avoiding it.

So over time you start to prefer the bigger menu, you get more comfortable with the idea of choice – you can always come back another time and have that dish you rejected last time – and you don't worry so much about making a poor decision once in a while. You find choosing easier and faster and you invest less in the decision-making process for a bigger return. Instead of the huge menu being a problem for you, the choices become something you look forward to – a source of possibilities instead of problems.

Developing a creative approach

You can increase your flexibility in generating options by giving yourself the opportunity to become more creative in all areas of your life. Your right brain is responsible for creative and flexible thinking. Research shows that when your right brain is more frequently fully engaged, you can amaze yourself with your ability to magically come up with all sorts of innovative approaches to solving problems. Left-brain thinking is fantastic for analysis and evaluation, so you need to employ your whole brain when making whole-life decisions.

Do you hold a limiting belief that you're not creative? Many people do. Everyone is born naturally creative, but creativity gets a little lost over the years as we focus on process, analysis and getting results. Everyday creativity is of the same nature as the spark of genius in all great artists. You can harness yours to widen your mindset, develop your flexibility and help you view your options in new ways.

Becoming more creative can be as simple as interrupting some of the patterns that keep you stuck in old grooves. But you may find it tricky to suddenly decide one day that you're going to approach your options in a creative way. A more effective strategy is to get your brain into training through regular creative activities that you can work in to your normal routines.

Here are some ideas to get your creativity going:

- ✔ Do you have young children or nieces and nephews? Join in their games from time to time, not as an adult but by really getting down and dirty in the sandpit!

- ✔ Move six objects from familiar locations in the house to unfamiliar places. What new connections come up for you as you see the familiar in a different context?

- ✔ Have a conversation with a complete stranger in a supermarket queue. What do you have in common? What's different?

- ✔ Take a different route to work five days in a row.

✔ Read a book on a topic that you would never normally be interested in. If you usually go for romantic fiction, pick up a popular science book, for example.

✔ Listen to music that is the complete opposite of your normal tastes – African drums rather than Mozart, or a score from a musical rather than hard-core rock.

✔ If you rarely take public transport, make a point of catching the bus or the train every day for a week and notice what goes on around you.

✔ Read a section of your newspaper that you normally avoid (business, sport, style – whichever is not your usual choice).

✔ At the weekend, go out to lunch at your favourite restaurant instead of eating out for dinner in the evening. Notice what's different.

✔ Walk down your high street and explore a shop that you've never been in before.

✔ Spend ten minutes every week thinking about ideas like this that you can try out in the following seven days and do the ones that take your fancy!

Doing most of these suggestions only requires tiny adjustments to your normal routines, so take a small amount of thinking time to build a creative strategy into your day. You soon start to feel changes in the quality and clarity of your thoughts that will pay dividends in your life. And you enjoy the day a lot more!

Playing with unlimited options

How can you use the ideas in this chapter to start creating a route map for your whole-life goals? First of all, get your whole-life goals clearly in sight. You may express them as a *desire statement* (refer to Chapter 8) that is all-encompassing or as a statement that relates to a particular aspect of your life. Consider the following desire statement:

> *I want to be a successful and talented businessperson, creating the wealth that I need to provide my family with the lifestyle that we all want.*

At this stage the desire statement isn't a tangible goal because it's not detailed enough. It is, however, a powerful intent that encompasses some key motivational values. If you have a strong desire like this, you already know that you have many options for achieving this outcome. In deciding which options you're going to take, you toughen up your desire statement to form it into a real goal that you can shoot for.

Here are the four stages of generating options from your desire statement:

1. What's possible?

Remember to think in a mindset of 'yes, and' not 'yes, but' (see the earlier section, 'Avoiding the 'yes, but' game'). Give yourself permission to accept that almost anything is really *possible* for you if you're willing to work hard enough on yourself and your resources. For each of the desire statements you have, think about all the different ways to get there. You may find it helpful to think in broad categories:

- ✔ **The fastest option.** Maybe you have an opportunity to go for a big promotion at your current work that you're pretty sure of getting. This option may be appealing for its certainty and security.

- ✔ **The scariest option.** Does the idea of setting up your own business scare you even though you can see the benefits that may result? Sometimes you can convert scariness into the kind of adrenalin that really motivates you.

- ✔ **The most difficult option.** Perhaps you can also consider going for that promotion and also setting up a small business that you focus on at weekends. This may be the most difficult option because you may struggle to balance your time. You may also see it as an approach that pays the biggest benefits for you.

- ✔ **The riskiest option.** You may think about the option of investing money in property development or stocks and shares. This may be an attractive option to you because of the potential for high rewards in return for high risk.

- ✔ **The most exciting option.** What about the option of selling your house and moving abroad, where you may be able to make more money from your skills? This may be appealing to you if you can also see the lifestyle benefits for your family.

Each of these options has upsides and downsides. What is safe, scary, difficult, risky or exciting for you? What impact does each of these options have on other whole-life goals? What factors do you need to take account of – responsibilities and commitments, current life conditions? Keep 'yes, and' in mind as you go through these options. Having flights of fancy and asking yourself 'what if?' is okay. Your inner coach (see Chapter 1) knows the questions you need to ask yourself to evaluate these options realistically and safely for you.

2. What am I capable of?

Notice what comes up for you as you think about your options. Do you get a sense of your own capability or do you find that unhelpful limiting beliefs keep popping up? If you find yourself thinking 'I couldn't possibly do that!'

ask yourself why not – is it just because you've never done it before, or that you believe you may fail, or perhaps that option conflicts with an important value that you hold?

3. Who can help me?

While you think about each option, consider the people you know who can help you with your plans. How can they help to move you forward?

4. Where can I get more information?

Where are the gaps in your knowledge or skills to help you formulate the exact route for each option? Where can you find ways to fill these gaps? Do you need to search the Internet, read a book, join a club or support group?

Having considered these four factors, you're now ready to re-craft your desire statement. Do so with all the options you've generated so that you can make a comparison. Frame your statement in the present tense to bring your goal even closer:

> *I am a successful and talented businessperson, creating the wealth that I need to provide my family with the lifestyle that we all want. I am achieving this through working towards securing a major promotion in my current role, whilst laying the foundations for my own business.*

Concerned that framing your statement in the present tense feels too far away for your current beliefs to be effective? That's quite common. Try it on for size and see if it begins to feel more comfortable. If not, simply start with the bridging phrase 'I am becoming' and notice how that may feel truer for you. You will find that all that 'becoming' soon becomes current reality!

Choosing the best fit

The time has come for you to choose the option that's going to be the best fit for you in your current life conditions. Chapter 10 focuses on really applying the rules of goal setting to create specific action steps for you; for now, simply check your options against your intuition to see which route is right for you. Ask yourself the following questions:

- ✔ **Which option is the most compelling for me?** Can I really see myself achieving my goal, despite any fears and doubts I may currently have?

- ✔ **What am I resisting?** Is there an option I'm resisting because of fears, doubts, concerns or lack of skills, knowledge or ability? Is this resistance coming from the harsh judgement of my inner critic or the wise counsel of my inner coach?

✔ **Am I honest about the consequences of my preferred option?** Is the option broadly in line with my values in other areas of my life? If I really want to choose that route, yet it seems to have undesirable consequences for me in other life areas, do I need to do more work first on my values and motivation to bring them into balance?

✔ **What exactly do I need to work on to move forward on this option?** Do I need to improve my skills, my knowledge or my beliefs?

Finally, ask yourself what the very first step is in galvanising yourself into action. Your first step may feel like a giant leap into the unknown, but more likely something very simple catapults you into action. Perhaps you simply need to pick up the phone and call someone who can listen to your plans, help you clarify them further and encourage you to go for it. Take note of what feels natural to you and make a promise to take that first step without delay.

Chapter 10

Planning Effective Action

. . . .

In This Chapter

▶ Being smart about goal setting

▶ Planning the route to achieving your goal

▶ Dealing with setbacks

. . . .

*A*fter you've decided on the goals you want to aim for (refer to Chapter 8), you're ready to formulate and take the specific actions that move you towards achieving your goals in life. The saying 'well begun is half done' is true – planning well and considering all the possible outcomes gets you off to a flying start. Taking action is so much easier when you've really looked at what you believe is possible for you, you're aware of the resources and options you have, and the values that guide you.

You also need to ensure that the circumstances you're in when you're taking these actions are those that make it easiest for you to succeed. This chapter takes a look at how you can build an effective action plan to sustain you through the ups and downs of your journey.

Smarten Up Your Goal Setting

You already have some compelling whole-life goals sitting on your horizon (if not, head to Chapter 8). At the moment, these goals are a broad vision of how you want your life to be at some point soon. You also have some possible options in mind to get you there (refer to Chapter 9). The first stage of taking action is to bring those whole-life goals into full sight and apply the SMARTEN UP goal-setting guidelines to the whole process (I explain this acronym in a moment). This process means getting up close and personal with the what, how, where and who associated with your goals.

Your brain needs clear instructions about what, how and when to achieve that which you want. The SMARTEN UP goal-setting model is a great method to help you on your way.

To be realistically achievable, your goal (or in some instances, you) must be:

- ✔ Specific
- ✔ Measurable
- ✔ Achievable or appealing
- ✔ Realistic
- ✔ Timed
- ✔ Enthusiastic
- ✔ Natural
- ✔ Understood
- ✔ Prepared

Here are all the elements of cast-iron, can't-fail SMARTEN UP goal setting in more detail.

Specific

Your goal must be specific. Saying that you want to 'get fitter' isn't enough because your brain has no clear way to interpret that type of instruction. Fitness for you may be getting slim, being more energetic, getting more toned, growing stronger or becoming free of disease. Or perhaps all of the above!

When you formulate your goals, think carefully about the aspects of each goal that are most important to you. You can give each aspect a priority ranking (refer to the values activity in Chapter 6) to keep you focused on what really works for you, or to help you pinpoint your hot buttons. Designing your plan to get fit then allows you to focus on the options that generate the most important results for you. If energy is vital, look at how you eat and the exercise you do to get the maximum impact in this area.

Measurable

Your goal must be measurable. If you want to tackle your smoking habit, you must quantify what you want to achieve. For example, this may be to cut out smoking completely from your life, or to reduce the number of cigarettes you smoke by a stated amount. Again, your brain needs a clear instruction or it doesn't know where to start and procrastination sets in.

Achievable or appealing

The *A* in SMARTEN UP can be 'achievable', but 'appealing' is often a more meaningful measure to apply to your goals. So, is a goal achievable because other people have done it? In the example of buying a French farmhouse, the fact that many other people have successfully moved abroad can be a great impetus for you. On the other hand, you're not 'other people' and thinking too much about this as a measure can sometimes get in your way. You may even prevent yourself from going for a goal that you can achieve because you lack a precedent. Think of Roger Bannister running a mile in four minutes – if he had applied the 'achievable' measure he never would have attempted to set this record because the whole world was telling him it was impossible.

Your goal must also be attractive and compelling for you. Focusing on the undesirable effects of continuing to overeat as a motivator for action only goes so far, and you may find that all the negative associations make you feel worse, not better. Instead, find a positive vision for yourself of all the benefits of eating in a healthy and controlled way – focus on how much you're likely to enjoy your new lifestyle and your slimmer, healthier body shape.

If you don't find your goal appealing, you can't get anywhere with it because the goal doesn't motivate you. If your goal is to lose weight because you think that your partner wants you to, but you're pretty happy with your body shape, you may well find getting fit a struggle. Make your goal appealing or find a new goal that makes you want to start the journey.

Realistic

External measures of what may be achievable, such as comparing your circumstances with those of others, may not be very helpful to you. Nevertheless, you must still ensure that your goal is realistic for you, in the current circumstances of your life and for your current level of ability. Having a big, stretching goal is wonderful, and you can always give yourself permission to reach way beyond your comfort zone, in the knowledge that really wanting to reach your goal helps you to succeed. But you need to ensure that you set yourself up for your own *success*, so take into account any constraints that you may be working with that may mean a longer journey or an adjustment to your plan.

Perhaps you have other commitments that you want to honour so your goal of travelling the world on horseback has to wait a while or be scaled down. Perhaps you have to look at a series of smaller goals to get you to the point where you have the resources you need to set up your own business.

Being realistic doesn't mean you have to set limits on yourself, it simply means that you need to figure out how to walk before you can run.

Timed

Your goal must be time bound or you may find you never quite make it. If you want to get a promotion at work, you succeed more easily if you set your sights on timed milestones to get to that point. You can start out by identifying the skills you want to develop and agree on certain dates when you can attend training or work with a mentor. Then you can set your sights on a role that is available to you and set yourself dates by which to prepare a new CV or practise your interview technique. You can always adjust these times as you gather more information, but the presence of timed milestones helps you to focus on the deadlines that are right for you. Having a time-bound goal that you are really excited about is one of the best cures ever for procrastination.

Enthusiastic

So as well as your goal being appealing to you, you must also be enthusiastic about the entire journey you take to it. You may want the end result very badly, but if the process of getting you there is too tough and painful, you may find it hard to keep going. You don't have to subscribe to the glib mantra of 'no pain, no gain'. Okay, achieving your goals may well involve some discomfort and sacrifice, but don't make it extra hard for yourself by never letting up. If you have explored your options well, you can always find a way of getting to your goal that increases your chance of success by boosting your enthusiasm along the way.

Give yourself regular small rewards – even making a call to a friend to celebrate an achievement along the way can give you a boost. Or approach the journey in a way that's fun for you – perhaps map out your progress on a large sheet of paper, pin it somewhere prominent and mark off achievements with coloured pens as you go along. And whatever you do, ensure that you think of ways to celebrate your success as you take each significant step of the way. You make the rules, no one else!

Natural

Your goal must work with your natural instincts. Harness your self-awareness and check all your goals against your intuition (see Chapter 15 for more on awareness and intuition). Is this goal really for me? Is it someone else's goal that I think I *should* want? Or is my goal so fundamental to me that putting off taking action is simply not an option? If you can't answer yes to that last question, check out your needs, values and beliefs and see what changes you can make to your goal to make it fully your own.

Understood

Your goals must be clearly understood by your significant others, whoever they may be – partner, friends, children, work colleagues. They need to know what you are trying to achieve and how they can support you. This doesn't mean you have to tell *everyone* your private thoughts and dreams. But you can help yourself by identifying the key players in your life and telling them what they need to know so that they can cheer you on your way. If other people play a big role in getting you to your goal, you need to make sure that they understand what you need from them and are able to support you or work with you.

Prepared

And finally, despite making sure that everyone is rooting for you, you must be prepared for setbacks and perhaps even for negative reactions from others. Even though your nearest and dearest want the best for you, they may find it unsettling to see you racing towards a stretching goal, especially if they wish they were doing as well with the goals in their own lives. Your loved ones may not mean to sabotage you, but they may quite unconsciously pull you back with a stray comment or a small temptation at just the wrong time.

Even if everyone around you is being incredibly supportive, you still may encounter some setbacks along the way. You need to be prepared for the fact that other people may not always be able to offer you the encouragement you need to pick yourself up and carry on. Your loved ones may want you to 'give yourself a break' and ease off your efforts for a while. That may be good advice, which you can choose to take. The key is to be prepared for the fact that other people are never as invested in you getting results as you are.

To see exactly how SMARTEN UP can work for one specific goal, consider the following objective (or desire statement – skip to Chapter 8 to remind yourself of how to craft these) that you might set yourself:

I want to sell my house and buy a farmhouse in France by May of next year.

- ✔ **Does the statement contain a specific goal?** Yes, you've expressed your goal as a plan to move to a specific place in a specific manner, rather than as a wish simply to 'move abroad', for example.

- ✔ **Is your goal measurable?** Can you know when you have achieved it? Yes, when you're the proud owner of a French farmhouse!

- ✔ **Is your goal achievable?** Yes, many people have done this kind of thing before. And appealing? Yes, you can really see yourself moving in!

- ✔ **Is your goal realistic?** Yes, you've investigated the property market on both sides of the Channel, and it seems to be perfectly possible for you to make the move in the current market and in your circumstances.

- ✔ **Is your goal timed?** Yes, you want to do this by May of next year, and you've checked that the timescale seems quite realistic.

✔ **Are you enthusiastic about the journey towards your goal?** Yes, you've already taken steps and started your research. And you've planned to spend two hours a week working towards your goal.

✔ **Is the goal a natural one for you?** Yes, you've spent many happy holidays in France, know the language quite well and feel at home there already.

✔ **Is the goal understood by the key people in your life?** Yes, your family is up for the change and look forward to spending long holidays there.

✔ **Are you prepared for the journey to your goal?** Yes, you've considered different contingency plans if your ideal farmhouse is out of your budget. You've thought through how you may need to adjust your strategy if the sale takes longer than expected or falls through.

After you've checked off your desire statement against SMARTEN UP, you're ready to rephrase your desire statement into the present tense. Something simple like:

> *I am selling my current house and buying a farmhouse in France, which I move to by May.*

Putting theory into practice

You can now write out your whole-life goals and use Table 10-1 to keep track of how they measure up to SMARTEN UP. Keep each whole-life goal as simply worded as possible – you want to be able to recall these statements quickly as you go about your day to keep your vision clear in your mind.

Table 10-1

SMARTEN UP Goal Setting

	Specific	Measurable	Appealing	Realistic	Timed	Enthusiastic	Natural	Understood	Prepared
Health									
Wealth									
People									
Career									
Growth									

Smartening up to lose weight

The following is another example of how to apply SMARTEN UP to your whole-life goals.

Louise had two young children under five and her lifestyle had changed so much as a result that she had acquired quite a lot of excess weight for the first time in her life. This added weight felt unhealthy to her, and she wanted to regain the energy levels that she had when she was slimmer. A secondary, and quite important, issue for her was that she wanted to wear a certain special outfit for a family wedding that summer. She decided to use coaching as a means to keep her focused.

Louise stated her whole-life goal for her health as follows:

> *Over the next nine months I will reach my natural body weight through a healthy eating programme and regular exercise. This will result in reaching my target dress size for the family wedding while building up my energy levels on a daily basis.*

This goal checked out against SMARTEN UP as *specific, measurable* and *timed* – Louise felt she didn't need to put an absolute end measure on her energy levels because she would be able to see that change through what she felt on a daily basis. Louise decided to focus on a specific dress size because that felt very real to her – she could see and touch the outfit she wanted to wear and this was a significant factor in making the goal *appealing* to her and maintaining her *enthusiasm* for the journey.

Louise's goal was *realistic* because she could lose weight slowly and this felt very doable in the context of her busy life. Her goal was a *natural* one for her because she had always hated the idea of having to crash diet and liked to eat well without depriving herself. And Louise made sure that her family *understood* what she wanted to achieve and that they were ready to support her. At the same time, she was *prepared* for the sustained effort that she needed to maintain, as well as the possibility of setbacks, and she had engaged a coach to support her through the process.

To help herself really focus on her goal, she created a present tense affirmation that she repeated to herself daily, as often as she could:

> *I am reaching my natural body weight and increasing my energy levels.*

Matching Your Options to Your Goals

So you have clearly defined your whole-life goals, and you have considered some of the options for getting you there (refer to Chapters 8 and 9). Now's the time to map out the stages of your route and the very first step is to match up specific ways of moving forward to the goals you've set yourself. Having applied SMARTEN UP to your goals, it may now be very clear that some options are better than others for your circumstances. But you can check this out by looking at your options in the context of SMARTEN UP as well.

Louise was happy with her whole-life health goal and now needed to look at the options she had generated for getting there. She planned two aspects – losing the excess weight and becoming more energetic through regular exercise. For the weight loss, she considered two main options: joining a local slimming group and following their recommended diet plan, or asking her local GP to suggest a healthy eating programme that she could follow herself. For the fitness aspect, she decided that some kind of aerobic exercise would generate the most energy for her. She had two main options: she could have access to a friend's exercise bike or she could join the local gym and follow a programme there. All her options passed the SMARTEN UP check in terms of being *appealing* and *enthusiastic* (and she could also check them out against *specific*, *measurable* and *timed*), so she now needed to decide which were most *realistic* and *natural* for her.

Louise considered her natural preferences. She liked the idea of following her GP's suggestions slightly more than joining the slimming group because doing so would gave her more flexibility of time. She also chose the option of going to the gym over using the bike because the option of the bike felt just a little too loose to keep her on track.

Setting milestones for your journey

Having a clear goal and preferred options mapped out is probably enough to propel you into taking the first step towards achieving your goal – maybe you need to book an appointment with someone, or check out times of a fitness or educational class. Making a start as soon as you can is key to getting momentum. But you also want to think about *milestones* now. Your milestones are the stopping-off points on your journey where you can celebrate your success so far. You can think of these stopping-off points as an oasis, where you can recharge your energy and enthusiasm for your whole-life goals and take a quick check of your coordinates to make sure you're still going in the direction you want to go in.

Touching the Void

This compelling docu-drama tells the story of Joe Simpson, an ambitious mountaineer who set off with his friend Simon Yates to scale the west face of Siula Grande in the Peruvian Andes. A terrible accident forces Simon to make the decision to abandon Joe, whom he believes is dead. Joe then makes an agonizing journey alone, with a broken leg across hostile terrain, fighting for his survival.

Joe's worst moments come when he begins to doubt for the first time that he can make the distance, faced with a seemingly impassable rock face and his own increasingly weakened physical, mental and emotional state. His survival strategy is to set himself small targets to reach a certain point ahead of him within 20 minutes, and he continues to set these 20-minute targets as he makes painful progress to each goal. By competing with the clock and through sheer determination, he is able to access inner strength despite his pain and fear. He describes it as:

'Quite clear … like a voice … a separate part of me telling me to do something. Do this, do this, and this, and you're going to get there.'

Joe survives and goes on to scale many more mountains.

During the course of Louise's nine-month programme, she set herself alternate milestones every six weeks. Every 12 weeks she was able to see a big result in either fitness and energy levels or inch loss. This period of time between milestone goals worked well for her because she felt that she was never that far away from an opportunity to monitor and celebrate her progress and because the big changes were very motivating.

Taking baby steps

You may be tempted to race towards your whole-life goals and try to achieve them as quickly as possible. Sometimes that's the right approach and you gain lots of momentum. However, most people find that lasting change comes about through small, incremental progress to your goal.

Here are some advantages of following the tortoise strategy for making it to your goals rather than joining the hare on his racetrack:

- ✔ You can fit your goals into the rest of your life without sacrificing other things that are also important to you.
- ✔ You can make small and significant adjustments to your route as you go along, instead of finding that you have to do a rapid U-turn at speed if something doesn't turn out as you wanted.
- ✔ You enjoy the journey much more because you have time to build in rewards and celebrations.

- ✔ You build habits that stay with you for longer and become part of who you are, making the change much easier to sustain after you've reached your goal.

- ✔ You take out a lot of extra stress and pressure from your life that could have undesirable effects for you.

- ✔ You are more likely to sustain progress because you aren't behaving in an extreme or uncomfortable way for your natural preferences.

Louise achieved better results from taking baby steps rather than racing ahead – her slow weight loss was better for her body's health overall and her skin adjusted along the way so she wasn't left with sags and wrinkles.

If you simply must join the hare, apply this racing-ahead approach to goals that cause minimum disruption to everything else in your life and take you a relatively short time to attain, where you know you can maintain your momentum. Getting fast results in this way may well kick-start your motivation but is unlikely to be sustainable. You need to consider the healthy option for you in the long-term, especially if you have a weight-loss goal. Some people even put a hold on other activities and go on a form of retreat or sabbatical to focus on their specific objectives. This approach can have advantages, but you usually need a lot of time and money, and you still need to consider how you're going to sustain your progress after the period of focus. I'm talking about *your* goals and *your* life – only you can decide what works best for you.

Keeping Your Promise to Yourself

Congratulations on setting out on your journey with a well-stocked kitbag and clear coordinates! If you continue to review your progress at each milestone, achieving your whole-life goals seems easy and effortless.

When events test your resolve, remember the promise you made yourself to achieve your goals. In this section I show you some simple things you can keep in mind to help you see your promise through.

Thinking like a hero

You don't have to scale mountains or fight dragons to be heroic. You are the hero in your own life. Your unique brand of heroism lies in living your life with your own sense of integrity in the way you want to live it. That may mean huge goals or small adjustments, yet the courage and commitment you need to do either is of the same quality. Your promise to yourself is ultimately accountable only to you, even though you may also choose to share your goals with others to garner support. All true heroes know that they have the highest standards for themselves.

Part of the deal of being a hero is that you are probably tested along the way and sometimes you may falter. Courageously reaching for your goals over and over again marks you out as the hero in your own life, a quality that is a long, long way from any absolute standard of perfectionism. Thinking like a hero in this way can sustain you at the toughest of times.

The following activity is a fun way to help you think about your heroic qualities.

Imagine your favourite movie director has phoned you up with the great news that he or she wants to make *The Film of Your Life*. You get first option on how the script is written and who plays you.

How does *The Film of Your Life* play out? Is it an action adventure with lots of cliff-hangers? A warm romance? A joyful comedy? A thoughtful reflection on serious issues? Or a mind-expanding fantasy/sci-fi extravaganza?

If you could choose anyone, famous or not, to play you, who would you pick? What qualities do they have that you see in yourself? What would be the peak performances, the scenes that take your breath away? What advice would you give to the main actor about how to approach the role?

What does this activity reveal to you about how you approach the drama of your life?

When life gets in the way of living

Taking steps towards your goal feels easier when life goes on around you in a fairly predictable manner. You've prepared well, so you have contingency plans for lots of eventualities along the way and you find that not a lot can deflect you from your course. And then you have One of Those Days. Every crisis you can possibly imagine rains down on you all at once – you collect parking tickets from nowhere, final demands turn up for bills that you thought you had dealt with and the people around you seem unwilling or unable to help you out with any of it. On top of that, your energy levels are low because you've been working hard and missed out on your usual quota of sleep and you're coming down with a nasty bug that makes you feel weak, fed up and sorry for yourself. The final straw is finding that you can't get a signal on your mobile to warn an important new client that you're stuck in traffic and are running late for the presentation.

Everyone has these days – sometimes they turn into weeks or even longer – and when you're in the middle of a challenging goal, sustaining your efforts is tough. Something has to give. Trouble is, if your goal gets sidelined, you may find it really easy to beat yourself up and that can create an even bigger setback.

At times you're playing the long game in your life. If you have to put aside your big goal in order to get through a bad run of luck or unusual series of events, then so be it. Accept that setbacks are a normal part of any change and keep focused on what you can do to deal with your current crises as best you can and get out the other side to the clear open terrain of your journey again. Think about ways to make progress, even in very small ways, such as looking for any unexpected opportunity in the situation. Chapter 16 helps you find ways of doing that.

During her nine-month journey to health and fitness, Louise encountered several setbacks and temptations along the way as other aspects of her life provided distractions. During the times when she had to miss her gym sessions to deal with other priorities, she kept her focus by writing in her journal for five minutes a day, considering a different benefit of maintaining her goal each time.

Exploding the myth of will-power

Suppose your setback happens because you succumb to temptation. You can often give in to temptation when you're making a change in your health – quitting smoking, getting fit, losing weight – but it can also happen in your other goal areas. Perhaps you're focused on getting a promotion at work but suddenly you find yourself slipping back into old, comfortable habits of procrastinating on essential tasks. Again, your inner critic is happy to berate you for your lack of will-power and causes you to wonder, 'What's the point in trying for this new role?'

You may be surprised to discover that the people who are most successful in achieving their goals in life often don't believe in will-power. Successful people often behave as if they have *no* will-power at all and make sure that they set up conditions around them to avoid temptations most of the time. When they do give in to temptation, they shrug their shoulders, enjoy the moment of indulgence and get straight back on track without any self-recrimination.

Think of will-power as a trait you can develop as you gain momentum and start to see results. If you're blessed with strong will-power, then that will certainly help to get you started with your goals. For most people though, seeing great results helps them to maintain their enthusiasm and progress.

Accept that you're human, and that you're going to fail from time to time. Don't accept that one failure is an excuse to carry on with a habit that takes you further away from your goal.

Dealing with jealousy from others

Setbacks can occur when people around you withhold approval or even express disapproval about you coaching yourself to achieve a goal. Sometimes this stems from jealousy that you are doing so well with your goal and it can be very unsettling.

When this happens, look for the positive intent behind the jealousy from the other person. She is probably afraid that by achieving your goal she may lose something valuable that she got from you. Perhaps you were the one who joined her for a cigarette at break time and she is unsettled by your new non-smoking conviction. Or it may be a family member who has got used to joining you as a couch potato in front of the television and feels bereft because you're spending more time at the gym. Maybe you used to be the person in the office who always seemed to sympathise when a colleague wanted to have a good old whinge about the boss, and now you're taking a different attitude to being a team player – your new approach takes the fun out of it for your colleague.

In all these examples, the people close to you miss the rapport they formerly had with you and the sense that you were in it together. Your new habits *are* changing your behaviour, and change is what you want. It may take a little time to readjust the relationships you had before you started making these changes. Some of those relationships may never be the same again and you can take the lead in changing your relationships for the better too.

Part III
Focusing on the Elements of Your Life

The 5th Wave   By Rich Tennant

"My wife and I were drifting apart, so we decided to go back to doing what we did on our honeymoon. We called her parents and asked them for money."

In this part . . .

In these chapters you turn the coaching spotlight on your work, your wealth, the people in your life, your health and your own personal growth. You can begin to make practical adjustments to whatever's out of kilter in the key areas of your life, and you start to see the big picture emerging.

Chapter 11

Career and Work

. . . .

In This Chapter

▶ Making proactive work choices

▶ Understanding the power of focus and feedback

▶ Looking to the future of your work

. . . .

*Y*ou probably spend a large proportion of your time at work. Or, if you're not currently employed, you may spend a fair bit of time and energy searching for work. If you're retired from a career or job, you may be in the process of redefining what can fill the gap that your work used to fill in your life. But the paid work that you do, or have done in the past, is only one aspect of what constitutes work for you over your lifetime. Your work as a parent, caregiver, volunteer and even your hobbies or interests are all facets of your natural drive to be involved in purposeful activity for your own or others' benefit.

A helpful definition of *work* is that it is the context in which you use your skills and talents in some way to give and (often) receive something of value, whether monetary, in kind, for your own satisfaction or as a duty of care. Having a career on the other hand, means that you also make choices that allow you to build on the skills and abilities you use at work so that you can take on bigger and/or more demanding roles. These roles are usually associated with pay rises and improved benefits because you're stretching the range of what you can offer, and as an employee you can command more value in return. Building your career may include self-employment and consultancy work where you create and generate opportunities for yourself in a broader market place.

Not everyone wants a career in this sense, and you may be happy to consider the work that you do as a lower priority in your life than, for example, your family or your commitment to your health. You may work simply to get enough money to fund the lifestyle that you want and so choose to invest most of your energy in areas that are more important to you than work. Chapter 1 helps you decide on the relative importance of these life areas for you. In reality, you're likely to alternate between thinking 'it's just a job' and having your work take centre stage.

This chapter focuses on three main aspects of your work and career: how satisfied you are with what you do; how much you feel your efforts are recognised through pay, promotion and feedback if you're in a paid job; and the extent to which you have opportunities to develop your skills and potential through your work or career. This chapter guides you through some of your options to improve these three areas and helps you identify aspects of your work and career that are fundamental for you in your life as a whole.

Assessing Your Attitudes to Work

I often hear people complain about 'that Monday morning feeling' when the sound of the alarm bell going off just makes you want to slide back under the duvet and go back to sleep. But work, maybe more than love, does seem to make the world go round. Even if you don't need to work for money, the instinct to focus on purposeful activity is still very strong. What's true for you right now? Do you work to live or live to work? Does your current work need to change to reflect your attitudes in life, or does your attitude to work need a bit of fine-tuning?

Playing your part in different work roles

When people ask 'What do you do?' your answer is probably to give your job title, or to talk about the company you work at or own. How much of your identity is attached to your paid work (or lack of it)? Imagine for a moment that you're actually forbidden from working for pay at all. Think about what your response would be when asked 'What do you do?' How comfortable would you feel answering that question? The degree of discomfort you feel may indicate the strength of your reliance on the work you do for pay as a strong validation of your success and self-worth. Nothing's wrong with that; recognising the other ways in which you use your talents to work is a great way of enhancing your overall skill set and becoming happier with the idea of work.

Balancing your different roles

Consider the three main work roles that you probably play:

- ✔ **Pay:** Work that you get paid for – your job or business.
- ✔ **People:** Work that you do for the people in your life and world – parenting, caring, voluntary work.
- ✔ **Passion:** Work that is linked to your interests and passions – activity in a hobby, learning a new skill, being a member of a club.

These three areas may well overlap for you, or you may see them as sitting in three different compartments of your life. The balance between these three aspects of work is rarely an equal split in terms of time. Most people spend more of their time in paid work, at least for certain periods of their life. But think about the times you don't have paid work – periods of unemployment, maternity or paternity leave, sabbaticals and retirement. What will define your idea of work then?

Perhaps you don't feel that you've identified passion work yet. If you spend a lot of time and energy on building your career, then you may have to put passion work at the bottom of your pile of priorities. Chapter 15 helps you understand why developing this aspect of your work and life can be so helpful in increasing your overall level of happiness.

The following activity can help you to see the links and differences in your attitudes to different work areas. Think of the roles that you carry out in the work areas of pay, people and passion, and answer the questions in Table 11-1, which uses Stuart, who runs his own business, as an example. In this example, I focus on one role within each work area, but of course you may have more than one (such as being a parent and also caring for elderly relatives in the people work area). Choose the roles that are most significant for you.

Table 11-1	Identifying Your Role in Different Work Areas		
	Pay	*People*	*Passion*
What is the main role I work at in this area?	Run my business.	Father of John and Sophie.	Member of local art group.
How much time do I spend on this work?	Too much! At least 50 hours during the week and I often work at weekends.	Not nearly enough . . . bedtime stories during the week. Weekends better but often interrupted by paid-work issues.	Have missed the last six meetings.
What value do I get from this work?	Money, stimulation, sense of self-worth and achievement.	Love, joy, laughter, sense of contribution to my family.	A real buzz from tapping into my creativity and helping to stage exhibitions of our work.

(continued)

Table 11-1 *(continued)*

	Pay	*People*	*Passion*
What feelings do I have about this work?	I veer between feeling very motivated and pretty stressed, depending on the challenges.	I feel very peaceful and calm in this role and find it helps me get perspective and de-stress.	I have a lot of fun in this role and feel alive and purposeful. My energy levels are higher after a meeting.
What is my current attitude to this work in ten words or fewer?	Takes more time and attention relative to the rewards I get.	I always get more out than I put in.	I've been taking this for granted and reducing its impact.
What do I need to change about this work to balance my portfolio?	I can be more disciplined, delegate more and reduce the time I give to this role. I probably only need to reduce my hours by an hour a day to make a significant difference. And I can cut out weekend working.	Freeing up time from paid work will allow me to devote more time to this role. I'd like to commit to organising family suppers at least twice a week.	I can make a regular weekly commitment here by giving it a higher priority in my life. I'll also investigate opening up the club to children occasionally so I can share my interest with John and Sophie.

Your answers to the questions in Table 11-1 highlight the relative importance you place on each area of work, the time you allocate to these areas and how they feed your most important values. Stuart's completed table shows clearly that the time he allocates to the most pressing one – paid work – drains the value he gets out of the other two. By recognising that, he can see ways to manage his paid-work time a little better and focus on the other two areas, which in turn help to re-energise him for his paid work.

Setting Your Work in Context

Adjusting the balance of your work areas helps you to identify ways to ensure that you get what you need from all aspects of the work that you do. The rest of this chapter focuses on improving what most people classify as work: your paid job.

Even if work is just something you do to pay the bills, you probably spend a fair amount of time doing it, so considering how work fits into your life and preferences as a whole makes sense. To what extent does your job match your natural abilities, fit with your beliefs about your world and support the values that you hold most dear? Why should what you do best in terms of skills determine the most natural choice of work for you? Would you get even more personal satisfaction in an environment where you were developing skills that are currently less strong for you? For the work that you choose to do most of the time – whether that be paid or unpaid – this section helps you to find your unique balance between being comfortable using your best skills and stretching yourself to your natural potential.

Making a conscious choice

Think for a moment about how you ended up in the role you currently hold, or the jobs you have formerly performed. What made you choose the work you currently do? Did happy or not-so-happy accidents result in your career choices? Were you influenced by a parent or an older adult? Did you get swept along by an interview process and suddenly find yourself accepting an offer? Would you choose your job again knowing what you now know?

Perhaps you're struggling with work issues, or you're in the wrong job, or you're not using your skills to best advantage, and you can't see how to get to the work that you're meant to do (or even decide what it is). All that experience, however uncomfortable, is preparing you in just the right way for what's around the corner. Whichever route you take – being open and flexible to opportunities or planning every move – use the detachment and questioning skills of coaching to ensure that you're heading in the right direction. You may choose to stay where you are for the moment, knowing that you need to gather strength (maybe a strong sense of self-belief and confidence) and resources (skills, knowledge and experience) to make a change. Making that choice in itself is part of the process of moving forward.

Evaluating your job

You may find that you get so caught up in the detail of your work, for good or ill, that before you know it another year has passed and you wonder what's changed for the better. You can adapt to almost anything, and you may find yourself settling for a role that you've long outgrown, or that imposes unhealthy pressure on you, simply because you haven't taken the time to ask yourself some searching questions on a regular basis. A high proportion of workplace stress is caused by the accumulation of lots of small irritations piled on top of each other and left to go unchecked. If you're ambitious and want to progress your career, you need to carefully assess where you are and where you're heading.

You can assess whether your skills and natural preferences are best suited to what you currently do by putting yourself in the role of someone who is evaluating the requirements, ups and downs, and perks and potholes of your job. See how you measure up against this evaluation. Don't think about your official job specification – often the things that aren't written down cause the most frustration or offer the most joy. Try the following activity and feel free to add other questions to tailor it to the context of your own work. (You may want to refer to Chapter 4 to explore your specific skills prior to completing this activity.)

- ✔ What is your main purpose for doing the work you do?
- ✔ What do you spend 80 per cent of your time doing at work?
- ✔ Which of your best skills do you use at work?
- ✔ Which of your skills do you never or rarely get the opportunity to use at work?
- ✔ What proportion of your time do you spend:
  - Feeling stressed?
  - Feeling bored?
  - Feeling stimulated?
  - Enjoying your work?
- ✔ To what extent do you feel in control at work?
- ✔ How often do you stretch your capabilities?
- ✔ How often do you coast along at work?
- ✔ How would you describe your working environment on a scale of 1 (= your worst nightmare) to 10 (= your idea of heaven)?
- ✔ Finish the following statement: 'I choose the work I currently do because . . .'

✔ Choose the statement that best describes how you feel about your work:

- 'I'm living my work dream – I don't even think of it as "work".'

- 'I feel challenged, stimulated and valued most of the time, and this carries me through the difficult bits.'

- 'Some days are better than others and on the whole, I can take it or leave it. Work is not a priority area for me.'

- 'I often get frustrated, anxious or bored at work, and this affects my enjoyment of the good bits.'

- 'I have to drag myself in every day; I'm ready to quit.'

As a result of this activity, what have you discovered about your work that needs to change? Perhaps you found that you spend 80 per cent of your time doing tasks that bore you or use skills that you least enjoy? Or you may have discovered that you feel bored half the time and stimulated the other half, and that overall the stimulation outweighs the boredom. Or perhaps you've identified that your attitude to your work is in the middle ground – 'take it or leave it' – and that this means you can put up with day-to-day irritations because work is a low priority for you. Look for common themes and links in your answers to the activity. Is your main purpose the same as the reason you chose the work you do?

When Stuart completed this evaluation, he described the main purpose of doing his work as providing financial stability for his family in a way that meant he was fully in control. The reason Stuart chose to do his work (running his own business) was because he naturally enjoyed being an entrepreneur. Stuart's work purpose therefore linked to his values (Chapter 6), and his choice of work had come about because of his knowledge of his best skills (Chapter 4).

Making adjustments at work

From the previous activity, you can identify the main areas that need change. Work often needs adjustment as a result of undesirable impacts in the following areas:

✔ **Beliefs.** Your beliefs about your work may be holding you back. Perhaps you think that you're entitled to be stimulated by what you do and need to rethink that belief so that you can be more proactive about finding ways to increase stimulation for yourself.

✔ **Motivation.** Your motivation may need readjusting by making a change in the way you approach work.

✔ **Freedom.** You may feel the need for more freedom and autonomy in your work.

✔ **Support.** You may require more support and recognition from those around you.

✔ **Pressure.** Your work may overload you and cause you unhelpful stress.

✔ **Responsibility.** You may feel disconnected from your work and want to take more responsibility in order for you to become more engaged in what you do.

✔ **Environment.** You may be unfulfilled with your current environment – from a simple issue of 'same desk, same four walls' to having really outgrown your current job and company.

Using Table 11-2 as your example, write down the commitment in each area that moves you closer to your ideal work. Here's what Stuart had to say about his paid work of running his own business.

Table 11-2	Commitment Statements to Move You Closer to Your Ideal Work
Change my beliefs	'The business will not collapse if I delegate more, in fact it will benefit from fresh energies directed at some areas.'
Focus on my motivation	'I'm looking forward to harnessing the creative energy I get from my art to see how I can solve business problems more effectively.'
Enjoy more freedom	'Setting a goal of getting home on time more often will stop me feeling chained to the business.'
Get more support	'My office manager (Jo) is ready for development and is really committed to the business – she will thrive on being asked to support me more and take on new responsibilities.'
Generate less pressure	'Spending time with my children will help me de-stress.'
Take more responsibility	'I want to be more responsible about my time. I'm shocked to see how often I coast along thinking I'm working hard. Staying late has become a habit.'
Change my environment	'Don't feel the need for a change here, although Jo has some ideas to move the team around to stimulate new work relationships. I'll keep an open mind!'

Improving Your Current Job

If evaluating your job has made you realise that your current work isn't meeting your needs, you may now be formulating a plan to make radical changes. You may decide that although you want to change certain aspects of your current role, it basically meets a lot of your requirements for a satisfactory work situation. On the other hand, you may feel ready to take a deep breath and search elsewhere for a new position (see the section 'Finding Your Dream Work'). But you probably have to serve notice, meet obligations and hand over projects before you can cross the next threshold. Even if your change is relatively organic – such as acquiring or developing a new skill so that you can progress to the next level in your current organisation – a shortfall remains between your ambitions and where you are now.

Keeping your focus

You need to work out how to focus your attention on the here-and-now at work while setting your sights on your next goal. And in the process of making the best of your current situation, you may also discover some new wisdom to inform your next step. You may realise that you can make changes in your current job that improve your situation.

Senti started coaching with one clear objective – to escape from her current role before she got fired! Although she admitted that she probably wouldn't really be fired (she was a careful and conscientious manager), she hated the relationship she had with her boss so much that she *felt* as if it were true. She was intensely unhappy because although she knew where she *didn't* want to be, she had no clue about the next best step.

During coaching, she worked through the steps she needed to take to resolve her stalemate. She realised that deciding exactly on her next career move was not the most urgent priority. She faced the fact that some of her own beliefs about herself were contributing to the poor relationship she had with her boss. Unless she found more assertive ways of behaving, she would find herself in a similar position in any new role she undertook.

Senti set herself two main goals – to identify and begin to take action to secure the job of her dreams, and to address her relationship with her boss. The second goal was hard work because part of her had already written off her current position and was focused on the future. She worked hard on her self-esteem and confidence, which allowed her to stop taking her boss's style personally. In turn, this helped her boss to see Senti's talents clearly at last. Three months later, he offered Senti a promotion to manage a new project.

After some thought, Senti accepted the new role. It would enhance her skills considerably and was in an exciting area of the business that interested her. Her biggest surprise was that she found that her new role took her pretty close to the dream job she'd begun to identify for herself. Using coaching, Senti's new-found self-confidence gave her the courage to identify business needs that she was uniquely fitted to address.

Like Senti, you may discover through coaching that the external factor that you think is the problem with your current work role – the pay; the way you're managed; the pressures of deadlines – may be secondary to the internal factors that you can control by applying and developing your natural skills. Here are some suggestions that can help you to improve your enjoyment of work:

- ✔ **Practise assertive communication.** If you feel frustrated at work, your needs are not being met (see Chapter 6 for more on identifying your needs). Be clear with yourself about what you need from your role – is variety more important to you than a fixed routine? You may find ways of creating a more varied structure to what you do, but you may need the okay from your boss to make changes. State what will work best for you clearly and directly as early as possible rather than fuming quietly over a situation. This helps you avoid any tense confrontations further down the line when the boredom has really got to you.

- ✔ **Remember what motivates you.** When you're clear on your values (Chapter 6), you can link all that you do to these motivating forces. If elements of your job feel stressful at times and you wonder why you stick with it, think about what your job gives you that helps you live your values. Perhaps your salary supports the lifestyle you want, or the recognition you receive for meeting deadlines feeds your sense of accomplishment and self-belief. Keeping a focus on the end result helps you put your job into a whole-life perspective.

- ✔ **Catch yourself 'being in the moment'.** A sign that you're performing well is when you get absorbed in what you're doing and lose track of time. With a little practice, you can place yourself in the moment even when you're bored or frustrated. Simply focus on what you are doing as if your life depended on it, or as if it were the most fascinating thing you've ever encountered, or try to recall the feeling you had when you completed this task for the very first time. This trick won't always turn a boring task into the highlight of your day, but making the effort to switch your mental state is often enough to jolt you out of negativity and help you deal effectively with the routine so that you can move on to more interesting tasks.

- ✔ **Remember that the only things that are ever fully in your control are your own thoughts, behaviour and actions.** No matter how little you deserve it, you sometimes fall foul of the bad mood of a colleague or boss. You can allow this to throw you off course or you can put yourself in their shoes and decide on a course of action that accommodates the unfavourable circumstance and still gets you where you need to be. Sometimes that means tackling the behaviour and sometimes it means giving the other person space to work through their bad mood without you taking it personally. Focus on what you can control – your *own* mood and behaviour – and you're more likely to help the other person get back on track too.

✔ **Check in with yourself every couple of hours.** If you know you tend to prefer the company of others rather than working alone, how can you inject some human interaction into your task to help you regain energy to continue? Think about the different ways you can carry out simple or routine tasks that increase your enjoyment. If you have a mailing to pack up for the post, can you get some other people involved to make it more fun? Or would you prefer to sit by a window with a nice view and let the routine task act like a calming meditation? These little choices can make a huge difference to how you feel about what you do and help to put you more in control of your work.

Dealing with negative situations

You may love your work but find that the people around you drain your energy and lower your mood, your confidence or your conviction in what you do. You can protect yourself from the most damaging effects of negativity by understanding that people often exhibit bad behaviour when they feel trapped and sense that they lack power and choice.

Boredom and disengagement can lead to apathy, which can put a damper on the enthusiasm and proactivity of entire teams. When you succumb to apathy you get hijacked by lethargy, cynicism and a feeling of pointlessness, and it's easy to pick this mood up from other people and join in. Coach yourself to avoid this mood by asking yourself, 'What am I feeling frustrated about? What is causing me to feel trapped and out of control? What can I do to positively support the team or proactively challenge this problem?'

A quite different form of negative behaviour results from the temptation to indulge in gossip and hearsay. Damaging gossip can stem from fear and self-protection, directing attention away from the gossiper. And the effects are often very negative – encouraging back-biting between departments and destroying trust. All this can be quite exciting – for a while – until the negative energy means that the biter ends up getting bitten. Coach yourself to steer away from indulging in gossip by asking yourself, 'How can I direct my energies to fuel a more productive fire?' Before you pass on information about a colleague to a third party, ask yourself three questions: 'Is what I'm about to say true? Is it positive and constructive? Is it useful and relevant to the person I'm talking to?'

Finding Your Dream Work

This section looks at the options you have when you know that progressing your career means leaving for pastures new. (Chapter 21 helps you assess the need and plan for a really radical upheaval in your working life and offers helpful strategies for when major changes such as redundancy and unemployment are imposed on you.)

Finding your dream work starts with knowing what you really love to do in a work context. The following activity helps you to identify what you relish doing at work.

Find a quiet spot and sit comfortably, taking a few moments to breathe deeply and relax. Close your eyes and ask yourself the following question:

> *If a miracle happened and when I open my eyes I have the perfect work for me, what would that look like? What would I do for the next 24 hours?*

Think about exactly what would happen, planning out each hour of the day exactly to your taste and preferences. You can include scenarios that may seem impossible and beyond your current grasp. The end result of your visualisation is not to create an accurate blueprint, but to give you clues to the key elements of your perfect work day.

What has your miracle created for you? Is it an extension of your current work, maybe just a few steps away from where you already are? Or is your dream work something so wildly different from your current job that you can't see how you can ever make it happen? You already have all the resources you need to get your dream job, no matter how many challenges stand in your way (read Chapter 23 if you don't believe me). Of course, the further away your dream job is from your current skill set and reach, the stronger your passion must be for pursuing it so that you can maintain the momentum when the going gets tough.

Make sure that your passion is well rooted in what's really important to you in your life as a whole before committing to the road ahead (refer to Chapter 6). Chapter 4 helps you explore your natural skills and abilities so that you can design a robust strategy to identify and secure this work of your dreams.

Start bringing your dream job closer to home by collecting adverts for roles that approximate or match it. Some may be a little out of your reach right now, but you can also include adverts in your dream-job folder that are a few steps closer to where you are currently. By researching and referring to your ideal role and thinking about how you can prepare yourself for getting there, you'll find that your goal becomes much more realistic.

Knowing your job-search goal

What did you discover about your dream job from the activity in the preceding section? To what extent is that role in your reach right now? Your strategy for exploring the job market differs depending on how many steps you need to take to get to your ultimate destination. Your goal may be:

- **Wanting change for its own sake.** You probably like elements of your current job a lot, as well as being frustrated over others. Essentially though, your main motivation for moving is to re-enthuse yourself in a fresh environment. Positive change for its own sake is really your key driver. You can make this change in your work fairly easily and quickly because you don't need to change many factors to re-enthuse yourself. Start by looking around at other departments within your company to get a fresh perspective. A secondment (temporarily transferring to another position) may be just the trick to satisfy your need for a change or springboard you to a new role.

- **Increasing your challenge.** You want to get to the next level, or even the one beyond that. Promotion and a rise in salary may be key motivators for you. You're ready to compete in the job market, demonstrate that you can stretch yourself and prove that you're worth the increased financial investment for a new employer. You need to prepare for the healthy competition you may face – think about your CV, your interview technique and the research into the market you need to do. When you've done this groundwork, change can happen quickly.

- **Expanding your horizons.** You have your sights set on a long-term goal of broadening your skills base. Maybe you see the next few years as a platform for ultimately setting up your own business, so your next move is about gaining lots of broad experience as preparation. You may need to move a little sideways to get the long-term benefit of a different skill set. This career goal may take longer to achieve because you want to change a number of factors and need to demonstrate that you can adapt to a whole new work arena.

If your dream job involves acquiring a new skill or retraining, take a look at www.learndirect.co.uk for a wealth of information and resources on practical study and qualifications to help you.

Creating the perfect CV

You don't have to have a curriculum vitae (CV) to find a new job. If you're confident in your ability to sell yourself and are aware of your unique selling points, the fastest and most effective way to secure a new role is to phone a targeted list of potential employers direct, with a view to getting an interview where you can impress the socks off them. Few people call potential employers in this way, which is why it's so compelling and powerful if you can pull it off.

However, a CV can spread the net wide when you're not being proactive on the phone. And even if you secured an interview without a CV, a prospective employer will probably ask for one further down the line. Here are some tips for creating a knock-out CV:

✔ Keep your CV concise and direct – three pages are ideal, or a little more if you have a very extensive track record. The longer your CV, the more you need to work at making the text visually compelling by using bullet points and clear headings.

Think of your CV in the same way as you think of how you dress for an interview – first impressions really do count.

✔ Spend more time on your recent experience and focus on the results you achieved in each recent role. The interview is the place to go into the background detail.

✔ Keep your CV fairly generic but design it so that you can tailor it for specific roles. Always write a concise covering letter for each application and refer to the needs you know that potential employer has (you pick these up from the advert or other research you've done). Your aim in the covering letter is to demonstrate very briefly how you can solve the company's problem and meet their needs.

See *CVs For Dummies* by Lois-Andrea Ferguson and Joyce Lain Kennedy and *Answering Tough Interview Questions For Dummies* by Rob Yeung (Wiley).

Working the market

When looking for a new job, you can go it alone by sending out speculative CVs to job adverts, posting responses on Internet job boards or working your networks (the following section is about using your current network of people to your advantage). You can also use recruitment consultancies. You may want the strength of an expert behind you who can give you support, advice and can market you with skill.

If you decide to use a recruitment consultancy, choose two or three and build up good relationships with your contacts there. Sign up to a consultancy with a national network to benefit from their extensive resources, and one or two smaller local consultancies who can give you the very best service. Agree how you'll keep in touch with your consultant – don't assume they'll call you. Be memorable and ensure you're at the forefront of their mind when a juicy role comes up.

Floating into a career change

For the last 30 years, Richard Nelson Bolles has published an annually updated manual for job hunters and career changers called *What Color is Your Parachute?* The manual contains some great exercises to identify specific skills and give you ideas on how and where you might apply them (although the manual is more specific to the US job market). Take a look at the companion website www.jobhunters bible.com, which has additional guidance on how to search the Internet for job-hunting resources.

Using your networks

A high proportion of career moves, especially at a senior level, are word-of-mouth introductions (the hidden job market). But you don't have to be a serial networker to take advantage of this route. When you're searching for your dream job, don't hold back from telling the people around you your wish list for your next move and ask them to consider people they know who may help you. Your acquaintances may not know a potential employer, but they may know someone in the right industry who can offer you helpful information to help you prepare. Or someone in your network may be able to practice interview techniques with you or review your CV. Ask yourself:

> *What do I need to close the gap between where I am now and where I want to be? Who can help me do that?*

Check out Chapter 13 for more about the importance of building up networks of people to support you while you make the changes you want in your life.

Getting Recognition for Your Work

Even the most high-minded and self-aware person needs the right kind of feedback and recognition in order to feel that their work is worthwhile. But giving and receiving feedback can be tricky. Sometimes you may fear to confront a problem or feel embarrassment at the idea of offering or receiving gushing praise. Many problems at work are caused by people hoping that the problem disappears or that they don't need to say 'well done' because you've obviously done a good job. However, studies show that even negative feedback, poorly delivered, is preferable to no feedback at all. (That's not an excuse to give negative feedback, of course, but it does show how lost people feel in a feedback vacuum!)

Coaching yourself to give and receive feedback at work not only helps you to develop your work abilities, but also enhances your own self-awareness, empathy and ability to come up with solutions.

Getting feedback

Do you look forward to getting feedback in appraisals and one-to-ones? Or do you simply find them pointless and irrelevant? Appraisals can sometimes feel too focused on looking at how you measure up to a common standard – and you are, of course, an uncommon, unique individual. While the company perspective is essential, both parties benefit when the review is really meaningful for the person being reviewed. Try to see your formal review as a free, and very powerful, coaching session and help your appraiser to tailor the session to your needs – you get a lot more out of your review and also project a proactive, professional image.

Ask yourself the following questions:

- ✔ What opportunities do I have to get formal feedback at work? How can I encourage more constructive feedback opportunities?
- ✔ What benefits do I currently get from formal feedback at work?
- ✔ On a scale of 1–10, how much do I enjoy this kind of feedback and feel motivated by it?
- ✔ How can I get increased benefits and feel even more motivated by formal reviews?

Here are three suggestions for getting more out of your formal review process:

- ✔ If you are nervous or apprehensive, explain so in good time so that your appraiser can come up with ways of reassuring you. This might be as simple as finding a less formal room to conduct the meeting in – facing your appraiser across a cold, forbidding boardroom table is off-putting for many people.
- ✔ Be clear about the focus for the feedback session well in advance and prepare any relevant documentation. If you have facts at your fingertips, you waste less time and present a good impression.
- ✔ Ask for specific examples of behaviour (good and bad) and an explanation of exactly why the behaviour did/didn't match up to expectations. Ask for suggestions for maintaining/improving your performance in the future.

If you're self-employed, you can still benefit from setting up a feedback process through self-coaching and listening to your customers and suppliers. Here are some annual review questions you can ask yourself:

- ✔ What were my successes over the last year? What has inspired me most?

- ✔ What have been my main challenges and how have I overcome them? What have been my biggest obstacles and what am I learning from these?

- ✔ What do my customers think about me, my business and my products/services? (Ask them!)

- ✔ How do my suppliers and partners feel about our working relationship? (Ask them!)

- ✔ What skills have I developed and what have I learnt about myself?

- ✔ What new personal goals can I set for the coming year?

- ✔ What support do I need?

- ✔ How can I measure my success?

What is your personal wish-list for an effective feedback session? What action can you now take?

Promoting your personal brand

Getting recognition at work is all about helping others to see what your unique contribution is. You may feel that selling yourself and your skills is egotistical, especially if you tend to be naturally modest about your achievements. Perhaps you tend to hide your light and find that over time you begin to feel a little resentful that people don't always notice or appreciate your good work. Or you may take the opposite view and grab the limelight as often as you can, only to find that those around you push you back down into place. Getting the balance right is tricky. You may feel that you have to adopt a different work persona and play office politics in order to be successful, but the truth is that most people hate spin, and the last place they want to have to deal with it is at work.

In what ways do you put up a façade at work? Do you sometimes present a show of blustery confidence when you're really quaking in your boots? At times this is helpful, but at other times it may prevent you from getting the support you need. If you manage staff, do you think you always need to know the answer to every problem? What impact does this have for you and the team, on those occasions when you don't know the best solution? How can you present an authentic you at work and maintain the respect of others?

Think of yourself as a business. What are your unique selling points? Yes, you have skills, but how do you package and present these skills to the world in a way that is unique to you? Getting used to thinking about how you project your personal brand can help you to develop versatility. After all, you are uniquely your brand and you can also change that brand as you wish, according to the market you're in. So you may choose to display your more extrovert image in a meeting or you may let people see your reflective, thoughtful side, depending upon your audience and what's required.

Looking to the Future

What are the trends you see developing in your work choices? You may feel you have to run to keep up with the pace of change, but if you regularly coach yourself through your work choices you can set your own pace and establish your own standards of excellence.

Progression in your work life need not always equate to promotion up the ranks. Progression may be more about finding ways to remain stimulated in what you do, perhaps taking a sideways move from time to time to re-energise yourself and your skills. Or progression may mean that you move to a different role in a new company every few years. If you've found the work that you feel you were meant to do, making progress may be easy.

Generally, you feel a sense of making progress when you're living your values at work and being your authentic self. And while all jobs have an element of routine in them, you usually feel more inspired if you can find new things to learn about yourself and your skills through work.

Here are three things that you can contemplate on a daily basis to measure your progress:

- ✔ **What were my wins today?** This could be successfully negotiating with a supplier or achieving a deadline.

- ✔ **What have I learnt today?** Maybe you added to your skills, picked up some new knowledge or discovered a way not to do something!

- ✔ **What can I change as a result of today?** Perhaps you want to revisit your time-management strategy as result of experiencing a bit too much stress meeting that deadline, or you decide that you're going to step into future negotiations more readily to take your confidence to another level.

Write down your answers so that you can reflect back on them and witness the cumulative power of these small daily successes, learning points and significant steps that you've integrated into your working life.

When you think about the work you plan for the future, how prepared are you for it? Do you have a dream to be your own boss or to create a working life that is independent of your source of wealth – by investing in property, for example – so that you have more freedom to choose your work on its own merits? You can think about your future work in the context of a SWOT analysis, considering your strengths, weaknesses, opportunities and threats, as follows:

- ✔ What are my **strengths** at work?

- ✔ What **weaknesses** am I aware of and how am I working on them?

- ✔ What **opportunities** do I have at work that match my whole-life goals?

- ✔ What **threats** at work may hold me back from meeting my whole-life goals?

Coach yourself for your future work by working through the following coaching questions (refer to Part II for more about these coaching approaches):

- ✔ **Powerful opening question:** What attitudes do I want to develop about work to fulfil my potential throughout my career?

- ✔ **Personal style:** What kind of work am I naturally drawn to? What do I thrive on? What demotivates me? What kind of environments suit me best? Where do I feel most at home when I am working?

- ✔ **Beliefs:** What negative beliefs do I have about work that prevent me from preparing for future challenges?

- ✔ **Motivation:** What image of myself at work is most appealing as my future vision? What would I reach for if I knew that I couldn't fail?

- ✔ **What's working:** What am I doing now to prepare myself for my future working life? How can I develop these behaviours and habits? What's getting in the way of fulfilling my potential? What trends do I see developing now that propel me forward or hold me back?

- ✔ **Exploring options:** What options do I have to expand my working range? What is the easiest route? What is the most challenging route? What more information do I need before I decide on my options?

- ✔ **Taking action:** What's my first step? How much time can I allocate to planning my approach? How do I know when I am making progress? What can I do to celebrate?

Chapter 12

Money, Wealth and Abundance

In This Chapter

▶ Putting money in its place

▶ Understanding wealth creation

▶ Living life with abundance

Money and wealth aren't necessarily the same thing. Most people have to work to earn enough money to buy the basics that they need and the luxuries that they want. Whether you have a little or a lot of money, your relationship with wealth is probably a significant factor in how content you are in your life.

However, money doesn't always produce more happiness. Some interesting research looked at lottery winners and people who had been severely handicapped in serious accidents and found that a year later, the lottery winners reported the higher levels of unhappiness. But, of course, many deliriously content multimillionaires live in this world too. What you do with your money and your personal relationship with it are what create or destroy some of your potential for happiness.

Wealth issues usually centre on the degree of basic financial security you have, the extent to which you can live the lifestyle you want and the provision you're making for the future. This chapter helps you put money in its rightful place, assists you in identifying what real wealth is for you and encourages you to explore how you can create your own sense of abundance. If you focus on what you want to have, do and be in your life, and arrange your financials around those goals, you may well find that the money then flows far more easily than those times when you put the money cart before the wealth horse.

Defining the Role of Money in Your Life

Most people have to work hard to develop a relationship with money that works well for them. If you live in the western world, you're already rich by the standards of developing countries and probably even those of your own forefathers many centuries ago. But you may not *feel* rich. Gadgets such as cars, mobile phones and computers are within your grasp, but when you've acquired the car or the phone or the computer, you may feel encouraged to set your sights on the bigger, better and newer version within a very short space of time. Discontent sets in very quickly if your definition of feeling wealthy is tied into the acquisition of material things.

Perhaps the simplest way to avoid being happy in life is to compare yourself with other people (who are probably comparing themselves with you and getting the same effect, by the way). Such comparisons are at their sharpest and most painful in the realm of money and material possessions. You can easily get blinded by the shiny results of having money and forget what you need it for in the first place.

Money is simply a commodity that helps you to:

- Acquire essential things such as food and heat
- Buy pleasurable commodities such as fancy new shoes and nice holidays
- Enhance the quality of your life by perhaps financing a business venture or donating to your favourite charity

Gross national happiness

The small Himalayan country of Bhutan now has a formal measure of gross national happiness as well as the financial measure of gross national product. Based on non-material values and a traditional Buddhist way of life, government ideology focuses on improving the quality of life for the people of Bhutan, not simply through wealth creation but also through maintaining cultural, social and environmental values. Is it working? Time will tell, but a number of international economists have already commented favourably on this approach to government strategy. This unconventional approach is likely to gain popularity as the world becomes more conscious of the damage that can be done when an excess of greed flourishes within societies.

Not having enough money can cause you anything from mild frustration to extreme distress, yet the pursuit of money for its own sake can have equally undesirable consequences and may cloud or dilute the enjoyment you get from the things that are truly important to the success of your life.

Wealth is very different from money. You usually can't feel wealthy without first feeling that you have abundant money, and entering the realms of the abundant is definitely trickier if you haven't fully defined the role of money and the meaning of wealth in your life.

What's the distinction between money and wealth for you? What has to happen for you to feel wealthy in your life? When has money in itself made you feel happier, more secure and more content?

Being Financially Secure

First things first – life coaching to get to abundance starts with developing your basic financial common sense. Enjoying life is pretty hard if you're wondering where to get the money to pay the bills or put food on the table. You may be familiar with the anxiety that goes with tough times, when outgoings completely outstrip income. Just starting out on your own and taking on rent or a mortgage for the first time, not to mention losing your job, experiencing a business failure or even going bankrupt all contribute to a feeling of financial insecurity. You don't always feel that you have much control over whatever financial hit is lying in wait.

The constant worry that you may lose your financial security can hold you back from fulfilling your dreams, and not fulfilling your dreams can in turn stop you from generating the wealth and ultimately the security you most want and deserve. You can avoid this vicious circle by putting in place your own lifetime strategy that allows you breathing space and the knowledge that you can always survive financially, no matter what's round that corner.

Drawing up your financial ground rules

Do you know the critical things you need to do on a regular basis to ensure that you are always financially secure? (You can find lots of detailed information on this subject in *Sorting Out Your Finances For Dummies* by Melanie Bien.) To get you started in coaching yourself to a new financial plan, here are some tried-and-tested guidelines that can help you think about exactly what's going to work for you:

✔ **Be honest with yourself.** Get out of denial. Do you know how much you actually spend? A client of mine decided to declutter and clear out six months' worth of accumulated paperwork. She was horrified to find that the only envelopes that were unopened were her bank statements. Spend a month writing down every penny that you spend instead of comforting yourself that you only indulge in the occasional bargain impulse buy.

✔ **Work out your budget.** Happiness is possible even on a reduced budget, but unhappiness seems almost guaranteed if you lose control of your spending, even if you have lots of money to start with. Your budget is a simple formula – your outgoings should never be more than your incomings – so start with two columns and list every item under each.

✔ **Aim to spend less than you earn each month.** After you set your budget, you can decide on your regular safety margin. By spending a little less than you earn each month, you know that you have some money left at the end of the month to act as a rainy-day contingency fund. You can then, at the end of the month, choose to spend some of the extra cash on a treat or reward if you like. By holding back a little, you reduce the worry that can turn money into an obsession that gets in the way of other, more significant life goals.

Reducing your spending may not sound much fun, but you can take a positive mindset to this and turn it into a challenge or game. Consider the choices you make in the supermarket – do you always go for certain brands when you could select own-label products? You could make a policy of visiting the shop at the end of the day when many products are reduced in price. Make a game out of finding the best bargains and see how much you can shave off your weekly shopping bill.

✔ **Try to save 10 per cent of everything you earn.** Instead of using the extra cash to indulge yourself at the end of the month, you may choose to let it work for your future financial security by saving or investing the money. Decide what proportion of your income you can save and aim for that. Stashing away a certain amount each month often works better than a feast-and-famine approach where you save like crazy when you get a big bonus and then abandon saving at other times. Make the transaction automatic so that you aren't tempted to change your mind and simply forget what you promised yourself.

Write down your new financial ground rules in your journal so that you can refer to them easily and reinforce your commitment.

How do you feel about developing a budget, spending less than you earn and saving a set amount of money each month? Perhaps you relish the idea of getting in control again. Or perhaps you recoil in horror at setting such constraints around yourself. Ask yourself what's causing this recoil. Is it that you value spontaneity and freedom where money is concerned and feel that budgets and savings plans would stifle this? What impact does having this freedom then have for you? If you experiment with a more structured approach, what can it give you that's better than what you currently have? You can find other financial ground rules that suit you and your life – rules that give you the same sense of freedom yet don't leave you panicking about final demands and unexpected bills. If other options exist for you, what are they? Whatever option you choose, you need some element of discipline to ensure that your spending stays in control over the long term.

Developing your financial survival plan

Coaching yourself in matters of money may result in a major decision to change your lifestyle or work. Or you may find yourself suddenly bereft of a major source of income through redundancy or business failure. What's your survival plan? Do you know how much money you need to get by and how long you're going to need to get things back on track? Financial advisors usually recommend having six months' salary in savings to tide you over in an emergency, but this figure will differ depending upon your spending habits and your circumstances. You'll almost certainly need more if you're thinking of setting up in business unless you're certain that your new venture will pull in cash for you very quickly. If you've already worked out your everyday budget, determining your contingency fund is a lot easier. Here are a couple of suggestions to get you motivated about drawing up your ideas:

- ✔ **Think of doing this as a freedom strategy rather than a survival plan.** If security is a strong value for you, then imagining yourself safe and secure when that rainy day comes is very compelling. But you may already be pretty financially secure and not feel the same drive to amass this contingency resource. If so, then allow yourself to daydream about the possibilities your savings give you if/when you wake up one morning and know with certainty that this is the perfect time for you to enjoy that sabbatical from work, go travelling for six months or take advantage of a business opportunity that has fallen into your lap.

  You can always think of your nest egg as both a freedom strategy and a survival plan – focus on whatever beliefs support you to take positive forward action.

- ✔ **Get help to design your plan.** A trained financial adviser or an accountant can discuss tax and investment issues with you. A trusted and level-headed friend can help you check your budgeting assumptions.

Paying the penalty for not knowing your budget

Rosie and Mark had a double income that was the envy of their friends and a lifestyle to match. Yet they were constantly miserable and stressed because their credit card bills just seemed to escalate every month, to the point where they had to take out a high-interest loan to clear them all and start afresh. They even stopped opening the envelopes containing their statements because they just didn't want to face the reality. The couple came to coaching and set goals to face their fear and agree on a budget. They eventually got back on track and found that they only then needed to make small adjustments to their spending to keep everything ticking along smoothly. Not knowing their budget had sent them over the edge and created a cumulative debt that they paid for dearly, both emotionally and in cash.

When Shami was considering establishing her own business, she had a figure in mind of what she needed to see her through the first year of trading when she didn't expect to be making much money. This was a pretty tidy sum and was beginning to sap her motivation. Exploring the issue with her coach helped her to look more closely at her figures and assumptions. Shami discovered that she didn't need nearly as much as she thought because of the savings she'd make on travel costs and expenses directly bound up with her current role at work.

Living Your Chosen Lifestyle

No matter how much you enjoy your work, you probably hold the belief that you'd rather be enjoying more leisure time. You look forward to eating out in nice restaurants, or playing a round of golf or lazing by the pool – and often these activities really do enhance your life. Sometimes though, your leisure pursuits don't give you what you expect. You may have occasionally experienced that flat feeling when you're on holiday, surrounded by the good things in life, willing yourself to have fun but in reality you're bored, restless and discontented.

Your lifestyle is an aspect of your wealth; you may need money to enjoy a certain lifestyle, but your enjoyment of your lifestyle doesn't have to be directly related to how much money you spend. How and where you get enjoyment are like drawing money out of a bank. If you choose wisely and build a lifestyle that connects with what fires you up inside, your leisure time is well spent and pays dividends, creating a feeling of richness to your life. If you focus on things that 'should' make you happy but never really fully engage with them, true wealth doesn't get a chance to grow. You feel empty and cheated. Think hard about your leisure pursuits and the money and time you spend on them. Perhaps you shell out your hard-earned cash on a gym membership that you never use. A weekly run in the park with your best friend would do the job of getting you fit just as well, while feeding the inspiration and energy you get from your friend's company.

Counting the true cost of your lifestyle

Like all tangible resources, money is not usually unlimited. If you fall into the trap of believing that the more money you spend on immediate gratification the happier you'll be, you end up being disappointed. And you deplete the financial resource that could be directed to areas to enhance your happiness, such as saving for your dream holiday home. You can probably remember the thrill of your first really big-ticket purchase – a car, a down payment on a house, a holiday abroad – but the truth is, you get used to things. That thrill may have been a little less intense with the second car, the third house move or the fourth exotic holiday. You may feel that you need to spend even more money to recapture that thrill. On the other hand, you may find that you continue to get a real buzz from trading up possessions, and that's fine too – don't be guilty because you love the material things in life and get real pleasure from acquiring the money to buy them.

Consider what you lose out on, or jeopardise, by choosing the lifestyle that you have. You may have convinced yourself that you aren't at all materialistic when secretly you'd love a fancy sports car but don't think you deserve one and couldn't possibly afford it. If so, perhaps you need to face up to the fact that money and what it can buy *is* pretty important to you and start to put strategies in place to attract more money into your life. Or you may swan around in the latest swanky car looking enviously at the couple strolling hand in hand to the bus stop to go shopping. Maybe in this situation you realise that material possessions don't make up for the lack of a loving relationship in your life, and you may decide to direct some of the energies you currently place in creating money wealth into securing relationship wealth.

Peace of mind concerning money issues often comes down to knowing where to direct your resources and when to recognise that retail therapy is often just a sticking plaster.

When you consider the things that are important to you, coaching reminds you to look beneath the tangible possessions that you have, such as money, to what that possession gives to you. If you love money, you no doubt love the security it offers you, or the joy you get from owning beautiful objects. Few people actually love money for itself – unless they have a passion for coin collecting.

Coach yourself to financial awareness by working through the following coaching questions (refer to Part II for an explanation of each approach):

- ✔ **Powerful opening question:** What is the true cost of my lifestyle?

- ✔ **Personal style:** How much money do I need to live my life according to the way that suits my natural preferences and my needs? How can I test how much money I need?

- ✔ **Beliefs:** What limiting beliefs do I have about money?

- ✔ **Motivation:** What does money buy me? What does the pursuit of money give me that I don't want?

- ✔ **What's working:** What's good about my attitude to money? What do I want to change?

- ✔ **Exploring options:** What ways of being around money help me to achieve my whole-life goals?

- ✔ **Taking action:** What's my first step towards using money to achieve my whole-life goals? How much time can I allocate to planning my approach? How do I know when I am making progress? What can I do to celebrate?

Permitting yourself to be rich

What assumptions about money do you hold? You may hold beliefs that stop you from generating the wealth you deserve. Do you think being poor is virtuous? How you manifest that virtue is what really matters and you can find some pretty mean-spirited poor people out there as well as some wildly generous and philanthropic multimillionaires. Do you think you don't deserve to be wealthier than you are? What cash price do you put on yourself that limits you? Or do you think you don't have the talent, the commercial acumen, the persistence or the drive to go out there and seek a glittering prize? Where is the evidence for your belief and what contrary evidence do you have? Where do your beliefs about money come from?

Ask yourself these questions:

- ✔ Can I allow myself to be rich? (Consider your beliefs.)

- ✔ Can I be rich and remain wealthy in all other areas of my life? (Consider your whole-life implications.)

- ✔ Can I be rich and keep my integrity? (Consider your overall contribution to your world.)

SPRINGBOARD

If I was a rich man . . .

If being rich fits with your other core values, then you need to set a money-making strategy. No single best way exists to build a personal or business fortune and anyone who tries to convince you of that wants to sell you something. Only *you* can find a unique mix to work its magic for you.

First you have to decide the context of making money – your job, a business venture, stock investments, property – the list is endless. To focus your research, choose three potential money-making methods that currently sit well with you. Imagine you're going to write the definitive book on each of the three subjects. Read, search the Internet, talk to role models and mentors, sign up for newsletters and join relevant associations. But the key is not to take a committed step until you reach the point where you know plenty about all three approaches. Money isn't something to squander, so take all the time you need and make the best decision. You may well end up with a portfolio of options that more than compensate in wealth potential for the time you took to do your research.

You may also be interested in reading *Investing For Dummies* by Tony Levene, and *Retiring Wealthy For Dummies* by Julian Knight (both Wiley).

If the answer to all three questions is yes, you've given yourself permission to take the steps you need to take to pursue riches *if* that's what you really want. In the case of riches, the old adage to be careful what you wish for lest it comes true contains much wisdom. Acquiring riches isn't actually the hardest part of the process; deciding why you want money, what you're going to do with it and then unblocking the thought processes that are holding you back from attracting it into your life constitute the real ground work. After you're clear on what you want and why, you're then ready to do the hard work and make the sacrifices that are required to make money.

Cultivating a Feeling of Wealth and Abundance

Feeling wealthy in your life because you have developed a range of resources (cash and otherwise) is a great goal to aim for and like all big goals, you need to keep focused on it. When you begin to feel wealthy (as opposed to simply well off) in your whole life, you can think about the next level – tapping into the abundance that you can create for yourself and your world.

Dancing through life with abundance

Making your life abundant is a great life coaching aim. Here are the steps of abun-*dance* for you to experiment with as and when the time is right for you:

✔ **Choose your partners for the dance.** You can generate a feeling of abundance with your life partner, friends, family or even strangers, such as those benefiting from a charity you donate to.

✔ **Dance on an uncluttered floor.** Give away what you don't need to people who may

need it more. Focus on, and appreciate, what remains, whether that is money or time.

✔ **Get caught up in the energy.** Abundance creates its own energetic momentum. Give your time and money frequently and without pressure. Over a period of time your reputation grows as someone who can be trusted, who is talented and who is generous. The more you do this, the more people give back in return, because they've seen and felt the value of what you give.

Here are some of the things you probably need to feel wealthy in the broadest sense of the word. How true are these statements for you right now?

✔ You have enough money to meet your bills and lifestyle choices. (This starts with sorting your everyday budget.)

✔ You feel secure in your future financial security and provision. (This comes from regular and consistent saving.)

✔ You are *time-rich* – that is, you use the resource of time wisely and proactively. (Chapter 20 has tips on how to balance your daily demands.)

✔ The investment you pay into looking after your health pays you dividends in vitality (hop to Chapter 14 for more).

✔ You give and receive friendship, companionship and love within your circle of people. (Chapter 13 explores the significant relationships you build in your life.)

Depending upon your own core values, the relative importance of these areas is unique to you. The priorities you place on the things that make you feel wealthy change over time. You may place higher importance on relationships and health as the real sources of your wealth as you get older.

Abundance means not only that you have all these things in the proportion that is right for you, but also that you have a feeling of plenty in your life. You have enough, in fact more than enough, and have a sense of wanting to share out the money, time and love. When you arrive at this point, it's pleasantly ironic that your philosophy of abundance very often means that you begin to get even more back than you give.

Giving It All Away

Expert marketer and multimillionaire Dan Kennedy said: 'Everybody starts out each day with 24 hours to invest as wisely as possible, for profit, for joy, for the benefit of others.' You can choose to give away your time and/or money, working towards a belief that the more you give out, the more you shore up for yourself.

Giving away your time or money relates to a combination of two seemingly contradictory statements – 'speculate to accumulate' and 'the giver gains'. These two expressions come from very different places. The statement 'speculate to accumulate' is linked with hard-nosed commerciality, saying that money begets money. For your investments to grow, you have to let go of money you already have and hope that doing so pays huge dividends. Yet you accept that you may lose your money for good if the stock market fails, the business crashes or the value of your property plummets.

The statement 'the giver gains' says the same thing in a more altruistic way. Giving away your resources of time, talents and/or money simply out of a spirit of generosity and goodwill to humankind can often result in huge dividends in the form of personal satisfaction and fulfilling your sense of purpose. Yet you must accept that people may take advantage of you and leave you feeling depleted and bruised. Like playing the stock market, if your motivation for giving is to receive equal value back, you may be disappointed – and those you give to may feel uncomfortable and that they don't know how to repay you. But if you reduce your reliance on the return, generosity and goodwill more easily flow back your way, directly or indirectly.

You can cultivate abundance in many ways, big and small, for example:

- ✔ Donating to a favourite charity.
- ✔ Doing sponsored walks and runs.
- ✔ Helping out at school fundraisers.
- ✔ Giving your time to a friend in need.
- ✔ Being a good neighbour.

Don't devalue yourself or your time. False modesty doesn't have a role in an abundant lifestyle and isn't helpful. If you're self-employed, you must set a fair price for your labour and be confident that you're giving value to receive it. Abundance means that you can be generous when you've met your essential financial needs. So you're then in a position to do *pro-bono work* (where you don't seek to make a profit) if you want, or you can gift your time to a good cause.

You can only cultivate abundance if you already have a strong sense of your wealth. Financial experts suggest that you only invest excess money that you're prepared to lose, not cash that you need for your own security and comfort. You can only give out your precious resources of time and talent when you have first given them to yourself and those dearest to you and have amassed a surplus of energy that you actively want to pass on for the good of others. Being abundant without taking care of the basics for you won't always make you happy, and may even make you feel resentful.

Financial advice from the heart

Jack's career as a financial adviser had been a bit of a roller-coaster. During coaching, he wanted to let go of a drive to competition that no longer sat well with his values of caring and concern for his customers. However, he also didn't want to lose opportunities to generate income.

'I remember the bad old days where we were trained and targeted to sell products and close the deal on the spot. I was quite young then and saw it as a game, I didn't think too much about the ethics of it all. Things are different now and the industry is so well regulated that lots of protections are set up for people. But still, the reason for being in business is to make money and that potential conflict troubles me at times.'

Jack's coach asked him what he wanted for himself out of his business:

'Well, I do want to meet certain targets, but it's also really important that I feel in myself that I give the right advice. I want to really get under the skin of a client's wealth needs as if I was advising my best friend or my son. Sometimes it becomes obvious quite early on that buying

a product isn't the right route for a client, but I can see bigger issues that they can address with their basic approach to money and I want to help them. I don't get commission for this and it can be time consuming, but I feel I'm cheating them otherwise. My business partner says I'm being commercially naive.'

His coach then asked him to consider how he could develop the business so that it was in complete alignment with what he wanted for himself and the world. This took place over a few coaching sessions and the end result was that Jack put in place a new fee structure in his business. He offered a low-cost fixed-fee session for clients who needed consultancy on their basic approach to money. The fee went some way to covering the cost of his time and had bigger benefits because he generated more referrals for more lucrative business as a result. His partner fully supported him and their different approaches became far more complementary, so the reputation of the practice grew. Both Jack's riches and his sense of wealth and abundance in his life and work increased significantly.

Chapter 13

People and Relationships

In This Chapter

▶ Establishing your relationship priorities

▶ Getting mutual support through friendship

▶ Networking to expand your circle of influence

*W*hen I worked in recruitment and the going got especially tough, we'd joke, 'If only we didn't have clients or candidates . . . or colleagues – this job would be perfect!' You can probably relate to this sentiment when you've had a particularly bad day and everyone seems out to get you, reject you or complicate your life. Really bad days are when the most meaningful relationship you want to have is with your DVD player so that you can escape from everyone!

Hopefully, most of the time you don't really want to escape from everyone. After all, many of your most precious and enjoyable moments stem from being with people you love, who stimulate you and you have fun with. Getting the balance right between give and take in relationships is tricky and is one of the biggest causes of discontent in life when the balance is askew.

Relationships fall into three main categories – your family and your partner if you have one, your friends and the wider networks around you at work and in your community. This chapter helps you assess what you want from your relationships with others and encourages you to define the roles you want love, friendship and community to play in your life.

Enjoying Loving Relationships

The psychoanalyst Sigmund Freud singled out work and love as the two most significant aspects of human experience that are most important to get right if you want to be happy. While the pursuit of meaningful work occupies a high proportion of your attention and time, your relationships with the people around you provide the main context for living well. And if work occasionally causes you angst, I'd bet that love – defining and finding it, sharing and nurturing it – has already presented you with even more bittersweet challenges.

Creating a relationship with yourself

When it comes to relationships, the only constant you have is the relationship that you build with yourself. Family members and friends may not always be there for you; you may never find 'the one', or you may be together for a while and then separate. Your children grow up and your relationship with them may change. Your wider networks may not always support you. You can deal with all this and you can accept that everything changes over time – as long as the certainty of your self-esteem remains.

If your self-esteem is strong, you're comfortable in your own skin and you don't feel the need to fill your time alone with distractions that may not enhance the overall quality of your life. If you don't manage to develop self-esteem, no matter how hard you try to please the important people in your life – and sometimes because of your efforts – you often find that real connection with them remains just out of your grasp.

Nathaniel Branden, an expert on self-esteem, describes self-esteem as 'the experience that we are appropriate to life and to the requirements of life'. This means that you feel secure about your place in the world and the challenges you face, even when they're tough. Self-esteem may equate to self-confidence certainly, yet self-confidence in itself is a fickle thing and is often tied in some way to external factors such as the approval of a partner or good feedback from a boss. But if you have high self-esteem, you can still march bravely into the unknown while quaking in your boots. Building reserves of quiet self-esteem is far more beneficial for you than any quick-fix boost of confidence. Real self-esteem comes from a mixture of healthy respect for yourself and a mature understanding of your role in the world. I've summed up Branden's six pillars of self-esteem:

- ✓ **Living consciously:** Being aware of the power of your thoughts and how your behaviour affects yourself and others.

- ✓ **Self-acceptance:** Knowing that you are bound to experience lapses and setbacks along with your successes and leaps forward.

- ✓ **Self-responsibility:** Accepting accountability for all that you do, even when that realisation is painful.

- ✓ **Self-assertiveness:** Knowing your needs and being able to express them clearly, directly and calmly to others.

- ✓ **Living purposefully:** Feeling that what you do (not just at work) is worthwhile and has meaning for you.

- ✓ **Personal integrity:** Knowing your values and always aiming to live up to them.

You can see that self-esteem can grow naturally from the self-awareness and growth you generally experience through coaching. When you focus on coaching yourself in self-esteem, you also enhance your success in many other areas of your life too.

Set aside some quiet time for this activity and write your answers in your journal so that you can keep an eye on your progress. Coach yourself to self-esteem by asking yourself these questions (based on the sections in Part II):

- ✔ **Powerful question:** What kind of relationship do I want to have with myself?

- ✔ **Personal style:** What factors naturally build my self-esteem? What factors drain it?

- ✔ **Beliefs:** What beliefs about myself stop me from appreciating myself?

- ✔ **Motivation:** How do I affect my self-esteem when I act according to my most important values? What is the reverse of that for me?

- ✔ **What's working:** What's good about my current level of self-esteem? What do I want to change?

- ✔ **Exploring options:** What actions and choices help me to build strong self-esteem? Which of these appeal most and fit with my natural preferences?

- ✔ **Taking action:** What's my first step? How do I know when I am making progress? What can I do to celebrate?

You can find more on building self-esteem and confidence in Chapter 19.

Finding your soul mate

If you're meeting your own needs and building your own self-esteem as a single person, finding a soul mate becomes a much less anxious pursuit. You're already presenting your best self to the world, which is naturally attractive and gives you the best chance of finding someone who is attracted to the real you. When you have high self-esteem you can make relationship choices that feel healthy and mature. You don't fall prey to flattery or insincerity that feeds your vanity, and you can enjoy each other's company without wondering if this is 'the one' relationship to bring you happiness – because you're already happy.

Are you holding on to an ideal of romantic love that may not be realistic? Do you feel that you're looking in vain for Mr or Ms Right? If this search is a source of unhappiness for you, think honestly about what a relationship can give you that you don't already have or can't get elsewhere.

If you find yourself alone after a separation or bereavement, you may feel uncertain about how to fill what feels like a big hole in your life. Certainly, people need people but not always in the way they think. The more clarity you have about why you want to meet someone, and the consequences of the choices you make, the better placed you are to forge the right kind of relationship with the right person for you. So quickly getting back into the dating game may be just the boost to your confidence that you need. But you also need to take account of the fact that you may not be ready to start a serious relationship for a while and may benefit from some alone time to sort out exactly what you want from your changed lifestyle.

Here are some suggestions to consider if one of your whole-life goals is to meet someone you can share your life with:

- **Check out your beliefs carefully.** Are you holding on to a romantic dream that only one person is out there for you and that you'll know instantly when you meet your soul mate? What pressure is that belief putting on you and the friendships you're building right now? Would changing that belief help you to see clearly your potential soul mate who lives right next door, or works in the next office?

- **Consider where you're looking for your soul mate.** For example, Internet dating works wonderfully for some people and for others it's an unmitigated disaster. Notice the patterns that occur for you and if you always seem to get the same kind of poor results, consider that you may be fishing in the wrong pool. Try different waters for a change.

- **Your soul mate is going to share some of your most important passions, so make it easy for them to recognise the passion in you.** If you love reading, you can join a book club. Maybe you won't meet a romantic partner there, but you may discover some great friends. And who knows who they may introduce you to?

- **Don't think that all your attached friends are gloriously happy while you are still single.** Every life choice has ups and downs, and your coupled friends may envy the freedom and fun of your single life. Remember that a true zest for life is one of the most attractive qualities around, whether you are looking for love or friendship.

Building and maintaining a strong partnership

Have you seen the episode of the sitcom *Friends* where Chandler and Janice break up? Chandler spends his time moping around listening to sad romantic songs, bemoaning the loss of their 'movie love'. Even though you can laugh at this, when it comes to your own view of how love and romance should be, you may find that you cherish similar tendencies. Being in love can make you giddy, wanting to edit out the realities of life and cut to the scene where hero and heroine kiss and ride off into the sunset together.

What happens beyond the sunset? Do the hero and heroine enjoy a fairytale marriage and produce perfect children who are sweet, funny and bright? Even if you're fortunate that your romantic life has broadly followed this kind of script, I'm sure that a lot of mess, confusion, worry and angst have simply refused to end up on the cutting-room floor along the way.

Biology may be partly to blame for the path of true love rarely being smooth. Human beings can be biologically attracted to people with opposite qualities and style to themselves, as nature attempts to mate two halves of a whole for the greater protection of future offspring. In the first flush of romantic love this dynamic is exciting and enjoyable, but over time these differences can be the very things that cause tension and disharmony. Coach yourself to a greater understanding and awareness of different styles. Check out Chapter 4 for more detail on how to assess your own and others' personal preferred styles.

If you're in a settled relationship, do you wonder how you're going to sustain your commitment to each other amid all the strains, stresses and temptations of modern life? The following activity can help you to identify areas of strength and room for improvement in your relationship.

Coach yourself in a committed relationship by asking yourself these challenging questions (refer to Part II for more detailed explanations of each of these approaches):

- ✓ **Powerful opening question:** How do I play my part in maintaining mutual love and respect in our relationship?

- ✓ **Personal style:** What behaviours do we have in common? What behaviours in myself and in my partner cause friction or tension?

- ✓ **Beliefs:** What beliefs about myself and how my relationship should be cause me to hold back, to blame or to behave selfishly?

- ✓ **Motivation:** What goals and values do we have in common?

- ✓ **What's working:** What are the great things about our relationship? What can be better? What isn't working very well? What must change?

- ✓ **Exploring options:** What ways can I begin to make changes? What options are most natural for both of us?

- ✓ **Taking action:** What's our first step? How do we know when we're making progress? What can we do to celebrate?

Mixing it up

The traditional path of love and marriage has broadened to include many tangents, detours and alternative routes. People now often marry later in life or may not marry at all, and many choose a same-sex partner or decide to remain childless. In the film *About a Boy*, the young son of a single mother starts out by trying to match-make his mum with an eligible bachelor because he feels that a family unit of three is stronger than one of two. His plan fails – mum and Mr Right are not remotely attracted to each other. However, by the end of the film, as a result of the boy's efforts to reach out to people around him, his new extended family is a delightfully untraditional mix of strong interdependent connections that offer him even more security and happiness than the old model may have done. The film has a Hollywood happy ending, but is rather more reflective of the complex social interactions you may see around you, or may already be a part of. As far as intimate relationships go, we live in a time of unprecedented uncertainty and few of the old rules now apply. This reality can be as bewildering as it is often exhilarating.

Deciding to leave a relationship

One of the hardest decisions to make is to leave a relationship, especially when children are involved. No matter how compelling the reasons are for a break-up, you're going to feel pain as you move away from the situation. You need to ensure that protection and support is available throughout the process for all concerned.

Chapter 21 can help you identify ways to make this tough decision and work out strategies based on finding solutions rather than focusing on problems. It also guides you through the sense of loss that you may experience as a significant relationship comes to an end.

Rebuilding or ending a very troubled relationship may require more than a coaching approach. The counselling service Relate began as an organisation to help couples through problems in their marriage and has evolved to offer a wide range of relationship counselling and therapies. Check out its website at www.relate.org.uk for resources and advice.

Nurturing Family Bonds

Close family members are likely to be the people who draw out the best and the worst in you. Siblings may drive you mad at times and parent-child relations can get fraught, but in times of crisis the bonds forged with your nearest and dearest often prove to be the strongest.

Sometimes the extremes of emotion generated within families can be hard to handle, however. You may feel you're making great progress with coaching yourself to an enlightened state of inner calm and goodwill to all humankind – and then your teenager walks muddy football boots all over the new cream lounge carpet for the fifth time in a month. Or you find yourself having one of those conversations with a parent where you feel like bursting into angry tears and flouncing from the room, despite the fact that you left childhood behind more than a couple of decades ago. Family members push your buttons more than anyone else and controlling your emotions is not always easy.

To deal successfully with any family upsets, take the time to stand back and look at how the relationship between you and members of your family has changed. You can easily fall into old patterns of unhelpful behaviour. Coaching can help you update your relationships with your family members so that you see each other for the evolving human beings you really are. (And you can still have a good flounce, but maybe in the privacy of your own home on your private stage!)

What role do you take in your family dynamics? What part do you have to play in ensuring that your relationships evolve in a mature and adult way, where all parties accept that change is inevitable? How can you use your energies so that your family becomes a support and inspiration, not a source of tension and play-acting?

You may decide to use your coaching skills to improve communication within your family (see Chapter 22 for more on this). And the information about behaviour preferences in Chapter 4 can help family members understand that differences of opinion and style are inevitable and can be a source of creativity and variety rather than conflict.

Peter lived some distance away from his father but spoke to him regularly on the phone and visited as often as possible. Peter's mother died many years ago when Peter was a teenager and his father remarried a few years later. The second marriage ended three years ago, and Peter's father now lived alone.

Peter and his father had always had a pretty good relationship and shared an interest in golf, but over the last year Peter had noticed that his father was reluctant to join his son in a game when he came to visit and seemed to prefer to stay home and watch daytime television. Peter found himself getting increasingly frustrated by his father's lethargy and tried several times to spur him on to more active pursuits, but to no avail. They quite often ended up arguing about it.

It took Peter a little while to see why he was so determined to force his father away from the television set. During a self-coaching session, he asked himself if he would feel so strongly if this weren't his father and the answer was a definite no. At first Peter thought his feelings were because he cared about his father's well-being, but as he probed deeper he realised that a part of him felt embarrassed that his lively, energetic father, who he had always looked up to, seemed to have given up enjoying his life. This realisation helped Peter to see the situation from a different perspective, and he decided to broach the subject with his father in a more neutral way. After all, if television was what really gave his dad pleasure, then who was Peter to judge? After Peter stepped back from his former hectoring stance, his father felt able to open up and admit that he had lost some confidence since his divorce. He now found it easier to stay home than face social situations, even at the local golf club where he was a well-respected and popular member.

Several months passed before Peter's father decided that he was ready to dust off the golf clubs, but their new understanding allowed Peter to provide the right kind of support for his father as he regained some of his natural self-confidence.

Setting family ground rules

If you run a business or work in a team, you're used to agreeing and setting boundaries that contribute to harmony. So why not do the same within your family unit?

Consider the following as starting points for your own family manifesto:

- **Banish blame.** Beating yourself up or accusing others of ruining your day is rarely the best or most enjoyable option. Notice what's really going on when tensions run high and be attentive to the emotions behind actions.

- **Watch your language.** Statements such as 'You make me feel so angry' may come from the heart, but they're not even very accurate. *You* choose your emotion and *you* control how you can change it, sometimes in a heartbeat. Acknowledge your primary role in generating your own emotions and let your language reflect this by not blaming others.

- **Devise get-out strategies for when things get out of hand.** Disagreements and conflicts can escalate simply because no one knows how to bring them to an end. Have a strategy in place that you can pull out of the hat when what started out as a friendly disagreement threatens to turn into tears before bedtime. This strategy could be setting time limits on heated discussions and agreeing to cool-off periods.

Giving and Receiving Friendship

I remember listening to an interview on the radio with a famous woman who'd been married several times, and who now, in her mid-fifties, had finally realised the real importance of her friendships. 'Do you know,' she said, 'I spent so much time wringing my hands over the men in my life and yet I now look back and over the years the people who gave me the most happiness, and who I had the most fun with, were my friends. I'm more content now than I ever was when I was chasing after that one single relationship that I felt would somehow define and satisfy me.'

Friends can come and go – you have probably lost contact with some, fallen out with others and are busy forging friendship bonds with new people. Whatever your approach to your friendships, they constitute a key part of the satisfaction you get from life. But finding ways to keep friendships alive and thriving can often be a real challenge in a hectic lifestyle.

Maintaining lifelong friendships

You may choose your friends because they share the same attitudes to life as you do. You're often attracted to people with very similar qualities to you. Bear in mind that your similarities mean that your friends have some of the same challenges as you. If you both tend to race through your days and never have enough time for the important, but not necessarily urgent, things in your life, then you can find that you've drifted miles apart before you know it. People sustain friendships when both parties get what they need and want out of the relationship. Sometimes knowing that people are there for you when you need them is enough. However, at other times your inner coach may tell you that you can usefully give a little more quality time to your faithful best friend.

Communicating through the levels

What do you get from your friendships? What you share when you talk to your friends often determines the quality of that friendship. The three main levels of friendly communication are:

- ✔ **Level 1:** You talk about the weather, celebrity gossip, your last holiday or a car you're thinking of buying. You may really get on with this person, but you haven't yet established a strong mutual trust.

- ✔ **Level 2:** You express your feelings and emotions, concerns and fears. Perhaps you're worried about job security, or have a mutual interest in a hobby. You find this person supportive and have developed good rapport with them.

- ✔ **Level 3:** You share the things that are most important to you – your values and beliefs, hopes for the future and your sense of purpose. You have developed strong mutual trust and may well be very much on the same wavelength with the things that are most important to your friend.

You may always have friends who stay at Level 1 throughout your life. And you may very quickly move to Level 3 with a new friend. Consider what levels your current friendships operate at. Are there any mismatches in the levels? Do you have a friend who communicates with you at Level 3 while you are holding back on Level 1, or vice versa? What impact does that have on the friendship for you both?

Staying in touch

Think about how you maintain your friendships. Some people have probably fallen by the wayside as you've gradually lost touch or moved out of the area, or you may have let someone go because of a heated argument or disagreement that proved painful at the time. Not all friendships are lifelong, of course, but sometimes the ones that deserve to be can fall foul of the accidental circumstances of life or the challenges of geography. Think about the friends you now spend time with and check that those relationships are healthy and nurturing rather than draining your energy.

Watch out when you hear yourself say 'We must meet up sometime soon!' Aim to fix a time and a place so that you don't both drift along and suddenly find another year has gone by without seeing each other.

Answer this powerful question: If you were throwing a party next week to celebrate all the people who had positively contributed to your life, who would be on the guest list?

Perhaps the time has come for you to reposition friendships in your life. What are the focus areas for you? Is it to nurture and develop the friends that sustain you, to step back a little from the people who may drain your energy or to consider how you can build bridges with those who have faded out of the picture?

For this coaching activity, write letters to four people from your present and your past:

- ✔ A friendship that ended badly – perhaps a trust was betrayed or feelings were hurt.

- ✔ Someone whom you have simply lost touch with.

- ✔ A good friend whom you know you often take for granted.

- ✔ Someone whom you now spend time with, but who tends to feed your negative thoughts.

Don't send these letters! Instead, use them to answer the following questions for yourself:

✔ What do I/did I get from this friendship?

✔ What can be different?

✔ How can I be with this person now?

Maybe you decide that you want to communicate some of the things you write in your letters. What is your inner coach telling you is the best first step?

Staying open to new friendships

Some people prefer to have a few close, lifelong friends, while others thrive on having a wide circle of people around them. Either way, making new friends can become less of a habit over the years, especially because your life is likely to be full enough already and you have to work pretty hard at maintaining the good friendships you already have. Or maybe you sometimes struggle to make new friends because you feel shy or self-conscious when meeting people for the first time. You may even think that encouraging new friendships reduces the time you have for other important people in your life. And you probably don't want to be the kind of person who adopts a new best friend at the drop of a hat. But remember these advantages to staying open to the arrival of new friends:

✔ All relationships settle and stabilise over time, and new people coming into your circle can re-energise the whole system.

✔ You are changing as you coach yourself to greater satisfaction, balance and fulfilment, so you may naturally widen the scope of the kind of person who attracts you as a potential friend and support.

✔ As you become more self-confident, you may find that you welcome the challenges and stimulation of people who are dramatically different from you.

✔ If you suffer from shyness, remember that people rarely pick up on how you're feeling inside and instead they simply enjoy the fact that you're listening to them. So don't put pressure on yourself to be fascinating and interesting – you already are those things, you simply express it in different ways.

How do you integrate new friendships into your circle? Do you keep certain groups of people separate because they're different? Consider mixing the groups up and watch the fun! You may see different things in old friends as they start to appreciate a new side to you too.

Building Productive Networks

Your wider networks are unique to you, and taking the time to build productive relationships with people outside your immediate circle of close friends and family can really pay off. Casual acquaintances, neighbours and work colleagues can turn into good friends – even if they don't, a little investment in the people around you helps to oil the wheels of your daily life.

Widening your circle of influence

The more people you have access to in a positive, mutually beneficial relationship, the more support you have when you need it. Not everything you want to accomplish in your life is within your power to complete alone, no matter how self-sufficient you are. If information is power, other people often hold the information you need.

Your *circle of influence* contains all the people you have contact with in your life, from those who are closest to you, to your casual acquaintances. You touch or influence the lives of all these people in some way, and they do the same for you. Consider for a moment the areas where your circle of influence is already extensive. Perhaps you already make the effort at work to get to know people in other departments or divisions, or you're particularly good at building relationships with customers and suppliers. Do you maintain personal contact with some of these people when you move on from that job or do you invest all your energies in a new circle of people? You have a limited store of time and energy, so it may be impossible and unrealistic to stay in touch with everyone, but you may be able to keep in contact with a few key people who you've established rapport and respect with. How can you continue to benefit from their influence and support over the years?

What about your neighbours? Communication breakdown with neighbours can lead to painful disagreements and strained relationships that become difficult to repair. How satisfied are you with the quality of your connections with your neighbours? What opportunities do you have to play a bigger role in your community, perhaps at a local school, a neighbourhood watch group or a social club?

This activity homes in on what your circle of influence looks like. Grab a large sheet of paper – maybe flip-chart size – and map out your circle of influence (see Figure 13-1). Put specific names on it. Stand back and look at your world of people. What areas need focus? How can you widen your circle of influence if you want to?

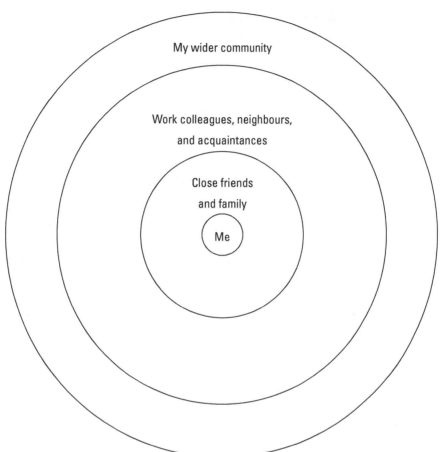

Figure 13-1:
Your Circle
of Influence.

Getting into the networking groove

Networking – the process of meeting new people and adding them to your circle for mutual benefit – isn't just for finding business opportunities. You can apply networking skills to any new social situation – a party, a fundraising event or chatting to other parents during the school run. Try out these tips for successful networking:

> ✔ **Be interested rather than interesting.** Use your coaching skills to ask open questions and really listen to the answers. Don't be tempted to cut in with a 'me too' story too quickly. People find you fascinating if you show that they fascinate you.

✔ **Look for ways you can help one another.** This might be in very small areas – perhaps passing on a useful article on an area of mutual interest – but it can be something pretty significant, such as a skill, resource or business introduction.

✔ **Play the host.** If you're among a group of strangers and want to break the ice, try to find ways of carrying out simple tasks that make people warm to you. Maybe you can offer to get them a coffee or fill up their glass.

Taking a role in your world

As you improve your relationships with the people around you, you start to notice some common themes that shed light on your unique qualities. Ask yourself what qualities people tend to get from you. Do they see you as someone who always knows the best restaurants, or can they rely on you for a good laugh when someone needs cheering up? The small gifts that you give out to the people around you can be more precious than you realise. You can develop a quality that you take for granted into something that helps you to define part of your role in your world. Sometimes this may even lead to a business opportunity – you bake a mean pie and find that people are prepared to pay you for it – but equally it can result in simple, effortless ways of using your natural gifts for your own enjoyment and the delight of those around you.

Chapter 14

Physical, Mental and Emotional Well-being

....

In This Chapter

▶ Choosing your best health

▶ Getting physical

▶ Ensuring optimal mental health

....

*B*eing in great health is about much more than physical fitness or freedom from disease. To feel on top form, you also want to be in good
mental health – managing the stress and pressures of everyday life. Well-
being results from taking note of your emotional health and keeping a check
on your emotions instead of letting them overwhelm or incapacitate you.
Health matters include both taking care of your physical body and building
your mental and emotional resilience. In this chapter you discover that the
small steps you take to integrate a holistic approach to your health can make
the most difference in how you look and feel on a regular basis.

Health and well-being is a critical area for coaching, because really big
changes in other areas of your life are often more possible when you have
good health as a foundation.

If spirituality is a part of your personal sense of well-being, read Chapter 15.

Choosing Your Health Goals

How have your feelings about your health changed over the years? Much
depends on how healthy you used to be and how healthy you are now. If you
were a strong, healthy child, you may feel that you'll always be strong and
healthy. But if you experienced a life-threatening or debilitating illness as a
child, you may not take good health for granted. When you consider family
members, the fact that your loved ones live long and remain disease-free
may comfort you. Or you may be very conscious of the sad losses you've

experienced due to heart disease, cancer or other fatal illnesses. Your previous experiences affect your current attitude to your health, and you need to take account of this in defining your health goals and focusing your motivation.

Defining your health goals

In choosing your health and well-being goals, you can ponder the following:

- ✔ **What's really important to me right now about my health?** Which areas of health have taken priority for me up to now? For example, your energy levels may be the priority right now. You may be looking for a way of being that promotes this rather than a short-term focus on losing weight fast for a forthcoming holiday.

- ✔ **What has to happen for me to feel healthy?** How has my definition of good health changed over the years? Good health at one time in your life may have meant having the stamina to burn the candle at both ends. Now, good health may mean giving your body rest and taking care of your mental and emotional well-being through gentle exercise and meditation.

- ✔ **How much time do I want to allocate to my health and well-being?** Reaching and maintaining fitness takes time and effort. Consider whether you want to devote a regular daily time slot to your health goals or if a weekly commitment is better. Planning your goal and preparing the ground also takes a little time, so consider how you want to schedule that.

- ✔ **What old beliefs may be getting in the way of my current health goals?** Perhaps you think that because everyone in your family smokes, giving up is impossible for you. Challenge this belief and seek new ways to build better ones (refer to Chapter 5).

- ✔ **What may I be in denial over in relation to my health?** Perhaps you always dress well to hide the excess pounds you carry and avoid having your photo taken so you don't have to face the reality.

- ✔ **How do I want to feel when I think about my health?** You can translate this desire into a positive affirmation such as 'I feel strong, energetic and full of vitality every day.'

- ✔ **What do I want for my future health and well-being?** Perhaps you want to be able to take your children swimming and play football with them, or simply want to be disease-free and able to enjoy life.

Digging deeper into your motivation

If your motivation is right, you can achieve even really challenging health goals. The time has come to consider exactly why you want to be healthy.

A wake-up call to lose weight

Maria was in her mid-40s when she decided to try coaching to address her health challenges. She had always struggled with weight issues and had never felt slim enough, even as a teenager, especially compared to her popular best friend who always seemed to get the dates. Now, Maria's life was very different. For 15 years she'd been in a long-term relationship, which had recently come to an amicable end. She loved to cook and entertain with family and friends and also had a good job as a marketing consultant – she often stayed away and ate out in restaurants. Over the years Maria had gained a great deal of weight, and with a family history of heart disease, her doctor advised her that her health would soon begin to suffer.

Over the next few months Maria experimented with new diet and exercise programmes that promised the weight loss she wanted, but with disappointing results because she continued to hang on to her old, indulgent eating habits.

Maria's coach asked her what future images she was holding as her main motivation for losing the weight.

'Honestly? Well, since my break-up I've been a bit of a recluse on the dating front – being my ideal weight may give me the confidence to get back out there. And of course I do want to be generally healthy and fit.'

Maria's specific focus on the dating goal was telling. Her coach asked her if being overweight was the only factor stopping her from dating. Maria thought for a long moment and then shook her head.

'Maybe not . . . I suppose I've been enjoying my own company and spending time with friends. But if I were slim then I'd be good to go when I do feel like dating again!' Maria laughed at what she had just said. She realised that she was relying on an outdated motivator (wanting to attract dates) to propel her forward. Maria's real wake-up call was the warning from her doctor about the impact on her health. Her beliefs about herself and the values she held at the age of 43 had evolved – eating well and enjoying the company of friends were important to her as was buoying up the vitality, energy and strength she needed to enjoy her lifestyle to the full.

To balance the two beliefs, Maria and a like-minded friend took turns planning healthy weekend dinner parties and signed up for a sponsored walk for a heart charity. A year later Maria had achieved her goal of losing weight while not cutting back on her fun lifestyle and had also become actively involved with the heart charity, which helped her keep a strong focus on maintaining her health. Although she still hadn't quite found time for dating, she did have one or two ideas for writing a book on healthy eating, gourmet style . . .

Think first about your core values (see Chapter 6 for more on this). Chances are that tying your health goal to your other values will help you to get motivation behind what you're aiming for. How does being healthy support you to live your best life? If your family is a core value for you, how does being unhealthy work against that? Are you in the best position to support your family and enjoy your lifestyle without good health?

Consider how much of your motivation is moving away from pain and how much is moving towards pleasure. For example, smoking may now cause you more pain than pleasure – perhaps it aggravates your tendency to asthma, so on top of knowing the long-term consequences, you now have immediate distress as a result of your habit. Focusing on the benefits of a new, healthier you is the most effective motivation strategy, but you can reach that point quicker if you really open your eyes to the negative consequences of any poor health choices.

Separate out the external factors that may be pushing you to be healthy and make sure that they aren't forming the foundation of your motivation. Do you think that you should be a certain body size? Are you giving up smoking purely out of a sense of guilt? Change has to come from within you, and while other people's opinions can be a positive catalyst for action, those opinions won't see you through the challenges ahead. You achieve your health goals more effectively if you feel good about yourself and your choices, so propel yourself into action, instead of being propelled by others.

Looking After Your Body

As far as your physical body goes, most people tend to underrate the positive attributes they already have and focus on the body bits that displease them. Unless you decide that radical cosmetic surgery is part of your strategy (and I say 'radical' for a reason), you simply can't change parts of your body. The body you were born with is sufficiently miraculous in its form and function without too much user interference. Your body deserves respect and loving care, so a great starting point for *holistic health* (the concept that physical, mental and emotional health are all connected and impact on each other) is getting used to being comfortable in your own skin and changing the way you think and feel about your body for the better. Substitute the negative thoughts about your body that pop into your head for positive ones. Instead of giving yourself a hard time about those love handles, think about your strong arm muscles. What can you already do, have and be as a result of the body you inhabit?

Coaching in health and well-being issues usually works best when you focus on what's already working and figure out how to do more of that or enhance what you already have. Focusing on how big you think your nose is compared to other people's only makes you more conscious of your nose. And plenty of people with tiny button noses wish they had more striking features like you!

Avoiding illness and disease

Suffering the occasional cold in winter or minor attack of hay fever in summer is annoying. But when it comes to debilitating illnesses that you or your loved ones have to cope with, you really begin to appreciate what it means to have good health.

Coaching works best by focusing on positive goals, but in areas of illness and disease you may need to imagine the consequences of becoming ill while you are relatively fit and healthy. By the time the problem is severe enough to cause you to want to make changes, the road to recovery can be an uphill one (literally and figuratively).

Hereditary and environmental factors affecting your health are not within your full control. But whatever your gene pool is like and no matter what kind of air you have to breathe, you can actively coach yourself on improving your diet and the exercise you get. Diet and exercise can make a massive difference to how healthy you are now and will remain throughout your life.

Filling your body with the best fuel

How should you eat for optimum health? The government and media offer such a bewildering array of (often contradictory) advice on food choices that you may opt to ignore it all and enjoy your food the way you want to. Alternatively, you may become a diet junkie and career from one holy grail eating plan to the next.

Weight loss is only one aspect of preventing illness and disease and is an important one if you're a long way beyond a healthy body weight. But think about other considerations. The food choices you make can affect your mood and your energy levels, and can be connected with allergies or have an impact on conditions such as asthma. Food can act as nourishment or poison, depending on what the food is and how you use or abuse it. If you plan your life, why not also take the time to design your approach to the fuel that enables you to live your life to the full? You wouldn't expect your car to run on below-par fuel, and because your body is a lot more valuable than any car, take the same care when making food choices to keep you healthy.

Most nutrition experts agree on avoiding processed foods, drinking lots of water, eating a balanced diet and practising moderation in your diet. Take a look at *Nutrition For Dummies* by Sue Baic, Nigel Denby and Carol Ann Rinzler (Wiley) for lots more practical advice on the options you have for healthy food intake. You need to make the right choice of fuel for your body, within the context of the lifestyle you want. Consider the following:

✔ **What makes you choose to eat certain foods that you know are unhealthy for you?** Do you reach for heaps of chocolate when you're feeling emotionally low? Or is alcohol a way for you to get in the party mood? What else can help fuel a feel-good factor apart from these things?

✔ **What habits do you have that support a healthy attitude to food?** Do you take time to enjoy meals without the distraction of the TV? Do you take time over cooking nice meals?

✔ **Do you use food and drink as a reward?** That's fine, as long as it doesn't go too far for your own good. What other rewards can sustain you in better ways?

✔ **Do you have to get into a mentality of 'going on a diet' in order to lose weight?** How can you change your attitude so that you permanently adapt your eating habits and integrate good choices into your life?

In this activity, coach yourself to healthy food choices by asking yourself the following questions and exploring the answers in a journal (see the chapters in Part II for a detailed explanation of each theme):

✔ **Powerful question:** What kind of relationship do I want to have with food and nutrition?

✔ **Personal style:** What are my lifestyle choices that affect the food I choose? (Do I love to entertain, spend time alone, take things calmly or race around?) How does my environment help or hinder me to choose wisely?

✔ **Beliefs:** What beliefs do I have about food and diet that stop me from attaining and maintaining maximum health? In what ways do I depend on eating habits that don't serve my best interests?

✔ **Motivation:** How can creating my own nutrition strategy allow me to live my life according to my deepest values? How can I be when I am living with respect for my body in this way?

✔ **What's working:** What's good about my current dietary choices? What foods make me feel healthy? What areas of my health does my current diet neglect? What must change for me to move forward?

✔ **Exploring options:** What health choices and lifestyle options can I explore? How can I stay objective? How can I check out the advice and guidance I get? Which of these options appeal most and fit with my natural preferences?

✔ **Taking action:** What's my first step towards healthy eating? How much time can I allocate to planning my approach? How do I know when I am making progress? What can I do to celebrate?

Avoiding sweat and tears: Finding the best exercise for you

Diet alone only goes so far in building your resistance to illness and disease. Your body is designed to be used, and activity through some form of exercise acts as the oil that keeps the machine in good working order. Benefits of regular exercise include increasing your resistance to infection and raising your level of *endorphins* (the naturally occurring chemicals in your body that block pain) so that you feel better.

Building very moderate amounts of exercise into your daily routine protects you from illness just as effectively as a sustained and extensive fitness programme.

What stops you from making a commitment to exercise? You may have genuine reasons for why scheduling and following through can be tricky. But if you're honest with yourself, you no doubt have some excuses that you trot out from time to time. Table 14-1 shows some of the common excuses, together with some suggested coaching questions and affirmations to help you break the cycle.

Table 14-1	Overcoming Your Excuses not to Exercise
Excuse	*Coaching Questions*
I never have time to exercise.	What can I stop doing three times a week for 30 minutes each time to free up my time? (For example, watching TV or staying up too late so you can't set your alarm a little earlier.)
Exercise is boring.	What kind of exercise would be fun for me? (For example, salsa dancing, skipping in the back garden, learning to box.)
Gyms are expensive.	How can I create a home gym on a budget and get my friends along for extra motivation?
I feel guilty spending time on myself.	When I am healthy and fit I offer more of my best self to the people I love and care for.
I feel embarrassed and self-conscious when I exercise.	No one is looking at me, and they certainly can't tell how I'm feeling.

The optimum secret to fitness success lies in building in regular daily exercises that stretch you just a little in speed or intensity, and that last for 15–30 minutes. You don't have to join a gym or invest in expensive exercise equipment. For example, you can walk more often, a little faster and for a little longer to get fitter. Walking is the perfect exercise for general fitness because it puts less strain on the joints than jogging or running, needs no special equipment other than good comfortable shoes and can be combined with other pleasant activities with family and friends, or simply built into your daily routine. A simple and inexpensive pedometer (a gadget to measure how many steps you take) is an optional extra if you like the idea of measuring your progress as you go about your day.

What simple daily activity can you build into your routine? What may be stopping you from making this a habit? What ways can you help yourself to build the habit? When can you make a start?

The following section has some more tips on choosing the right exercise option for you.

Building energy, strength and fitness

If you're already fairly healthy, you may want to coach yourself on taking your fitness to the next level. If this is your health goal, then you need to move up a gear and commit to a sustained programme that allows you to participate in your chosen exercise for 30–60 minutes for five out of seven days to achieve a real change in your fitness level.

Why do you want to be fitter? Is it to have more vitality on a daily basis, to strengthen bones and joints, to become more toned, to look and feel younger, to reduce stress, to be able to join in games with your children, to have a great posture? All these aims and more are within your grasp through a well-chosen fitness strategy. If you want to achieve all these benefits, bear in mind the following:

- Choose a number of different forms of exercise.
- Set yourself realistic long-term goals.
- Accept that you need to spend a high proportion of your time pursuing your health goals, perhaps at the expense of other priorities.
- Choose the form of exercise that works for you and inspires and motivates you to keep going with it.

Exercising with intent

Research shows that the best fitness results come from full, focused attention on whatever exercise routine you've chosen, for the period of time you've chosen to do it. So those people you see at the gym reading a magazine while pedalling or chatting away on the treadmill are probably getting more pleasure out of their visits than actual results. (And that's fine, if that was their main goal – gyms can be a great way to build a social life!) Focusing your attention on exercise is only possible if it has the potential to grab your attention in the first place, so pick a sport or activity that really interests you.

As with diet, the coaching approach is concerned with making the choice that works for you, in the circumstances you currently find yourself. For cardio/aerobic results, you can choose walking, running, sports such as tennis and squash, five-a-side football, belly dancing, swimming and many more. For strength and toning, you can look at disciplines like yoga, Pilates, weight/resistance training or the martial arts. Indeed, many of these also combine the effects of cardio and strength/tone benefits when you practise them at an advanced level.

This activity can help you to choose the exercise options that work best for you. Identify up to six different types of exercise that you think may help you achieve your fitness goal. Research them all a little to check whether they're suitable for your current level. Choose appealing options – if you loathed eye/hand coordination games like tennis and netball at school, you'd be a bit of a masochist to decide that's the route you want to go down now. Instead, get creative and start combining possibilities:

1. **Write out all the fitness options on six separate slips of paper.**

2. **Jot down the people you can get to join in and support you on six different pieces of paper.**

3. **Research and make a note of the timings and context in which you can carry out the activity on six further pieces of paper.**

4. **Shuffle the three piles separately and take the top slip from each pile.** What do you get? Is it a workable and appealing option? Take the next three pieces of paper and see how that combination pleases you. Go through to the end and then shuffle again until you hit on a combination that you really want to do. This way you are likely to come up with a new angle that has you rushing for the phone to get the chosen option all arranged and in the diary as quickly as you can.

Your initial choices may look something like the ones shown in Table 14-2:

Table 14-2	Your Fitness Options	
What	*Who*	*How*
Belly dancing	Friends	Mornings
Running	Family	Lunchtimes
Walking	Alone	Evenings
T'ai chi	Neighbours	Weekly class
Swimming	Work colleagues	Intensive course
Tennis	Join a club	Weekends

Taking Care of Your Mental and Emotional Well-being

Recent research on happiness suggests that 50 per cent of what makes us happy in life comes from personal characteristics such as our outlook on life, flexibility, openness to change and resilience. A hardy personality bounces back from setbacks quickly and generally remains positive. You have inherited some of your attitude to life from your gene pool, but you can do a great deal to develop your mental and emotional health. Coaching forms a great foundation for improving your emotional well-being, because you're constantly questioning unhelpful thought patterns and behaviours, as well as setting yourself challenging goals that help you to stay motivated and fulfilled in your life.

Managing your emotions

Do you feel comfortable expressing your emotions or do you bottle things up only to find they explode at just the wrong moment? Do you notice what your emotions are all the time, or do you find you sometimes feel upset but can't really put your finger on why? Knowing your emotional range takes practice, and being able to describe how you feel to others can be tricky until you become clear on exactly what these feelings are for you. Marshall Rosenberg, a specialist in conflict resolution, pioneered an approach called *non-violent communication*, which advocates speaking from the heart in all interactions. Doing so helps you to become more assertive, to say what you really mean and need in a factual way that doesn't threaten other people. The starting point to non-violent communication is working out what your heart feels. Think of how you feel when your needs are being fulfilled – glad, joyful, proud, inspired, motivated, amazed, eager, thankful. Each emotion feels slightly different to you, but you may be used to attaching a single label to many of them, such as, 'I'm feeling happy today.' Now think about how you feel when your needs are not being fulfilled – angry, frustrated, puzzled, annoyed, lonely, bitter, disappointed.

The more specific you can be in identifying what you're actually feeling, the clearer you can be in expressing what you need out of a situation to move yourself to a more positive emotion. The following activity helps you to identify specific emotions:

1. **Write down as many positive emotions as you can think of.** Recall some times when you've experienced these emotions and describe what the physical feeling is for you. Perhaps 'joy' is like 'pride' for you and for both you feel a warm sensation at the back of your throat. Or 'motivated' feels like a pleasant tension in your abdomen. Notice the similarities and differences between each positive emotion.

2. **Do the same with the negative emotions that you experience.** Maybe 'anger' causes your shoulders to tense while 'lonely' gives you an empty feeling in your stomach.

3. **Recapture some of the pleasant emotions you've identified by focusing in on the thoughts and memories that trigger the physical feelings for you.** As you recall the moment when you felt 'pride', notice how you can recapture the same warm sensation at the back of your throat even though you experienced unpleasant reactions only a moment before. Notice how quickly you can begin to affect changes in your body that directly affect your mood. Keep practising this – sometimes you need some time to really tune into managing your state in this way.

4. **Armed with this awareness, catch yourself as you go about your day and notice your feelings.** When someone cuts you up on a roundabout, what do you feel? Angry? Frustrated? Rejected? You might be surprised at the real emotion behind the trigger, and that it can change depending on the mood you're in to start with.

Recognising your emotions is half the battle. Expressing them in a way that gets the message across clearly and moves the situation forward in a positive way is the next step to healthy emotional well-being. Think about the last time you were in a heated argument with someone close to you. Did you say – and hear – things that were hurtful and hard to forgive? In a calmer mood, you realise that you didn't really mean some of what you said. Although getting things off your chest is good, letting strong emotion exaggerate the drama of a situation is rarely helpful.

Chapter 17 has more on creating happy emotions for yourself.

Take some of the sting out of arguments by staying mindful of what your needs really are. Perhaps you feel neglected or frustrated in a relationship. Choose to express yourself by describing the specific reasons that make you feel that way, without resorting to a blanket accusation such as 'You never have time for me'. Help the other person by explaining what action they can take to resolve matters.

Don't forget to celebrate your happy and positive emotions. You can make a big impact on your emotional well-being by simply noticing the things that make you feel good and going out of your way to make sure they're part of your life. Those mornings when you wake up full of enthusiasm for no particular reason don't come out of nowhere. Certain triggers help you to feel that way – maybe a smile from a stranger or a supportive email that you didn't really notice at the time. If you can work out what those triggers are, it's like bottling up your own personal happiness formula for your future use.

Getting out of getting into a state

Emotions release chemicals in your body that directly affect your physical state. Worry and anxiety can produce symptoms such as a dry throat, clammy palms and feelings of nausea that often serve to make a difficult situation worse for you, especially if you're about to make a major presentation or speak at a meeting. Just as you can affect your physical body by switching your thoughts (see the preceding section), you can change your emotional state by altering your physical state. Here are some suggestions:

- ✔ **Don't just think about your positive affirmations (refer to Chapter 5) – find a private corner and shout them to the rooftops.** Throw your whole body into it and let rip. Yes, you feel silly, but afterwards you feel better too. If that turns you cold, writing down your affirmations and pinning them where you can see them regularly can do the trick too.

- ✔ **Act 'as if'.** When you feel tense inside, your body tenses up too. Breathe deeply and slowly, expand your chest, walk tall and hold your head high as if you were the most confident person on earth. As you feel the oxygen coursing through your veins, you begin to feel the tension leave your body too.

- ✔ **Take a short brisk walk or jog if you can.** Five minutes may be enough to change your physical state. Better still, listen to an upbeat piece of music and dance along.

✔ **Have a good belly laugh at a joke or comedy show.** Not only does laughing change your physical state, but also humour works directly on your brain to change your mental state. Comedy works because it overturns your expectations – showing you something bizarre or outrageous, or surprising you with a twist in a punchline. Comedy is a key element of creativity, which is a great aid to changing unhelpful thought patterns and feelings (refer to Chapter 15).

Developing mental resilience

Everyday emotional health stems from your level of mental resilience and how quickly you can bounce back from setbacks. If you feel that you're wobbling on the edge of breaking down due to external pressures and feeling out of control, you're not alone. Many people who seem to be very good at coping have at some time or other suffered from stress and depression.

People are a lot less open about emotional and mental instability than they are about physical illness. Spotting the signs of stress that can lead to depression or physical illness is the first step towards dealing with the problem. Chapter 20 has more information on how you can strike the right balance between healthy, forward-propelling stress and unhealthy, debilitating symptoms.

What gives you mental strength? If you're living the life you want and are in control of what you are doing, you're likely to feel strong and resilient. What drains you mentally and how can you reduce the impact of this?

Developing mental resilience begins with four basic strategies that can help you grow stronger:

✔ **Get support.** Talk to people who can help you when you hit problems. Sometimes you simply need a friend who can be there for you. You don't get a bravery award for going it alone. Enlist the advice of a doctor or trained counsellor if your low feelings become persistent and overwhelming.

✔ **Keep a focus on your priorities.** You may need to practise saying no from time to time. When you feel less mentally resilient you may try to please people more, or go in the other direction and get angry at the demands they place on you. Knowing your goals and reminding yourself of them often can be the sanity check you need to assert your needs.

✔ **Schedule a regular activity that builds your mental and emotional muscles.** Take note of activities that leave you with a sense of peace and perspective and make sure that they have a priority in your life. The activity may be meditation or an active sport.

✔ **Take the performance pressure off yourself.** You are the most important person in your world, but everyone around you is far too caught up in their own performance anxiety to notice yours. Remember that you don't have to be perfect – be content with being good enough.

Dancing for happiness

A team of six social science professionals conducted a fascinating experiment for a BBC documentary called *Making Slough Happy*. Fifty volunteers were given their own Happiness Manifesto (a kind of mission statement of how to be happy) to incorporate into their lives. Some of the top tips for action that came out of the experiment were very simple ones, such as enjoying nature, setting aside time to have a good natter with a friend or partner and enjoying a small treat every day, such as 30 minutes of me-time, or an inexpensive impulse buy.

Interestingly, the top negative factor that reduces happiness was watching too much television. Although a pleasurable activity for many people, watching the box for long periods of time is passive and makes people feel sluggish and fed up.

A surprising result on the activity front is that barn dancing was found to promote a lot of happiness. Perhaps some of the reasons behind this discovery are that barn dancing is highly physical, everyone can join in and it's almost impossible to get through an evening of barn dancing without having a good laugh. So take your partners by the hand, it's time to dosey-do . . .

Chapter 15

Developing and Growing

In This Chapter

▶ Developing yourself through change

▶ Understanding your powerful brain

▶ Putting play and purpose into your life

*T*he changes that you make through coaching not only give you better results; they help you grow as a person. In fact, even without the goal of improving your life situation, you constantly need to find new ways to grow, adapt and change, otherwise your enjoyment of life over time can diminish because you become used to the status quo. Coaching is a fantastic mechanism for personal growth. You can apply coaching to the process of your personal development, enhancing your ability to acquire new skills faster and more effectively, so that becoming wiser and more self-aware in itself becomes a whole-life goal.

How well you take on board new information and ideas, how much you seek to gain from fun and leisure time, and your focus on your spiritual well-being are all aspects of personal growth. This chapter focuses on how you can accelerate results in all areas of your life by harnessing your natural talents to soak up new experiences and integrate them into your world – and how you can discover what truly has meaning and purpose for you.

Thriving on Learning

Get one thing clear for starters – learning in the context of your whole life has very little to do with anything you may have experienced at school. Learning is simply a cycle of assessing the information available to you, making decisions, taking action and reflecting on your results to take better steps next time.

Over the last 20 years, research into *accelerated* or brain-friendly learning has identified some fascinating stuff that may explain why so many people switch off and don't get as much out of their early schooling as others seem to do. *Accelerated learning* (also known as *whole-brain thinking*) means you employ the strengths of both the left and right sides of your brain (the later section 'Harnessing your brain power' has more). Exciting times are ahead as schools, adult learning centres and the workplace begin to integrate these new theories fully. The potential of accelerated learning has massive implications for improving the quality of lives and the effectiveness of organisations.

Being your best

Is it really important for you to aim to become competent at everything you do, to stay at that stage and to enjoy the fruits of your labours? Well, becoming competent at something is a great goal. But a higher level is always ahead and, sooner or later, if you want to grow to become your best self, you have to come to terms with letting yourself become incompetent on a regular basis – allowing yourself to struggle at the higher level for a while. This process is like a spiral taking you to ever higher levels, as shown in Figure 15-1.

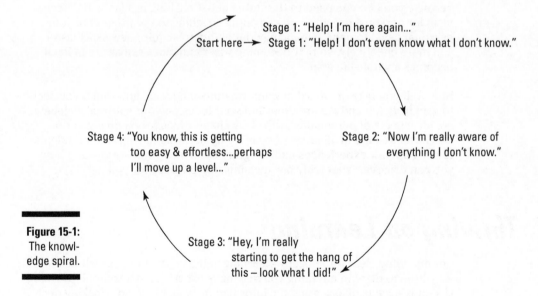

Stage 1: "Help! I'm here again..."

Start here → Stage 1: "Help! I don't even know what I don't know."

Stage 4: "You know, this is getting too easy & effortless...perhaps I'll move up a level..."

Stage 2: "Now I'm really aware of everything I don't know."

Stage 3: "Hey, I'm really starting to get the hang of this – look what I did!"

Figure 15-1: The knowledge spiral.

Try applying the knowledge spiral to taking driving lessons. You may experience some of the following:

Stage 1: You're enthusiastic, ready to learn and blissfully unaware of the scope of the challenges ahead. Anyway, other people make it look so easy. You don't yet know what you don't know!

Stage 2: You start to feel a bit panicky and confused, and are suddenly conscious of how clumsy or ignorant you feel. You have a lot to study and remember – both theory and practice – and you wonder why you thought driving was going to be easy. You are all too aware of the things you don't know and can't do properly.

Stage 3: You're gaining confidence now and feeling proud of your progress, although you may still crunch the gears or forget a road sign occasionally.

Stage 4: A good while after passing your test, you can now spend long stretches not thinking at all about how you drive the car but just doing it. You feel great most of the time, but you do wonder sometimes if you're as good a driver as you were the day you passed your test. Time to enrol in an advanced driving course maybe?

Getting to Stage 4 is often a mixed blessing. You feel comfortable because you're so good at what you do, but if you stay too long at that stage, bad habits can creep in, as well as boredom and complacency. Think about the different areas of your life now. What stages are you at? If you're in a brand-new work role, you may be experiencing the heady optimism of Stage 1 – but how are you preparing for the potential frustration of Stage 2? Are you in a long-term relationship where you think you know everything about the other person? Perhaps Stage 4 complacency has set in – how can you take your relationship to the next level and discover new things about each other? Or you may be working hard at your fitness goals and honing your technique in a new sport. What can you do to accelerate yourself to Stage 4 so that you can have the feel-good factor that comes from being unconsciously competent?

Harnessing your brain power

The choices you make and the actions you take determine the results you get in life, and your choices and actions stem from how you think and use your brain power. You naturally develop preferences and grooves of thinking that work well most of the time, so you may not see the need to stretch yourself. Unless you change how you think, you continue to get pretty much the same results as you always have because you probably choose the same actions and behaviours. But you can develop different ways to think and get different results by engaging other parts of your brain.

In very simple terms, you can think of your brain as two halves of a whole that work together to produce your best results. Table 15-1 summarises the differences between your left brain and your right brain.

Table 15-1	Differences Between the Left and Right Sides of Your Brain
Your Left Brain Focuses on:	*Your Right Brain Focuses on:*
Detail first, then big picture	Big picture, then detail
Fact	Intuition
Logic	Imagination
Theories	Experiments
Structures	Patterns
Organisation	Spontaneity
Seeing what's tangible	Asking what's possible

The left side of your brain is brilliant at processing small bits of data, working out sequences and structures, coming up with theories and applying logic and analysis to problems. Your left brain is really handy for a task such as doing a 5,000-piece jigsaw puzzle. You separate the pieces out, look for the edge ones first, assemble the frame and then begin to put small pieces together. Then (five months later) you finally succeed in assembling the big picture. Your left brain gathers together information logically from the parts to the whole. Left-brain activities tend to dominate most traditional schooling, in part because they're easier to measure than right-brain activities.

The right side of your brain is fantastic at glimpsing the big picture and making those intuitive leaps that seem to come from nowhere. Your right brain helps you stand back, look at the half-completed jigsaw for a second or two, pick up a new piece seemingly at random and somehow know exactly where it goes. Your right brain breaks down information intuitively from the whole to the parts. If you have a strong preference for using your right brain, you may have been the kind of child at school who learned best from imagination and unstructured activities and you may have found it difficult to tune into the logic and order of left-brain learning.

Relying on intuition (right brain) alone doesn't get the jigsaw completed any quicker than using your left brain. Ideally the parts of your brain work together, so you apply logic and process along with those flashes of intuitive brilliance.

Just by comparing the two lists in Table 15-1 you can probably see which of the two sides your brain tends to favour, and areas you can now focus on to get enhanced results. Do you want to get all the facts before you make a decision about something? Maybe you can coach yourself to listen to your intuition from time to time to see how that affects the results you get. Or you may prefer to dive into a task and go with the flow. Try applying more organisational structure to improve your results.

An ability to handle facts, data, and logic, and to pass exams, is only one aspect of being successful. Accelerated learning leads to balanced behaviours that get significantly better outcomes for you overall.

Coaching yourself means opening up options for yourself, trying out new things and exploring different routes. In doing so, you discover better ways of getting what you want and need in your life. Harnessing the sleepy side of your brain and getting it up to speed with the side that's happily whirring away means that you can achieve at least twice as much as you ever did before.

How can you develop your whole brain capability to help you get better results, in coaching and in your life? Here are a few suggestions:

- ✔ **When you formulate your goals, take time to write them down (left-brain activity) and also to visualise or draw them (right-brain activities).** This helps your whole brain to recognise the instruction you're giving it.

- ✔ **Take up crossword puzzles or sudoku to train your whole brain.** Cryptic crosswords in particular are very whole-brain friendly because they make you apply logic and language as well as leaps of intuitive thinking. And sudoku isn't just about numbers (left brain), but about pattern recognition (right brain). Take a look at *Su Doku For Dummies* by Andrew Heron and Edmund James (Wiley) for some real brainteasers.

- ✔ **Build in rest periods for your task.** The optimum period to concentrate fully on a task for your whole brain efficiency is around 90 minutes, after which your brain needs to rest for 20 minutes. (A change really can be as good as a rest, so this doesn't mean a quick snooze at your desk!)

Playing in the Game of Life

Can you remember how you used to play as a child? You'd be fully absorbed in what you were doing, engaging with others, freely moving from one activity to another, coming up with all sorts of imaginative approaches that defied logic. Play enabled you to socialise and interact with others, and it also helped you acquire new skills without feeling anxious and under pressure.

Play can bring you back to life

Some fascinating research among a group of orphans indicates that, far from being a frivolous activity, play is crucial to human development and maybe even survival. In 1999 the Sighisoara Paediatric Hospital in Romania secured the services of the country's first playworker – someone trained in enabling children to learn through play – who trained at Leeds Metropolitan University's innovative Playwork programme. The children at the hospital had all suffered such terrible trauma and neglect that they were used to spending all their time sitting and rocking, trapped in their own solitary worlds. Indeed, all the children had been diagnosed as severely retarded and were destined for a children's mental hospital.

Through the playworker engaging with the children in play activities over a few short months, all of them made the sort of progress that many experts had asserted was impossible with such severe cases of disturbance. A very high proportion of the children were subsequently adopted or fostered, and it seems clear that their rapid transformation was primarily due to the introduction of purposeful play activities.

If play is so important to a child's development, think about what it can do for your adult development.

Humans learn at the most concentrated level in their first seven years. When formal education begins, you start to learn other skills – how to reason and apply logic. Both play and logic are helpful in life, but developing through play is much more right brained and hard to measure, so the education system favours measurable left-brain activities. You leave behind childish things as you grow and feel a little foolish if you go back to them. Even though you may secretly still love joining your niece or nephew with crayons and paints, you may feel you can't possibly whip out your own colouring book when no children are around!

What did you love to do as a child that you have grown out of? What have you lost as a result? In what ways can you integrate this back into your life? You may have replaced simple activities such as cycling with friends with more 'adult' pursuits such as trips to the gym – all well and good, but recapturing the sense of fun you had in child-like activities can bring unexpected benefits.

Benefiting from a playful approach

Coaching yourself to a more playful approach to life has practical benefits, including:

✔ **You enjoy enhanced creativity in the solutions you come up with for your life.** Apply a little childlike imagination and ask yourself a non-logical question from time to time. For example, 'If this problem were a colour/animal/city, what would it be?'

✔ **You begin to see things more clearly.** Children are often brutally honest about what they see in their world. However, they quickly learn not to point out to Great Aunt Ethel that she's got a very wobbly bottom, so they discover diplomacy and how to keep quiet. This develops into telling little white lies to avoid hurting people's feelings. You may have become so used to the truth being a bit of a chameleon that seeing what's going on clearly is sometimes tricky. Young children are generally honest with themselves until they learn otherwise. This innate talent can help you take anxiety out of everyday mishaps and problems. Ask yourself, 'What's really true for me here? In what way am I glossing over the truth to avoid facing something?'

✔ **You enjoy your journey more.** Ask yourself 'Am I having fun yet?' from time to time to stop you from taking yourself or your task too seriously. Look for ways to liven up whatever you're doing.

✔ **You begin to probe beneath the surface more often.** Play the Game of Five Whys with yourself from time to time. This game (inspired from the eternal question children ask) simply means that you explore an issue for yourself by asking 'why?' five times in a row, to really get to the heart of the problem. For example: *Why* am I still doing this job I hate? To earn money. *Why?* So I can have more holidays. *Why?* So I enjoy myself more. *Why?* Because I feel miserable most of the time. *Why?* Because I keep turning up to this job I hate!

Making the most of your leisure time

The habits you get into during your leisure time have a lot of impact on how much you enjoy your life as a whole. Weekends and holidays may be the main way that you rebalance the frantic pace of the rest of your life. You may feel that the last thing you want to do is take on more challenges. Your perfect vacation may be lazing by the pool – this may be just the thing to send you back to your daily routine relaxed and recharged.

But check your assumptions once in a while. What's the best holiday you've ever had and why? Do you go back to the same resort or have a similar holiday every year because that's what feeds your soul or because that's become a habit? Do you find that you need or want to take longer and longer to recharge? Do you find that a week or so of inactivity leaves you feeling less, not more, energised? You may be reaching a tipping point where the stress in certain areas of your life is getting to be a little more than is good for your healthy balance (if so, check out Chapter 20 for stress management and rebalancing strategies).

Your lack of energy may have another explanation. Do you know people who never seem to stop doing things? They take on numerous projects at work and at home and then spend their holidays learning to sky-dive or climbing minor mountain ranges. Sometimes, the more you do, the more energy you have.

Look closely at your leisure time and see how you can get the best of both worlds, relaxing *and* action-packed. So you've been promising yourself to learn another language? Rather than sign up for an evening class that may be hard to schedule into your busy week, you can investigate joining in with some classes on holiday abroad, spending the morning having fun in school and the afternoon sightseeing or relaxing. In terms of variety, for example, if you usually holiday with your family, consider taking a solo short break to reconnect with your own sense of self.

Your leisure time is a great opportunity for personal growth, as well as a blissful space where you can simply be for a while, before you get right back into the thick of the action.

Find a quiet spot and ask yourself these questions to coach yourself to more enjoyable leisure pursuits:

- ✔ **Powerful opening question:** What role do I want leisure to take in my life?

- ✔ **Personal style:** Am I naturally active or reflective? Do I favour left- or right-brain activities? What gives me energy?

- ✔ **Beliefs:** What beliefs do I have about time out that may be restricting my enjoyment? What constraints do I put around holiday time? How do I reduce the priority of leisure in my life?

- ✔ **Motivation:** What can I achieve in my personal time that supports my key values? What is a compelling goal to aim for that enhances my enjoyment of my core interests?

- ✔ **What's working:** What's good about the choices I make about how to spend my leisure time? What compromises do I make that I resent having to make?

- ✔ **Exploring options:** What ways can I find to experiment with different approaches to my leisure time? How can I test the choices that are right for me?

- ✔ **Taking action:** What's my first step? How much time can I allocate to planning my approach? How do I know when I'm making progress? What can I do to celebrate?

Getting in Touch with Your Spiritual Side

Part of gaining knowledge and growing is getting in touch with and developing your spiritual side. One of the greatest benefits to come out of coaching is a growing sense of self-awareness. You begin to accept yourself as human, unique, capable, sometimes flawed and yet endlessly resourceful. You become comfortable in your own skin, you accept yourself and you begin to get a feeling for what is really important for you. (Part II of this book has lots more on this process of self-discovery.)

What is spirituality for you?

Here are some of the things that you may associate with spirituality:

- Feeling touched by something you see or experience – perhaps a glorious sunset, the wingspan of a bird in flight or a baby's smile.

- Sensing that you're contributing to something bigger than yourself.

- Being willing to connect with others openly for no other reason than that they share the same air as you.

- Feeling in flow with what you're doing at that exact moment and that your attention is fully focused.

- Wondering at the ultimate mystery of the world around you.

- Noticing how often the opportunity to have what you most want presents itself to you unexpectedly without you actively seeking it.

What are the characteristics of spirituality for you? Spirituality may be connected with your religion or faith. The two concepts are not the same, although for many people religion is a powerful mechanism to access their spirituality.

Bless you!

Whenever I want to connect with the concept of blessings to support myself in my life journey, I go to www.mayyoubeblessedmovie.com. This inspirational short film reinforces my strong, positive life-coaching beliefs about myself and my world. (You can ignore the page at the end asking you to pass on the address – it's the film itself that's inspirational.)

Accessing your spirituality

Coaching helps you to realise that you can deal with anything. Having a strong sense of self enables you to handle even the worst events and you begin to learn the truth in the saying 'what doesn't kill you makes you stronger'. You create your world through what you choose to focus on and do. Coaching can result in changes in your thoughts, behaviours and actions to build a life that sits well with your authentic self (refer to Chapter 4). And that can lead to a search for your true role in the world, whether on a big or small stage. For many people, all this self-discovery in itself can become a spiritual journey.

Even if you feel that spirituality is not part of who you are, self-coaching can be immensely joyful, challenging and fulfilling. No matter what stage of the journey you're at, or what level of awareness you've achieved, you're connecting with something quite indefinable in yourself that many people describe as their spirit or essence.

How can you access your spirituality? Here are some ideas:

- ✔ **Meditate.** Meditation relaxes you, helps you to feel grounded and is a great way to empty your mind of everyday concerns so that you become more open to the big questions and connections that form the basis of spirituality. Sitting comfortably and gazing at a candle is a simple form of meditation.

- ✔ **Get out in the natural world and take a good look around.** Think about how long the oak tree in the woods has stood, when the hills were formed and how often the waves crash against the shore. Your head will soon start to spin but you'll get some perspective on the challenges in your life.

- ✔ **Take up a physical practice such as yoga, Pilates, or t'ai chi.** Or combine your spiritual quest with a fitness goal through running and jogging if that's more your style. By giving the body purposeful movement you also free up your mind.

- ✔ **Read as much as possible.** Fiction, poetry, humour, philosophy – read whatever takes your fancy as long as it challenges you a little and broadens your horizons.

- ✔ **Feast on art, music and dance whenever you can.** All great artists express their bigger purpose in some way through their art, and you can catch some of their magic dust as you appreciate the beauty of their work.

Take a look at *Spirituality For Dummies,* 2nd Edition, by Sharon Janis and *Mindfulness For Dummies* by Shamash Alidina (both Wiley).

Exploring spirituality through coaching

Coaching is about finding ways to enjoy what you have and to attract more of what you want. Coaching is also one of the most powerful mechanisms to explore what gives meaning and purpose to your life. Throughout this book – and especially in Chapter 24 – you can find powerful questions to help you switch on the light for yourself.

Think of the things that are most precious to you. Your values are a big clue here (see Chapter 6). What makes your life worth living? What puts a spring in your step? What gives you the feel-good factor? When do things feel most right for you? What's going on for you on those occasions when you're in your element and you're really glowing?

Don't be afraid to ask yourself the really big questions: What's life all about? Why am I here? What's my true gift to the world? What's the one thing I would change in the world if I could make it happen? Philosophers through the ages have asked the same questions – you have just as much of a chance of answering them as they do, and a far greater chance of finding the right answers for you.

INSPIRATION

Staying true to the vision

Tim found his life purpose as a coach who works with people and organisations to help them realise their vision of success. The story of his journey has all the elements of a spiritual awakening – a sudden clear vision of life purpose, a determination to do the right thing whatever the sacrifice and the beauty of *synchronicity* (similar events coinciding in time, although seemingly unrelated). This was the powerful question that prompted Tim's self-transformation:

What great dream would you dare to dream if you knew it was guaranteed to come true?

Tim immediately got a picture of himself standing at the centre of a crossroads, with signposts pointing in four directions, and footprints leading out along each path. He saw himself guiding people along their way and out of this image came the affirmation, 'I am helping people move along their chosen path in life.'

In the late 1990s Tim became one of the very first full-time coaches in the building and manufacturing industries, turning his back on the prospect of the operational directorship that he had long set his sights on because of the strength of his new conviction. After he'd made that decision, a whole series of events and signs supported him and helped him shape what would ultimately become his own successful coaching business.

Looking back, Tim realises that he made the choices he did because he felt such a strong sense that this was what he was meant to be doing and who he was meant to be. Tim's life purpose is to show the way to help people transcend to their best selves. He retains a down-to-earth, practical business focus, but he freely admits that the feeling he gets of being the right person, in the right place, at exactly the right time adds a deeply spiritual dimension to his life.

Part IV
Working with the Themes of Coaching

"I think my body's energy centres
<u>ARE</u> well balanced. I keep my pager
on my belt, my mobile phone in my right
pocket, and my palmtop computer in
my inside left breast pocket."

In this part . . .

You explore the important coaching themes of happiness and success. You'll hopefully answer the big questions about what happiness and success really mean to you. You also get heaps of advice on tackling procrastination and low self-confidence – the common blocks to your coaching journey.

Chapter 16

Attracting the Life You Want

In This Chapter

▶ Getting in the flow and releasing resistance

▶ Appreciating the present moment

▶ Tuning into positive emotions

*W*hen you coach yourself effectively, you always aim to keep a balance between heading towards what you want and enjoying the journey of getting there. No matter how much you plan and how good your route map, you can never be absolutely sure that your destination will be all that you hoped for. And sometimes even when it is, you may find that it doesn't fully satisfy you. This isn't depressing news – just realistic. You change and grow all the time, and every decision you make is only as good as the wisdom and insight you have at that moment.

Focusing exclusively on the future – 'things will be better when . . .' – makes no more sense than harking back to the past. Attracting the life that you want is about creating great results in your life with eager anticipation combined with present-centred appreciation of everything you already have. And I do mean *everything* – the good, the bad and the plain ugly!

In this chapter I show you how to coach yourself to attracting the life you want by wanting what you have so that your life truly flows. Are you truly ready to attract your best life? Everything in this book will help you to do that, and applying the knowledge and techniques in this chapter in particular will assist you to get into a wonderful state of flow that helps you move effortlessly through life. Even when it really isn't all plain sailing.

Mastering the Art of Acceptance

Do you know people who simply seem to flow with their lives? Everything seems effortless and they always appear to get exactly what they want, when they want it. They may seem luckier than other people and are always experiencing happy coincidences or synchronicities that open up doors for them. At the same time, they don't ever seem to strive for anything and when things don't go so well, they can shrug their shoulders and turn their attention elsewhere. These people are often generous of spirit and you feel good around them. What's their secret?

Well, they've probably mastered the gentle art of *acceptance* – a way of being that lets good things flow towards you. And the first step towards allowing or attracting good things is to coach yourself to let go of resistance.

Letting go of resistance

The saying goes that what you resist, persists! Think of a time when you were in a confrontation with someone. You may have vigorously defended your stance, only to find that your adversary fought back even harder. You were both resisting what *is* – the fact that you held differing viewpoints. The solution you can both find is to simply accept the situation with curiosity. It only takes one person in the resistance tug of war to let go of the rope. If you've ever done that – simply remained silent as the other person railed against you – you'd probably have noticed that the torrent stopped short. Where there's nothing to fight or grab against, there's no struggle, and a more collaborative solution can emerge in the space that is created.

Whatever the weather

One of the most ridiculous things we humans tend to do is complain about the weather. No one can control the weather!

It's understandable that you feel disappointed when spring rain stops play, or when the damp summer heat wave brings out the midges in full force, but some people make complaining about these things into an art form! There's no point complaining; the weather will be exactly as it is. And resisting what you can't control takes up energy that's better applied to positive action in your life.

Simply because it is – literally – a force of nature, accepting the weather is a great way to practise letting go of resistance. Catch yourself next time you find yourself getting into a blue funk about the wind and the rain and switch your thought process around. Start by simply shrugging your shoulders and accepting it.

Then take a closer look. What's pleasant, awe-inspiring or at least leads to a positive benefit about the weather that you are witnessing? There are no rainbows without rain, for one. I recently spent a week on the Isle of Skye and noticed how stunning the clouds were even on the dullest of days. 'We just don't seem to have that kind of light back in Yorkshire,' I remember thinking to myself. You know what? A week later I was looking at the sky in my home town and thinking how pretty the clouds were and, yes, it was the dullest of dull days.

Acceptance, as well as practice, makes perfect!

You may be resisting good things in your life in all sorts of ways. Although it may seem strange behaviour, maybe you have sometimes found yourself resisting feeling happy because you think you don't deserve to be happy or haven't earned it.

And think about when things don't go your way. Do you feel a tightness in your body, frustrated or even angry? Do you rail against fate, bemoan your luck, kick the cat or snarl at your work colleagues? Do you get into a 'poor me' state and feel that everything you do is doomed to failure? All of these are symptoms of resistance. Whatever it is that has happened, shouldn't have happened and you're fighting against it with all your might.

Where does that get you? Generally, not very far at all. You can make progress by standing back from the situation and focusing on positive, resourceful actions. You allow that things don't always go your way and accept what is, making the best out of whatever hand life has just dealt you.

If all that sounds easier said then done, ask yourself these seven powerful questions to coach yourself from resistance to acceptance. To do this activity effectively, remove yourself from all distractions and have a pen and paper at the ready. Speak each question out loud and write down whatever answer comes up. Stop writing as soon as you start to sense your inner critic saying 'yes, but . . .' and move quickly onto the next question.

1. What am I resisting right now?

2. What negative impact is that resistance having on me?

3. What positive impact is that resistance having on me?

4. How would I feel if I let go of my resistance?

5. How specifically would I think and behave if I simply accepted this situation/person/unpleasant emotion *as it is?* (Allow yourself to really get into the feel and sense of how this state would be for you before moving on to the next question.)

6. How can I retain the positive aspects of my resistance?

7. What right action now comes to mind? (You know a right action because it is probably a more creative and yet simpler step to take than any that you were formulating in your state of resistance. Trust your intuition if it feels right, no matter how wacky it might appear, and find ways to test it safely if it takes you out of your comfort zone a little!)

Being present

Where are you when you're not fully present to each moment? Chances are you're stuck in the past (fretting over some mistake or injustice) or worrying about the future (how to pay the gas bill, what to do about your suddenly surly significant other). Living in the past or for the future disrupts the flow of your life and can keep you stuck in unpleasant thoughts and emotions. Imagine a river that silts up with mud. The mud is your attachment to dwelling on past and future events. How smoothly does the river of your life flow?

But what about pleasant memories and optimistic forward planning? These are much more helpful to flowing in life, surely? Yes, indeed – but only up to a point. Think about it for a moment. If you live nostalgically in the past, you are in fact *re*-living – repeating what has already been created – and you don't get the space to create new memories. And focusing pleasantly on what will be in the future can lead to all planning and no action. Your memory and your imagination are also very selective, so you're not even very accurate in how you see both past and future.

I'm not at all advocating that you shut out past and future completely. You can use past positive experiences to provide the evidence and the foundation for present action, and visualising your goals taking place in the future is a key way to make them a reality. However, by staying fully present to each moment for the great majority of your time, your life flows more. You notice more, you appreciate more and you learn more. You're more open to the opportunities that (excuse the pun!) present themselves. You start to attract the life you want. So how do you coach yourself to do it?

This activity has two parts. I recommend you really take the time to complete Part One before moving on. In my experience (and I include myself here!) people tend to think they're much more present-centred than they actually are. It's helpful to revisit Part One of this activity on a regular basis to keep track of your progress and avoid complacency.

Part One

Choose a week where you can carry around an alarm (perhaps on a mobile phone), a notebook and pen and make regular brief notes at intervals during the day. Choose a week where you are working or going about activities quite a lot on your own, because that's when your thought patterns tend to go into habitual grooves.

For the whole week, set an hourly alarm during the day and when the alarm goes off, simply ask yourself:

- ✔ **Where are my thoughts now?** Are your thoughts in the past, the present or the future? Record your answer.

- ✔ **Where have my thoughts mostly been for the last hour?** Record your answer.

Don't analyse these results yet; simply move on. At the end of the week summarise and review your results. Where have you been living mostly – past, present or future?

Remember two things during this activity:

✔ **The importance of an honest assessment.** You often think you're in the present, but when you look at what you're actually thinking of, it's about the past or the future. Perhaps you're thinking: 'What does Rose think about this business decision?' which sounds pretty much in the present. But the thought behind that might really be 'Rose disagreed with me in last week's meeting (past), so I wonder what she'll say about this decision (future)?' Remember that nothing's inherently bad about this, and in fact you do need to take account of the past to plan for the future. But this exercise shows up the predominant thinking focus for you.

✔ **The act of measuring something often tends to get positive results in itself.** The simple fact of focusing on how much you're being present may naturally incline you to be more so, without you being in any way conscious of that. So when you review your results, be aware that they're probably better than they are when you're not monitoring your attention in this way!

Part Two

When you know how present-centred you are, you can begin to make small changes to be more in the moment. Even if you're pretty pleased with the results of your experiment above, you can still improve, because being present-centred isn't just about the amount of time you focus on right now – it's also about the quality of your attention.

You may need that trusty alarm again to build the habit, or simply make a commitment that you'll do this activity at specific times of the day.

For a week, set your alarm (real or imaginary) five times a day. At that time, perhaps on the hour, simply stop whatever you're doing (as soon as is safe of course!) and focus on your breathing. Bring your attention to any one of your senses – taste, smell, the feel of your clothes on your skin, hearing or sight. Or close your eyes if you wish because what you see tends to be more of a distraction than other experiences.

Do this for a minute. That's all, just 60 seconds. If your attention wanders, simply focus back on your breathing. And then come back into your usual awareness and look around you. Simply notice, without making any judgements or turning your attention to your to-do list in your head. You're observing the world exactly as it is. Do the exercise again for about a minute – longer if you like. Don't force it. If your attention really begins to move away from simple observation of your breath, just get back to whatever you were doing.

As you practise this activity, you'll find that you become seriously addicted to it. It's a simple form of meditation and can really de-stress you if you make a habit of it. You'll also notice that you gradually become more and more in the moment, both when you're doing the activity and at other times. Feel free to do this activity much more regularly than five times a day – it's really easy to pause like this very frequently – but to maintain the habit of attention I find that even a couple of times a day works really well.

Mindfulness For Dummies by Shamash Alidina (Wiley) has some more wonderful tips for staying present in order to enjoy your life more fully.

Wanting What You Have

If you truly want your life to flow and attract your best life, you need to appreciate everything that shows up for you, even and *especially* the things you can't control, don't want and positively abhor!

Sounds contrary? Well, maybe a little counter-intuitive I agree. Still, let me share a very important secret with you, based on my own experience and that of so many of my clients. *If you can coach this aspect of wanting what you have into your life, even if you do none of the other things I suggest in this book, you'll dramatically enhance the quality of your life.*

I covered letting go of resistance and getting into acceptance as a way of flowing with your life earlier in this chapter. Mastering the art of acceptance doesn't just make you feel better in a bad or challenging situation (although it does). The deeper truth is that everything that happens to you has the potential to open you to even more joy and happiness, *especially* the seemingly bad things in your life. You have no doubt already had experience of a twist of fate for the worse that turned out to be for the better. Perhaps you were made redundant and now you run your own successful business. Be aware now that this wasn't an exception, it's the rule! Shifting your perspective so that you want what you have – even the so-called negative aspects – will pay huge dividends in your life.

The trick is in stepping back and identifying the lesson in whatever has happened and allowing yourself to change, grow and evolve. You can't do that without letting go of resistance and getting into acceptance, covered earlier. Beyond that then, if you come to believe that everything has a positive intention for you (the cloud's silver lining, if you like) then you move into a state of being appreciative of all that happens, because you trust that the silver lining is there to be found, and it will be worth more than all the heartache. Trust is a key factor here, because it might indeed take some time before you can see how the lesson plays out for the positive.

Are there exceptions to this? The really painful events of life, like the death of a loved one, don't have silver linings. Even so, you can allow the process of grieving and coming to acceptance to change you in healthy and positive ways. You may come to appreciate and value your life and your relationships more, knowing that every moment is precious.

So a key to flowing is wanting exactly what you already have, for the love of it, or the lesson in it, or the deeper gift, knowing that by doing this, it opens up the potential for you to create more, or different, or better. And where it feels impossible to want what has happened, know that by accepting it, you can allow yourself to grow and evolve.

Wherever you are right now is perfect, even when it's not!

And if that scrambles your brain, that's okay too. Take a moment now to reflect on that statement and begin to feel how it may be true for you. The following sections go into more detail about how you can start to really want what you have.

Practising gratitude

The best way of getting into the groove of wanting what you have is to perfect the art of being grateful.

It's not too difficult to feel grateful for the good things in your life – perhaps your health, your children, pets or your home. But how can you be grateful for things that are unpleasant, uncomfortable or even frightening? It can feel challenging to start with, but as you practise building the habit of gratitude, it becomes stronger.

Whatever situation you're facing, it's usually possible to imagine one worse. For most everyday challenges, this is enough to turn you towards a feeling of gratitude, even a small one. It's really all down to your sense of perspective.

But what about the tougher stuff you may have to face, such as the death of a loved one, or a life-threatening illness? I know from personal experience how difficult it feels to connect with any good feeling in these situations.

Yet even in the darkest hours there are bright lights that shine, if you turn your attention to them. You can honour your loved one best by focusing on those bright lights, even amidst painful feelings. And your resources to face serious illness will strengthen if you tune into what you can be grateful for. You get what you focus on, and the more grateful you are, the more things you will attract to be grateful about.

When you've connected, however slightly, with a feeling of gratitude, you can begin to strengthen it by journaling, reflecting or meditating on all the other things in your life that you have to be grateful for. Start with the first thought and write, or say to yourself:

I am grateful for . . .

Then create a list in your journal or in your mind, all beginning with that simple phrase. Make it even more powerful by adding more positive phrases, for example:

I am so happy and grateful for . . .

It won't always feel authentic to add that extra dose of positivity, especially if the challenge you're facing is a tough one. As you stay with the feelings though, you may often find that you move naturally towards feeling grateful. Don't ever feel guilty about feeling good. As long as your good feelings are coming from the wisest and highest part of you, don't hold back on them.

Notice how, as you gain momentum, your gratitude list becomes longer, the things on it become bigger and more heartfelt, and you start to really *feel* happier and more grateful. Keep a special Gratitude Journal that you can go back to over and over again to get a fix of gratitude.

Check out my website www.reachforhappiness.com for more tips and techniques on building habits of gratitude.

Tuning into your positive emotions

Gratitude in particular allows you to flow with your life and attract more good things. Any positive, resourceful emotion allows you be open to more of the same.

Did you know that in general, unless you consciously switch them, your emotions are around 60 to 80 per cent negative? By negative, I mean unhelpfully so – some negative emotions can be important and healthy. Attracting more good things to your life means regularly and consistently moving your emotions along the line from negative/unhelpful to positive/resourceful, and here's how:

You're about to take a walk across the Bridge of Emotion!

Take these steps across the bridge when you notice an unpleasant emotion coming up:

1. **Identify the emotion.** Do you feel anger, confusion, disappointment or simply sadness? Don't worry about labelling it 'correctly' – go with your instinct about what you're experiencing.

2. **Ask yourself what the emotion is telling you, in a positive way, that you need to learn.** Perhaps you feel angry about a perceived slight from a colleague. When you think about it, you realise the lesson might be to let go of making assumptions. Again, don't worry if you don't get a clear answer at this stage. Simply by assuming that there _is_ a way for you to develop in this, you help yourself to move to a more positive state and allow your unconscious mind to start looking for the constructive lesson. And don't spend too long on this side of the bridge. Remember the concept of acceptance – you simply feel the way you do right at this moment.

3. **Consider what positive emotion you'd really _like_ to feel, even if it seems out of reach.** If you feeling _anger_ about your colleague, perhaps you really want to be feeling _enthusiasm_ so that you can get on with the project in hand. There are no 'right' emotions to aim for – the one that you _want_ to feel is important; the one that will help you be most resourceful and happy.

4. **Visualise a bridge ahead of you.** Make it the kind of bridge that is attractive to you, so it could be a wooden bridge over a river, or even an impressive actual structure like the Golden Gate Bridge in San Francisco!

5. **Imagine that positive emotion you identified is waiting for you just on the other side of the bridge.** Look ahead from where you are and mentally judge the distance between the negative emotion you're currently standing in and the lovely positive one waiting for you on the other side.

6. **Consider what emotion would take you one step nearer to your ultimate positive emotion.** If you started out with _anger_, for example, perhaps you decide on _irritation_ as the next step. Still not a great feeling perhaps, but better than anger. Imagine yourself taking that step onto the bridge. Feel how different that emotion is for you.

7. **Do this as many times as you need to in order to arrive at your positive emotion goal.** Every step takes you a bit closer to where you want to be. Each time, make sure you really notice and feel the difference of standing in the new emotion. So your next step might be _frustration_ and the one after that could be _confusion_. Maybe you'll then find that _curiosity_ pops up and then _excitement_ and finally . . . ta da! you arrive at positive _enthusiasm_ waiting eagerly for you on the other side of your Bridge of Emotion!

Chapter 17

Coaching Yourself to Happiness

· ·

In This Chapter

▶ Understanding the happiness factors

▶ Becoming more optimistic

▶ Creating your happy life plan

· ·

> *If you search the world for happiness, you may find it in the end, for the world is round and will lead you back to your door.*
>
> — Robert Brault

*H*appiness is no laughing matter; in fact, it's a serious business! Take a moment to think about the reason behind all that you do. You set goals for better health, wealth, a great career and brilliant relationships. Why do you do all of that? Chances are, it's because you believe that attaining these goals will make you happier, or at least enhance your current level of happiness. Even truly altruistic goals – where you make a contribution to the world and to others, perhaps at some personal cost – still contribute significantly to your feelings of happiness.

The best goals make you feel happy by a combination of a great outcome that really motivates you and a process of getting there that is, at least in part, an enjoyable one.

Even so, happiness can still be elusive and fleeting. Things that you think should make you happy sometimes don't, and you can find true happiness in unexpected places. This chapter helps you make sense of the happiness conundrum. Applying what you learn here can help you coach yourself to *your* definition of enduring happiness – and that's the one that counts after all!

Discovering Your Happiness Formula

We live in a scientific age, so you might expect that you can now apply a formula to your happiness, in much the same way that you can solve a quadratic equation (if you happen to be good at maths, that is). It hasn't always been so. Philosophers, sages and religious figures throughout the ages have always offered wisdom and insight about how to live a good and happy life. And while all that knowledge combined does seem to come down to some common truths, it's only been in the latter half of the twentieth century that the new science of positive psychology has found ways of measuring levels of happiness, both in a subjective way – how people feel – and in terms of what we see at a neurological and physical level. Their findings are fascinating, both for how they back up what you might know intuitively but in some cases run counter to that.

Coaching yourself isn't about slavishly following anyone else's advice, including mine! And applying the happiness formula isn't quite as simple as a decent mathematician solving a quadratic equation. Knowing how a formula works is just a starting point – the real skill is in reflecting and exploring these ideas and coaching yourself through making them work in *your* life.

Getting into the flow

The fabulously named psychology professor Mihaly Csikszentmihalyi conducted groundbreaking research on something he termed *flow*, which has also been referred to as 'being in the zone'. Csikszentmihalyi discovered that the happiest individuals have many flow experiences in their lives; periods when you're absorbed in something so that you lose track of time. You might not actually be comfortable doing the thing at the time (perhaps climbing a mountain or writing an essay), but you're using your skills and talents to the full. You might be a bit out of your comfort zone, but you're well enough equipped to be up to the challenge and, more importantly, the activity is something essentially enjoyable and worthwhile for you.

Flow experiences can occur a lot in a career context, because that's where you tend to be using your skills and talents more frequently. But they can also occur just as significantly in a leisure pursuit, when making love or in parenting.

The characteristics of flow are that you:

  ✔ Are engaged in an activity where you're clear about your goals and you can get immediate feedback on your progress, from others or from yourself.

✔ Are intensely absorbed in what you're doing to the extent that time seems to stand still and yet expand. You are fully present.

✔ Become one with the tools you're using. For example, if you achieve flow through painting or writing, then you might feel that the paintbrush or the pen is part of you, making the action effortless.

✔ Are challenged and are using your skills at their limits, yet you have confidence in your ability to succeed.

✔ Lose self-consciousness and may not even be fully aware of all the steps you take. Afterwards, you feel a stronger sense of self.

✔ Are doing whatever you're doing because you want to rather than because of an end goal, although the end goal is also important.

Sounds like a great state to be in doesn't it? Flow occurs in your peak experiences, and these aren't always everyday occurrences. When they do occur, either because you create them or when they simply happen, your sense of flow contributes massively to your overall level of happiness.

When you're coaching yourself to happiness, think of how you can build in more opportunity to experience flow moments in your life, such as engaging in a hobby that allows you to build your skills and being open to opportunities in a work context to stretch just a little outside of your comfort zone in an area of personal strength. The more routine aspects of your life can give you a flow experience too. Being very present and attentive to whatever task you have in hand can also lead to a feeling of flow, such as gardening or cooking a meal, especially where a little extra challenge and skill is involved like designing a new flowerbed or cooking a new dish for a dinner party.

Delving into positive psychology

The father of positive psychology is considered by many to be Martin Seligman, from the University of Pennsylvania. Seligman challenged the perspective of traditional psychology with its focus on the question *What's wrong?* by asking instead *What's working?* He began to research the tangible things that make people feel good and came up with the happiness formula:

$$H=S+C+V$$

In this formula, H=Happiness, S=Set point, C= the Circumstances of your life and V=the factors under your Voluntary control.

Considering the pleasure principle

Is happiness all about pleasure? The answer seems to be *no* – if you believe that pleasure means simply making sure your senses are well satisfied with treats. But it's also *yes* if you think of pleasure as being about choosing activities and pursuits that give you a varied journey of pleasant emotions from mild enthusiasm to blissful joy, taking a lengthy stop at contentment along the way.

The answer can also be *not only*. Happiness can coexist with painful emotions and quite often it *must* for you to have a full experience of happiness in your life. Many things that create feelings of happiness in your life – such as living according to your values and purpose – also include challenges that may not be at all pleasurable. So your enduring level of happiness over time may be significantly reduced if you keep too strong a focus on pleasure. Feeling good, however, is always a choice, even in the most challenging of situations.

Here's what they mean (Figure 17-1 shows the percentages as a pie chart):

✔ Your **set point** for happiness is dependent on your genes by around 50 per cent – what you inherit from mum and dad. Bad news, you might think, for anyone born into generations of Victor Meldrews, but in reality you benefit from a mix of optimistic and pessimistic genes. Opposites tend to attract, after all, so Moaning Minnie quite often ends up marrying Sunny Simon. And of course, Minnie has her magic moments too, whilst Simon occasionally suffers. Overall, evolution has seen to it that there are no unhealthy extremes.

Your set point tends to remain quite stable over your life time, and big bursts of happiness or depression don't affect it in the long term because you tend to return to your set point once the initial euphoria or misery has abated a bit.

✔ The **circumstances of your life** account for only 10 per cent of your happiness potential. A tiny percentage really, considering that many people think that a big blow like redundancy, divorce or financial ruin would affect their happiness dramatically. These things do have a big affect – for a while – but you tend to return to your set point in due course. How long that takes is down to the last part of your happiness formula.

✔ The **factors under your voluntary control** – how we *choose* to think, feel and act is a massive 40 per cent. You can improve even the worst of situations by a change of mindset, which leads to you feeling better, which in turn can generate positive action.

Happiness is in very large part a choice – *your* choice.

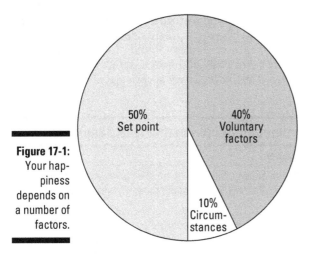

Figure 17-1:
Your hap-
piness
depends on
a number of
factors.

50%
Set point

40%
Voluntary
factors

10%
Circum-
stances

Identifying the elements of happiness for you

You can't rewrite the happiness formula, but you can take comfort from how much your happiness is under your control at any point in time. Coaching yourself to happiness is made easier because you now have a lot of evidence about the specific things you can do to affect your happiness.

Taking the good with the bad

One of the most compelling pieces of research around happiness involved a study of two very different groups of people. The first were lottery winners and the second were people who had become quadriplegic (limbs paralysed) as a result of an accident. As you might expect, immediately after the win, the lottery winners all reported increased feelings of happiness, and the quadriplegics reported the reverse after their own life-changing event. However, a year down the line both groups on average had returned to their normal set point level of happiness. This is known as *Adaptation Theory* – over time you adapt to anything, good or bad.

Interestingly, both groups had people who felt significantly happier *because* of their experience. So winning the lottery may or may not make you happier, just as suffering a tragic accident could mark the end of your normally happy way of life or the beginning of new possibilities and meaning. It all depends on your set point, and how you then choose to deal with whatever life has offered you.

So now's your chance to browse the happiness store and see what you already have well in stock and what extra provisions you might need to acquire. Table 17-1 shows some of the key things researchers have found make the most difference to happiness. Table 17-2 shows some of the factors that haven't been found to contribute to happiness. The findings may surprise you!

Table 17-1	Factors that Contribute Positively to Happiness
Factor	*Explanation*
Doing work that stimulates you	Purposeful activity, paid or unpaid, that gives you satisfaction and interests you most of the time, is a strong factor in happiness.
Being extroverted	Even if you have a more introverted preference, you're likely to have more happy feelings when you allow yourself to be extroverted in the way that is right for you. For example, a strongly extroverted person might feel happiest at a party when chatting to as many people as possible, while a more introverted friend chooses to connect with fewer folk and to listen more. They're both being extroverted at the level enjoyable for them. (See Chapter 4 for more on extroversion/introversion.)
Having leisure time	Having hobbies that engage you, or simply making some time for yourself to do what you want to do, significantly increases your happiness level.
Being optimistic	Always choosing an optimistic perspective, no matter how bad things get, helps you feel better and builds your resilience to life's challenges.
Having good social networks	Close friendships and loving relationships play a huge part in happiness. It doesn't matter if you go for quantity or quality – or both! – what matters is that you feel connected to people who are important to you.
Looking after your body's physical needs	In particular, sleep is essential to healthy well-being and exercise boosts the endorphins (those happy chemicals) in your body.
Having a comfortable standard of living and social status	You don't have to take yourself from rags to riches to be happy. But a comfortable standard of living is high on the happiness agenda. Research suggests that more isn't necessarily better, however.
Being married	Perhaps a little surprisingly, marriage (as opposed to committed cohabiting) still seems to come out better in terms of happiness. However, being in a marriage that is *not* working scores highly on unhappiness compared to being divorced or single.

Factor	Explanation
Having a religious faith or sense of spirituality	Having a sense of a bigger or higher purpose is a great source of happiness.
Taking a positive attitude towards your health	Happiness isn't about the actual state of your health, more about how you view it. So a chronically ill person can be happier than someone who's physically as fit as a fiddle, because he chooses to relate differently to his physical condition and makes the best of what small progress he makes in getting to well-being.

Table 17-2	Factors that Don't Seem to Contribute Positively to Happiness
Money	You need to have basic financial needs met, but beyond that, happiness doesn't seem to increase the wealthier you get. More money can certainly bring more pleasure, but you quickly get used to having more and even the pleasure factor reduces the more you acquire.
Education level	Having a Ph.D. won't make you any happier than leaving school without a qualification to your name. Getting the education you want can usually be achieved (one way or another) at any stage of life, if qualifications are important to you.
Having children	Children certainly bring joy, but they also bring stress, worry and pressure. Having children can make life more meaningful and for very many people the joys outweigh the challenges. But it's not a sure-fire factor that contributes positively to happiness.
Being physically attractive	You only have to look at the misery of many of the beautiful people in the celebrity spotlight to understand this one. *Feeling* attractive is much more likely to make you happier.
Age	The research is a little inconclusive here, but on the whole, you're not more likely to be happy at any particular age. Again, the important factor is how you choose to think about your age.
Gender	Overall, neither men nor women have the monopoly on happiness. However, women tend to have steeper peaks and troughs than men, so they can be more blissful but also more depressed at different times than the blokes, who maintain a more even level.
Moving to a sunny climate	You really do take the weather with you! Short-term boosts to happiness tend not to be sustained when you move to a sunnier climate, and if they are, the effect tends to be very small.

How's your happiness trolley looking? Chances are, you already have basic stocks of a lot of happiness ingredients, but perhaps in a few areas the cupboard is a bit bare. Grab yourself a cuppa (that's a mini happiness factor for me!) and try the following activity to identify your areas for improvement:

1. Imagine you're the happiness researcher of your own life. What factors (from the previous tables or unique to you) have consistently contributed significantly to your own happiness? Identify five factors from your past. For example, travelling to different countries may be something that has consistently helped you to feel happy.

2. Think about the present moment. What are the small things you do (whether or not you do them consistently) that give you happiness? Again, think of five examples, like taking a walk or allowing yourself to find time to relax and read a good book.

3. You now have a mix of happiness factors, some of which are to do with life choices and others which are habits or behaviours. Tear a sheet of paper into strips or use sticky notes.

4. Write each positive happiness factor on a piece of paper or a sticky note.

5. Arrange the happiness factors into priority order for you. Which factors feel the most important (whether or not they are currently in your life)? Write the ranking from one to ten, with one being the most important, against each factor.

6. Think about how satisfied you feel about each factor in your life now, in terms of both quality and quantity. Take a different coloured pen and rank your satisfaction level for each. This time, let one be the lowest score and ten the highest.

7. Take a look at your scores and see which of the factors both score under five to identify a factor that is of great importance to you but currently has low satisfaction.

8. Finally, consider what steps you need to take to improve your satisfaction with your happiness factors. Refer to Chapters 9 and 10 for ideas about how to implement your ideas as goals in your life. Remember to take one significant step within 24 hours of completing this activity and preferably choose a step that you can take within an hour. For example, you may have identified that the biggest area of potential improvement for you is in developing your friendships, so your first step might be to phone someone to reconnect.

Making yourself miserable over factors you can't fully control is futile! For example, while 'being married' is more strongly correlated to happiness than cohabiting, remember that the essence of this finding is about feeling a strong sense of commitment and security within a relationship. So for you, living with a long-term partner may be perfect bliss, or you may know that the single life is your idea of heaven. You can also find an equivalent depth of connection in close friendships or other family relationships. Check in with yourself honestly to see how you really feel and refer to Chapter 6 on values to get a sense of what is truly important to you.

All the research shows that taking action over things you *can* control makes you far happier than trying to change other people to meet your own needs.

Discovering Optimism

In all the findings about what makes for a happy life, the most important one seems to be that optimists fare better than pessimists. And that's because positive emotions are better for you than negative ones. You're simply more resourceful, more creative and more resilient when you feel optimistic. You see things differently and that helps you do the things that get better outcomes for you – one of those lovely virtuous circles.

For the pessimists in the corner who are saying that being optimistic all the time just isn't realistic – no one is taking away the value of realism in life. It's even good to have a healthy dose of pessimistic thinking. You don't want to be an airline pilot who calmly assumes all will work out for the best even when every warning light is flashing in the cockpit, nor would you last long as a lawyer if you only saw your client's case through rose-tinted spectacles. Humans are conditioned to look for danger and problems so that we can flee, fight or fix them and that's just fine. But living in a constantly pessimistic state is the surest way to set yourself up for worry, stress, ill-health and misery.

Optimism is determined partly by that genetic set point explained earlier, but you can try out new behaviour in terms of how you think, choose to feel and act, no matter how dour and gloomy you are by nature!

Sweet dreams

Getting enough sleep is absolutely vital to your happiness. Psychologists Joe Griffin and Ivan Tyrrell discovered that interrupted sleep patterns may be associated with depressive states. This is because during sleep your brain processes all the things which, in the previous 12 or so hours, you were unable to act on consciously. It's thought to be the reason why you dream metaphorically, because it's a safe way of acting out things that in real life you'd never

do. If that process is interrupted abruptly – say, by an alarm clock in the depths of a winter morning – Griffin and Tyrrell suggest that the brain's natural processing job can be hindered and this may lead to depression. Waking up more naturally, as we tend to do in the lighter months, allows the process to flow. So if you tend to find your moods are lower in winter, consider investing in a dawn simulator version of a morning alarm.

Taking charge of your mindset

The saying 'It's all in the mind' is true. What you think creates how you feel and what you feel leads to the action you take. If you can begin to notice the flaws in your thinking, you're well on the way to cracking the job of learning optimism.

Pessimists believe that negative events are:

- ✔ **All about me.** Taking things personally.
- ✔ **All encompassing.** Believing that one event will impact badly on many or all other areas of life.
- ✔ **For all time.** Being convinced that the situation will last forever.

Table 17-3 takes a bad event – being made redundant – and shows how the two types of thinking differ.

Table 17-3	Optimistic and Pessimistic Thinking	
	Pessimist	*Optimist*
All about me	'**I'm** being let go from my job.' (Something I did wrong.)	'**My role** is being made redundant.' (It's not a reflection on me.)
All encompassing	'It's going to affect all areas of my life.'	'It's not going to affect all areas of my life; I can contain the negative effects.'
For all time	'I'll never get another job like this/at my age.'	'This is a temporary setback; I'll soon find another good or better opportunity.'

Pessimists take things personally and think that the bad condition is going to affect everything and last forever. But optimists detach themselves from the situation and are able to keep a sense of perspective.

Practising the positive

Is optimistic thinking really as simple as choosing different thoughts? Actually, yes, in most cases it is – if you do it consistently. Here are some ways you can practise positivity in your life on a daily basis:

✔ Listen to how you talk to yourself when bad things happen. If you fall into pessimistic thinking about something, actively choose to rephrase what you're saying to make it impersonal, contained and temporary, as Table 17-3 showed.

✔ Each night before you go to sleep, think of three good things that happened that day, however small, and replay them in your mind like a film.

✔ Focus on good news over bad news. That doesn't mean you have to blind yourself to what's happening in the world, but be aware that most news in the media is problem-centred, and a constant diet of it takes you very far from positivity. Turn off the news on TV and avoid reading newspapers for a week and see how it affects your mood.

✔ Savour your experiences more. Surprisingly, research suggests that *more* of a good thing won't necessarily make you happier. If you can delay gratification a little, you enjoy pleasurable experiences more and feel more positive generally. You get the experience of looking forward to something and you then get to really savour it when it happens.

✔ Play to your strengths. A happy life is one where you're doing the things you do best most of the time. Check out Chapter 4 for more on identifying and coaching yourself to your strengths.

✔ Honour your positive true values daily. A happy life is one where you know what's important to you and do the right thing for you. Skip to Chapter 6 for more on values and ideas for how can you build in simple ways of keeping a focus on your values each day to boost feelings of positivity.

Planning Your Happy Life

A happy life is built from your unique blend of three main things:

✔ **Feeling good.** Having frequent opportunities for pleasurable activities and positive emotions.

✔ **Doing good.** Playing to your strengths and living a life in tune with your deepest values.

✔ **Creating good.** Making a contribution to the world and leaving a legacy, whatever that means for you (Chapter 24 has more about creating a legacy).

Time to draw up your Happy Life Plan:

1. Write 'Feeling good', 'Doing good' and 'Creating good' on separate sheets of paper.

2. Spend 15 minutes capturing all the things under each heading that you currently do that help you feel happy. What makes you feel good? What activities play to your strengths and feed your values? What makes you feel that you're making a difference?

3. Notice the overlaps. Are there activities in your life that do all three? Create a goal to build in even more of these. These activities are likely to be the ones that help you achieve a flow state.

4. Notice the gaps. Is one list sparser that the others? Is that a challenge for you? Would you like to have more experience of *making a difference*, for example, and if so, what would fill that gap? (Don't worry if one list is shorter than the others. Remember the key question to ask yourself is, *Is that okay for me?*)

Making time to be happy

You only ever have this present moment to be happy. All your memories and all the things you can imagine doing are all created in a single moment of time – right now. Now is the only time to be happy, and the more you can bring your attention back to that, the happier you're likely to be. Here are some suggestions for making time to be happy:

✔ **Set your alarm.** I'm not being flippant here. Whole days can drift by without you being consciously aware of what you're doing and whether or not it makes you happy. So set your alarm two or three times a day and ask yourself the question, *Is what I am doing right now helping me to be happy?* If the answer is no, you have three alternatives:

   • Change your activity.

   • Change the way in which you do it, to make it feel more enjoyable.

   • Change your perspective so that you connect with the happiness that will result when it is complete.

Any or all options will do. If an activity isn't giving you pleasure, it may be helping to grow your strength and develop your values, or it may be something that helps you contribute in your world. Just realising that can increase your sense of happiness. And if it isn't any of these – well, you know which option to choose!

✔ **Join the Fun Police.** You may need to bully yourself and others into making time for happiness. Agree with a trusted friend or co-coach some simple happiness promises and arrange times to check up on each other.

✔ **Take a few moments in the day to be still.** Find a little space, a breath even, between activities and you'll find that your experience of the day will be happier. Being still allows you to tune into the present moment and connect with what is important to you. Chapter 17 helps you stay present.

Keeping faith and focus on happiness

As I finish writing this chapter I am deeply sad due to the sudden loss of a dear relative who has left us all far too soon. At times, life offers us events and challenges that seem to take us further away from our connection with happiness.

Yet if you go within, as I am doing now, and tune into the wisest part of yourself, you'll know that happiness is always there for you, even amidst feelings of pain and sadness.

I am happy for the experience of having known my loved one. I am happy for all the many gifts of inspiration that she gave me. I am happy knowing that she is here right now in my heart, helping me to write these words and to live my life.

In the toughest of times you can truly learn what happiness is and how to reach for it in a way that gives you joy.

> 'There is no way to happiness. Happiness is the way.'
>
> *Buddha*

Happy resources

The following websites can help you to explore the state of happiness as you coach yourself to define your own happy vision.

✔ **www.happiness-project.com** Author Gretchen Rubin spent a year test-driving every happiness principle, tip, theory and scientific study she could find, encompassing ancient and modern wisdom. This blog is a treasure trove of her reflections and contains countless practical tips for making happiness a daily project in your life.

✔ **www.happiness.co.uk** Created by an array of psychologists, life coaches, business leaders, spiritual ministers, doctors, artists and writers, this website offers happiness techniques and inspiration galore to help you lead your happiest life.

✔ **www.findhappiness.org** For a Buddhist perspective on how to achieve inner peace and happiness through meditation, check out this website, which has easy-to-follow advice on building meditation into your life.

✔ **www.authentichappiness.com** The website for happiness guru Martin Seligman, where you'll find lots of free tests that help you assess your level of optimism and identify your strengths for a happier and more fulfilled life.

✔ **www.reachforhappiness.com** The second of my websites, where you're inspired to build lasting habits of happiness.

Chapter 18

Defining True Success

. . . .

In This Chapter

▶ Building on your strengths

▶ Modelling success

▶ Changing your thinking

. . . .

> *What you get by reaching your destination is not nearly so important as what you will become.*
>
> — Zig Ziglar

*E*verything in your life changes and evolves, including and especially *you*. Nothing stays still, and even if you locked yourself away in a dark room for several years and did nothing at all, you'd emerge completely different.

The natural instinct is to strive to become more successful – in your career, your relationships and in all aspects of your life. No one sets out to become *less* successful after all. And yet all too often the drive for success turns out to be a little shallow and empty.

If you coach yourself to a definition of success that is truly meaningful for you, then you find that success and happiness march hand in hand down the road of your life. If happiness is mostly an inside job (Chapter 17 is all about happiness), being and feeling successful is a way to allow your gifts to shine to the world. A perfect partnership!

Knowing Your Value in the World

A lot of great inspiration and motivation is attached to the philosophy of success, but some messages seem to encourage you to be better than others, aim for number one and go to the top of the pile. But you'll always judge some people as being 'better' than you.

Comparing yourself to others is a sure-fire way to unhappiness. When you do that, you're likely to underestimate your achievements and focus instead on what you lack. And you get what you focus on!

Defining true success starts with knowing that you already have huge value in the world. You're starting from where you are right now and becoming more of who you are. No one can ever be a better version of you than YOU.

Create your success treasure trove! You need a box large enough to contain images, photos and objects that represent success for you. Take an afternoon out to sort through photo albums and other memorabilia and select items that are associated with real value in terms of success for you in your life. Maybe you have a photo of yourself winning a competition, or a CD containing a song that reminds you of a summer you spent working towards a good outcome in an exam. Perhaps you have a pebble from a beach where you had a fantastic holiday, paid for out of a promotion or pay rise. Or a memento of a great friendship you forged or romantic relationship you created and enjoyed. Aim to get lots of tangible reminders of how you've created value for yourself in your life so far.

Whenever you feel a little blue, open up your success treasure trove and know that what you have already created is just the start.

Adopting the personal qualities of success

Your success treasure trove is your evidence that you know how to be a success in different areas of your life. But how do you *be* successful on a consistent basis?

Successful outcomes are generated from regularly adopting the personal qualities or behaviours that get good results. While you do this best according to your natural preferences, the way to enhance your success is to deepen your strengths and to develop your less strong areas so that you become more consistent and balanced overall.

In Chapter 4, I explain the four styles that make up your behavioural preferences, using the metaphor of nature (go to Chapter 4 to take the simple quiz to see how your preferences combine):

✔ **Mountain style:** You focus on tasks in an outgoing (extroverted) way. This aspect of yourself is all about getting practical results.

✔ **Sun style:** You're people-oriented and outgoing. Sun style focuses on enthusiasm, spontaneity and inspiration.

✔ **Sky style:** If you're strong in this preference, you favour task completion in a more reflective (introverted) way. You like to plan, attend to the detail and ensure quality.

⮞ **Ocean style:** Here, the focus is on people in a more reflective (introverted) way. This preference is all about team working, patience and support.

Remember that you combine all of these aspects, although some are stronger for you than others.

Here are 12 personal qualities that combine beautifully in your most successful self, together with some definitions of how they might operate for you:

Mountain success qualities:

- **Courage:** The way in which you face your fears and embrace issues that arise as you reach for your goals.

- **Confidence:** Feeling sure in yourself so that you can say yes to opportunities that arise, even when they take you beyond your comfort zone.

- **Perseverance:** Having the tenacity to follow through on tasks and projects and knowing that small rejections along the way are part of a learning process.

Sun success qualities:

- **Positivity:** Maintaining an optimistic approach at all times, both within yourself and as you relate to others.

- **Passion:** Being really connected to a goal and enthusiastically working towards it.

- **Faith:** Having a strong and certain belief in yourself and your capabilities.

Sky success qualities:

- **Focus:** Keeping your sight on what is important – your goal, intention and the big picture.

- **Integrity:** Being honest and authentic in all that you do.

- **Attention:** Letting go of unhelpful distractions so that you can tune into each task along the way.

Ocean success qualities:

- **Calmness:** Being grounded and centred as you move towards your goals.

- **Patience:** Knowing that getting results takes time and that each small success builds on the next to move you closer to your dreams.

- **Compassion:** Taking account of others as you progress, and especially showing compassion and forgiveness to yourself when things don't turn out the way you anticipated.

The other personal quality that enhances your chances of achieving success is *consistency*; understanding that little and often of the same good actions are better than occasional erratic bursts of activity. Think of digging a garden over – if you do ten minutes each day you achieve more than if you save it all up to the weekend, only to find the prospect of more than an hour's work too daunting. You can apply consistency to all the qualities above.

As you contemplate this list, some of these traits may feel quite natural to you, while others are frankly alien. Remember that no human being on the planet has all of these 12 qualities in abundance all the time! Think of this list as a guide to your successful self. Even quite small shifts in a positive direction in each area can make for dramatic changes in the great results that you get. And because these are qualities of *being*, you feel more successful too.

For this activity, choose a goal or intention that you're working towards, or would like to work towards. Consider each quality in turn and in the second column in Table 18-1 (Where am I now?) rate yourself out of ten, with ten being the highest score. In the third column, set yourself a numerical target of where you want to be, out of a maximum possible ten. Remember the objective of developing your personal success qualities isn't to set yourself impossible targets, so think realistically about the gap between where you are now and where you want to be. The difference between the two columns is probably no more than two or three steps at this stage.

Table 18-1	Adopting the Personal Qualities of Success	
Success Trait	*Where Am I Now?*	*Where Do I Want to Be?*
Courage		
Confidence		
Perseverance		
Positivity		
Passion		
Faith		
Focus		
Integrity		
Attention		
Calmness		
Patience		
Compassion		
Consistency		

Now that you have an honest self-assessment of your current success qualities and have made a commitment to moving that forward a few points, it's time to make that commitment more tangible:

1. For each of the qualities, write in your journal one example of a behaviour or action that you already exhibit in relation to that goal. Say your goal is to organise a summer fair for a local charity. Under the quality of Courage, you may identify that you volunteered for it in the first place even though it's something you've never done before, and you've always been a little bit intimidated by the previous organiser.

   When you've done that (and no matter how low some of the original scores look to you!), give yourself a metaphorical pat on the back. You have a starting point.

2. Now consider what one thing you'd be doing if you were at your absolute best in terms of this quality; if you were at a perfect ten. Perhaps you decide that your success quality of courage would be boosted by inviting a celebrity name to open the fair. It would be really facing your fears and translating them to excitement if you could identify and directly approach someone well known to contribute to the success of the fair.

3. Look at the realistic target you set yourself in the third column. Taking into account where you are now and the difference between your perfect ten for each quality, what action or behaviour feels right? Perhaps your perfect ten score of hunting down and signing up Madonna feels a bit too much of a reach, but you can adjust the action by fixing on a more local celebrity, or by getting the former organiser of the fair (the one who's just a tiny bit scary) to help you network.

Defining your success is about knowing how far you need to stretch each of these qualities – building the muscles of success – not setting yourself impossible targets all at once.

Set yourself timescales on making your changes – you can hop to Chapter 10 to refresh your ideas on planning effective action.

Modelling excellence

You can draw on help from others to boost your character traits of success. Looking at Table 18-1 again, identify a trait that has a fairly low score for you; perhaps Perseverance. You've honestly assessed your own qualities and feel that the main thing that's stopping you from being more successful is a tendency to give up a little too quickly at times, or in certain situations. But you have a colleague whose motto seems to be 'Never give up!' What an inspiration!

Giving success its proper name

Lucy seemed to struggle with the idea of success, although she had experienced lots of great results in her life such as the many promotions she'd gained over the years as a result of successfully managed work projects. Still, she found that whenever she thought about what it meant to be successful, she got bogged down with ideas of striving, being competitive and making sacrifices. Looking back, quite a lot of her tangible successes had been created in just that way, and while she had accepted the pain with the pleasure over the years, she'd really had enough of the downsides; so much so that she was holding back on going for a much desired promotion at work.

As Lucy started working with her values during coaching, she noticed that her main success value – Achievement – was a lot lower down the priority list than it had ever been. (You can identify and prioritise your values in Chapter 6.) Looking at it now, it even seemed a bit detached from her, as if it was something she *did* rather than an aspect of herself. During coaching, she played around with other names for that value, which felt more comfortable, and finally arrived at Accomplishment. When she thought about a particular goal in the context of Accomplishment rather than Achievement, she could feel the enjoyment and thrill. She had no sense of striving, competitiveness or sacrifice associated with the newly named success value, although the tangible results were the same.

In fact, overall Lucy got much better results simply by *being* accomplished rather than *doing* achievement, Lucy's experience of going for and winning her promotion made for a much happier experience of success.

Modelling excellence is about finding a trait that someone else excels at, observing how she does it and then connecting that to what is naturally within you until it feels authentically yours.

You can ask your persevering friend or colleague directly about how she cultivates that trait, and you'll probably get some good answers. However, some of the 'how' may be so instinctive that she can't honestly pinpoint the steps. So it's up to you to play detective and observe what she does.

1. Ask your friend or colleague for permission to observe her when she's engaged in an activity that requires perseverance (or whichever trait you want to model). If that's not possible, ask her to recall a specific time when she really needed to persevere.

2. When you're observing, position yourself where you can watch and take notes discreetly. Perhaps your colleague is making follow-up phone calls to clients to book appointments following an e-shot.

3. Observe your colleague's body language as she makes the calls. Is she upright or slouched? What is her expression? What pace and tone of voice does she use? How quickly does she move on to the next call?

Do any little rituals take place between calls, or does she change body position? Simply note down everything you see for now.

4. After you've been observing for a while and when she's finished, ask your colleague to talk you through what she's experienced. Identify the moments when she drew on the success trait you're modelling.

5. When you've identified a good example of one of these moments, ask more detailed questions. Perhaps your colleague had made ten calls without success and you noticed a slight change in her body language that meant discouragement. Ask your colleague what she experienced. Was it a feeling, a thought or an image? How did she then move past that? Did she say something to herself, create a different image or change the feeling? You're drawing out a strategy here, and it really pays to keep asking the question *what happened next?* so that you can get the detailed steps down.

6. When you have a full strategy, try it on for size yourself, adapting it to make it your own. For example, your colleague's full strategy might be something like this:

'I always sit upright in my chair before making calls and I take a few deep breaths to settle me and get calm and relaxed. I imagine the clients who are waiting to hear from me and I picture them looking forward to speaking to me. I make sure that I move quickly on to the next call whatever the results and that keeps me feeling energised. As I do this, I occasionally say to myself 'It's a marathon, not a sprint.' And when I reach a point where I feel discouraged because I haven't yet had a positive result, I stand up for a moment, stretch and recall all the times when I've had good results – I kind of see them all playing out like a series of images. That gives me a feeling of confidence and I say to myself 'Keep going, the next opportunity is waiting for you.'

When you try this strategy, it may work differently for you, so tweak it until it works. For example, your images of successful outcomes may be more like a movie than a series of images. Or your self-talk may be slightly different.

You can apply this modelling to any of the personal success qualities, and indeed any behaviour that you want to adopt as your own.

Getting the Results You Want

As you work at developing your success qualities, you're experimenting with applying them to a whole range of goals and outcomes in your life to get certain results. However, you don't have a crystal ball, so your expectation of success may differ quite a bit from the reality. So get clear on what your big picture is for success, and then begin to focus your energies on the goals that really make you feel successful.

Developing your inner success compass

Think for a moment about what success really means to you. You may choose to reflect quietly, write in your journal, paint, draw or find some other way of representing your definitions. Choose whichever means of expression is the most natural and compelling as you consider the following questions:

- What does true success mean to you in your life? Is it achieving material goals, enjoying the moment, building wonderful relationships? What will your life look like when you've achieved your vision of success?

- What has to happen for you to be and feel successful? How will you know when you're successful? Perhaps you realise that you need the assurance of others to feel successful? The more your success depends on other people's approval, the trickier success is to achieve and maintain.

- What are the consequences to you and your loved ones of holding this meaning of success? You may feel that your success must come at a price – a coveted promotion versus less time with loved ones, for example. Think about how your definition of success fits into the rest of your life. What tensions may be created by holding values that are at odds with each other?

After you identify your answers to these questions, summarise your vision in a single statement:

Success for me means _____. I measure my success by _____.

Here's an example:

Success for me is setting and achieving personal goals that stretch me, both at home and work. I measure my success by asking for feedback and by recognising the inner satisfaction I get for a job well done.

Thinking Yourself to Success

Your inner critic wants to keep you safe and that doesn't involve letting you leap off the cliff into the adventure of a new success goal. How often have you talked yourself out of your own success? Everything that's created in reality is first created in your thoughts and your imagination, so it stands to reason that holding yourself back from success happens that way too.

Celebrating the private victories

Joe was at a pretty low point when he first came to coaching. He had recently lost his job and his finances were in a mess. He had never felt so unsuccessful in his life and admitted in the first session that he had lost so much of his get up and go that he was finding it really hard to stay positive about getting a job.

As Joe explored his various options, he came to see that his *thoughts* about his situation were causing the majority of the problems. He began to understand that he was getting himself in a negative loop. Joe had always relied on external feedback to judge himself and his achievements, and so he felt at a complete loss as to how to move himself from where he was. After all, not much was going on in his external world that allowed him to feel good.

After a little while, Joe began to accept that the only opinion that really counted was the one he held of himself. If he could begin to focus his evaluation of his success on his private victories, then he could begin to break the negative loop. At first he found this difficult and continued to underestimate every little achievement – such as doing a job application – because no external signs told him he was making real progress.

Joe's breakthrough came when he began looking at certain examples of success and failure in his past and realised that other people's opinions had rarely been consistent. Some things he'd considered to be okay were considered by others to be magnificent, and examples where he thought he'd set the world alight had sometimes gone almost unnoticed. He now saw that judging himself by what he thought others might think held no real certainty, but the one thing he could be certain about was his own standards.

He adopted a daily strategy of celebrating the personal stuff and began making detailed lists of everything he did that he was proud of. At first the lists contained very small things – like getting up an hour early to take a brisk walk – and his inner critic really tried to make fun of him. But he persevered. He'd think to himself, *for where I am right now, that's a success*. As his self-esteem improved, his inner success compass began to point him in the right direction and within a few short months he was in a new job he loved.

Observing your thoughts

Your thoughts create your reality, because they generate the emotions that help you stay happy and resourceful – or the opposite! (Check out Chapter 17 for more on working with your emotions.) The key to your success lies in thinking the thoughts that lead you to success.

Try this activity to become aware of your thoughts.

1. Find a quiet spot where you can sit undisturbed for ten minutes. Sit comfortably and close your eyes.

2. Focus on your breathing. Take five or six deep breaths, concentrating on the inhalation, holding for a second and then focusing on the exhalation, holding again for a moment.

3. Continue to focus on your breathing. Notice as thoughts come into your mind and just let them drift away.

4. After ten minutes, open your eyes and make a note of the most common thoughts that came up for you.

What did you discover from this activity? Chances are, most of your thoughts were practical to-do list kind of stuff, or worry-wart issues. Of course, you may have had some very pleasant thoughts too, but overall, most people find that the former predominate.

Now consider – are these thoughts leading you towards or away from success? Some of your thoughts may well be quite productive – but did you notice how quickly they seemed to be associated with the worry-wart thoughts and feelings?

Consider your definition of success. What thoughts would you have if you were moving towards this? Perhaps they'd be something like *'Setting and achieving stretching personal goals helps me feel and be successful. I enjoy getting feedback to help me develop my success. I hold realistic standards for myself for a job well done and know that the inner satisfaction I gain helps me build even more success into my life.'*

Having identified these new, more positive thoughts that are linked to your personal vision, you can repeat the exercise. If a less helpful thought comes to mind, let it go and replace it with your resourceful thought.

You can practise this exercise often, and as you increase your awareness of what you're thinking, consciously choose to observe and then change the nature of your thoughts frequently during the day to those which create your vision of success.

Creating positive outcomes

Build the habit of creating positive outcomes by starting with small daily successes. You can practise with something very simple, like finding a perfect parking spot or a supermarket checkout with no queues on a busy Saturday. Simply visualise the outcome that you want – really see the space where your car will drive into and the empty checkout, and feel as you would when that becomes a reality.

You don't have to believe in magic for this activity to have a powerful impact on your life. As you try it more and more, you may be astonished at how often things turn out exactly as you imagined. In doing this, you're training your mind to focus on a positive expectation and belief. Maybe what you want doesn't always happen. That's fine too, and you can begin to take the view that maybe there's a reason for that, one that you don't yet know, such as teaching you patience and perseverance!

As you connect more and more with creating your own daily successes, you'll begin to see that success, like happiness, really is an inside job!

Chapter 19

Tackling Common Blocks

In This Chapter

▶ Overcoming procrastination

▶ Combating conflicts within yourself

▶ Banishing self-doubt

*Y*ou're unique, so any blocks you have to your progress are individual to you. That said, you're likely to come up against three key blocks that can threaten your progress more than you'd like.

Perhaps you think you've got it all sorted with a plan, project, goal or intention, yet you can't seem to get started or you keep delaying completion. Or perhaps you feel conflicted about a choice or decision and want seemingly opposite things? Or perhaps your level of confidence keeps you feeling glued to the status quo?

If procrastination, conflict or lack of confidence feels familiar, this is the chapter for you, and you can tackle these very common blocks in the following pages.

Kicking Procrastination into Touch

Procrastination has been called 'the thief of time', and it can certainly feel that way. You put off doing something to the point where you finally have no choice and end up burning the midnight oil to do what you need to. The effort expended can leave you feeling time-poor long after you've done what needs to be done, and the cycle starts again.

Here are some statements you may say to yourself when you're justifying (or at least trying to understand) your procrastination:

✔ 'I'm a perfectionist, that's why things take longer for me to complete.'

✔ 'It isn't fair that I have to do this.'

✔ 'I'm not really able to do this thing well.'

✔ 'I don't want to do this.'

✔ 'This is too hard.'

✔ 'I haven't got enough time.'

✔ 'I don't have the knowledge.'

✔ 'I don't want to fail.'

✔ 'I don't want to look stupid.'

Do any of these statements resonate with you? Make a note of those that do and prepare to eliminate these excuses with some probing coaching!

Getting to the root of why you procrastinate

Quite often when you have a habit like procrastination you're not being entirely truthful with yourself about why. Don't worry, that doesn't make you a bad person! Procrastination so often masks fear – of success, failure, embarrassment or rejection – and dealing with fear is a challenge. It can be easier to accept the first thing that seems sensible as a reason – that you're just not that organised, or you don't particularly enjoy a certain task – rather than admit that you're really engaging in self-sabotage and holding yourself back out of fear.

But becoming self-aware about the patterns you run is liberating. After you understand the *why* of it all, you have a choice. You can carry on procrastinating, with all the damage it does, or you can take simple steps to change.

Here's an activity to help you get to the root of your procrastination. You need some quiet time and a big sheet of paper and a pen.

1. Place both paper and pen in front of you as you sit back and relax for five minutes. Close your eyes and focus on your breathing to clear your mind.

2. Bring to mind the current thing in your life or work that you're procrastinating over. Perhaps you're holding back on writing the content for a new business website. Allow yourself to experience it in whatever unpleasantness it currently holds for you. Notice any feelings in your body, and images and self talk in your mind.

3. Ask yourself the question *What is my fear?* Start to write whatever comes up – single words or short phrases only. Perhaps initially things might come up like *I might fail in getting my message across, people might criticise my style, I haven't really got enough expertise to demonstrate.* Keep

asking yourself the question over and over as quickly as you can. You might find some strange things come out and that's okay. Gradually you may find that some deeper fears pop up – maybe you don't feel you deserve to have success in business so putting off the website development prevents you from failing. Your unconscious is helping you to get to the root of it all.

4. When you feel you've come to an end, ask yourself the question *What else?* until you really feel you've exhausted all possibilities.

5. You now have a number of possible fears behind your procrastination. Take a good look at the list and ask yourself which statements feel strongest. If you have, say, ten statements, number them one to ten with number one being the biggie.

6. Starting with number ten, carefully consider the statement and ask yourself *Is that true?* On a separate sheet make a list of all the reasons and evidence why it is true and alongside each one, why it isn't. As you complete this, ask yourself *What do I want to believe about myself?*

7. Cross out all the negative statements. Now focus on the positive statements. You can add new ones as you recall more and more evidence to support what you want to believe about yourself. Remember to make these positive, personal and present focused, for example, *I am hard-working, I am succeeding.* You know that these are true because you have the evidence and you're choosing to focus on these aspects of yourself.

8. By the time you get to the number one fear on your list, you'll already have lots of positive statements about yourself and your ability to tackle your fears. Repeat all the positive statements to yourself out loud before going through the same process with fear number one.

9. Finally, sit quietly for five minutes and visualise yourself completing the task in hand, armed with all of the positive energy that your resourceful statements have given you.

This activity can really help you face the fears behind your procrastination. Take a check on how you're feeling as you complete this exercise. Did it throw up some things that are a bit scary?

Self-coaching is a great way of moving yourself forward, but at times you may benefit from getting someone else's help on the topic. This is appropriate if you found it really hard to come up with positive evidence and found that you continued to beat yourself up for procrastinating. You can repeat the exercise in getting to the root of procrastination with a friend who may be able to see your positive qualities more clearly than you. And if your fears are still looming, especially if you come back to feeling things like '*I don't deserve this*', get in touch with a professional coach or counsellor who can support you further.

Maintaining momentum

The previous sections helped you get a better understanding of why you procrastinate and enabled you to create some strong positive statements. Here are some simple things you can do to gain momentum for achieving your goal. Choose the pointers that fit your natural style best, but also play with some that you haven't tried before to see if they do the trick:

- ✔ If achieving your goal seems daunting, make the tasks look small and easy to accomplish in your mind and remind yourself of times you've accomplished even bigger tasks.

- ✔ Promise yourself to just make a start and that you only need to do something for five minutes and then you can choose to stop.

- ✔ Tell someone you respect that you're going to do part of your task at a certain time to give yourself a little bit of extra accountability.

- ✔ Get the help of a friend to work with you on the sticking point.

- ✔ Look at your environment – can you make small, quick changes to get you in the mood for overcoming procrastination?

- ✔ Can you delegate a part of the task to someone and still make that part of your journey?

- ✔ If time is an issue for you, what can you lose from your schedule to free up even a small amount of time to get started on your goals? Question all your assumptions about how important it is that you do *everything* yourself.

- ✔ Do the easy bits first and gather momentum from small successes.

Sorting out wishing from wanting

You might have identified that your tendency to procrastinate is about perfectionism and are now working with accepting that sometimes 'good enough' *is* quite good enough. Or perhaps you uncovered a fear of failure (check out Chapter 18 on defining success if that's the case). But what if you still procrastinate? It could be that you simply don't *want* to do the thing that you think you should be doing, so maybe it's time to get honest with yourself.

Some subconscious self-sabotage works this way – if you put something off then maybe you'll end up rushing and doing a bad enough job that you won't have to do it ever again. A clue is in how you talk to yourself about the task in hand. If you say a lot of 'shoulds' and 'musts' to yourself, then you're not really taking instruction from your best and truest self but from some other set of rules – other people's perhaps, or even your own idea of how you wish you were.

Climbing the ladder to tackle procrastination

Martin, a coaching client, had worked on his habit of procrastinating for some time and had made a lot of progress. He said that unpacking the reasons for him choosing to procrastinate felt very much like climbing a ladder.

Martin first identified that his habit of putting certain work tasks off until the last minute was a strategy that got his adrenalin going so that he turned out his best work. As that didn't always get the right result because too many other things suffered – such as his relationship with his frustrated and long-suffering colleagues – he decided to find other ways of keeping his motivation high to pace himself better. Looking back, he described his promise to find alternative motivators as 'the first rung of the ladder' and agreed that for a while it worked really well. But Martin still procrastinated in certain areas, and he felt that he hadn't really got to the bottom of why.

During coaching, Martin discovered that he held a strong belief that if he left things to the last minute and then failed to deliver, he could always say that he hadn't given himself enough time, so could not beat himself up for not being good enough. This realisation was 'the second rung' for Martin, and he then worked hard on improving his self-esteem so that he had no need to procrastinate.

But a third rung arose for Martin. Despite tactics to maintain his motivation and raise his self-esteem, he also found that he put off some things, like the monthly sales budget, because he wasn't fully engaged in their outcome. Martin started to examine the reasons for this and found that he wanted to change the focus of his career to recapture the sense of energy and drive he used to have. He went after a different role in his company, which was closer to his true passions.

By working through all the levels of this apparently simple behaviour issue, Martin was able to fine-tune a solution. Getting to the third rung of his ladder without climbing the other two would have been impossible, and the ultimate solution was the better fit for him because of the work he had put into getting there.

How you deal with this depends a lot on what the plan, project, goal or intention is, of course. Avoiding everything that doesn't immediately please you isn't all that realistic and many routine or challenging tasks can become really enjoyable if you can break everyday procrastination. When the procrastination-busting strategies in this chapter don't work, and you're just forcing yourself to get through something, you have to question your intentions.

Identifying your intentions can help you let go of unrealistic expectations. When you *wish* for something, it's a little idealistic. You might imagine yourself doing something but it feels a bit distant or disconnected from you, and the immediate first steps aren't very clear. When you *want* something, the image is clear and bright; you feel really part of it and you want to take action towards it.

You *can* move from wishing to wanting. A way to do that is to step into the wish you have for yourself. Imagine vividly all the things you want to do. Make the pictures and images big and bold with vibrant colour and light. Feel excited about your actions and notice how your motivation changes.

If you're still left with the habit of procrastination, ask yourself again, *Do I really want to do this?* and face the consequences of your decision. If your decision means that you feel you're letting others down, you can coach yourself to understand where the 'shoulds' are in sticking with your goal. Better to be open with people and admit you don't want to follow through with something, mitigate any resulting problems and let go, than to force yourself down a route where your heart isn't engaged.

Clearing Up Confusion

Do you sometimes feel that you want opposite things? You want chocolate cake *and* you want to be slim and healthy. You want adventure and surprises in your life *and* you want the contentment that comes from a stable lifestyle. Your personality is made up of all different elements, so a certain amount of conflict is perfectly normal. However, this can cause you to veer from one extreme course of action to another, or it can keep you stuck, unable to make a decision.

Knowing why you feel conflicted

In the case of the chocolate cake dilemma, the answer may be in deciding whether your need for momentary pleasure is greater than feeling a bit unhealthy.

More serious conflicts within you aren't always so clear cut. You may feel that both adventure and contentment are strong positive values for you. Chapter 6 can help you prioritise which value is more to the fore for you. Quite often, simply knowing the priority of a value helps you move forward – even if it is only to fulfil the secondary value in a different way until you are better able to bring it into full play. For example, you might choose adventure holiday breaks to meet the need and provide a little spice in the comfortable routine of your life.

If conflict remains, dig a bit deeper. All your different experiences of life result in strong emotional reactions, but these can operate largely unconsciously. For example, if you were bottom of the class in a test at school and felt very humiliated, the part of you that still feels that pain may want to prevent you from going for a tough job interview in case you fail, even though you also feel excited about the interview. You may think you've dealt with that childhood stuff, or perhaps you suppressed the memory. If you go for an interview, the part of you that is fearful of failure may unconsciously create an illness or subtly leave you open to running so late that you hit traffic.

Although confusion, conflict and feeling stuck don't get great outcomes, in fact a positive intention for yourself is behind everything you do. The trick is to bring your conflicting parts into harmony rather than denying or rejecting any of them.

Finding common ground for forward motion

If you go deep enough, you find that what each seemingly conflicted part of you really wants is often exactly the same in some very important respects. The part that failed the test wants success and so does the part that gets excited about the interview. This activity helps you stay focused on the positive intention that each part has for you.

Ideally, find a friend or partner who can guide you through this activity and keep notes for you. This enables you to really focus on the answers that are true for you without getting distracted by recording your own responses. Your unconscious is more likely to come out to play and you're less likely to over-analyse the responses as they come through.

Find a quiet place where you won't be disturbed and keep your eyes closed as you work through the activity.

1. Visualise an empty stage in front of you, well lit and uncluttered.

2. Think of two parts that are in conflict, such as the part that's frightened of failing tests and the part that's excited about going for job interviews.

3. Give a name to each of those parts. Go with your first instinct. Choose simple names like 'Fearful' and 'Excited'. Perhaps the names you choose aren't that logical, and that's okay too.

4. Invite Fearful and Excited on to the stage to stand side by side, facing you.

5. Acknowledge that these parts are an aspect of you. Look closely at each of them and imagine them as separate personalities. Take a few moments to really step into their world and see, hear and feel what they might experience.

6. Ask each part *What do you want for me?* Keep asking the question until you find that each part is giving very similar or even the same responses. The answers need to be positive so ask again if a negative comes up. Here's an example of how the responses might look as you work through:

Fearful	*Excited*
I want you to be safe	I want you to show your best side
I want you to do well	I want you to be successful
I want you to play to your strengths	I want you to have fun and be happy
I want you to be happy	I want you to reach your potential

7. Now that you've identified quite a lot of common ground, invite each part to tell the other what it has to offer to help it achieve the common positive intentions. For example, Fearful might say *I can help you make sure that you know exactly how your strengths are suited to this job so that you feel prepared and safe.* And Excited might say *I can help you inject some fun into preparing for the interview so that you feel happier.*

8. Watch as Fearful and Excited face each other. They walk slowly together and merge, becoming the new you that is fully integrated.

Transforming Self-doubt into Self-esteem

A happy and successful life is one where you're able to connect with feeling confident and content within yourself. If you have a foundation of inner confidence, you trust yourself and can handle any worries and anxieties that come up. When you doubt yourself, moving forward is hard.

Accepting yourself as you are

The saying goes that the opposite of a great truth is also true. So while coaching yourself to greater success, glorious goals and amazing achievements is often a rewarding and joyful part of your experience of life, so is leaving well alone and knowing that everything about you is already just as it should be. No matter how much you grow and develop, aspects of yourself may always feel like they lag behind a little, because your expectations of yourself might be at a higher level than before. You aren't going to arrive at a point where you're an enlightened, all-knowing, benevolent being for the rest of your time on earth. In fact, your very human qualities – the mistakes you make and the many missteps you may take – contribute to a full and rich life.

You can't appreciate light without having experienced darkness. The world is made up of opposites that allow you to experience these differences. So it is with you – you have many positive qualities that you display regularly, and you also have a shadow side. Perhaps sometimes you're lazy, or petty or you lose your temper, and that makes you feel bad about yourself. Actually, these things aren't *you*, but aspects of how you sometimes behave.

All behaviour is a choice. What do you focus on when you make a poor choice? Do you make it personal by describing yourself as lazy, petty or aggressive? When you make a mistake, do you castigate yourself for not being smart enough? All of this kind of self-talk intensifies your feelings of self-doubt. Imagine you were saying these things to a small child – how would that child feel, and what would it do to his confidence?

So imagine that your inner confidence is that small child. He needs nurturing, right? In just the same way as you nurture a baby as he grows into a toddler, or as you might care for a kitten or a puppy, your self-confidence grows the more you talk kindly to yourself.

Consider the quality of compassion. You're probably very compassionate to your friends when they've made an apparent mess of things. You can always see something to praise and encourage. Well, you can also apply that compassion to yourself. At any point in time you're always doing the best you can.

Here's an activity to help you connect with self-compassion. Find a quiet spot where you have about 12 feet of clear floor. Choose a room with a window, preferably one that opens out onto a view that pleases you in some way. You're going to take a walk back into your past to find your compassionate self!

1. Stand about three feet away from, and facing, the window in the room. This represents the present moment for you. The space ahead of you is the future.

2. Take a few moments to come fully into your body. Bring your attention to the crown of your head and then gradually move down your body – face, neck, shoulders, arms, chest, legs, feet and finally toes. Appreciate your body as you do this, remembering all the great things it does to support you.

3. Now ask yourself the question *When have I felt compassion for myself or others?* Start walking slowly back as if you're walking back through your life and stop as you recall an event. (Make sure the space behind you is clear so you don't bump into things!) As you find an experience, relive it, reminding yourself of the thoughts, feelings and images that were associated with it. Where do you feel that compassion in your body?

4. Keep walking back until you have at least two or three examples. Notice which of these feels strongest for you. It doesn't matter whether the feeling is for yourself or another person or situation. Whichever experience is the strongest, walk back to that point and connect again with it. Intensify and amplify the feeling, imagining yourself seeing everything that happened. When the feeling is at its most intense, walk slowly forward to the point that represents now, imagining as you do that you're walking that quality of compassion into the present moment.

5. Give yourself permission to carry this feeling of compassion into your future. Still connecting with the feeling, walk slowly forward until you're standing close to the window. Look out of the window and see an imaginary future ahead of you. See yourself taking the best actions you can and kindly accepting whatever results you get.

6. A great test of whether this activity is working for you is how you feel as you bring your conscious attention back to the room. Whatever is happening just outside the window, notice how your connection with compassion softens it.

Knowing that you're worth it

If self-doubt plagues you from time to time, you might well tend to put other people's needs ahead of your own. Serving others can help you feel good about yourself, and if it's balanced with serving your own needs that's perfectly fine. But constantly putting others' needs before you own can increase your feelings of self-doubt.

Try these simple tips to build your sense of self-esteem on a regular basis:

✔ Give yourself five minutes each morning before you get out of bed to appreciate and feel grateful for your body. Even if you feel some aches and pains or have an illness of a more serious nature, find positives to focus on to build a sense of value.

✔ As you go about your day, look for opportunities to catch yourself doing something well and take the time to congratulate yourself. Ask yourself how you can do more of this and enjoy that feeling of well-being more frequently.

✔ If you take a false step, ask yourself what you can learn from it. Imagine looking back on the event from a future date and seeing it as less significant, or even as the moment when you made an important breakthrough.

✔ Accept compliments from others. Don't fall into the trap of devaluing the gift that has just been given to you. Smile and say thank you.

✔ Create positive affirmations for yourself to say frequently. Choose areas that you know are more of a challenge for you. If you rarely make time for your own relaxation, try something simple like _I deserve to rest and relax._ You may want to stick these affirmations to a bathroom or bedroom mirror, knowing that as you look in the mirror at your wonderful self, you're giving yourself gentle instruction to be kind, compassionate and loving to the person whose regard is most important to your happiness and success – you!

Flush the doubt away!

Julia came to a coaching session full of a hundred and one reasons why she didn't deserve to apply for the training course that would help her change career. Some of those reasons seemed practical – she couldn't afford it, she didn't have time, there was a lot of additional travelling to do – but actually, when she began to examine what was behind every one of those reasons, it came down to the fact that she doubted her own value. She just wasn't prepared to invest in herself. We decided to write the doubts out so that she could see them for what they were – simply thoughts that she was choosing.

Then playing the role of her own best friend, Julia role-played a conversation with herself, reminding herself of all the reasons why she had permission to put herself first. She also created strong positive affirmations to support her new resolve.

Julia decided that not only were the doubts now redundant, but also they were even laughable. She wanted a way of taking the sting out of them and reclaiming her own power in a humorous way, so she rewrote them on a single sheet of loo paper and literally flushed them away!

Part V

Creating a Harmonious Whole Life

The 5th Wave   By Rich Tennant

"We've tried adjusting your diet, and prescribing medication for your anxiety. Now let's try loosening some of those bolts and see if that does anything."

In this part . . .

You discover how to create your own balancing act to serve you well in the crazy pace of your life. You explore the scary crossroads of 'no going back' change, and navigate it without getting run over. And you see how you can use your coaching skills to help others.

Chapter 20

Achieving Balance

. . . .

In This Chapter

▶ Finding your balance point

▶ Using daily strategies to rebalance yourself

▶ Developing a long-term stress-busting strategy

. . . .

*I*n life coaching, having *balance* means that you have a sense that all the parts of your life form a harmonious whole. Balance is different for everyone, and even different for you at various stages of your life. You may work long hours, but if that produces your desired rewards and allows you enough time to enjoy some leisure pursuits, then you're likely to feel balanced and stable. When you're off-balance, on the other hand, the smallest thing, such as an unexpected deadline, can send you over the *tipping point* – when things get overwhelming and you lose your balance.

Balance can be a tricky thing to catch and hold onto in your life. Simply trying to stand firm and hoping that you can keep all those plates spinning isn't really going to work for long, because something is sure to come along, knock you over and send the plates crashing to the ground. The key to balance is to be in control of yourself and your goals, to keep moving in a forward direction and yet to accept that sometimes you need to take a backwards or sideways step to maintain your momentum.

This chapter helps you to get a sense of what balance really means for you, where your tipping point is, what your stress triggers are and how you can choose the best practical steps for you to regain balance.

Finding Your Balance

Your sense of balance changes with your life priorities, as the excitement of new roles begins to fade a little and as you become more comfortable with who you are. You may be prepared to put lots of energy into your work and social life when you're a young adult because it may be very important to you to prove yourself, to earn the money you want and to have fun. In your forties and beyond, you may well have achieved a lot of your material goals and find you want to spend more time rediscovering yourself and trying out new things. You may consider money with fresh eyes and you may change the ways you go about having fun. Coaching yourself regularly to identify the overall impact that your daily choices have on your whole life will help you find your balance point at any point in time.

Integrating the Goldilocks theory of balance into your life

Goldilocks, the heroine of the fairytale *Goldilocks and the Three Bears*, was a great natural self-coach on the subject of balance. She took a long, hard look at the three bowls of porridge in front of her and made quite sure she tested them all out thoroughly before she settled down to enjoy the one that was 'just right'. She knew instinctively that trial and error was the best approach to making sure that she got exactly the right quantity and quality of porridge for her, and guesswork just wasn't an option.

Do you find yourself making assumptions about balance in your life? Here are some thoughts you may carry around with you:

- Not enough money
- Too much stress
- Not enough time
- Too many demands
- Not enough fun

Many of these assumptions may well be true for you at certain times in your life, and often you instinctively know what changes can improve your sense of balance. But you may find that you make the adjustment (by freeing up some time or dropping a hobby that demanded too much of your attention) and things don't improve. Or perhaps you discover an unexpected negative consequence of your adjustment that outweighs the benefit you have gained. You may actually miss the adrenaline rush and sense of achievement you got from handling all those demands at work. You won't always get your balancing actions right first time – quite often it's the process of making adjustments that tells you exactly what and how much you need of certain things in your life.

Think hard about whether you have too much or too little of something in your life. In fact, you may have good reasons why you made the balance tip in a certain direction. You may thrive on the adrenaline you get from your demanding job and feel you should want to spend more time with your family. But if the quality of the time you do spend with your family is good for all concerned, maybe you can let yourself off the hook a little? And you may love the role of the giver in your social group – the one who always has time for other people's problems – but feel that you ought to be more assertive and less willing to drop what you're doing for a friend in need. Be honest about what you want and don't want in your life.

This activity provides you with a visual way to check how balanced you are right now.

1. **Take a sheet of paper and draw a circle in the middle of the bottom of the page.** Label this circle 'My Centre of Balance'.

2. **Draw two arms coming out of the circle, one to the left and one to the right.** Label the left arm 'Too Little and Not Enough' and the right arm 'Too Much and Too Many'.

3. **Load up the two arms with things that are 'too much' for you and things that you have 'too little' of in your life.** Load up your arms as if each separate thing was a box and stack them on top of each other. Not having enough of something feels just as heavy as having too much.

4. **Now draw a triangle at the top of the page, in the middle, above your Centre of Balance.** Call this triangle 'My Ideal Life'. Imagine that this triangle contains all of your whole-life goals. You can get creative by deciding on a symbol that represents this for you. Perhaps you choose a heart, a star, a tree or a house – pick whatever best represents your life at its most balanced. Imagine standing in your Centre of Balance, with your arms stretched out and your sights firmly set on your Ideal Life.

5. **Write 'Just Right Zone' below your Ideal Life triangle.** The space in between your Centre of Balance and your Ideal Life is the Just Right Zone. Things that are just right for you feel light and airy, like wispy clouds that let you see through them to a clear view of your ideal life. Draw clouds in your Just Right Zone and within the clouds write down the things that are just right for you at the moment.

6. **Look at the balance between Too Much and Too Little.** If you have too much or too little of a lot of things, your focus is probably on the balancing act itself, keeping your energy from moving forward and preventing you from focusing on your ideal life.

7. **Consider what action you could take from each arm that would move something into the Just Right space and take the load off one or both of your over-burdened arms.** Maybe you have too much time spent on housework and not enough fun?

8. **Write out your actions in your journal and redraw your balanced whole life as it now looks.**

Take a look at Figure 20-1 for an example of a completed Centre of Balance activity.

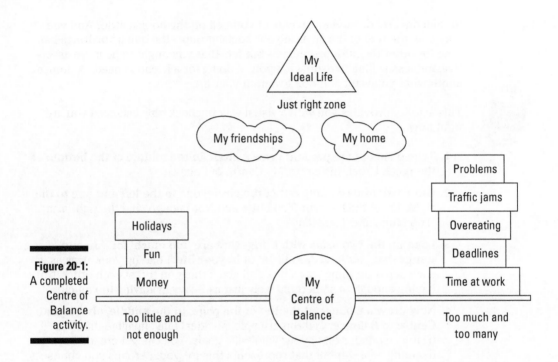

Figure 20-1:
A completed
Centre of
Balance
activity.

Checking out your daily energy balance

Remember the old chestnut: 'It's better to wear out than to rust out'? You'd probably prefer to be active and fully engaged in all that you do rather than feel lethargic and bored. So you may instinctively push yourself that little bit harder on a regular basis in order to avoid feeling rusty. But actually, the opposite of rust-out is burn-out, so don't push yourself too far.

Take a look at the Balance Curve in Figure 20-2. Generally, you experience high levels of energy when you're fully engaged in what you're doing. This energy is sometimes created by good stress – feelings of excitement, the sense of adrenalin pumping to help you meet a deadline, a target or other desired goal in your life, especially a goal that has a time-critical factor. This good stress only becomes bad stress when the pressures reach a tipping point – when you feel that you're not coping so effectively and maybe begin to doubt your own judgement. The tipping point may be an actual event or simply your own state of mind. Beyond that tipping point, you feel stressed and your energy often dips, which compounds the feeling of stress.

Imagine a typical work day. You start off pretty calm perhaps, having enjoyed a good night's sleep. As you race around the house preparing yourself for the tasks ahead, your energy picks up and the good stress starts to rise. You negotiate the traffic, get to your destination and start ploughing through your task list. You tackle challenges, work towards deadlines and solve problems. Your energy matches the rise in good stress that you feel, so you see some good results.

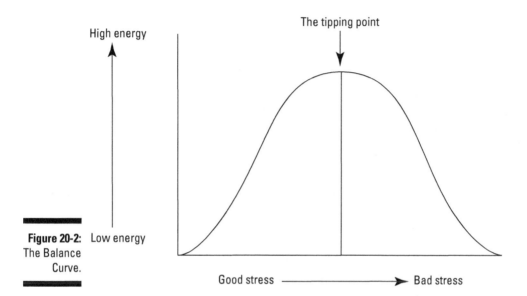

Figure 20-2:
The Balance
Curve.

Then you hit a real puzzle that halts you in your tracks. Perhaps you have a genuine project crisis, a perceived immovable obstacle, some unpleasant feedback or a call from home to say the boiler has exploded. Whatever the trigger, it's just enough to send you over the top of the curve and now you're feeling bad stress – out of control, unsure what to do for the best, beginning to doubt your own opinion and actions. And your energy levels start to drain as you begin to feel paralysed by the situation. In reality the trigger event may be no different to all the other stuff you've handled well up to that point, but just the little bit of overload pushes you over the curve – your tipping point.

This type of thing won't happen every day, of course. Often, you stay just the right side of the curve so that you're firing on all cylinders, harnessing your adrenaline to help you maintain your energy and get lots done. And some-times the bad stress keeps you focused on something very important just long enough to pull it off.

But have you ever revisited something you did when you were on the wrong side of the curve? Your work may be below standard because your productive energy levels were dissipated and all that anxiety got in the way of your cre-ativity and vision. Think also of the harmful effects of stress on your physical and mental health. (See 'Spotting your danger signs' later in this chapter.)

Where is your tipping point? Think back to days when you felt out of balance and identify your external and internal triggers, which may include:

- ✔ An unexpected time-critical demand
- ✔ A crisis you didn't foresee
- ✔ Something someone said to throw you off-track
- ✔ Starting to doubt yourself
- ✔ Something taking too long to complete

Adjusting your daily balance often starts with changing your attitude to the stress trigger before going on to take whatever action you need. Try these seven simple steps when you feel overwhelmed or out of kilter during the day:

1. **Ask yourself *exactly* what you're feeling and what *specifically* is the trigger.**

2. **Think about where you are on the balance curve.** Sometimes momentary anxiety can be set in context very quickly as you focus on the good energy you still feel.

3. **Change your physical state rapidly by taking a few deep breaths, a brisk walk round the room or having a long stretch.**

4. **Imagine yourself standing back from the anxiety you now feel.** Ask yourself, what would this feel like if it was curiosity instead of anxiety? Changing your state of mind from anxiety to curiosity helps you get into the mindset of problem-solving and reduces the tension in your body.

5. **Consider what you need to do now.** Do you need to act, explore or reflect on the challenge?

6. **Take your first small step towards resolving the challenge.**

7. **Review your feelings and position on the balance curve and repeat Steps 1 through 6 if you need to.**

Centring yourself

Finding your sense of balance can result in doing things that initially feel like going against restoring order. You're running up against a crucial deadline, you're tired, irritable and panicky because you have three hours to finish something that would normally take six. The last thing you can afford to do is take a break, and yet a balanced approach suggests that having a quick rest is vital to give yourself the best chance of delivering a quality piece of work.

Do you know what it feels like to be centred? Think of a strong-rooted tree with its flexible branches waving in the wind. Grounding yourself physically gives you clues to understanding your emotional and mental balance. Notice what your body does instinctively when you're not in motion. Do you slouch, lean on one leg, cross your arms or even find yourself contorting your body into a combination of all three? Standing tall, firm and straight feels quite weird if you're used to slouching. But not only does making like a tree help your body physically, it can also act as a gentle meditation and a reminder of the importance of staying grounded.

The following activity is a five-minute balancing act that you can carry out at any time.

1. **Stand with your feet shoulder-width apart.** Check that your toes point forward and not to either side.

2. **Let your arms drop loosely to your sides, leaving a little space between them and your body.** Pull your shoulders back comfortably.

3. **Take a few deep breaths so that your chest expands.**

4. **Look straight ahead of you, keeping your chin up as you do so.**

5. **Bring your attention to the strong physical centre of your body, just below your navel.** You may want to repeat an affirmation or mantra to yourself, such as, *'I am strong, centred and balanced.'* Imagine the strength of the roots that support you and the resources that sustain you.

6. **Continue to stand centred for a few moments, breathing deeply and with control, until you're ready to reach out to your next challenge.**

Regaining Your Balance

In this section I explore the three main ways you can recapture your sense of balance: how you approach the management of your time, what you choose to let go of and how clear you are in expressing what you need.

Managing yourself and your time

Time seems so rigid and finite, and yet I'm sure you've experienced the strange way that time seems to speed up or slow down in contradiction to what the clock actually says! You can't manage time, but you can manage yourself and what you want to do in each 24 hours. Every day you have 24 hours available to you, and you have choices about how you're going to use them. Ask yourself the following question regularly throughout each day to bring yourself back on track:

What can I let go of right now so that I can regain my balance?

Your answers may surprise you. Sometimes you can drop a tangible thing such as an item on your to-do list that you can easily delegate. But often you can simply let go of a feeling of tension and anxiety that you've built up without realising. Reflecting on what you can lose may help you to let go of that feeling, knowing that you're capable of whatever challenge you face.

Don't worry – you don't need to be firing on all cylinders every second of the day, with no time to take a break. Sometimes you want to be full steam ahead, taking action on your goals, and other times you want to be still, calm and quiet, or having fun at a party.

You can find loads of tools to increase your effectiveness in managing yourself and your time, but before you race to book yourself on a time-management course or invest in more books, consider the kind of person you are:

- ✔ Do you enjoy working with the same systems or processes or do you get excited by new time-management tools (a different diary system, the latest personal digital assistant, colour-coded task lists) but then find you lose interest quickly? You may be the type of person who needs to chop and change their time-management systems to get the best out of your time.

- ✔ What times of the day do you usually get the most done? You may be an early-bird lark or a night owl, so play to your body-clock strengths and adopt a system that encourages you to be most proactive when your energy levels are highest.

- ✔ Do you prefer to spend a block of time working to complete a big task, or is it better for you to break it up into digestible chunks? Time yourself on a big project and see when your attention and productivity start to wane. People usually need some kind of break every 45 minutes, even just a few moments staring into space, but your own clock may work to a different rhythm.

- ✔ Are you a self-starter or someone who needs to be prodded – do you respond better to the carrot or the stick? Some people are spurred on by rewards and others need a push to propel them into action. As a rule (although you create the rules, remember), you are best served by 70–80 per cent pull motivation versus only 20–30 per cent push tactics. Some tasks may need more push, especially if they're tough ones for you to get really motivated about, in which case remember to play to your attention-span strengths and get more support.

✔ Are you an optimist or a pessimist when it comes to the amount of time you have available to complete tasks? Do you often under- or over-estimate how much time you need, potentially causing yourself too much pressure on the one hand or too little challenge on the other? Some people believe that it's better to under-promise and over-deliver and this might earn you a few brownie points at work (until your boss gets wise to the technique). However, the most respected approach, and the healthiest one for your own balance, is to become more skilled at making accurate estimates of the time you need for a task. This takes practice and close observation, so keep trying.

Think about your daily choices in the context of being *reactive* (responding to events and people) or *proactive* (taking the initiative and thinking ahead). Usually when you're aiming for your goals, you work proactively. But how much time do you spend being reactive to tasks that you're given? You can't avoid being reactive sometimes; you simply have to do certain things because you have responsibilities you must fulfil. But because this reactive approach is so much a part of everyday life, you may find it hard to get out of autopilot. Ask yourself if you can add anything a little more proactive to the process to move you further towards your goals.

Khan was responsible for the hour-long morning school run for his two young children. He enjoyed the time he spent in the car with the young ones, but found that their high energy levels at that time of the morning were distracting. In addition, he expressed a concern during coaching that he was rarely finding time in his busy days to reflect on his goals and build on them. During the morning drive, Khan's mind was full of the things that he needed to put on his task list for that day, which, combined with the two boisterous forces of nature bouncing around, didn't help him arrive at work calm and collected. He decided to write out his task list for the next day just before he went to bed instead of when he arrived at work.

For Khan, this small proactive change had a remarkable effect. Instead of his head buzzing with all the problems he needed to solve that day, possible solutions started popping up during the drive. It was as if his brain had processed all the challenges during the night and was now delivering neat outputs into his brain. This enjoyable outcome nearly matched his children's energy because it felt positive and upbeat.

Learning to love delegation

Delegation – sharing your load by assigning some of your tasks and responsibilities to others – isn't simply a skill that you use in a business or work context. One of the best ways to regain balance in your life is to delegate.

Coaching yourself through your options and choices in different situations is one way to do this – you're engaging with your inner coach to help you solve problems, so it's as if you already have two heads working on finding the solution. Also, simply talking things through with a trusted friend can give you some of the effects of delegating, as you also harness their energy to help you see things from a different perspective. You can also employ the real skill of delegation in very practical ways in your life as a whole.

Here are some pointers for delegation:

- **Find tasks to delegate that other people can do even better than you.** You may be used to being the capable one in the household or work-team, but you become more valued, not less, when you help other people to show their own talents. A son or daughter may discover an unexpected skill for gardening after you delegate mowing the lawn to them and a work colleague's success in completing the month-end report reflects well on you too.

- **Be clear about what you need and the support you can still offer.** You remain responsible for ensuring that the person to whom you delegate has the resources they need. You can help your son or daughter understand how to use the lawnmower safely, and you need to share the protocols involved in distributing the month-end report with your colleague.

- **Agree how you'll review progress.** Offer praise on a well-cut lawn or a well-turned-out report. You can give constructive feedback for the future, maintaining your input, but still delegating!

Choosing to let go

Self-coaching on the balance in your life may lead you to the conclusion that you have to give something up in order to regain control or enjoyment of your life. If that something is a major decision for you – such as leaving your job, selling up and moving abroad, or ending a relationship – then go to Chapter 21 for ideas about how to make this kind of major change with the least pain and most gain all round. But perhaps you've found that you can let go relatively small things from your life to significantly improve your sense of balance. And while it may be a no-brainer – you really have realised that you can do without the extra night-shift at work – sometimes you encounter resistance in yourself because you're used to a certain way of being.

Who made up the rule that only you are capable of loading and unloading the dishwasher in the right way? Where is it written that you are the only person at the meeting responsible enough to summarise and distribute the minutes? Ask yourself whether you're hanging on to tasks that someone else can do better than you – from fear that they will!

Reframe some of the beliefs you hold about letting go:

- ✔ 'If I want something done properly, I have to do it myself' becomes 'I trust that other people can approach this task with standards as high as my own.'

- ✔ 'If I give this task away, I lose control' becomes 'If I give this task away, I can do more of what I love and my control over my life may increase.'

- ✔ 'If I can't handle it all, I'll be a failure' becomes 'My success comes from knowing how to channel my resources and when to ask for help.'

What beliefs about delegation can you reframe to give yourself breathing space?

Saying what you mean

Living your most balanced life is only really possible when you learn to identify what your needs are and ask for them clearly and assertively. Otherwise you run the risk that other people load you up with demands, questions and challenges.

What's the balance between what you give and what you receive from other people? If you give so much of your time and resources that you have nothing left for key priorities or are beginning to feel used and abused, how can you find gentle ways of asserting your needs? Saying what you really mean isn't about expressing the negative emotion that's been bottled up inside you. You need to look behind the emotion for the real meaning and express that as positively and clearly as possible. You can practise with the following statements:

- ✔ **At work:** Instead of 'I'm far too busy with the month-end report to help you on that project, I can't believe you even asked!' try 'I'm happy to help you with this project and in return you can give me some support on the month-end report. It's been defeating me this month and I'd welcome your fresh perspective on it.'

- ✔ **At home:** Instead of 'You're so selfish, making your room into such a mess! Don't you think I'm entitled to have a little bit of time to myself instead of clearing up after you?' try 'When you don't keep your room tidy, it means I have to spend extra time cleaning up and I feel resentful towards you because I have less time for myself. I don't like to feel that way, so what can we do to make sure that your room stays tidy and I get some of my me-time back?'

✔ **With friends:** Instead of 'I hate going to a nightclub every week, it's so loud and I end up drinking too much and staying up too late' try 'I love spending time with you and I've been thinking that when we go out to a nightclub, we have less chance of really talking and I often feel tired and hung-over the next day. So I'd like to ring the changes and go to a restaurant every other week instead.'

Managing Longer-Term Stress

Good stress is the fuel that helps you to deliver your great results. This good stress is more a feeling of excitement, a sense of urgency and a willingness to push out of your comfort zone, despite the butterflies in your stomach or your fears of failure. The kind of stress that you need to manage is really *di-stress*, when you feel overwhelmed by the enormity of what you have to do and your energy recedes instead of grows. You can often deal with distress on a daily basis, but at other times, no matter what you do, you seem to be under the kind of sustained pressure that dissipates your enjoyment of life for a while. Don't allow yourself to come to boiling point slowly, without even realising the cumulative effect of pressure piled on pressure on a regular basis. Learn to spot your danger signs and have a plan of action ready to put in place.

Spotting your danger signs

You have your own danger signs that warn you when you're under too much pressure. Spotting these signs at an early stage is vital for your physical, mental and emotional well-being.

Your danger signs may include:

✔ Not sleeping well

✔ Feeling anxious

✔ Always being tired

✔ Having lapses of concentration

✔ Experiencing extreme mood swings

✔ Feeling low

✔ Having trouble with memory

✔ Eating for comfort or drinking to excess

✔ Noticing unpleasant physical symptoms (headaches, stomach pains, cold sores)

Many of these symptoms can have other underlying causes, but if you're experiencing several of them at the same time, you're probably living on the wrong side of your balance curve.

You can start regaining balance by changing your attitude to the stress in your life, but that may have limited impact. The only effective long-term solution when matters get to this stage is to change the situation in some way. A sign that you really need to change the stressful situation can be when you're adamant that you can't implement change or deny that you need to, so be honest with yourself. Extreme stress, the kind that leads to depression and other diseases, is often accompanied by a feeling of being locked into the bad situation and bereft of choices.

Apply the following three-point plan to launch yourself into action:

1. **Ask yourself what options you have that can reduce the ongoing stress without increasing negative stress in another area.** Imagine an ideal solution, even if at this stage you don't really believe it's possible. If your job is causing you stress, these ideal solutions may include working part-time, taking a sabbatical, finding a new job, giving up work entirely or getting extra support in your role. For each solution, ask yourself, 'What will happen if I do this? and 'What will happen if I don't do this?'

2. **Ask yourself what further information you need to move forward.** You may find you need more information from your boss or the Human Resources department. Perhaps you can get information on your contract of employment via a website or need to check out with your bank manager if you can secure a loan to fund a sabbatical.

3. **Ask yourself what resources and support you need and what's stopping you from enlisting that help.** Apart from the people you need information from, you may want to consider who can lend a supportive ear and help you think through your options. If you're having professional coaching, your coach is a great start, and so are family members. Perhaps you need to start with your boss, but worry that you'll come across as uncommitted to your job? You can approach this conversation by thinking through the benefits for the organisation of getting to a better working situation for you.

Don't hesitate to get more help in stressful situations. This isn't a time for going it alone and your energies are best employed pulling in other resources and fresh perspectives.

The website of the International Stress Management Association has some great resources on the topic of stress and time management. Check out www. isma.org.uk.

Coaching your way through stressful situations

Stressful situations have a habit of driving out logical thought and creating panic. Taking the time to coach yourself through these occasions pays dividends because the next time stress hits, you'll find making the best choices for you a little easier. The following tips focus on the use of powerful questions to help you stand back from the panic and get some perspective. (Chapter 7 has more on crafting powerful questions.)

Here are some rules of engagement for when stress attacks you:

- **Be clear on your values, your vision and your goals.** Take time to see the clear vision of your life and measure every choice you make against this vision.

  Powerful question: What do I really want now in my life?

- **Hold your goals lightly and be mindful that changing circumstances may change the goal and the steps you need to take to get there.** Accept that stressful times do occur and give yourself permission to make the adjustments to your goals that you need.

  Powerful question: Where can I be more flexible now?

- **Ask yourself frequently what you can let go of, and what you don't need any more.**

  Powerful question: What's getting in the way of my best interests?

- **Take only actions that enhance your self-esteem and personal integrity.**

  Powerful question: How does this action or decision make me stronger?

- **Understand that you will have situations you can't change, people you can't help and results you can't achieve.** You can win other battles instead.

  Powerful question: What can I accept with graceful humility?

- **Tap into the goodwill of others.** Don't let your ego stand in the way of joining forces with your best allies.

  Powerful question: Who can support, encourage or inspire me?

- **Have a contingency plan, or two, or three.** Get into the habit of thinking through your contingency plans for the really key areas of your life, or really stressful situations.

  Powerful questions: What are my options? What else can I do? What option can't I yet see?

Chapter 21

Making a Life-Changing Decision

· ·

In This Chapter

▶ Plotting your life stages

▶ Spotting the signs that you need to change your life

▶ Making your decision

▶ Embracing the changes

· ·

*Y*ou make life-changing decisions every single day – some bigger than others. Even the decision to make no decisions at all is life changing. In the film *Sliding Doors* the central character plays out two contrasting versions of her life, which hinge on the difference between catching a certain train and missing it by a few seconds. You can probably look back on some of these 'sliding door' moments in your own life. Perhaps, for example, you can attribute your current romantic relationship to a chance meeting following an inconsequential decision you took to visit a particular café on a specific day, when you could so easily have stayed at home with a cup of instant coffee.

But some decisions, such as deciding to have children, change career or move abroad, make it very plain that they are both *big* and *important*. These decisions *feel* life changing, and they occupy a fair amount of your energies at all stages of their resolution. You may resist, battle with them and agonise over your conflicting feelings about them for what seems like an eternity. Then, you finally reach the point when you say to yourself, 'Enough, no more – the time is right now!' And you take a leap into the relatively unknown, for better or ill.

This chapter helps you to take the leap more safely and with more control. You'll find ways of making those momentous decisions while maximising your gains and minimising the pain of what you inevitably have to let go of in the process.

Knowing How Your Stage of Life Affects Your Attitude to Change

Did you know that a mid-life crisis can occur at any age? It's a popular misconception that the only time you experience the upheaval of a major transition is around your fortieth birthday.

You'll probably experience at least three or four periods of transition during your lifetime, as shown in Table 21-1. (The table is adapted from the work of the psychologist Daniel Levinson who studied the 'seasons' of the lives of two groups of men and women during the 1980s.) Your individual transitional periods occur at the ages and stages that are unique to you, of course, but similar general trends do appear in many different life paths. Knowing the principle of how you move from your own transition periods to stable phases can be helpful in understanding why some periods of your life feel chaotic and confusing whereas others just seem to tick along smoothly.

Table 21-1   Common Transitional and Stable Periods in Your Life

Age	Stage
Late teens to early 20s (Transitional)	**Finding your adult self** You may be identifying your voice as a young adult, making and testing out friendships and romantic relationships, considering what kind of work may be best for you.
Mid- to late 20s (Stable)	**Choosing a path** You may be making commitments in your field of work and with friends and romantic partners.
Late 20s to early 30s (Transitional)	**Exploring options** You may be clarifying or adjusting your earlier decisions. Perhaps changing career direction or entering into new relationships. Maybe considering marriage and/or parenthood.
Mid-30s to 40 (Stable)	**Settling down** You may have recommitted to or chosen new options and again throw yourself into the busyness of your life.
Early to mid-40s (Transitional)	**Mid-life questioning** You may see this milestone as similar in some ways to your first transition into adulthood and are once again questioning who you have become and what you really want out of the next phase of your life.

Age	Stage
Late 40s to early 50s (Stable)	**Renewal** You may have made some significant changes and are beginning to feel that you're evolving and developing. You're likely to see that some of your values have shifted in priority as you make sense of what's truly important to you.
Early to mid-50s (Transitional)	**Exploring options** You may arrive at this transitional stage more confident in your expanded sense of self and are considering what will be the key focus areas for you during the rest of your life. You may be thinking ahead to a second career or retirement options.
Mid-50s plus (Stable)	**Focus on meaning, purpose and legacy** You may have found a stronger sense of purpose, a new vocation or be keen to pass on a legacy of some sort through your unique gifts.

These stages aren't set in stone and aren't the same for everyone. You may speed through these stages in a couple of decades, or on the other hand find yourself still searching for stability in your fifties. So much depends on the choices you make in your life and the experiences you have that shape you and move you on. For example, Levinson showed that, for women, the phases were more strongly tied to the family life cycle. And both stable and transitional phases can last a long time for a particular person. If you settled down to marriage and a family at a very early age in your twenties, you may stay in a stable state for years, only hitting a major transition when the children grow up, leave home and give you some mental space to ponder 'what now?' That transition period can feel very significant, chaotic and confusing to you, compared to someone who has moved through a number of evolving phases and so has had time to get used to the roller-coaster. On the other hand, if you're in your forties and have felt in transition for the last 15 years, you may feel anxious and panicky that you'll never find the life you truly want.

Accepting where you are, why you're there and why you feel the way you do about being there is a really good starting point to help you move on to the inevitable big life-changing decision that will take you to your next phase.

The following activity can help you recognise where you are in your life stages.

1. **Take a sheet of paper, at least A4 size, preferably larger.**
2. **Draw a straight line horizontally in the middle of the page.** This is your personal life-line.

3. **Consider the major events in your life and draw a line peaking at the periods of transition and dipping at your more stable periods.** If you like, you can indicate your age when these transitional experiences (which may be good or quite traumatic) occurred.

4. **Think about these peaks and troughs and consider the main feelings and emotions you experienced.** You can decorate your life curve with images, or smiling/frowning faces to indicate your perception of these periods of your life, or you can simply jot down one or two words against each phase that describes how you felt about it (as shown in Figure 21-1).

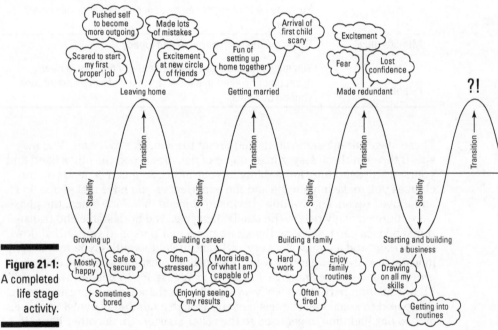

Figure 21-1: A completed life stage activity.

5. **Ask yourself some powerful questions.** What trends have you identified in your life stages? Do the stages have more similarities than differences? Have you had a relatively stable life so far or has it been a roller-coaster? What have you discovered about how you handle change? What do you have yet to learn? Do you look forward to the transitions in your life? Or do you seem to enjoy stable periods more than transitions? What's your prediction for the next big transition? How will you prepare for it?

Recognising Your Need to Make a Radical Change

Some radical changes come about via a wake-up call – a strong emotional reaction to your circumstances, events in your life or choices to date. The wake-up calls often seems like life or death. Consider the difference between going on a short-term diet because you can't fit into your favourite jeans anymore, and completely changing your lifestyle – your eating, drinking and smoking habits – because you've had a life-threatening heart attack and you need to make radical changes fast.

Changing jobs to fit with your career plan is a different kind of change to the one that occurs when you realise that your true vocation in life lies in a totally different field and your current role is sapping your best energies and making you ill. Big changes often occur because you feel you have no better choice. You may have to set aside all your rules of balance and moderation to focus on survival – whether it's the survival of your physical body, that of your mental and emotional health or when your core values or the people and things most dear to you are threatened.

Not all radical change is prompted by negative factors. You can be essentially happy with your lot in life and also know that you need a major change to take you to the next level. Deciding to have children or marrying someone who has a ready-made family; moving abroad; or taking a sabbatical from a career to make a contribution to a cause dear to your heart – all are examples of scary steps into the unknown that are driven by positive motivating forces.

Perhaps you have a compelling drive to move towards something positive, such as a total career change or a burning sense of purpose to fulfil. Although the motivation is a positive one, you still feel that you *must* make the decision because the consequences of remaining where you are cause you pain – because of the absence of the pleasure that you glimpse ahead of you.

These sections help you to work out ways to retain some balance and moderation in your change process.

Moving from pain to pleasure and purpose

People often continue to put up with things in their life until the moment when the pain of continuing to suffer them becomes greater than any pleasure they may get from them, such as a bad relationship or harmful habits. It may seem strange to think that any situation that is causing you a lot of angst can also be a source of pleasure – after all, nothing is particularly joyful about a relationship or job gone sour, or addictions to habits that drain your health. But making choices to move away from painful situations can be tough for many reasons. You may have invested many years into that relationship or job and are loath to walk away from those responsibilities. You may derive a lot of immediate comfort from continuing to overeat, drink or smoke too much. And a part of you may even feel more comfortable having difficulty paying the bills every month rather than taking your courage in both hands and fighting for a better, richer life. Struggling through these and other painful situations may actually feed part of the sense of self that doesn't want to quit or that wants to comfort and protect you.

Think about the sources of pain in your life for a moment. What do you really get from them, good and bad? What will you miss if you leave these sources of pain behind?

Major change comes about when the pain is so great or the call to pleasure and purpose is so compelling that you must take action – and when you're prepared to face and deal with all the consequences.

Noticing the clues in your emotions

You often know the time has come to make a radical change because your emotions tell you so. When the change is prompted by pain, you may experience any or all of the following:

- ✔ Irritation
- ✔ Resentment
- ✔ Anger
- ✔ Detachment or disengagement

Notice the frequency and intensity of these feelings and how far they move you away from being in harmony with your job, your key relationship or other aspects of your life. Watch out for irritation turning into resentment. This may happen at work, when you find yourself increasingly resentful at being overlooked in meetings and it becomes harder to let the feelings go and enjoy the good things about your relationship with your boss and peers. As soon as you become angry, you find ways to rant and rail against the unfairness of whatever painful situation you're in. But actually the killer state is often detachment, or a blocking of feeling. If you get to the stage where you feel that your actions are pointless and make no difference, you may completely withdraw from any kind of harmony in that situation and find it hard to see the positive side of things.

Wanting to be a better person

Melvin, the central character in the film *As Good As It Gets*, starts out seemingly beyond redemption. His public face is that of a sensitive romantic novelist, but in private he avoids all human contact, displays obsessive-compulsive behaviour towards routine and cleanliness, is vindictive to his neighbours and even attempts to dispose of his next door neighbour's dog down the rubbish chute in his luxury apartment block. The dog is rescued and Melvin gets his just desserts when he is forced to look after the animal when its owner is hospitalised after a brutal mugging. This, together with the relationship he starts to build with a compassionate local waitress and her sick son, becomes a turning point as he starts to glimpse the possibility of living his life a different way. For Melvin, a radical change is something as simple as allowing himself to step on the paving stones he has ritually avoided all his life and this symbolises his new approach to love, trust and a meaningful relationship with the people around him.

Everyone experiences periods of extreme negative emotions from time to time, but ask yourself how frequently and for how long you suffer with these feelings compared to the good times you experience.

You can make a life-changing decision more safely if you begin to tackle it before you settle into the stages of anger and detachment and they become the norm for you. Neither of those feelings is conducive to high-quality decision-making. Be aware of the nature, frequency and intensity of your emotions to help you coach yourself back into harmony with your current situation or make an informed decision to move on.

Your emotions give you different clues when the change is based on moving towards pleasure or purpose. A move abroad, to a new culture and lifestyle, may evoke a range of feelings such as:

- ✔ Excitement
- ✔ Anticipation
- ✔ Hope
- ✔ Passion

Although these are positive emotions, they're often accompanied by apprehension and fear as you make the transition. Even though the strong positive emotions can often carry you through the change, watch out for your inner critic instilling fear and doubt in you by whispering thoughts that you may not be up to the challenge. Refer to Chapter 5 to strengthen your positive beliefs, and to Chapter 13 to remind yourself how to bolster your self-esteem at these times.

Deciding to be your authentic self

You take on many roles during your life such as worker, parent, child, friend and neighbour. People may see different qualities in you depending on what kind of person you strive to be when you're with them. You may even feel you have to act a certain way in some of the roles you take on. Sometimes the most radical change you can make in your life is deciding to be truly authentic (see Chapter 4 for more on developing your unique qualities). That's not to say that certain people and situations can't bring out different aspects of your true self, but it does mean living your values with integrity.

How far away are you from being your authentic self and how much do you compromise your core values? The balancing acts of your life may mean living with a certain amount of compromise – perhaps the job you do is pretty soulless, but the money it gives you supports your value of security, which may have a higher priority for you at certain times of your life. But at other times you may know that you're not fully living up to your own standards. You may find yourself sometimes justifying means by ends and cutting a few corners to get a result, such as delivering a lower quality piece of work on time rather than admitting you need more time to produce a higher quality outcome. What do you really believe in and what is your purpose in life? Do people see your values shining out like a beacon in everything you do? What discomfort and pain are you prepared to go through to do the right thing? Would you stick your neck out for something you believe in? What would that something be for you? What impact on your life would that have?

Making Your Best Decision

You've finally decided that a radical decision must be made. Perhaps you've decided that an unhealthy or painful relationship or a job that's stifling the best of you has to change. You know you have to act, soon, and in a big way. What are your options? Take a look at the pros and cons of tackling your decision from a problem-based view first.

Fixing it

Fixing a bad situation does have huge benefits to you. First, and most obviously, doing so solves your problem. Secondly, and maybe more importantly, fixing a bad situation does wonders for your self-esteem. You get to be the hero in your own life who draws on all your reserves of strength and talent to come up with resourceful options for saving your own world. The benefits will continue, because you discover so much in the process of change that you can apply your problem-solving skills more widely. Yet you may also reach a point at which trying to fix something indicates stubbornness or even low self-esteem rather than wisdom. Staying in an abusive relationship that shows no signs of changing despite all your efforts is an extreme example of this.

Ask yourself the following powerful positive questions about fixing a bad situation:

- ✔ What would my life be like if a miracle happened overnight?

- ✔ What would I gain and what sacrifices would I need to make?

- ✔ What impact on my whole life would fixing it have?

- ✔ What support do I need?

- ✔ Where can I start and how can I maintain my commitment?

Fleeing from it

Fleeing from an unpleasant situation sometimes seems like the only viable option and it's often an agonising choice to make. If you're in a bad relationship, have tried to fix it to no avail, but can't bear the thought of finally ending it, you may be tempted to seek out the catalyst for change in the form of another person. So you may think about or actually start an affair, which then becomes the excuse to leave your bad relationship without actually resolving the underlying problems. Of course, people do fall in love and as a result may choose to end existing relationships; that's a bittersweet fact of life. But falling in love with the right person is easier when you've had a chance to work out why things went wrong before.

Ask yourself the following powerful challenging questions about fleeing from a bad situation:

- ✔ What am I escaping from?

- ✔ What am I using as a distraction from facing the real issue?

- ✔ What impact is this choice having on my self-esteem?

- ✔ What would it be like to move away from this situation?

- ✔ What beliefs do I have that cause me to take the line of least resistance at present?

- ✔ How can I learn from this bad situation?

- ✔ What environment can best support me to grow from my experience?

INSPIRATION

Fleeing to Florida

Tina was sick of her well-paid but boring job and was fed up with playing the dating game to no avail. She felt that a lifestyle change was just the thing to kick-start her energies and so she gave up her job and flat to spend an extended period of time in Florida, where she had had some wonderful holidays. Tina was relying so much on an overnight transformation of her fortunes that she was bitterly disappointed when she didn't step off the plane filled with renewed vigour to focus on a new career and find the man of her dreams. Instead of revitalising her, the constant sunshine drained her and she felt that she was dragging around all her old problems with her wherever she went.

After identifying that the Florida trip was her way of fleeing from her situation, Tina began to feel a lot better. She cut short her stay, found a life coach and began to investigate what options really excited her. (Check out Chapters 2 and 3 for info on finding a life coach.)

In fact, Florida came back into the frame six months later when Tina secured a temporary contract as a holiday rep. She was still in transition and making decisions about her life, but this time she really threw herself into her new experiences, knowing that she wasn't running away from anything at all.

Building on strength

Often the most constructive approach to making your best decision is to take your focus away from the problem and begin to draw out the elements of what's working for you in your current situation as a starting point for major change. You don't want to throw out the baby with the bathwater, and this is a real danger when you're contemplating brand new horizons, whether for negative or positive reasons. Think about a major change, such as becoming self-employed, and consider the following example of a coaching conversation you might have with yourself:

Q: What's great about my current situation that I want to retain?

A: I have financial security, great team relationships and fixed working hours.

Q: What is my dream for my working life?

A: To add in greater freedom and autonomy. I want to make more of my own decisions, choose how to spend my budget and develop my creativity in new markets.

Q: How can I design a new working life that combines the best of both worlds?

A: If I begin to identify potential working partners now, I'll be ready to trade at a profit in a year's time when I plan to resign my current role. I can begin to develop ideas for products and services in my spare time, which will help me identify my learning needs in the new market. If I work towards reduced hours within six months, I'll have more time to consolidate these beginnings so that I'm ready with a solid foundation financially and personally.

This positive approach, based on a coaching technique called *appreciative inquiry*, can help you move away from problems and into the more fertile land of possibilities.

When a major change seems big and far away, you can measure your ongoing progress by the following questions:

✔ On a scale of 1–10, where am I now in relation to my goal?

✔ What would move me closer to a 10?

✔ What positive attributes are helping me to achieve the number I'm at?

✔ How can I enhance these positive attributes?

Appreciative inquiry is often used in organisations to help create positive change. Find out more at www.appreciative-inquiry.org.

Letting Go and Integrating the New

A major change can occur at any stage of your life, whether self-motivated or through external, largely uncontrollable factors such as redundancy or bereavement. You may be on the receiving end of someone else's major life change, and if you're not at the same stage, separation and divorce can result, which will of course throw you into radical change as well.

Whether you choose your life change or have it imposed on you, you need to make sense of it all.

Working through the change

Even when your radical change is positive and you have actively chosen it, you actually go through a grieving process similar to bereavement. You're saying goodbye to a part of your life and even when you feel relief and happiness, you can also feel deeply uncomfortable and sad.

Think about the following scenarios:

✔ Vimla has just heard rumours that the company she works for has been bought out by a competitor who has a cut-throat, highly commercial approach to business.

✔ Peter's partner of many years reveals she has fallen in love with someone else and wants a divorce.

✔ Maria is deciding whether to leave her career as a corporate lawyer and secure a qualification to teach English as a foreign language to fulfil her ultimate goal of living and working in Portugal.

✔ Jonathan is about to hand in his notice on his well-paid managerial role in a big company so that he can set up in business for himself for the first time.

Now consider how each person manages the bereavement process of denial, anger, emotional negotiation, sadness and acceptance:

1. **Denial:** Vimla is horrified at the takeover news and initially can't believe it's happening. She thinks of all the reasons why the takeover news can't be true and can't accept that the board of directors has sold out in this way.

2. **Anger:** After his initial shock and denial, Peter feels extreme anger towards his partner for the betrayal of trust. He is furious that she has been having an affair behind his back and finds it difficult to see past this to discuss options calmly and clearly.

3. **Negotiating:** Maria initially fought against both her need to retain her status and her urge to start again in a new career. She experienced anger that she couldn't have it all before arriving at a negotiating stage where she accommodated both options in her mind. She comes round to the idea that a break from the law profession is going to be best for her in the long run so that she can really focus her energies her new goals.

4. **Sadness:** Jonathan went through denial about how he could ever set up his own business and anger in the form of extreme frustration at his unhappiness. He also experienced negotiating as he attempted to weigh up his real options clearly. He now feels sadness that he is saying goodbye to a feeling of security that has served him well for a long time. Handing in his notice feels like a huge step, and he is not yet ready to look forward to the next stage.

5. **Acceptance:** All four finally arrive at acceptance and are ready to let go of the old path for the possibilities of the new. Even negative outcomes – Vimla does lose her job, and Peter does get divorced – are easier to bear because the people concerned have accepted and processed those outcomes during their acknowledgement of the changes that are occurring.

Evolving to the next stage

After you accept that a major change is inevitable and work through the stages of loss to arrive at acceptance, you then begin yet another journey. The following steps walk you through the period of transition.

1. **Start with closure, or the end.** Accept the passing era of your life. You may choose to symbolise it in some way, either visually or by a clear-out or bonfire of paperwork or objects you no longer need that are associated with the passing phase. You now distance yourself from the past, in order to embrace the future. You're probably relieved that you're free to move on, but may also be fearful of what is to come.

   Vimla, who lost her job as a result of a company takeover, moved through to acceptance with the help of supportive friends and family networks. She realised that she had stayed with her old company out of fierce loyalty, even though she now saw that she had been quite bored by the routine. She was getting excited about fresh fields, although she hadn't a clue how she was going to find the confidence to get back on the interview circuit.

2. **Flow through your transition.** The transition from old to new may be chaotic, as you adjust and discover the consequences of your new choices. Your energy rises as you grow in confidence that you're on the right path, even if you don't have all the answers quite yet. You may be tempted to stay in this phase for a long time without making a definite commitment to the new start as you explore rather than make commitments to action.

   Vimla spent her transition period working with a career coach. At first she was surprised that the coaching focused less on interview techniques and writing a great CV than on exploring what she really enjoyed about her work and what helped to build her confidence in all areas of her life. Vimla quickly got into the flow of her transition and was soon picking up the phone and researching potential new employers.

3. **Begin the new.** You arrive at a position of certainty and realign yourself with your new goals. This is a time of high energy, commitment and action. You feel strong and empowered and can look on your past self, your struggles and challenges, with acceptance.

   After quite a short time, Vimla secured a number of interviews and got two job offers in one day! On the day she started her new job, she wrote a short note to the new owner of her old company, thanking him for making her redundant and giving her the opportunity to spread her wings.

Chapter 22

Applying Your Coaching Skills More Widely

In This Chapter

▶ Checking out your natural coaching talent

▶ Focusing on listening and building rapport

▶ Coaching others responsibly

▶ Building coaching into your relationships at home and at work

*A*lthough coaching is a skilled profession, the key skills stem from certain basic human qualities that everyone already possesses. Using the ideas in this book, you can improve your ability to self-coach and may even develop the desire and expertise to take those skills to a wider audience. Coaching others isn't for the fainthearted and requires integrity, dedication and humility. But if you're inspired by your experiences of beginning to transform your own life through coaching, this chapter may be the starting point for you to enrich the lives of other people in similar ways, whether that's with your friends and family or at work.

This chapter begins with building coaching skills and goes on to explore how to use them. If you want to take your coaching skills to the next level, the appendix has information about becoming a professional life coach.

Thinking beyond Self-Coaching

Think back to a time when you saw a film that really made an impact on you or read a compelling page-turner of a book. You probably couldn't wait to tell your friends about it and perhaps you even insisted that it was a 'must see' or a 'must read'. If coaching has worked its practical magic for you, you may already be thinking about letting the world in on the secret. Perhaps you're even considering that coaching may be the profession for you. Many professional coaches found their calling through experiencing coaching themselves initially, and subsequently changed their vocational goals to train and practise full time.

A big difference separates experiencing your own coaching journey and facilitating that of someone else, especially if you're hoping to make your living in this way. Your starting point in deciding what wider role coaching may play for you is whether you are, or can become, a natural coach – someone who's passionate about supporting others to achieve their goals and who can apply a high degree of expertise and dedication to doing that.

A natural coach lives and breathes their values in all that they do, and you may already display the behaviours that are likely to make you competent at coaching other people, informally or professionally. Here are ten indicators of a natural coach:

- ✔ **You show commitment to self-development.** A natural coach walks the talk and constantly wants to develop self-awareness and build their skills. You self-coach, and are also coached regularly, both personally and professionally, because you know how effective coaching is for personal transformation. The chapters in Part II have more on enhancing your self-development.

- ✔ **You communicate skilfully.** A natural coach asks powerful questions and often probes and clarifies to check their understanding. You listen actively to others and with total attention. Your communication is clear, direct and positive, and you give honest and constructive feedback. Chapter 7 explains the skill of asking powerful questions. The section 'Hear, hear! The art of listening' in this chapter looks at effective listening skills.

- ✔ **You display empathy for others.** You easily put yourself in someone else's shoes and see different perspectives. You never allow your own view of the world to get in the way of facilitating progress for other people. Understanding your own preferred behaviours (Chapter 4) is a great starting point for understanding others.

- ✔ **You build rapport easily.** You match another person's natural style with sensitivity to ensure they're comfortable. You encourage mutual respect and trust. (I talk more about rapport in the later section 'Building rapport'.)

- ✔ **You challenge the status quo.** A natural coach helps others to see new perspectives and possibilities, and challenges assumptions and outdated or unhelpful thinking patterns. Your questioning skills are invaluable here; and so is the way you're able to turn the spotlight on an unhelpful belief (refer to Chapter 5).

✔ **You facilitate understanding.** You don't set out to be the expert, and instead facilitate people to make sense of situations and arrive at new and better conclusions for themselves. Refer to Chapter 1 for some definitions on what role a good coach plays in lighting the way to the right solutions.

✔ **You motivate and inspire action.** A natural coach always encourages positive action and expresses a strong belief in the other person's ability to make effective changes. Your sense of the values that motivate people stand you in good stead here (Chapter 6 has more on values).

✔ **You see situations objectively.** You never become personally or emotionally involved when supporting others. You are able to create a balanced and calm space where you can stand back from situations and see them clearly. You may want to refer to Chapter 14 to get some ideas on managing your emotions.

✔ **You understand and employ accountability.** You help others to define the results they want and encourage *self-accountability* – taking responsibility for your own actions and results.

✔ **You encourage long-term solutions.** You never rely on the quick fix, but seek to facilitate the most balanced and holistic solution.

Use Table 22-1 to rate your current skills on a scale of 1 (not at all competent) to 10 (extremely competent). Use column A for your own perceptions and ask someone who knows you well to fill in column B. What are the differences?

Table 22-1	Natural Coaching Competencies	
	A	*B*
Shows commitment to self-development		
Communicates skilfully		
Displays empathy for others		
Builds rapport easily		
Challenges the status quo		
Facilitates understanding		
Motivates and inspires action		
Sees situations objectively		
Understands and employs accountability		
Encourages long-term solutions		

Developing Key Skills for Coaching Others

You have already built up an impressive toolkit of skills by coaching yourself. You're in tune with the voice of your inner coach (check out Chapter 4), you use powerful questions to challenge your own assumptions (see Chapter 5), and you're facilitating a real awareness of what's important to you and then creating the conditions for the changes you want (covered in Chapter 6). All these skills are used in coaching others, but you need to hone a couple more skills – listening and building rapport – if coaching is going to play a wider role in your life. The great news is that these two skills are essential to developing productive human relationships, so your efforts to enhance your listening skills and rapport won't be wasted even if you never use them specifically to coach other people.

Hear, hear! The art of listening

Listening has been called the 'forgotten skill', although some people never really master it very well in the first place. Take notice of your listening skills and see how often you slip between the three levels of listening.

Level 1 listening

Level 1 listening is when your focus isn't really on the other person but on how what you hear applies to yourself. Perhaps you're introduced to someone new and she starts to tell you about the time she went scuba diving. Partly because you want to build rapport with her, you're keen to respond with your views on the subject and offer some of your own wet water stories. You have heard the information and understood the essence of the conversation enough to have a dialogue with her. But you may miss details because your attention is already focused on your own stories and what you're going to say next.

Level 1 listening is fine for most daily interactions but, just as when you self-coach, you need to listen harder in certain situations in order to start to make sense of the whole picture and really see its significance for that person. You're too busy applying your own filter, like the old conversational joke, 'But enough about me, what do you think of me?' When you begin coaching, you can be so anxious that you're doing it right and asking the right questions that you're really seeking validation in the other person's response more than really listening.

Level 2 listening

Level 2 listening is focused listening. Your full attention is on the speaker and you don't interrupt her, although you may ask questions to find out more or to clarify what she is saying. If the conversation is face to face, you engage in frequent eye contact and your body language shows that you're attentive to the other person. Focused listening is a wonderful gift to give someone because they feel really 'heard'. In a similar way to when you let your inner coach truly listen, without judgement, to your own internal dialogue, focused listening enables other people to sort out what they think for themselves as they relax into the space you create for them. (An added bonus is that focused listeners get the reputation of being fascinating people, because they allow others to be fascinating!)

Level 3 listening

The more Level 2 listening you do, the more you begin to get flashes of inspiration that can help the other person. Level 3 listening is when your intuition kicks in as you extract meaning from the conversation, including what the other person is not saying, and the feelings and emotions that she is subconsciously projecting. Combined with gentle and effective questioning skills, you can make suggestions that can assist her to clarify her thinking and identify workable options.

Building rapport

Rapport occurs when you show respect for another person and sensitively match what she does so that she feels comfortable in your presence. Rapport is essential for coaching others, but it doesn't mean that you try to become everyone's new best friend. You can build rapport with someone in four ways during coaching.

Non-verbal communication

If you interact or coach face to face, your body language reveals just as much as what you say or the way that you say it. Coaching is a relationship of equals, so forget settling yourself in a position of power that sets you up as the expert. Sitting behind a table feels formal; as if you're conducting an interview. Instead, sit alongside or slightly at an angle to your friend or colleague, to seem natural and conversational.

Your body language needs to demonstrate that your full attention is on the other person without invading their personal space. Be sensitive to others' personal space boundaries. Watch for tiny signs that people are uncomfortable that you're too close or too distant. People instinctively move away or move closer to get comfortable in their personal space, and if that doesn't achieve the result they want, the rapport may break as they give up on the effort.

Aim to match body language without mimicking it and to pace if the other person seems initially tense. *Pacing* means to demonstrate a relaxed style to encourage the other person to follow you, loosening up the tensions she feels. So be open and comfortable, with frequent but not intense eye contact.

Listening with one ear

Before I knew anything about modalities and preferences, I had a boss who was hugely auditory versus my strong visual/kinaesthetic bias. I recall an early meeting with him where I was passionately trying to get a pitch across for a project very dear to my heart (you see – kinaesthesia coming out!). I desperately tried to engage eye contact and get him interested in my great graphs, pretty pictures and oh-so-impressive pie charts. But he continued to go through his pile of invoices, his head tilted away from me, mumbling 'Uh-huh' from time to time. I finally exclaimed that he wasn't even listening to me. He smiled and pointed to his right ear, which was directly in front of me. This was his way of concentrating on my pitch, even though it looked pretty rude to me. We both made some adjustments to increase rapport and our relationship improved a lot. (He never did really buy into any of my pet projects, but that's another story!)

Using your voice

Your vocal qualities are vital for life coaching. Aim to match the pitch, tone and volume of the other person's voice as closely as possible to hold rapport and establish trust. Pacing here may mean that you help the other person to change to a more resourceful state by using your voice. If your friend or colleague becomes a bit disheartened during the course of a coaching interaction, you may hear this in the tone of her voice as well as the words she uses. You can move this forward by asking a powerful question (refer to Chapter 7 for more on powerful questions), and you can accelerate the impact of that question by injecting a more upbeat energy into your voice.

Using silence

Silence can be just as beneficial as dialogue during coaching. Most people need a little time to reflect on answers before they speak their thoughts aloud and other thoughts can emerge a few seconds later. If you're too preoccupied with keeping a flow going and filling all the gaps with splendid powerful questions, the other person doesn't have time to reflect and figure things out.

Adopt the three-second rule – wait for three seconds for an answer before assuming that your question needs to be clarified and allow another three-second space when the other person has stopped speaking. Much more extended periods of silence during coaching can be helpful too. One coach said that the longest period of silence she experienced during a coaching session was 30 minutes, and the client said that the session was one of the most productive ever! Be attuned and flexible enough to give the other person what she needs, not what you think she should have.

Choosing language

People tend to take meaning from their world in one of three ways, known as *modalities*. Modalities are really just a posh name for your senses. Being aware of the other person's preferences – whether she thinks in terms of sight, hearing, feeling or a mixture – really helps you to choose the most appropriate language to build rapport. Take a look at *Neuro-linguistic Programming For Dummies* by Romilla Ready and Kate Burton (Wiley) for more about modalities. Here are the three main modalities:

- ✔ **Visual.** Visual people work with pictures and images in their mind and often express it through their language and actions. Phrases such as 'I see what you mean' or 'What's the big picture?' stem from a visual preference. Visual people often like to make lots of notes, doodle a lot and often want to see concepts on the printed page. Most people tend to be visual and this can be either very image based or more visual/verbal (creating pictures in the imagination from words). If you say the word 'green' to a visual person, she may see an image of something green, like grass, or she may see the word green spelled out in her mind's eye. A visual person may have a preference for a face-to-face session, or may like to complete exercises as part of it, which can help her 'see' the process of coaching.

- ✔ **Auditory (Hearing).** Auditory people are often naturally comfortable with telephone-based coaching. Their trigger phrases may be 'I hear what you're saying' or 'How does that sound?' When considering her goals, an auditory person may come up with audible associations – hearing a voice saying 'Well done', or the sound of applause as she walks on stage to collect an award.

- ✔ **Kinaesthetic (Feeling).** Sensations and emotions are the drivers for kinaesthetically oriented people. They use 'feeling' words and phrases such as 'It doesn't feel right' or 'That doesn't sit well with me.' Coaching a strong kinaesthetic person often means getting in tune with the emotion behind what she says and helping her to detach from the feelings that cause pain and anxiety, building up instead a strong armoury of feel-good triggers to associate with her goals.

You can build rapport rapidly when you have sensitivity to the preferred modality of the person you're communicating with or coaching. Failing to pick up her signs can be a huge rapport breaker or even lead to anger and frustration.

Using Your Skills Ethically

Coaching is a very powerful mechanism for change and that carries a responsibility to ensure that you act responsibly and sensitively. If you're going to apply coaching in your life on an informal basis, follow these guidelines to ensure that you coach ethically:

- **Check out your intention.** Why do you want to use coaching skills? If any ego is attached to your motivation, back off. Effective coaching is impressive to experience and watch, but it's not a circus show and the objective should always be to help facilitate the right result for the other person.

- **Don't advise on anything you're not qualified in.** Are you vigilant about spotting danger signs that you may be getting out of your depth, such as if someone mentions that they sometimes feel suicidal? If you do get out of your depth, explain to the other person that you feel that she needs a different kind of support and you can use your coaching skills to help her explore the other support options she has, such as counselling. Do you have access to people who can help you if this happens?

- **Enable the other person to find her own answers.** Are you clear that your role is not to mentor or advise, whatever the strength of your feeling about the rights and wrongs of a situation? Of course you can help someone generate options if she feels really stuck, but you must be very clear that the suggestions you make are in no way preferred or advisory – only the other person is in a position to make that decision and you're there to help her clearly see all the possibilities. Are you also clear that you'll do all in your power to build self-reliance in others and not foster dependency on you?

- **Keep informed of coaching developments.** Are you committed to staying abreast of best-practice techniques, regardless of whether you coach professionally or informally?

If you choose to become a professional coach or to build coaching actively into your job, your professional body or training provider requires you to subscribe to a code of ethics. See the Appendix for more.

Developing a Coaching Role in Your Life

How do you begin to apply the skills you've gained? Sometimes the obvious starting points can be the trickiest. This section sheds some light on starting to coach other people informally.

Coaching friends and family

Your coaching skills, integrated into your life and behaviours, can significantly enhance the quality of your relationships with your loved ones. And if your loved ones are on a similar journey to you and are open to working with you, then friends and family can be excellent co-coaches. They can provide familiarity and support as you try out new ideas and techniques with each other.

However, you may also encounter strong resistance and experience more difficulties in adopting a coaching approach with your nearest and dearest precisely *because* they're so close to you, and you've built up longstanding patterns of behaviour with them. If you're likely to be very emotionally involved in coaching family and friends (and it's sometimes hard not to be), I strongly suggest you do not attempt it and look at alternatives. Perhaps you're co-coaching with someone who can work with a family member instead of you?

Here are three principles that may help you to integrate coaching into your personal life and family unit sensitively:

- ✔ **Practise really listening before you do anything else.** Of all the people you communicate with, your family and close friends may be the ones that you've got out of the habit of hearing in a meaningful way. You may be surprised at what you hear and learn about people when they get used to the new you that holds back from giving advice, however well meaning, and simply allows them to work out their own solutions in a calm, quiet space.

- ✔ **Work hard on suspending judgement, both within yourself and in the way you express yourself.** It's tempting to rush to fix things with close ones and to be overly critical or a little too indulgent. Adopting the same curious approach that you use with your own inner dialogues will help you to help your loved ones steer a true path. Get into the habit of asking the other person what impact a particular decision or choice has for her. You need to find your own language to put this across in a way that fits with how you all like to communicate as a family. Encourage your loved ones to be objective and to think about the consequences, good and ill, of choosing a certain route. Use your powerful questions with care (refer to Chapter 7) and be alert for signs that your family member or friend needs a professional coach or other appropriate support.

- ✔ **Set a quiet, shining example.** You're not a saint, a martyr or the next new guru. You're a human being of great potential, with both amazing talents and frustrating flaws. Don't set yourself up as having arrived at a mountaintop that no one else has yet scaled. You don't know how difficult someone else's terrain is. A natural coach accepts with humility that her role is to facilitate change but that change is only really possible when the time is right. You don't have to be perfect around your loved ones to show them how powerful coaching is. You do have to be self-aware and willing to continue with your own journey, despite relapses, setbacks and periods of low motivation. Dr David Hawkins, psychiatrist and writer on spiritual philosophy, said: 'We change the world not by what we say or do, but as a consequence of what we have become.'

Building coaching into your job

You can adopt any of the coaching techniques in this book to great success in your work, whether you're a manager or a team member. If coaching is an unofficial part of your role, the same guidelines as for family and friends are often appropriate (see the preceding section). You don't want to be someone fired up with sound-bites and a sudden injection of can-do/will-do juice. At the very least you can set yourself up for a fall if you can't sustain that enthusiasm, and at the worst, you may turn people off the whole concept of self-development. Don't mistake the sizzle for the substance; instead, use your enthusiasm and passion to look for ways to enhance what already happens in your workplace.

Here are some areas where you can consider using your coaching skills:

- ✔ Consider how meetings are conducted at your workplace. What opportunities do you have to contribute your coach's objectivity and questioning skills?

- ✔ Think about one-to-one time at your work. Do you have constructive goal and objective setting? How can you encourage self-responsibility rather than an environment where goals are imposed?

- ✔ Catch people doing things right and help your colleagues understand what makes them successful. People often deliberate too much on the mistakes they make and take their accomplishments for granted. As a natural coach, you can help your colleagues explore what factors contribute to their successful performance.

- ✔ Think of yourself as 'leader as coach' and work to get the best out of the whole person. Many organisations have a bit too much modelling of the more obvious leadership styles. Do you see leadership as brave and bold and charging over the mountainside? Well, yes, it can be. But a natural coach follows as well as leads, and can make that a leadership quality. So look around for the quiet, shining examples of good practice in your teams and offer appreciation and encouragement.

Making a difference, one person at a time

He often walked along the beach in the morning, planning the day ahead. One day he went in a different direction. This stretch of beach was more isolated, though still bleakly beautiful. He thought he had the place to himself until he saw a solitary figure way ahead in the distance. She seemed to be collecting shells. Curiously, she cast them straight back into the sea. He wondered why, and quickened his pace to catch up with her. Then he saw clearly just what she was doing.

Not shells, he thought, *starfish*. He smiled to himself. Admirable, of course, to want to give the poor things a chance to be where they can thrive, but surely it was pointless in the face of the hundreds, perhaps thousands of starfish littering the beach? Not a chance of making a difference to that number.

The starfish thrower looked up for a moment, almost as if she read his thoughts. She smiled. He smiled back, a little embarrassed, and carried on walking.

Days passed. He spent some time in the city, which he also loved, working. At first, he didn't think much about the starfish thrower as he strove to solve problems, meet demands. Somehow he solved very little and the demands seemed even greater than usual. He often felt like giving up. More and more, the image returned to him of the woman reaching down and throwing starfish in a smooth arc to where the sky and the sea and the sunlight joined. By the end of his long week, the image was too insistent to ignore and he returned again to that stretch of beach.

The starfish thrower was there. This time, he stood beside her and bent to reach for starfish. His cast made a precise arc in the bright, harsh sky and he thought to himself, 'Well, we made a difference for that one.'

He reached again . . .

Part VI
The Part of Tens

The 5th Wave   By Rich Tennant

"How can you not feel confident? You're wearing Versace sunglasses, a Tommy Hilfiger sweater, Calvin Klein jeans, and Michael Jordan gym shoes. Now go on out there and just be yourself."

In this part . . .

Instant inspiration at your fingertips! Need a great powerful question to focus you? Crave a daily balancing act? Keen to know where you can top up your motivation for your own development? Look no further: this part is for you.

Chapter 23

Ten Life Coaching Beliefs about Yourself

In This Chapter
▶ Understanding your uniqueness
▶ Realising your resourcefulness
▶ Accepting your freedom to act

> *The thing always happens that you really believe in; and the belief in a thing makes it happen.*
>
> Frank Lloyd Wright

*B*eliefs you hold about yourself help you to move forward or keep you stuck. You can choose to hold or reject every belief you hold about yourself. This chapter gives you ten truths about yourself that you can use to replace any old, unhelpful beliefs such as 'I'm lazy' or 'I never succeed at anything'. Read Chapter 5 for loads more about how coaching can positively affect your beliefs.

At first, you may find it hard to hold these new beliefs about yourself, but persevere to make them come true for you.

You Are Unique

> *What lies before us and what lies behind us are small matters compared to what lies within us. And when we bring what is within out into the world, miracles happen.*
>
> Henry David Thoreau

Even if you have an identical twin, no one in the world is quite like you. No one has ever been quite like you, or ever will be again. This doesn't mean that you're more special than anyone else. It does mean that no one can know what your potential is until *you* realise it. It's never too late to begin to identify what your uniqueness is. History is full of people who didn't discover this for themselves until late in life and then went on to achieve greatness – look at Grandma Moses, for example, the American artist who didn't begin painting until the age of 75 and became famous for her work after her first exhibition in New York when she was 80. Or the writer Mary Wesley, who was in her seventies when she published her first novel, went on to write ten more and was awarded the CBE (Commander of the Order of the British Empire) for her contributions to literature.

Greatness doesn't have to mean fame and fortune – greatness is often simply being the best that you can be, a quiet role model in how to live your own life. Be inspired by Chapter 4, which explores uniqueness more deeply.

Your Whole Life Is the Canvas for Coaching

I've learned that you can't have everything and do everything all at the same time.

Oprah Winfrey

How many times have you heard people say something like, 'My life would be great if I could just get that job . . . or find a life partner . . . or afford more holidays . . . or . . . or . . . or'? When you achieve the elusive missing element in your life, you sometimes experience consequences that you didn't expect. The job brings extra stress and that affects your previously blissful time spent with a significant other. Or you find your life partner and discover that you miss the solitary things you used to do when you only had yourself to think about. You may beat yourself up about this, because it seems you are never satisfied and happiness always eludes you.

Through coaching, you can begin to accept that this balancing act is a function of being alive. Recognise the three elements that you need to live your best life – your enjoyment (achieving the things that make you happy), finding meaning (what gives you purpose in your life) and balance (making peace with the sometimes messy process that gets you there). So although coming to coaching with a specific life area in mind is quite normal, only when you take your whole life into account can coaching really work its magic.

Chapter 1 has more about these three key elements that drive you and how they fit into your life.

You Hold Your Own Agenda

You will recognise your own path when you come upon it, because you will suddenly have all the energy and imagination you will ever need.

Jenny Gillies

You may find it odd to think that you'd ever hold anyone else's agenda during coaching, but you can fall into this trap surprisingly often. Are you losing weight because a partner thinks you should? Have you volunteered for a spot of executive coaching because it pleases your boss? Do you think you ought to give up smoking because your friends complain about it? Do you even want to get good results to please your coach?

All these situations are powerful motivators for change, and they may have their place in your tool-kit from time to time. But coaching starts with what *you* want more of, or less of, in your life. You can't be nearly as whole-hearted about change if your main driver for that change is someone else's agenda and sooner or later the cracks start to appear. Begin with your own core desires, then add in all the other good reasons for change and you've got a really robust strategy for success.

You Are Resourceful

Don't be timid and squeamish about your actions. All life is an experiment. The more experiments you make, the better.

Ralph Waldo Emerson

Remember how good you were as a child at getting what you wanted? You had all the elements of success – single-minded determination, creativity and imagination, flexibility to change tack as needed, irresistible persuasive qualities, even the element of surprise on occasion. And all that to get to stay up a little later or secure an ice cream. The adult world was no match for you when you really wanted something.

Well, all of those resources and more are still inside you. And you don't have to resort to a temper tantrum in the street to get what you want! Coaching helps to unearth those resources from the dusty attic and polish them off, ready for action. You acquire more ways of being resourceful all the time.

Check out Chapter 8 for more clues to your own resourcefulness.

You Are Capable of Great Results

Change your thoughts and you change your world.

Norman Vincent Peale

Have you ever surprised yourself by what you can do? Maybe you passed an exam in a subject that you were really struggling with, or snatched a promotion in the face of stiff competition. Perhaps you started a fitness programme and found after 12 weeks that you can run for 30 minutes at a time when the most you ever managed before was a 30-second dash for the bus. Or perhaps you overcame a fear of public speaking to stand up at a wedding reception and deliver the best man's speech.

Regardless of how good the end goal made you feel, often simply the feeling that you pushed your own boundaries gives you the greatest buzz. Coaching aims to harness the energy of those moments where you achieve your own brand of exceptional results, so that you are constantly delighting in achieving more than you could possibly have imagined for yourself. *Your* definition of 'great results' is important – no one else's.

You Can Generate the Right Solutions for Yourself

All truths are easy to understand once they are discovered; the point is to discover them.

Galileo Galilei

This truth can often take a bit of believing. When people come to coaching, they may think they need an expert to tell them how to fix something in their lives that isn't so good. After all, if you've been chewing around the problem for a long time with little or no success, you would have come up with the answer by now, right?

In reality, coaching frees you to approach your problems and goals differently so that you can access the answer that has always been there for you. One of the joys of coaching is that perfect solutions are always in you for the finding. This is because no one but you can live your life. Coaching allows you to explore options, play with ideas and try on solutions until you get the right fit. Take a look at Chapter 9 for more about how you generate solutions for yourself.

You Are Free from Being Judged

Some people find fault like there is a reward for it.

Zig Ziglar

Whether someone else is coaching you or you're coaching yourself, you need to suspend judgement about what seems to be right and wrong. This doesn't mean that you have free rein to break the law, of course. The kind of judgements that aren't helpful to coaching are full of 'shoulds', 'oughts' and 'musts'. Very often this kind of authoritative language is a big clue that someone else's judgement is a powerful influence. Coaching allows you to look at what's going on in a curious, almost neutral way. That way you are more likely to get at what's really going on.

You Can Make Powerful Choices

If you limit your choices only to what seems possible or reasonable, you disconnect yourself from what you truly want and all that is left is a compromise.

Robert Fritz

The feeling that you are stuck in a dead end without choices is one of the most miserable feelings around. You can feel trapped in a job you hate because you feel that no other employer values your skills. Perhaps the money is good, and you can't see how you'd be able to maintain your financial responsibilities if you take a pay cut to do work you love or to retrain. These are difficult choices to make, and it can be hard to see the benefits of giving up the security you have for something you don't know so much about. At times you have to make a choice to sacrifice something you want for something you want even more. You can't always have everything and, oddly enough, if you do manage to retain everything, you may find it all comes at a cost you're unwilling to pay.

Trust that you can come up with new choices that move you forward in unexpected ways. Perhaps you can reskill yourself over a longer period out of work hours or reduce your hours very slightly to free up some time to think about and plan your options. You may be tempted to think in terms of big, bold gestures to resolve the issues in your life, but the smaller choices that you make are often the most powerful, as well as the most workable.

You Take Responsibility for Your Results

> *It is not only for what we do that we are held responsible but also for what we do not do.*

> Molière

Coaching doesn't guarantee a 'right first time' result. Because coaching is about giving yourself permission to experiment and play with options, there's a fair chance that some of those options don't give you exactly the result you want. What they do give you is increased knowledge and self-awareness, and that's often more important and can prepare you better for the next challenge. Coaching is sometimes hard, and you may sometimes feel that you aren't getting anywhere fast. But as long as you're taking positive action and accepting responsibility for the results of those actions, you *are* getting somewhere and before very long you find your patience is rewarded.

You Trust Your Senses

> *As soon as you trust yourself, you will know how to live.*

> Johann Wolfgang von Goethe

For much of the time you use your conscious mind to think through your problems and design your strategies, which works well. Coaching suggests that you supplement this analytical strategy by taking note of your other senses. What do you *feel*? What *images* are associated with whatever you're dealing with? What *sounds* and *sensations* accompany your thoughts about your problems and goals? All your senses can give you clues on a more sub-conscious level about the options you can take and the actions that are right for you.

Learning to trust your senses takes time and practice. Start by simply notic-ing what's going on for you and before long you start to make connections that help you arrive at answers that come not just from your rational mind, but also from the clues your body gives you. For example, maybe you agree to take on a new responsibility at work that your manager tells you is exciting and worthwhile. But you have a nagging feeling – a gut reaction – that trouble is ahead. Pay attention to the feeling: it may be natural apprehension about a new challenge, or it may be a warning for you to dig a bit deeper and be sure about what you're letting yourself in for.

Chapter 24

Ten Questions to Keep Your Life on Track

....

In This Chapter

▶ Navigating your day with powerful questions

▶ Challenging your assumptions

▶ Moving yourself forward

....

*W*hen you begin a new exercise routine, you may ask your instructor what single exercise can most benefit you if you do it on a regular basis. With life coaching, one of the best routines you can get into to keep yourself on track is to ask yourself powerful questions as you go through your day.

The questions in this chapter can produce that light-bulb moment when you can suddenly see your situation more clearly or from a new perspective.

Write these questions on to small cards that you can keep in your wallet or diary so that you can refer to them often. When you feel that events are controlling you, or you feel uncertain about what you're doing, pause to ask yourself one of these questions. This helps you to refocus and get a sense of where your priorities lie.

And I've included an inspirational and thought provoking quotation at the start of each section.

What Would I Do If I Knew I Couldn't Fail?

Courage is being scared to death – but saddling up anyway.

John Wayne

Failure is many people's biggest fear. Failure can paralyse you into inaction so that sometimes you may prefer to avoid a challenge rather than face it.

But failure is all in the mind. Chapter 5 explains why fear of failure is really an illusion and how you can manage your Fear Foes. Still, it's true that the idea of failing can hold you back from being your best. One great way to sidestep this is to put the fear to one side and imagine what life would be like if you didn't feel it.

Ask yourself on a regular basis what you'd do if you knew you just couldn't fail. Doing so allows you to daydream about big, bold dreams stripped of the constraints of narrowing fears of failure. Imagining yourself successfully overcoming the odds lets you try out your dream safely and helps you decide if you really want to pursue it.

As well as the big things in life, the small fears of failure that drain your energy also benefit from this question. Perhaps you hold back from making a point at a meeting because you think you sound stupid. Maybe you talk yourself out of starting up a conversation with an interesting stranger because you worry about them thinking you too forward. See yourself doing these things without the straitjacket of fear of failure and you find that taking the first step becomes easier.

Who Am I Becoming?

We did not change as we grew older; we just became more clearly ourselves.

Lynn Hall

Who you are right here, right now, is made up of the sum total of your choices to date. Every cell in your body renews itself over time and in a very real physical sense you are not quite the same person you were ten years ago. Emotionally and mentally you change and develop, and you learn new skills over the years too. Ten years ago, did you imagine yourself as the person you are today? When you think about the next ten years, what sort of person do you see yourself becoming? Do you like the trends that you see developing? Perhaps you see someone who is becoming more tired and worn out with an unbalanced work/home life.

You always have the choice to become a different version of yourself, no matter how far you feel you have drifted down a path you don't much like. *You* set your course for the future you who is happy, fulfilled and enjoying life in your small daily choices.

What Am I Doing Right Now to Honour My Core Values?

If your success is not on your own terms, if it looks good to the world but does not feel good in your heart, it is not success at all.

Anna Quindler

Your values are the essence of who you are. When you live your life in tune with your most important values, you feel in harmony with yourself and your world. Asking yourself the above question every day can stop you short in the middle of activities that move you away from your values. You may ask yourself this question in the middle of gossiping with a friend where you're dissecting the behaviour of an absent third and find that the things you're saying are not what you would say if they were present. Or perhaps you get so focused on a tight deadline at work that you cut corners in ways that damage your own feelings of integrity.

After you've identified the values that are most true for you (refer to Chapter 6), consider finding or creating a visual symbol of them to remind you of your inner compass. You may choose a family photo that reminds you of the importance of love in your life, or a pebble you collected on a run to keep you focused on fitness goals.

What Am I Settling For?

I've arrived at this outermost edge of my life by my own actions. Where I am is thoroughly unacceptable. Therefore, I must stop doing what I've been doing.

Alice Koller

How many times a day do you put up with a compromise or go along with the line of least resistance? Maybe you are settling for a job that doesn't fulfil you, a friendship that drains your energies, a romantic relationship that saps your spirit. Chapter 21 helps you to make the major changes in your life when you have to let go of something big. But perhaps the problem is something as simple as an untidy work space, a garden that never gets tended or a bedroom that needs repainting. Getting the simple things in your life right can sometimes have as much power to motivate you as the huge, more challenging things. And taking small steps towards putting your needs first can give you the courage to do this more often for yourself. Where's that paintbrush, then?

What Is My Legacy?

Be the change you want to see in the world.

Gandhi

Your legacy need not be something that becomes evident after you have shuffled off this mortal coil. Your legacy is what you contribute to your world right now. It may be seen in bringing up children, supportive friendships, caring for older family members, voluntary work, a thriving business, a work of art or daily small acts of random kindness. Chapter 18 has more about how you can weave a coaching approach into the fabric of your life.

Your legacy takes shape each day as you find ways to share your energies with others.

Where Do I Focus My Attention?

Energy is the essence of life. Every day you decide how you're going to use it by knowing what you want and what it takes to reach that goal, and by maintaining focus.

Oprah Winfrey

If you spend many hours each day bemoaning your lot, no matter what your justification is, you're likely to find that your lot gets worse, not better. Your life becomes what you focus on. Thought habits (the pattern of your every-day thinking) create the texture of your life. If you continually indulge in pessimistic thoughts about all the disasters that may be awaiting you round the corner, you feel drained and nervous all the time. Visualising your whole-life goals on a regular basis is not only a more pleasant way to think, but also it actually helps to train your mind to take the action required to reach those goals.

Chapter 8 helps you to understand where you focus your attention and to direct that to the positive goals that serve to steer a true course for you.

How Am I Using My Gifts?

If you have a talent, use it in every way possible. Don't hoard it. Don't dole it out like a miser. Spend it lavishly like a millionaire intent on going broke.

Brendan Francis

You have talents that are uniquely yours – no one else can employ them in quite the way that you do. Lots of people can hold a tune, but you may have a way of expressing yourself when singing that lights up a room. Or you may have a seemingly mundane talent that you don't even recognise yet for what it is. You may take for granted your natural gift for choosing just the right colour combination for your house re-vamp, or your instinct for creating a wonderful, warm environment at a dinner party.

How are you using these gifts to enhance your life and your world? Don't play to your weaknesses when people all around you envy the natural gifts that you already have. One of the most effective ways of becoming happier in your life is to look for more opportunities to play to your strengths and oper-ate in your natural element. You attract greater success with less effort and you enjoy yourself far more.

Chapter 4 has more about using your natural gifts to your best advantage.

What Am I Holding on to That I No Longer Need?

The problem is never how to get new innovative thoughts into your mind, but how to get old ones out. Every mind is a building filled with archaic furniture. Clear out a corner of your mind and creativity will instantly fill it.

Dee Hock

Do you own a wardrobe full of clothes you never wear? Paperwork you hang onto 'just in case'? Old magazines and journals, because you never know when you might want to dig out an article? Books, videos, CDs and DVDs that you bought but never much liked? Spring cleaning is incredibly liberating because you offload stuff that causes clutter in your physical space. If you can find a good home for these items and benefit others, you also get a virtuous glow. And you often find that afterwards your mental space opens up wide.

Are you holding onto more significant things than tangible bits and bobs? An old belief, a habit that doesn't serve you, a pattern of behaviour that has become destructive? As you make changes in your coaching journey, you find it easier to let go of the things you no longer need because you want that space for more congenial travelling companions. Hike to Chapters 16 and 17 for more.

How Much Time Do I Spend with People Who Inspire Me?

The meeting of two personalities is like the contact of two chemical substances: if there is any reaction, both are transformed.

Carl Jung

The people you spend most time with have a strong influence on you. If you are in a soul-destroying job, surrounded by people who feel as if they're the living dead, you can't help but absorb some of that sadness and negativity. Before you can change any of that, you need to get a good dose of inspiration from people who are truly alive and energised. Who are the most inspiring people for you? Are they among your friends, co-workers, family members? Do you go to different people for different kinds of inspiration? Do your friends know how and why they inspire you and how much you value them? Make a promise to yourself to maintain and extend the network of stars in your life who boost your strength and motivation.

What One Thing Would I Change for the Better?

Desire creates the power.

Raymond Holliwell

Perhaps your one positive change would be losing weight, or giving up smoking, or moderating your alcohol consumption. Maybe you'd choose to improve the quality of your relationships. Or maybe you'd pick getting promoted or setting up your own business. What is the thing for you that would have the most benefits if you changed it? What's been stopping you from making that change? What small step can you take today towards making this great thing happen for yourself?

Identify the one thing you want to change for the better and get inspired by reading Chapter 2.

Chapter 25

Ten Daily Balancing Acts

In This Chapter

▶ Taking time out

▶ Building the habit of balance

▶ Giving yourself the gift of self-care

*T*aking ten short moments through your day to balance your energies pays dividends out of all proportion to the effort you expend. And doing so is the fastest way to build self-coaching into your life. Try out the simple tips in this chapter and see how your daily life improves. Happiness is a habit, not a destination.

See a Clear Vision

Take a moment to recall the vision of your whole-life goals at least once a day and whenever you feel stressed (refer to Chapter 8 for more about planning your life goals and how you can create that vision). You can call this reflection day-dreaming or creative visualisation, but the more you create your perfect day in your mind's eye, the more you encourage yourself to move towards it. The simple act of enjoying the luxury of seeing, hearing and feeling your ideal future helps you to relax, refocus and get back to the fray of your everyday life.

See with clarity.

Take a Gratitude Tonic

All strong emotions have a physical effect on your body that lasts for up to six hours. When you feel extreme anger, frustration or anxiety, the ill effects ripple around in you long after you've technically got the better of the nasty emotion and moved on. All this unwelcome stuff can contribute to stress and depression. But good, strong, positive feelings also stay in your emotional bloodstream. You can counteract the effect of all the toxins you encounter during a normal day by the simple technique of counting your blessings.

Anna Maravelas, an author and corporate consultant, describes how counting her blessings helped her overcome uncontrollable anger that once had her throw a chair out of a second-storey window:

> *By focusing twice a day on consciously counting my blessings, I created new circuitry in my brain for gratitude. Now everywhere I go I can tap into positive energy, just in myself; I don't need other people to bring it to me.*

 You consider taking a painkiller if you're in extreme physical pain, so for an effective barrier to the effects of emotional pain, spend five minutes twice a day loading yourself up on good emotions that release well-being throughout your system. First thing in the morning is a great time to ponder all the blessings you have in your life and all that you feel grateful for, even if those things are simply the warmth of the duvet and the gentle snoring of your pet at the bottom of the bed. Top up with another gratitude tonic around mid-afternoon to see you through the rest of the day.

Think with care.

Do a Kind and Thoughtful Act

You quite rightly spend a lot of your time focusing on your own needs and goals. Balancing this with a random act of kindness on a regular basis is an amazingly powerful way to inject a feel-good factor into your life and help you to get things in perspective. Here are some ideas:

- Let someone out at a road junction.
- Pack shopping for the pensioner in front of you at the supermarket.
- Praise a call-centre agent for their excellent communication skills.
- Email thanks to your boss for supporting you at a tough meeting.
- Pick up a bit of street litter.
- Leave a pound coin in the shopping trolley for the next shopper.

You don't notice the loss of what you give away, but you do notice the new spring in your step. And watch out for the good turn coming back to you in the spirit of 'the giver gains'.

Give with abundance.

Soak Up Wise Words

Words have the power to change minds and lives. Plenty of wise words are available to you to guide you to your own truths. Collect inspiring quotes and affirmations and keep them to hand. You can refer to the quotes and soak up their wisdom when you're feeling at your most derailed.

Read with wisdom.

See-saw between Action and Reflection

You can have too much of a good thing, so even when you're firing on all cylinders and motoring along the fast track of your day, you need to switch to reflective mode regularly to provide balance. Taking time out for reflection on your experiences also helps your decision-making abilities. Similarly, if you've spent a long period reflecting, theorising or mentally exploring options, switch to action mode often to redress the balance.

You can even automate this see-saw effect so that you don't forget – a gentle alarm on your phone every hour or so reminds you to change the energy. The alarm doesn't have to break your flow; even a small change in state stirs up the creative juices for you. You feel a lot more centred if you see-saw through the day and you almost certainly get more done.

Play with action and reaction.

Take a Deep Breath

Breathing deeply and with control is like taking a long, cool drink of water on the hottest day of the year. Deep breathing instantly revives you, calms you and centres you. Simply focusing on your in and out breaths for five minutes every so often really helps to centre you, especially when you feel anxious, stressed and wound up.

Find a quiet spot (even the toilet!) and breathe deeply. Focus especially on the out breath. Say the word 'out' quietly in your mind with each exhalation, and as you do so, imagine all the negative stress leaving your body bit by bit until it's all gone and you feel calm and relaxed.

When you feel tired and drained, claim that quiet spot and focus this time on the in breath. Say the word 'in' quietly to yourself and visualise taking positive energy into your body, leaving you bright and alert, ready for action.

Breathe with purpose.

Share a Smile

Laughter is a wonderful balancing act and even a simple smile can dissolve tensions and create ripples of harmony. Have you ever noticed that smiling at someone without getting a smile in return is almost impossible to do? So when the energies from those around you feel less than harmonious, redress the balance with a beaming smile. If nothing else, they may wonder what's put you in such a good mood and will probably respond in kind!

Smile with passion.

Give Yourself a Treat

Your busy routine benefits from the injection of the occasional spontaneous gift to yourself. As well as setting up rewards that are associated with progress on your goals, you can also aim to find or do something each day that reminds you that you're worth a bit of tender loving care on a regular basis.

Make your treat small and significant to you. Create a moment that you treasure as much for the experience as for what you give to yourself. Here are some ideas:

- Buy a postcard and send it to yourself.
- Find the juiciest peach in the shop.
- Put your headphones on and listen to your favourite music with your eyes closed.
- Dance with your cat or your childhood teddy bear.
- Bake a tiny cake just for you.
- Give yourself a gold star.
- Lie still and calm and look at the sky.
- Place a single flower in a small vase in front of you as you eat your breakfast.

Be with yourself.

Stretch Out

Do a 2–5-minute stretch every morning to have a positive effect on your balance for the day.

Simply stand tall and stretch your arms out above your head, reaching as far as you can. Feel your body being pulled up from the top of your spine by a strong silken cord. Hold for 20 seconds, release and repeat as you want.

While you stretch, feel your body strengthen and lengthen and remind yourself of all the great goals you're reaching for.

Reach with energy.

Get Natural

I bet some forces of nature really get you back into a good, stress-free mood. Maybe your balancing act in nature is the smell of the earth after rain, a lungful of fresh air or the sight of a plant or flower. Maybe you love walking barefoot on the grass. Perhaps a screensaver of a landscape reminds you of a great holiday or adventure.

You don't have to hug trees to commune with nature. But contemplating a strong, solid oak tree for a few minutes really gives you some perspective on everything you get so wound up about on a daily basis.

Take in the beauty of the natural world.

Chapter 26

Ten Inspirational Resources

In This Chapter

▶ Getting a fix of inspiration

▶ Staying open to the influences around you

▶ Trying out a few new styles

Coaching helps you to evolve your unique philosophy of life. You can create and innovate in much the same way as a novelist, a screen-writer, a self-help guru or a poet does – and you need inspiration to do so. Sometimes your *a-ha!* inspirational moments come from your own life and sometimes they come from another perspective such as books, films and poetry. All influences are resources for the self-coach. (Even watching reality TV can help you work out how you *don't* want to lead your life!)

This chapter guides you to a treasure chest of inspirational resources, all of which can help to motivate you along your way.

Your Life Is a Journey

> It's true; life really is generous to those who pursue their destiny.
>
> Paulo Coelho

Paulo Coelho's book *The Alchemist* is a fable about a young shepherd boy, Santiago, searching for the treasure he has dreamt so vividly of finding. He follows his dream and goes on a long journey, picking up wisdom and knowledge on his way. Alas, he gets to his destination and is bitterly disappointed when the expected riches are nowhere to be found. But that's not the end of his journey, and he finally finds his treasure in the most unexpected of places.

Santiago's determination to do what it takes to find his treasure and learn from his experience is a great example of facing the realities of living your dream, and ultimately discovering that the journey is also its own reward.

Get Out of Your Mind

There are no ordinary moments.

Dan Millman

Dan Millman used his own experience as an award-winning US college gymnast to write *Way of the Peaceful Warrior*, an inspiring story of the meaning of true success and achievement, also made into a film, *Peaceful Warrior*. The central character initially follows a typical striving and competitive path to glory, only to suffer a devastating accident that seems set to ruin his glittering career for ever. An unlikely mentor appears in the form of a petrol pump attendant he nicknames Socrates, and Dan's new education begins. Dan learns to let go of his attachment to winning at all costs and to focus instead on his love of his sport, getting out of his own head and tuning into his inner wisdom.

Whether you choose the book or the film, the simple and profound philosophies of *Way of the Peaceful Warrior* can remind you that success is a natural result of being attentive to the present moments of your life and true to your own greatness.

See Things as You Want Them to Be

Think about what you want, not what you fear.

Brian Mayne

Brian Mayne's enchanting fable for children of all ages, *Sam the Magic Genie*, takes its young hero Joseph on a magic carpet ride through his own mind, introducing him to the wonders of the Tree of Self, Faith the Dolphin and the Pool of Confidence. Sam finally encourages Joseph to brave the Fingers of Fear so that he reaches his own Sea of Potential. The book's messages are that you create your own reality by what you choose to think about and that self-love is the starting point for personal growth.

Choose Happiness

You keep on rowing; I'll keep on smiling.

Poppy in *Happy-Go-Lucky*

Mike Leigh's film *Happy-Go-Lucky* tells the story of Poppy, a born optimist who refuses to let anything get her down. Her gift is making the most of life, and she always looks for ways to let go of the irritations, frustrations and disappointments of everyday living.

When she meets her new driving instructor Scott, her natural exuberance collides with his troubled and narrow life perspective. The film is a great example of the importance of choosing a positive perspective. As Scott gets deeper and deeper into his negative frame about life, Poppy's cheerful approach helps her create good outcomes in her life and increase her own happiness. It's a warm, sensitive film about how in any ordinary life you can choose to determine your own happy luck.

Feast Your Senses

No one can teach you how to see.

Neytiri in *Avatar*

James Cameron's film *Avatar* takes you on a breathtaking journey to the imaginary planet of Pandora, whose inhabitants live in complete harmony with nature. Watch it on a big screen in 3D to feel immersed in the colours and richness of a spectacularly beautiful world. Allowing yourself to get lost in the amazing special effects of this film lets your creative right brain out to play – it's one reason why so many people who have watched it have said that for such a long film, time seems to pass really quickly!

Avatar has a serious environmental message too, so perhaps you'll be inspired to a deeper connection with nature yourself, for the good of the planet and your own pleasure!

Value Your Life Experience

Maybe it is written . . .

Jamal Malik in *Slumdog Millionaire*

Slumdog Millionaire is a rags-to-riches tale with a difference. Jamal Malik, an 18-year-old orphan from the Mumbai slums, hold audiences riveted as he competes in India's *Who Wants to Be a Millionaire?* television programme and astonishes everyone with his ability to answer the questions. It turns out that Jamal's life experience on the streets has uniquely and bizarrely qualified him as each seemingly obscure question comes up.

It's a story of determination, the courage of the human spirit, the redeeming power of love and of course, the value of all the experiences that you have in your life – even those that you wish had not occurred!

Poetry Creates Motion

Poems make the reader less settled yet more whole, more alert to the world, more alive, more in touch with being human.

Neil Astley

Poetry isn't all that fashionable these days. You might think poems are obscure, difficult and irrelevant to your life. But take time to find the kind of poetry that speaks to you, and you discover a wonderful resource for lifting you beyond your everyday worries and cares. The fact that a poem can sometimes take a bit of unravelling can even become the attraction, giving your brain a bit of a workout. And good poetry leaves footprints in your mind, even if you don't immediately understand all the meaning.

A poem takes less time to read than a novel, has the same effect as meditation in calming your mind and is ready for you to pick it up at any time of the day when you have a spare few moments. Almost convinced? Try two great anthologies, *Staying Alive* and *Being Alive*, edited by Neil Astley, which offer some of the best examples of modern poetry and are a good place to start to discover what styles hit the mark for you.

No Place Like Home

Birds fly over the rainbow, why then, oh why can't I?

Dorothy in *The Wizard of Oz*

In *The Wizard of Oz*, Dorothy, the Scarecrow, the Tin Man and the Lion set out on the Yellow Brick Road to seek the wisdom of the Wizard. They discover that they already have all the brains, heart and courage they need, and that Dorothy can find her way home at any time she chooses with a smart tap of her ruby slippers. *The Wizard of Oz* is a timeless classic book and film about journeys and friendship, self-awareness and personal growth. And you can sing along to the movie too.

Your Life Is Significant

All endings are also beginnings. We just don't know it at the time.

Mitch Albom

In the book *The Five People You Meet in Heaven*, Mitch Albom tells the story of Eddie who dies in a tragic accident trying to save a little girl. Eddie awakes in Heaven to discover that he has an appointment with five people he knew on Earth who explain the point of his life to him. Throughout the inspirational story of his meetings with his five people, the question remains – did Eddie really save the little girl or was his last act on Earth in vain?

The story is inspirational because it drives home the message that everything you do has significance, and that by being uniquely yourself you're fulfilling your own purpose in life.

Let Your Inner Coach Come Out to Play

Each of us defines for ourselves what it means to be successful.

Spencer Johnson

Of all the inspirational resources available to you, perhaps the greatest one is your own willingness to experience your world in the present moment. So learn from your past, set your sights on your future dreams and then make your dreams come true in the here and now. Read Spencer Johnson's *The Present* to get a timely reminder of how to give yourself the greatest of gifts – full focused attention on the present moment – that repays you in enjoyment and success in all that you do. Catch yourself frequently as you go about your day and tune into what you see, hear and feel. Revel in the chance to just be.

Appendix

Considering a Future as a Professional Life Coach

●●

*L*ife coaching is an incredible profession, and for me there's no going back. Work feels like purposeful play, my life has meaning, and I'm able to contribute to making a difference in the most powerful way to people's happiness and success – it's an amazing feeling!

Becoming a professional coach isn't for everyone. Just because you feel the power of coaching doesn't mean you'll find a market demand for coaches that's defined and easily accessible. Coaching really works in life and in business, but many people still see it as fluffy and new-agey, so you need to do a fair bit of leg work to educate your market about the benefits. Don't embark lightly on a career as a professional coach – as well as loving life coaching, you must also be ready to love the hard slog of setting up and maintaining a successful business.

Getting Started

Training programmes vary enormously in rigour and quality. Coaching Certificate or Diploma programmes usually offer a mix of residential and distance learning. The initial residential part – anything from a day or weekend to longer – usually focuses on practising core skills (such as effective communication) and knowledge (understanding basic coaching models, values and beliefs). The distance element involves completing assignments and modules to demonstrate your learning. You also participate in coaching practice with others from your training group, in duos or trios, just like a co-coaching group, and this forms part of your qualification evidence. Most courses ask for a short *thesis* (extended essay) on a coaching-related topic. You may also need to pass a *viva* (oral examination), where you're assessed on your live coaching style.

Allow anything from three months to a year to obtain a relevant qualification of this kind, depending on the course you choose and the amount of time you can commit to it.

SPRINGBOARD

Training options

There are now a large number of organisations which provide coach training and here are just a few to get you started on your search. You can get a flavour from these of what's available, from short vocational courses to more academic programmes of study. Remember, there's no single right route, so compare several options as well as getting in touch with former graduates if you can, to ask about their experience before making any decision.

✔ www.ncl-coll.ac.uk Newcastle College in the UK offers a distance-learning package, which was developed by Fiona Harrold, one of the UK's leading coaches. You can complete a Certificate or Diploma in life or performance coaching very cost effectively this way.

✔ www.the-coaching-academy.com The Coaching Academy is the largest UK school for coaches and offers a range or qualifications and short courses from personal and life coaching to business and executive coaching, at Certificate and Diploma level. They run two-day taster sessions to help you decide if it's the right option for you. Their programmes are a mixture of distance learning and residential modules and are designed for people wanting to establish a coaching practice as they learn.

✔ www.resultscoachingsystems.co.uk Results Coaching Systems is an International Coach Federation (ICF) accredited training provider that trains new and developing coaches in their own successful coaching model. They have a strong emphasis on helping their trainees to build a sustainable coaching practice and they offer a one-day taster programme.

✔ www.coachu.com CoachU was founded by the 'father' of life coaching, Thomas Leonard, and is a distance learning option. Also ICF accredited, their programmes are popular internationally and range widely across personal, business and executive coaching.

✔ www.brookes.ac.uk For the more academically inclined, Oxford Brookes University offers a postgraduate Certificate and Diploma in coaching as well as a Master's and a Doctorate programme. Numerous short courses can be taken without leading to a specific qualification.

✔ www.hull.ac.uk Another great academic option is the Master's (MSc) in Personal and Corporate Coaching, which is a two-year part-time programme at Hull in the UK. This is a good way of easing into building up a coaching practice while remaining in employment, or of developing coaching expertise to take back to the workplace.

You can also choose to embark on a more academic programme via a postgraduate degree. Currently, many programmes on offer cover coaching in its broadest sense and cater to people mainly interested in coaching within a business environment. Postgraduate degrees focus much more on understanding the theories behind coaching and seeing coaching in the context of other human resource development, as well as relevant aspects of psychology and organisational behaviour. These courses often have a strong practical element too. Many postgraduate courses need a time commitment of two or three years (especially if you attend on a part-time basis), and the workload is fairly heavy in terms of assignments, lectures and tutorials.

 When you start providing life coaching, consider getting the right support from a professional coach trainer who can help you with skills, knowledge, practical coaching experience and guidance on professional ethics. You can find more information about coaching qualifications in Chapter 2.

Considering Your Niche

Even before you start practising as a life coach, you'll find it really helpful to think about the *niche* (specialist area) that you want to work in. All too often coaches begin practising without thinking about their niche, out of fear that they'll narrow down opportunities for themselves. Actually the opposite is often true, because the absence of a clear niche makes it hard for people to understand who and what you are so that they can refer people to you.

When you're first building a practice, you'll probably want to welcome any suitable potential client that comes your way, out of a genuine desire to help, learn and have a variety of experiences. That's okay, but in the long term use this time to assess which type of client really interests you, is attracted to you and who you can best serve, and you'll be much better placed to build a sustainable practice.

How to find your niche? Consider two main things:

- ✔ **Your past experience.** Building on the expertise you already have makes sense. When I first began coaching, I focused on themes of career, mainly because I was building on a 16-year career of my own in recruitment. Over a period of a couple of years, that developed into guiding people to their vision of happiness, using some of the ideas and research within positive psychology. So if you're an engineer, your professional niche may be in that field, where you already have knowledge and networks.

- ✔ **Your passions.** Perhaps what you did in the past feels quite irrelevant to your future as a coach. Of course, whatever experience you're building on is never wasted, but for some people, their previous environments hold no fascination for them anymore. Instead, you might be drawn to what you're really passionate about – perhaps an activity or interest that has occupied you in your spare time or something connected to a sense of purpose. Maybe you've always wanted to work with young people and want your niche to be coaching within education. For me, the passion element of my own coaching comes into play because I have an interest in learning and personal growth, especially in a spiritual sense, so happiness is a theme that suits my own search for meaning as well as helping to attract clients who are also on that journey. My own niche is very broad and that suits me; however if you want to grow a practice fast, a specific niche is the best starting point to keep you focused.

After you've considered these two aspects, you can begin to home in on your ideal or target client. Take as a starting point any coaching experience you already have, or of working with people in a coaching style. You may want to check out Chapter 22 to get some ideas about incorporating coaching into your existing life and work, and I recommend this as the first step for any potential new coach before taking the plunge. As you're gaining this kind of informal experience of coaching, consider the following:

- ✔ **What themes seem to keep coming up when you use coaching skills with others, or when people come to you for support?** Are they around life areas – health, wealth or relationships, for example – or are they more topic-based – values, beliefs, searching for meaning and purpose?

- ✔ **Is there a pattern in terms of gender?** Some coaches like to narrow their focus in this way, or simply find that they naturally attract a more masculine or feminine bias to their practice.

- ✔ **What about age?** The issues that a twenty-something has to deal with are quite different to those of the fifty-plus generation. What resonates with you?

- ✔ **Are there particular professions or backgrounds that appeal to you?** You may have always been fascinated by writers or actors, for example, and are interested in coaching them through their particular issues. (It's generally easier of course if you have a background in that profession or a strong passion in that area.)

- ✔ **What about geography**? There's a big difference between the coaching themes that come up for people working in cities as opposed to rural locations. There could well be a promising niche for you if your interests are especially geared towards burnt-out executives, or towards supporting people living and working in the back of beyond.

Spend some time visualising the kind of practice you'll be running in, say, two or three years' time. Trust your intuition to help you get a clear picture and feel for your ideal client.

Doing the Business

If you're establishing a life-coaching practice, then you're running a business. What kind of business will that be? Ask yourself honestly what you want to achieve. How important are the financials for you? In common with many start up businesses, new life coaches take a couple of years to reach the earnings level that they'd like. Here are some things to think about:

- ✔ **Check out your local Business Link (www.businesslink.gov.uk) for oodles of resources and free courses to help you acquire the business skills you need.** They'll also help you put together a business plan and check out if any funding is available for you to start up.

- ✔ **Scout out a good accountant to help you get started.** If you're going to be self-employed, then in theory you can do your own numbers, but good advice from the start can pay big dividends further down the line.

- ✔ **Consider your mix of clients.** If you have the relevant background, you may be able to attract corporate work, as a coach or a trainer/facilitator. For many new coaches, this is an obvious choice because it allows work variety and offers steady income as they build up the practice. Build into your business plan realistic projections for how much corporate and personal work you want to do. If you're set on only taking on personal life-coaching clients, think about what financial cushion you need and over what time period, bearing in mind that personal coaching rates are usually around half or less that of corporate rates. And while you're training, you're likely to be charging a lower fee in any case.

- ✔ **Think about insurance.** As a coach in practice, you need Professional Indemnity insurance to protect you against loss or damage by a client if you make a mistake (see www.businesslink.gov.uk for an explanation of this type of insurance). You may need extra home insurance if you decide to work from home.

- ✔ **Decide on where you'll work.** Resist the temptation to secure office space straightaway. If you're going to be telephone coaching, then working from home is usually the most viable option. Even if you plan on doing a lot of face-to-face and don't want to or don't have home-based facilities, you can hire out small meeting rooms cheaply without needing to take on the additional risk and commitment of premises. As you grow your practice, you can also consider hot desking at a custom-built office unit that can provide telephones, computers and admin support.

- ✔ **Subscribe to professional associations.** These include the Association for Coaching, the International Coach Federation and the European Mentoring & Coaching Council. They offer member benefits (for example, you can get discounted professional insurance via this route) as well as continuing professional development. They are also great avenues for meeting other new, developing or established coaches with whom who you may be able to create joint ventures and collaborations.

If you decide to work from home and do most of your coaching on the telephone, your start-up costs are pretty low. And it's possible to practise part-time (evenings and weekends) while retaining the security of your day job until you're ready to commit full time. Most new coaches begin by offering free life-coaching sessions to build their expertise. Attracting your first clients through referrals from family and friends may be easier than you think!

Marketing Yourself

The right training provider can usually help you with marketing your business after you've qualified. Certainly by the end of the programme, you'll have built up relationships with other new coaches and can really benefit from those new networks while you begin to practise in earnest. If you plan to practise solo to begin with, don't underestimate your need to have like-minded people available to you to share your experience and lend support.

The starting point for marketing yourself is to be 100 per cent certain that this is the profession for you and that you absolutely believe in the value of coaching. If your new career is fully aligned with your values (take a quick detour to Chapter 6 if you need to check!), then you'll do whatever it takes to let the world know what you can offer. There are always ways of reaching your market that suit your preferences, and if you hate the idea of touting for business, you can find more natural ways to use your rapport to attract the right people to you. But marketing is hard work and takes every ounce of your dedication, energy and commitment, just like any new business does.

Knowing your offering

Coaching can be an intangible concept for people to grasp, so it's up to you to make it real. What are you really offering here? Knowing your offering is about being clear on what the benefits are to your target audience. People don't buy *coaching* as such, they buy the *outcomes* of coaching – being happier, more successful, more productive, more balanced.

Even having identified these outcomes, they're still high-level values and you need to make them much more tangible. A great way to do that is by using case studies and testimonials. So right from the start, whenever you use your coaching skills for others' benefit and they acknowledge that, ask if they'd consider writing you a short testimonial. This makes it real and helps you to market the results that you help people to get in their lives.

Choosing the right marketing methods for you

Some new coaches feel uncomfortable with the idea of marketing and selling, and it can be a big barrier to getting work that you love. Everyone sells in some way: the key is to shift your thinking. You're offering a valuable service that you're passionate about and the world deserves to know.

Don't think that because you have to build a business you have to make cold calls. Actually, that approach is unlikely to win you coaching clients anyway. A softer and more natural approach is required, and the very best way forward is to choose marketing methods that excite you and are natural to you.

Here are some things to consider:

- ✔ **Promotional materials.** Business cards are handy for networking and you may want to invest in a basic tri-fold flyer that describes your service. It's a good idea to have web presence, because many people search on-line for coaches. A simple website of between one and three pages will suffice to start with, and if you combine that with a blog, you'll start to attract a crowd of potential clients.

- ✔ **Networking.** If you're new to networking, then explore all options and discover whether you enjoy the really focused kind where you meet every week and pass qualified referrals to each other (check out business network website www.bni-europe.com for a great example of that). Or perhaps you might prefer more informal 'learn and share' type networking events, where you listen to a speaker and then chat and swap business cards. Go to networking opportunities that really interest you. Key to networking success is keeping a focus on where your target clients are likely to hang out, and also to recognise that *everyone* you meet may be able to put you in touch with someone interested in what you have to offer.

- ✔ **Writing and speaking.** Marketing is a communication exercise, so if your gifts are in the written word, then you can convey your message through writing articles and submitting them to article directories like Ezine Articles (http://ezinearticles.com) with links back to your website. As you gain expertise and confidence, you can also source opportunities to present at relevant groups and meetings through co-coaching, networking and conferences of various kinds.

- ✔ **Social media.** Increasingly social media – via websites Twitter, Facebook and Linked-In – is proving really effective in all kinds of business marketing, and especially if you're a personal or life coach, because you're very likely to reach a good proportion of your ideal client market via this route.

For heaps more marketing ideas, advice and even templates for marketing material, see *Marketing Kit For Dummies* by Ruth Mortimer, Greg Brooks and Alexander Hiam.

Making Up Your Mind

In the true spirit of coaching, you can ask yourself the following questions before making your decision about becoming a life coach:

- ✔ What will becoming a professional coach give me in my life? What will I lose if I choose this path?

- ✔ Do I have the financial stability to make any lifestyle changes that may be required while I build up my practice? Will I gradually build a practice part-time while I continue my usual job or will I fully commit from the outset? Am I convinced of the financial value of what I'll be offering? How will I decide on pricing? How will I market myself?

- ✔ What will the values of my business be? Am I ready to do whatever it takes, with integrity, to be the best coach I can be and reach the people I need to reach?

- ✔ What skills do I still need to develop to be the best coach I can be? What kind of training will suit me best? Is a short residential course, distance learning or an academic qualification in coaching going to provide me with the best platform?

- ✔ Am I ready to manage my own time and resources, and how will I ensure that I remain self-motivated and focused? Do I want to work closely with other coaches who can support me?

- ✔ Will I specialise in a certain area, such as career or relationship coaching?

Two excellent websites offer extensive resources for further research into becoming a professional life coach. They also have information on the codes of ethics that are emerging within the profession:

- ✔ **Association for Coaching:** www.associationforcoaching.com
- ✔ **International Coach Federation:** www.coachfederation.org

Get plenty of wide-ranging advice, do your research thoroughly, ask powerful questions and make sure that being a coach is something you *really* want. There's no room for half-hearted coaches in the world; the job is too important to you and to the people you'll have an impact on. If, after all that, you decide that becoming a life coach is the route for you – congratulations on your choice and welcome to a truly life-changing career!

Index

• A •

abundance. *See also* money; wealth
  cultivating, 177–178
  defined, 176
  relationship of wealth to, 169, 178
  as step beyond wealth, 175
  steps of abun-*dance*, 176
accelerated learning, 208, 211
acceptance
  being present, 223–226
  benefits of, 221–222, 226–227
  bereavement stage, 296
  letting go of resistance, 222–223
  of weather, 222
  of yourself as you are, 264–266
'achievable' element of SMARTEN UP, 133
achievement, fear of, 78
actions. *See also* results
  'as if', 204
  baby steps for, 139–140, 321–322
  balancing with reflection, 327
  closed questions resulting in, 100
  coaching conversation as call to, 19
  as coaching journey stage, 44
  completing assignments, 40
  doing versus stopping, 65
  email confirming, 40
  handling life demands, 141–142
  heroic qualities for, 140–141
  intentions versus results of, 109–110
  learning from results of, 109–110
  in life-coaching circle, 41
  milestones for, 45–46, 138–139
  refining after a session, 40
  stage of change, 14
  will-power over-rated for, 48, 142–143
activities. *See also* questions
  areas for coaching, identifying, 20–22
  assets and liabilities, 106–108
  behavioural style, discovering, 61–64
  being present, 224–226
  belief payoffs, 71

beliefs, discovering, 69–70
beliefs, reshaping, 73
Bridge of Emotion, 228–229
Centre of Balance, 273–274
centring yourself, 277
circle of influence, 190–191
competencies, discovering, 58
creativity, discovering, 125–126
desire statement for whole-life goals, 118
discovering where you are, 44–45
dream work visualisation, 158
eating well, 198
emotions, identifying, 203
engaging your inner coach, 18
Film of Your Life, 141
financial awareness, 174
fitness options, 201–202
focusing on the positive intention, 263–264
friendships, 188–189
gratitude, practising, 228
happiness, identifying areas for
    improvement, 238
imagining emails from the future, 117
influences, noticing, 124
job evaluation, 152–153
leisure pursuits, 214
life stages, 287–288
modelling excellence, 250–251
needs, understanding, 85
observing your thoughts, 253–254
procrastination, root of, 258–259
question funnel, 103
relationship, maintaining committed, 183
relationship with yourself, 181
results of actions, understanding, 110–111
self-compassion, 265–266
success qualities, adopting, 248–249
success treasure trove, 246
values, understanding, 87–91
work area roles, identifying, 149–150
writing hand, changing, 59–60
Activity icon, 4
Adaptation Theory, 235

advice, taking, 106
advising, in life coaching, 11, 306
affirmations or mantras, 72, 73, 204, 266
agenda, holding your own, 315
agreement, coaching, 32
Albom, Mitch (*The Five People You Meet in Heaven*), 335
Alchemist, The (Coelho), 331
Alidina, Shamash (*Mindfulness For Dummies*), 216, 226
anger (bereavement stage), 296
answers to questions
  energy levels aiding, 103–104
  listening to, 102–104
apathy at work, 157
'appealing' element of SMARTEN UP, 133
Armstrong, Neil (astronaut), 69
'as if', acting, 204
assertive communication
  expressing your needs, 281–282
  non-violent, 202–203
  as pillar of self-esteem, 180
  practising at work, 156
assets and liabilities, 106–108
assignments, completing, 40
Astley, Neil (editor), 334
attention (success quality), 247–248
attracting the life you want
  art of acceptance for, 221–223, 226
  being present, 224–226
  wanting what you have, 226–229
auditory modality, 304, 305
authentic self. *See* best self
Avatar (film), 333
awareness. *See* self-awareness

• *B* •

baby steps, 139–140, 321–322
Baic, Sue (*Nutrition For Dummies*), 197
balance
  of action and reflection, 327
  assumptions about, 272
  centring yourself, 276–277
  changed by life priorities, 271–272
  checking yours, 273–274
  of daily energy, 274–276, 325–329
  delegation to maintain, 279–280

between doing, having and being, 12
dynamic process of, 271, 272
as element of best life, 314
expressing your needs, 281–282
Goldilocks theory of, 272–274
letting go to regain, 278, 280–281
as life coaching benefit, 27
managing yourself and your time for, 277–278
stress management for, 276, 282–284
tipping point for, 271, 274, 275, 276
of work roles, adjusting, 151
of work roles, identifying, 149–150
Balance Curve, 274, 275
Bannister, Roger (runner), 69
barn dancing for happiness, 206
behavioural styles
  attitudes toward, 63
  benefits of awareness of, 60
  challenges for changing, 64–65
  choosing new behaviours, 65
  described, 63, 246–247
  discovering yours, 61–64
  effect on relationships, 64
  elements of, 60
  experimenting with opposite, 64
  flexible approach to, 64
  mix of, 63
  Mountain, 62, 63, 246, 247
  Ocean, 62, 63, 247
  Sky, 62, 63, 246, 247
  success qualities of, 247
  Sun, 62, 63, 246, 247
Being Alive (Astley, ed.), 334
beliefs
  affirmations or mantras for, 72, 73
  change blocked by, 67
  changing yours, 72–75
  commitment statement for work adjustment, 154
  considering others', 72
  defined, 68
  discovering yours, 69–70
  examples of overcoming, 69
  about failure, changing, 77
  fear at the root of, 73–75
  health goals blocked by, 194
  to hold about yourself, 313–318
  incomplete or misleading, 69

of inner critic, 68
limiting, payoff of, 70
limiting, reshaping, 72–73
origins of, 68–69
payoffs of, 71
positive versus negative, 42
results affected by, 67–68
about romantic partner, 182
about work, 153, 154
bereavement stages, 296
Bergman, Ingrid (actress), 110
best self
behavioural style of, 61–64
deciding to be, 291, 292, 320–321
key to being, 55
preferences of, 58–65
unique gifts of, 53–58
Bhutan, quality of life in, 168
Bien, Melanie (*Sorting Our Your Finances For Dummies*), 169
blame, avoiding, 186
Blink (Gladwell), 112
blocks to progress. *See also* inner critic; setbacks and relapses
beliefs, 67, 70
confusion or conflicted feelings, 22, 96, 97, 262–264
fear, managing, 75–79
handling life demands, 141–142
most common, 22
pace for sustaining progress, 140
procrastination, 22, 67, 257–262
seeing problems, not possibilities, 120–122
self-doubt, 22, 264–267
trapped feelings, 119
'yes, but' game, 120–121
blogging, 124
body language, 303
bold type in this book, 2
Bolles, Richard Nelson (*What Color Is Your Parachute?*), 161
boredom with work, 153, 157
brain, thinking with whole, 208, 210–211
Brandon, Nathaniel (self-esteem expert), 180
breaking up with partner, 184
breathing deeply, 327
Bridge of Emotion activity, 228–229
British Psychological Society, 64

Buddha, 243
budget, 170–171, 172
Business Link website, 341

• **C** •

calmness (success quality), 247–248
Cameron, James (director), 333
cancellation charges, 33
career. *See* work
Cast Away (film), 122
Centre of Balance activity, 273–274
centring yourself, 276–277
Certificate in Coaching, 33
change. *See also* blocks to progress
baby steps for, 139–140, 321–322
in beliefs, 68, 72–75
bereavement stages, 296
building on strength, 294–295
choosing new behaviours, 65
choosing one thing, 324
commitment to, 37, 38
doing versus stopping for, 65
evolving to the next stage, 297
fixing a bad situation, 292–293
fleeing from a situation, 293–294
for its own sake, 159
jealousy from others about, 143
life stages and attitude toward, 286–288
moving from pain to pleasure and purpose, 289–290
in priorities, handling, 94
radical, recognising the need for, 289–292
readiness needed for, 12, 37–38
resolve aided by coaching, 15
stages of, 13–14
will-power over-rated for, 48, 142–143
charges for coaching, 32, 33
circle of influence, 190–191
circumstances, in H=S+C+V formula, 233–235
clarifying questions, 99, 100, 101
closed questions, 99, 100, 103
coaching conversations, 10, 19
coaching journey
anticipating setbacks and relapses, 48
beginning, 41–44
discovering where you are, 44–45
enjoying, 29–30, 115, 139, 213

coaching journey *(continued)*
gifts discovered on, 14
life-coaching circle, 41–42
marking your progress, 45–50
survival kit for, 42–43
coaching promise. *See* promise to yourself
coaching questions. *See* questions
co-coaching, 35, 36
Coelho, Paulo (*The Alchemist*), 331
comfort zone, 53–54, 58–60
commitment
closed questions resulting in, 100
to coaching time, 39
email confirming, 40
promise to yourself, 37, 38, 140–143
statements for work adjustment, 154
compassion
self-compassion, 265–266
success quality, 247–248
competencies
applying, 56–57
defined, 56
discovering yours, 58
examples of using (table), 57
of life coaches, 300–301
list of, 56, 57–58
compliments, accepting, 266
concentration, optimum period for, 211
confidence. *See also* self-esteem
accepting yourself as you are, 264–266
developed by focusing on strengths, 54
low (self-doubt), 22, 264–267
relationship of self-esteem to, 180
as success quality, 247–248
conflicted feelings. *See* confusion or
conflicted feelings
conflicts, family, 184–186
conflicts of motivation, 92–94
confusion or conflicted feelings
as block to progress, 22
defined, 22
focusing on the positive intention, 263–264
questioning, 96, 97
understanding the reasons for, 262–263
consistency (success quality), 248
consolidation (stage of change), 14
contemplation (stage of change), 13
contract, 32
conventions in this book, 2

counselling
life coaching versus, 10–11
Web resources, 184
courage (success quality), 247–248
creativity
discovering yours, 125–126
flexibility increased by, 125
for generating options, 125–126
intuition linked with, 113
playfulness enhancing, 213
Csikszentmihalyi, Mihaly (psychologist), 232
curiosity, 42, 48, 111, 112
curriculum vitae (CV), creating, 160

danger signs of stress, 282–283
decision making
belief in your power of, 317
choosing options, 128–129
choosing your best self, 291, 292
about coaching career, 344
evolving to the next stage, 297
expanding your range of options, 124–125
fixing versus fleeing versus building on
strength, 292–295
life stages and attitude toward change,
286–288
recognising the need for radical change,
289–292
working through the change, 295–296
deep breathing, 327
delegation to maintain balance, 279–280
Denby, Nigel (*Nutrition For Dummies*), 197
denial
bereavement stage, 296
financial, 170, 172
about health, 194
stage of change, 13
depression, 31, 87
desert island scenario, 121–122
desire statement
for generating options, 126–129
SMARTEN UP model for, 131–137
for whole-life goals, 118
developing yourself. *See* learning and
growing
diet (eating well), 197–198
dieting. *See* weight loss

Diploma in Life Coaching, 33
disease, avoiding, 197. *See also* physical
    health
doing
  being versus, 250
  stopping versus, 65
drawings, tracking progress using, 49
dream work. *See also* work
  CV creation for, 160
  folder for, 158
  job-search goal, 159
  matching to values, 158
  networking for finding, 161
  recruitment consultancies for, 160
  training and qualifications information, 159
  visualising, 158
  Web resources, 159, 161
Dyson, James (inventor), 69

• E •

eating well, 197–198. *See also* weight loss
Edison, Thomas (inventor), 69
education. *See* training
email
  confirming actions after session, 40
  from the future, imagining, 117
embarrassment, 77
emotions. *See also* confusion or conflicted
    feelings; fears; well-being, mental and
    emotional
  allowing for your state, 48
  with assets and liabilities, 107, 108
  basic emotional needs, 84
  changing, by altering your physical state,
    204–205
  conflicted feelings, 22, 96, 97, 262–264
  expressing for positive results, 203–204
  identifying, 203
  lightening your mood, 113
  managing, 202–204
  negative, gratitude tonic for, 325–326
  non-violent communication about, 202–203
  positive, celebrating, 204
  positive, tuning into, 228–229
  price for fulfilling needs, 84
  signalling need for change, 290–291
  thoughts leading to, 253
  trapped feelings, handling, 119

employment. *See* work
ending a relationship, 184
energy balance, daily, 274–276, 325–329
energy lows, 103, 104
'enthusiastic' element of SMARTEN UP, 134
environment, work, 154
ethics, 178, 306
excellence, modelling, 249–251
exercise and fitness, 199–201, 204
experience of coaches, 34
exploring options. *See* options, exploring
extroversion, 59, 60

• F •

failure. *See also* results
  changing beliefs about, 77
  fear of, 77, 320
  as learning situation, 109
faith, 243, 247–248
family. *See also* relationships
  challenges of, 184–185
  coaching role with, 307–308
  ground rules for, 186
  improving communication with, 185–186
  role in, 185
fears
  of achievement, 78
  behind procrastination, facing, 258–259
  beliefs rooted in, 73–75
  beneficial, 75–76
  of embarrassment, 77
  of failure, 77, 320
  managing, 75–79
  motivating versus blocking, identifying, 76
  naming, 76–78
  reducing or eliminating, 78–79
  of rejection, 78
  resisting options due to, 128
feedback at work, 161–163
feeling conflicted. *See* confusion or
    conflicted feelings
feeling modality, 304, 305
Film of Your Life activity, 141
finances. *See* abundance; money; wealth
fitness, 199–201, 204
Five People You Meet in Heaven, The
  (Albom), 335
fixing a bad situation, 292–293

fleeing from a situation, 293–294
flexibility, 64, 124–125
flow (the zone), 113–114, 232–233
focus (success quality), 247–248
freedom, 153, 154, 171
Freud, Sigmund (psychoanalyst), 179
friendships. *See also* networks;
   relationships
  coaching role in, 307–308
  expressing your needs in, 282
  importance of, 186–187
  levels of communication in, 187–188
  maintaining life-long, 187–189
  new, staying open to, 189
  staying in touch, 188–189
frustration, questioning, 96, 97–98
funnel for questions, 99–100
future. *See also* goals
  enjoying the journey toward, 115
  focusing on, 116
  health and well-being in, 194
  imagining emails from, 117
  inner coach representing, 16, 17
  work, planning for, 165

• G •

Game of Five Whys, 213
gifts, developing, 14, 53–58, 192, 323
Gladwell, Malcolm (*Blink*), 112
goals. *See also* options, exploring; tracking
   progress
  attaining, as coaching benefit, 26–27
  baby steps toward, 139–140, 321–322
  choosing people to cheer you on, 47
  commitment to, 37, 38
  disappointment after attaining, 115
  encouraged by inner coach, 19
  enjoying the journey toward, 115, 139, 213
  finding your soul mate, 182
  happiness as purpose of, 231
  for health, 193–196
  heroic qualities for achieving, 140–141
  job-search, 159
  knowing what you really want, 114–118
  mapping values to, 92
  matching options to, 138–140
  meaningful achievement of, 29–30
  milestones, 45–46, 138–139

not needed at outset of coaching, 25
possible goals for coaching, 26
questions to ask about, 27
reviewing before session, 40
right and left brain formulation of, 211
SMARTEN UP model for, 131–137
sustaining progress toward, 140
whole-life, desire statement for, 118
whole-life, visualising, 117, 211, 325
will-power over-rated for, 48, 142–143
for work, setting, 155–156
Goldilocks theory of balance, 272–274
gossip, avoiding, 157
gratitude, practising, 227–228, 325–326
gross national happiness, in Bhutan, 168
growing. *See* learning and growing
guilt as motivation, avoiding, 47

• H •

H=S+C+V formula, 233–235
habits
  building, for achieving goals, 140
  for healthy diet, 198
  practise required for changing, 73
happiness
  Adaptation Theory of, 235
  art of acceptance for, 221–223
  balance needed for, 12
  barn dancing for, 206
  as element of best life, 314
  factors contributing to, 236–237
  factors not contributing to, 237
  faith and focus on, 243
  flow for, 232–233
  gross national, in Bhutan, 168
  H=S+C+V formula for, 233–235
  Happy Life Plan, 241–242
  identifying areas for improvement, 238
  leisure not a guarantee for, 172
  lost by comparing yourself to others,
    168, 245–246
  making time for, 242
  money not a guarantee for,
    167, 173, 235, 237
  optimism leading to, 239–241
  pleasure compared to, 234
  practising the positive for, 240–241
  as purpose of goals, 231

sleep vital to, 239
success versus, 110
Web resources, 243
wise choices for, 172–173
Happy Life Plan, 241–242
Happy-Go-Lucky (film), 332–333
health. _See_ physical health; well-being,
    mental and emotional
hearing modality, 304, 305
heart's desire, 93–94
heroic, being, 140–141
Heron, Andrew (_Su Doku For Dummies_), 211
hesitation, questioning, 96–97
higher needs, 84. _See also_ needs
holistic approach to health, 196
honesty
  in children, 213
  financial, 170, 172
hypothetical (presupposing) questions,
    101–103

• I •

icons used in this book, 4–5
illness, avoiding, 197. _See also_ physical
    health
inner coach
  engaging, 18
  future, imagining emails from, 117
  future represented by, 16, 17
  goals encouraged by, 19
  inner critic versus, 16, 17, 98
  inspiration from, 335
  listening to inner critic versus, 102
  positive viewpoint of, 16–17
  questions asked by, 19
  with relaxed focus, 114
  ways you are supported by, 17–18
inner critic
  absent with relaxed focus, 114
  accepting yourself as you are, 264–266
  change blocked by, 291
  inner coach versus, 16, 17, 98
  journal record of, 49
  listening to inner coach versus, 102
  low energy loved by, 103
  negative beliefs favoured by, 68
  success blocked by, 252
  wrong questions asked by, 98

Inspiration icon, 5
inspiration, sources of, 324, 327, 331–335
insurance for life coaches, 341
integrity, 109, 180, 247–248
intention
  of coaching, 306
  focusing on, 263–264
  results versus, 109–110
International Stress Management
    Association, 283
introversion, 59, 60
intuition
  checking options against, 128–129
  in level 3 listening, 303
  relaxed focus for, 113–114
  as right brain thinking, 210
  tips for developing, 113
  trusting your gut feeling, 112
  value of, 112
italic type in this book, 2

• J •

James, Edmund (_Su Doku For Dummies_), 211
Janis, Sharon (_Spirituality For Dummies_), 216
jealousy from others, 143
job. _See_ work
job search. _See_ dream work
journal keeping, 40, 49, 90
journey. _See_ coaching journey
judgement, suspending, 317

• K •

kinaesthetic modality, 304, 305
kindness, random acts of, 326
knowledge spiral, 208–209

• L •

labels, 53, 68, 108
laughter, 113, 205, 328
learning and growing
  accelerated learning, 208, 211
  character traits for, 55
  developing confidence, 54
  developing intuition, 113
  from failure, 109
  identifying areas for coaching, 20–22

learning and growing *(continued)*
  knowledge spiral, 208–209
  in leisure time, 213–214
  mindset for, 54
  networking for, 192
  playfulness for, 211–214
  from results of actions, 109–110
  self-awareness for, 29
  spiritually, 215–217
  from success, 109
  whole-brain thinking, 208, 210–211
leaving a relationship, 184
left brain, 210
legacy, yours, 322
Leigh, Mike (director), 333
leisure time, 172–173, 213–214
Lennon, John, 11
letting go
  creating space for change, 323
  to regain balance, 278, 280–281
  of resistance, 222–223
  working through change, 295–296
Levinson, Daniel (psychologist), 286
liabilities and assets, 106–108
life coach
  experience of, 34
  finding, 31–35
  non-directive approach of, 11, 34
  qualifications of, 33–34
  questions to ask yourself about, 35
  specialists, 34
  usefulness of working with, 29
life coaching
  advising in, 11, 306
  benefits of, 25–30
  business considerations, 340–341
  challenges of, 30
  co-coaching, 35–36
  competencies for, 300–301
  contract or agreement for, 32
  conversation topics, 10
  counselling or therapy versus, 10–11, 31
  deciding to be a coach, 344
  defined, 9
  developing a coaching role, 306–309
  developing skills for, 302–305
  duration of programmes, 32
  ethics of, 306
  with friends and family, 307–308

gurus versus coaches, 9
history of, 15
marketing yourself, 342–343
mentoring versus, 11
niche for practise of, 339–340
non-directive, 11, 34
principles of, 307–308
prioritising areas for, 20–23
readiness for, 37–38
self-coaching, 36–37, 259
specialist areas of, 34
terms and conditions of, 32–33
training programmes, 337–339
vigilance during, 31
at work, 308
life stages
  balance changed by priorities in, 271–272
  common, 286–287
  recognising where you are, 287–288
life-coaching circle, 41–42
lifestyle
  allowing yourself to be rich, 174–175
  as aspect of wealth, 172–173
  leisure time, 172–173
  materialistic, 173
  single life, 182
  true cost of, 173–174
light heart, living with, 113
listening, 102, 189, 302–303
low energy, 103, 104

• *M* •

Making Slough Happy (documentary), 206
mantras or affirmations, 72, 73, 204, 266
marketing yourself as a life coach, 342–343
marking progress. *See* tracking progress
marriage. *See* partner or soul mate
Marvelas, Anna (consultant), 326
materialistic lifestyle, 173
Mayne, Brian (*Sam the Magic Genie*), 332
meaning. *See also* purpose
  as element of best life, 314
  as life coaching benefit, 28
  of objects, 50
  of values, defining, 91
'measurable' element of SMARTEN UP, 132
meditation, 216

mental well-being. *See* well-being, mental and emotional

mentoring, life coaching versus, 11

milestone goals, 45–46, 138–139

Millman, Dan (*Way of the Peaceful Warrior*), 332

Mindfulness For Dummies (Alidina), 216, 226

mindset
  changing, as coaching benefit, 28–29
  for learning and growing, 54
  optimistic, 240

modalities, 304, 305

modelling excellence, 249–251

moment, being in. *See* present, being

money. *See also* abundance; wealth
  allowing yourself to be rich, 174–175
  being rich versus feeling rich, 168
  budget for, 170–171, 172
  defining its role in your life, 168–169
  ethics of making, 178
  financial security, 169–172
  giving away, 177
  happiness not guaranteed by, 167, 173, 235, 237
  identifying areas for coaching, 20–22
  paid work, 148, 149–150, 151
  pursuing riches, 175
  savings, 170
  spending less than you earn, 170
  true cost of lifestyle, 173–174
  uses for, 168
  wealth versus, 167, 169

monofont type in this book, 2

motivation
  changing priorities affecting, 94
  commitment statement for work adjustment, 154
  conflicts of, 92–94
  defined, 81
  fear as, 76
  for fitness, 200
  guilt as, avoiding, 47
  for health goals, 194–196
  heart's desire, 93–94
  individual differences in, 82
  needs as, 84–85
  shallow or empty sources of, 81
  theories of, 82
  values as, 42, 86–92
  as vital for success, 81
  for work, 153, 154, 156

motivation map
  changing priorities affecting, 94
  personal, need for, 82–83
  in relationships, 94
  values as coordinates for, 91, 92

Mountain behavioural style, 62, 63, 246, 247

• N •

'natural' element of SMARTEN UP, 134

nature, communing with, 216, 329

needs
  for delegated tasks, 280
  emotional, 84
  expressing yours, 281–282
  fitting with your values, 85, 86
  higher, 84
  price for fulfilling, 84
  questions about, 85
  selfishness as result of, 86
  values compared to, 86, 88

negotiating (bereavement stage), 296

networks. *See also* relationships
  building, 123, 190–192
  circle of influence, 190–191
  developing your gifts, 192
  for finding your dream job, 161
  marketing yourself as a life coach, 343
  networking skills, 191–192
  productive, 190–192
  six degrees of separation idea for, 123
  supportive, 123

non-directive life coaching, 11, 34

non-verbal communication, 303

non-violent communication, 202–203

Nutrition For Dummies (Baic, Denby and Rinzler), 197

• O •

objects, significance of, 50

Ocean behavioural style, 62, 63, 247

open questions, 99, 100

optimism, 239–241, 279

options, exploring
  choosing the best fit, 128–129
  as coaching journey stage, 44
  considering the help available, 128
  creative approach, 125–126
  desert island scenario, 121–122
  desire statement for, 126–129
  expanding your range, 124–129
  finding information, 128
  increasing your resources, 123–124
  in life-coaching circle, 41
  matching options to goals, 138–140
  matching options to SMARTEN UP
    model, 138
  requirements for results from, 15
  seeing possibilities, not problems,
    120–122
  seeing what is possible, 127
  seeing your capabilities, 127–128
  supportive networks for, 123
  'yes, and' attitude for, 121
  'yes, but' game, avoiding, 120–121
outcomes. *See* results

● *P* ●

pace for sustaining progress, 140
pacing, in communication, 303
paid work. *See also* work
  adjusting the balance of, 151
  balance with people and passion work,
    149–150
  defined, 148
pain
  moving to pleasure and purpose from,
    289–290
  signalling need for change, 290–291
partner or soul mate. *See also*
    relationships
  alternative paths, 184
  breaking up with, 184
  counselling or therapy information, 184
  finding, 181–182
  idealism about, 181, 182
  questions to ask yourself, 183
  sustaining your commitment, 182–183
passion
  sharing with soul mate, 182
  as success quality, 246–247

passion work, 148, 149–150, 151
patience (success quality), 247–248
payoffs
  of assets and liabilities, 107, 108
  of beliefs, 71
peak experiences, 233
people. *See* friendships; networks;
    relationships
perseverance (success quality), 247–248
personality profiles, 64
pessimism, 239, 240, 279, 322
physical health. *See also* weight loss; well-
    being, mental and emotional
  avoiding illness and disease, 197
  changing view of, 193–194
  coaching activities regarding,
    197, 201–202
  as critical area for coaching, 193
  defining goals for, 194
  eating well for, 197–198
  exercise and fitness, 199–202
  focusing on what is working, 196
  holistic approach to, 196
  identifying areas for coaching, 20–22
  motivation for achieving goals, 194–196
pictures, tracking progress using, 49
Pilates, 216
playfulness, 113, 211–213
pleasure
  happiness compared to, 234
  moving from pain to, 289–290
poetry, 334
positive, practising, 240–241
positive psychology, 233–235
positivity (success quality), 247–248
possibilities. *See* options, exploring
postgraduate degree in coaching, 33
powerful questions. *See* questions
preferences
  behavioural styles, 60–65
  changing your writing hand, 59–60
  comfort zone with, 58–59
  extroversion versus introversion, 59
  for options, 129
  task-focus versus people-focus, 60
preparation
  for coaching session, 39–40
  stage of change, 13
'prepared' element of SMARTEN UP, 135

present, being. *See also* self-awareness
   activity for, 224–226
   benefits of, 223–224
   intuition aided by, 113
   at work, 155, 156
pressure, relieving, 154
presupposing questions, 101–103
pricing for coaching, 32, 33
prioritising
   activity for, 20–22
   areas of coaching, 20–23
   balance changed by priorities, 271–272
   coaching time, 39
   for developing mental resilience, 205
   handling changing priorities, 94
   values, 89–90
   work, 147
   work roles, 149–150
probing questions, 99, 100, 103
pro-bono work, 177
procrastination
   beliefs resulting in, 67
   as block to progress, 22
   climbing the ladder of, 261
   defined, 22
   getting to the root of, 258–259
   maintaining momentum, 260
   moving from wishing to wanting, 260–262
   statements justifying, 257–258
professional associations, 341
progress. *See* blocks to progress; tracking
      progress
promise to yourself
   being heroic, 140–141
   checking readiness for, 37–38
   framing, 38
   handling life demands, 141–142
   simple commitment versus, 37
promoting yourself at work, 163–164
psychometric tests, 64
purpose. *See also* meaning
   as call to change, 290
   emotions signalling move toward, 291
   as life coaching benefit, 28
   moving from pain to, 289–290
   as pillar of self-esteem, 180

• *Q* •

qualifications of coaches, 33–34
questions. *See also* activities
   asked by inner coach, 19
   child-like curiosity for, 42
   for choosing options, 128–129
   clarifying, 99, 100
   closed, 99, 100, 103
   about confusion, 96, 97
   for discovering where you are, 44
   about eating well, 198
   effectiveness of asking, 95–96
   for feedback at work, 162, 163
   for financial awareness, 174
   about fixing a bad situation, 293
   about fleeing from a situation, 293
   about frustration, 96, 97–98
   funnel for, 99–100
   Game of Five Whys, 213
   for generating options from desire
      statement, 127–128
   about goals, 27
   for health goals, 194
   about heart's desire, 93
   about hesitation, 96–97
   for inner success compass, 252
   for job change, 158, 161
   to keep your life on track, 319–324
   about leisure pursuits, 214
   about life stages, 288
   in life-coaching circle, 41
   listening to answers, 102–104
   measuring progress at work, 164
   about needs, 85
   open, 99, 100
   about partner or soul mate, 183
   planning for future work, 165
   presupposing, 101–102
   probing, 99, 100, 103
   about procrastination, 258–259
   purpose of, 19
   reflective, 101
   for regaining balance, 278–279
   about results of actions, 110–111
   about self-esteem, 181
   for stress management, 284
   tell me your secret activity, 103
   for time management, 278–279

questions *(continued)*
  for tracking progress, 295
  wrong, avoiding, 98

• *R* •

random acts of kindness, 326
rapport, building, 303–305
rates for coaching, 32, 33
reading, 216
realism
  about optimism, 239
  about romance, 181, 182
  SMARTEN UP element, 133
  wanting versus wishing, 260–261
recognition for your work
  getting feedback, 162–163
  promoting yourself, 163–164
recruitment consultancies, 160
reflection, balancing action with, 327
reflective questions, 101
rejection, handling, 78
relapses. *See* setbacks and relapses
relationships. *See also* friendships;
    networks
  behavioural style based on, 60
  behavioural styles' effect on, 64
  building supportive networks, 123
  choosing people to cheer you on, 47
  ending, 184
  expressing your needs in, 281–282
  family, 184–186, 307–308
  finding your soul mate, 181–182
  friendships, 186–189
  help for options from, 128
  identifying areas for coaching, 20–22
  with inspiring people, 324
  motivation maps in, 94
  non-violent communication in, 202–203
  partner or soul mate, 181–184
  six degrees of separation idea, 123
  at work, cultivating, 157
  at work, handling negative situations,
    156–157
  work for people, 148–150
  with yourself, 180–181
relaxed focus, 113–114
Remember icon, 5
resilience, mental, 205–206

resistance
  letting go of, 222–223
  noticing for options, 128
resourcefulness, belief in, 315
resources. *See also* Web resources
  increasing yours, 123–124
  for inspiration, 324, 327, 331–335
responsibility
  self-responsibility, 180, 318
  at work, 154
rest during tasks, 211
results. *See also* failure; success
  belief in capability of achieving, 316
  beliefs' effect on, 67–68
  creating positive outcomes, 254–255
  focusing on, 110–112
  intentions versus, 109–110
  learning from, 109–110
  questions about, 110–111
  ways of viewing, 108–109
Return to Love, A (Williamson), 78
rewards, 46, 328
rich, being. *See* abundance; money; wealth
right brain, 210
Rinzler, Carol Ann
    (*Nutrition For Dummies*), 197
Rosenberg, Marshall (conflict resolution
    specialist), 202
Rubin, Gretchen (happiness expert), 243

• *S* •

sadness (bereavement stage), 296
Sam the Magic Genie (Mayne), 332
savings, guidelines for, 170
scheduling coaching time, 39
scrapbook, tracking progress in, 49
security, financial, 169–172
self, best. *See* best self
self-acceptance, 180
self-assertiveness, 180
self-awareness. *See also* present, being
  of behavioural style, 60–64
  of beliefs, 69–70
  benefits of, 43
  of competencies, 58
  of conflicted feelings, 262–263
  creating a relationship with yourself,
    180–181

discovering where you are, 44–45
of fears behind beliefs, 73–75
of fears behind procrastination, 258–259
financial, 174
focusing on results, 110–112
of heart's desire, 93–94
intuitive, 112–114
as life coaching benefit, 29
in life-coaching circle, 41, 43
need for, 105–106
needed before taking advice, 106
of needs, 85
as pillar of self-esteem, 180
about success, 108–110
of values, 87–91
of what you really want, 114–118
of your assets and liabilities, 106–108
self-coaching, 36–37, 259. *See also* inner
    coach
self-confidence. *See* confidence
self-doubt, 264–267
self-esteem
  accepting yourself as you are, 264–266
  building, 266
  flushing doubt away, 267
  questions to ask about, 181
  relationship of confidence to, 180
  six pillars of, 180
selfishness, 86–87
self-promotion at work, 163–164
self-reliance, belief in, 316
self-report, 64
self-responsibility, 180, 318
self-worth, work validating, 148
Seligman, Martin (happiness guru), 243
senses, trusting, 318
set point, in H=S+C+V formula, 233–235
setbacks and relapses. *See also* blocks to
    progress
  anticipating, 48
  handling life demands, 141–142
  jealousy from others, 143
shyness, 189
silence, in communication, 304
single life, 182
six degrees of separation game, 123
Sky behavioural style, 62, 63, 246, 247
sleep, 239
Slumdog Millionaire (film), 333

SMARTEN UP goal-setting model
  'achievable or appealing' element of, 133
  checking goals against (table), 136
  'enthusiastic' element of, 134
  matching options to, 138
  'measurable' element of, 132
  'natural' element of, 134
  overview, 131–132
  'prepared' element of, 135
  'realistic' element of, 133
  residence change example, 135–136
  'specific' element of, 132
  'timed' element of, 134
  'understood' element of, 134–135
  weight loss example, 137, 138, 139, 140
smiling, 328
Socrates, 105
Sorting Our Your Finances For Dummies
    (Bien), 169
soul mate. *See* partner or soul mate
space for coaching, 40
specialist areas of coaching, 34
'specific' element of SMARTEN UP, 132
spirituality, 215–217
Spirituality For Dummies (Janis), 216
spouse. *See* partner or soul mate
Springboard icon, 5
stages of life. *See* life stages
starfish story, 309
Staying Alive (Astley, ed.), 334
stopping, doing versus, 65
strengths
  building on, 294–295
  challenges for concentrating on, 54–55
  comfort zone with, 53–54
  concentrating on, 54
  as unique qualities, 55
stress management. *See also* balance
  bad versus good stress, 274, 275
  changing attitude toward trigger, 276
  daily energy balance, 274–276, 325–329
  powerful questions for, 284
  spotting danger signs, 282–283
  three-point plan for, 283
  tips for, 284
  Web resources, 283
stretching, 329
Su Doku For Dummies
    (Heron and James), 211

success. *See also* competencies; results
  adopting personal qualities of, 246–248
  behavioural styles and personal qualities
      for, 246–249
  being instead of doing, 250
  big picture for, 251
  building muscles of, 249
  celebrating private victories, 253
  changing your thinking for, 252–255
  comfort with, 78
  comparing yourself to others, avoiding,
      168, 245–246
  creating positive outcomes, 254–255
  fear of achievement, 78
  fear of failure, 77
  happiness versus, 110
  inner compass activity, 252
  knowing your value, 246
  as learning situation, 109
  modelling excellence, 249–251
  motivation as vital for, 81
  as natural inclination, 245
  redefining, 108–110
  treasure trove activity, 246
  vision of, 217
  ways of viewing, 108–109
  work as validation for, 148
sudoku, 211
Sun behavioural style, 62, 63, 246, 247
supervision for coaching, 34
support
  building network for, 123
  commitment statement for adjusting, 154
  for developing mental resilience, 205
  when delegating tasks, 280
  at work, 154
supportive awareness. *See* self-awareness
survival kit for coaching journey, 42–43
survival plan, financial, 171–172

• *T* •

t'ai chi, 216
task focus, 60
telephone-based coaching, 32, 36, 40
terms and conditions of coaching, 32–33
therapy, life coaching versus, 10–11, 31

thinking
  emotions resulting from, 253
  observing your thoughts, 253–254
  problems resulting from, 253, 322
  whole-brain, 208, 210–211
time
  allocating for health and well-being, 194
  for happiness, 242
  investing wisely, 177
  leisure time, 172–173, 213–214
  managing, 277–279
  optimism versus pessimism about, 279
  questions to ask about, 278–279
'timed' element of SMARTEN UP, 134
tipping point for balance, 271, 274, 275
Touching the Void (film), 139
tracking progress. *See also* blocks to
      progress; setbacks and relapses
  anticipating setbacks and relapses, 48
  choosing people to cheer you on, 47
  journal for, 40, 49
  milestone goals for, 45–46, 138–139
  pace for sustaining progress, 140
  patting yourself on the back, 47
  questions for, 295
  at work, 164
training
  for dream work, 159
  as life coach, 337–339
trapped feelings, handling, 119

• *U* •

'understood' element of SMARTEN UP,
      134–135
uniqueness, yours, 55, 313–314

• *V* •

values
  absent from your life, 89
  activity for understanding, 87–91
  defining the meaning of, 91
  depression from avoiding, 87
  fitting your needs with, 85, 86
  heart's desire, 93–94
  honouring and dishonouring of, 91, 321

identifying, 87–89
journal considerations for, 90
knowing what you really want, 114–118
knowing your value, 246
list of, 86
mapping to goals, 92
matching job-search to, 158
motivation due to, 42
as motivation map coordinates, 91, 92
needs compared to, 86, 88
positive, honouring, 241
prioritising, 89–90
probing questions revealing, 100
as unselfish, 86–87
wealthy feeling dependent on, 176
vigilance during life coaching, 31
visual modality, 304, 305
visualising
  Bridge of Emotion activity, 228–229
  dream work, 158
  tracking progress, 49
  whole-life goals, 117, 211, 325
vocal qualities, 304
voluntary control, in H=S+C+V formula, 233–235

• W •

wanting versus wishing, 260–262
wanting what you have
  benefits of, 226–227
  practising gratitude, 227–228
  tuning into positive emotions, 228–229
Way of the Peaceful Warrior (Millman), 332
wealth. *See also* abundance; money
  abundance as next step, 175
  being rich versus feeling rich, 168
  identifying areas for coaching, 20–22
  lifestyle aspect of, 172–173
  money versus, 167, 169
  relationship of abundance to, 169, 178
  requirements for feeling of, 176
  types of issues for, 167
weather, accepting, 222
Web resources
  blessing movie, 215
  Business Link, 341

competencies list, 57
depression information, 31
finding a coach, 32
for happiness, 243
International Stress Management
    Association, 283
for job search, 161
job training and qualifications, 159
life coach training, 338
life coaching profession, 344
motivation theories, 82
psychometric tests, 64
relationship counselling information, 184
values list, 86
website for this book, 5, 15
weight loss
  baby steps in, 140
  handling life demands, 142
  matching options to goals, 138
  milestones for, 139
  motivation for, 195
  for preventing illness, 197
  questions to ask yourself, 198
  SMARTEN UP model for, 137
well-being, mental and emotional. *See also*
    physical health
  changing your emotional state, 204–205
  as critical area for coaching, 193
  defining goals for, 194
  focusing on what is working, 196
  holistic approach to, 196
  identifying areas for coaching, 20–22
  managing your emotions, 202–204
  mental resilience, 205–206
What Color Is Your Parachute? (Bolles), 161
whole-brain thinking, 208, 210–211
whole-life balance. *See* balance
whole-life goals. *See* goals
Williamson, Marianne (*A Return to Love*), 78
will-power, 48, 142–143
wishing, wanting versus, 260–262
Wizard of Oz, The (book and film), 334
work
  apathy about, 157
  assertive communication at, 156
  balancing roles in areas of, 148–150
  being in the moment at, 155, 156

work *(continued)*
boredom with, 153, 157
checking in with yourself at, 157
commitment statements for, 154
conscious choice for, 151
curiosity in job roles, 112
CV creation, 160
dream job, finding, 158–161
dream-job folder, 158
evaluating your job, 152–153
expressing your needs at, 281
feedback, getting, 162–163
focus for, 155–157
getting recognition for, 161–164
gossip at, avoiding, 157
handling negative situations, 157
identifying areas for coaching, 20–22
identifying areas needing adjustment, 153–154
improving your current job, 155–157
job-search goal, 159
life coaching at, 308
life coaching professionally, 299–309, 337–344

motivation for, 153, 154, 156
for passion, 148–150
for pay, 148–150
for people, 148–150
people conflicts at, 156–157
planning for the future, 165
prioritising, 147
pro-bono, 177
progression in work life, 164
recruitment consultancies for, 160
as validation for self-worth, 148
work, defined, 147
working out what's working, 41, 43

'yes, and' attitude, 121
'yes, but' game, avoiding, 120–121
yoga, 216

• Z •

zone, the, 113–114, 232–233

FOR DUMMIES®

Making Everything Easier! ™

UK editions

BUSINESS

978-0-470-74490-1

978-0-470-74381-2

978-0-470-71382-2

REFERENCE

978-0-470-68637-9

978-0-470-68837-3

978-0-470-74535-9

HOBBIES

978-0-470-69960-7

978-0-470-68641-6

978-0-470-68178-7

Anger Management For Dummies
978-0-470-68216-6

Boosting Self-Esteem For Dummies
978-0-470-74193-1

British Sign Language
For Dummies
978-0-470-69477-0

Business NLP For Dummies
978-0-470-69757-3

Cognitive Behavioural Therapy
For Dummies
978-0-470-01838-5

Cricket For Dummies
978-0-470-03454-5

CVs For Dummies, 2nd Edition
978-0-470-74491-8

Divorce For Dummies, 2nd Edition
978-0-470-74128-3

eBay.co.uk Business All-in-One
For Dummies
978-0-470-72125-4

Emotional Freedom Technique
For Dummies
978-0-470-75876-2

English Grammar For Dummies
978-0-470-05752-0

Flirting For Dummies
978-0-470-74259-4

Green Living For Dummies
978-0-470-06038-4

IBS For Dummies
978-0-470-51737-6

Lean Six Sigma For Dummies
978-0-470-75626-3

Available wherever books are sold. For more information or to order direct go to www.wiley.com or call +44 (0) 1243 843291

13061 p1

FOR DUMMIES®

A world of resources to help you grow

UK editions

SELF-HELP

978-0-470-74830-5

978-0-470-74764-3

978-0-470-68472-6

STUDENTS

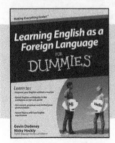

978-0-470-74747-6

978-0-470-74711-7

978-0-470-74290-7

HISTORY

  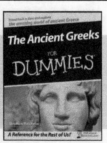

978-0-470-99468-9

978-0-470-51015-5

978-0-470-98787-2

Neuro-linguistic Programming
For Dummies
978-0-7645-7028-5

Origami Kit For Dummies
978-0-470-75857-1

Overcoming Depression For Dummies
978-0-470-69430-5

Positive Psychology For Dummies
978-0-470-72136-0

PRINCE2 For Dummies, 2009 Edition
978-0-470-71025-8

Psychometric Tests For Dummies
978-0-470-75366-8

Raising Happy Children
For Dummies
978-0-470-05978-4

Reading the Financial Pages
For Dummies
978-0-470-71432-4

Sage 50 Accounts For Dummies
978-0-470-71558-1

Starting a Business For Dummies,
2nd Edition
978-0-470-51806-9

Study Skills For Dummies
978-0-470-74047-7

Teaching English as a Foreign
Language For Dummies
978-0-470-74576-2

Teaching Skills For Dummies
978-0-470-74084-2

Time Management For Dummies
978-0-470-77765-7

Work-Life Balance For Dummies
978-0-470-71380-8

FOR DUMMIES®

The easy way to get more done and have more fun

LANGUAGES

978-0-470-68815-1
UK Edition

978-0-7645-5193-2

978-0-471-77270-5

MUSIC

978-0-470-48133-2

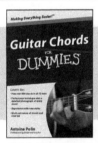

978-0-470-66603-6
Lay-flat, UK Edition

978-0-470-49644-2

SCIENCE & MATHS

978-0-470-59875-7

978-0-7645-5430-8

978-0-7645-5325-7

Art For Dummies
978-0-7645-5104-8

Bass Guitar For Dummies, 2nd Edition
978-0-470-53961-3

Brain Games For Dummies
978-0-470-37378-1

Christianity For Dummies
978-0-7645-4482-8

Criminology For Dummies
978-0-470-39696-4

Forensics For Dummies
978-0-7645-5580-0

German For Dummies
978-0-7645-5195-6

Hobby Farming For Dummies
978-0-470-28172-7

Index Investing For Dummies
978-0-470-29406-2

Jewelry Making & Beading
For Dummies
978-0-7645-2571-1

Knitting For Dummies, 2nd Edition
978-0-470-28747-7

Music Theory For Dummies
978-0-7645-7838-0

Physics For Dummies
978-0-7645-5433-9

Schizophrenia For Dummies
978-0-470-25927-6

Sex For Dummies, 3rd Edition
978-0-470-04523-7

Sherlock Holmes For Dummies
978-0-470-48444-9

Solar Power Your Home
For Dummies, 2nd Edition
978-0-470-59678-4

The Koran For Dummies
978-0-7645-5581-7

Wine All-in-One For Dummies
978-0-470-47626-0

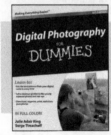